Annabella Fick
New York Hotel Experience

American Culture Studies | Volume 19

Annabella Fick (PhD) works as an academic advisor for Cusanuswerk, a scholarship program for highly gifted Catholic students. Her research interests include American History, New York and Hotels.

ANNABELLA FICK
New York Hotel Experience
Cultural and Societal Impacts of an American Invention

[transcript]

This dissertation project was supported by Cusanuswerk

Bibliographic information published by the Deutsche Nationalbibliothek
The Deutsche Nationalbibliothek lists this publication in the Deutsche Nationalbibliografie; detailed bibliographic data are available in the Internet at http://dnb.d-nb.de

© **2017 transcript Verlag, Bielefeld**
transcript Verlag | Hermannstraße 26 | D-33602 Bielefeld | live@transcript-verlag.de

All rights reserved. No part of this book may be reprinted or reproduced or utilized in any form or by any electronic, mechanical, or other means, now known or hereafter invented, including photocopying and recording, or in any information storage or retrieval system, without permission in writing from the publisher.

Cover layout: Kordula Röckenhaus, Bielefeld
Cover illustration: Book page 15, »The Old Waldorf-Astoria Superimposed on the New«; from The Unofficial Palace of New York: A Tribute to the Waldorf-Astoria, 1939.
Leonard Schultze (American, 1877-1951) and S. Fullerton Weaver (American, 1879-1939), architects.
Lloyd Morgan (American, 1892-1970), renderer.
Francis Welch Crowinshield (1872-1947), editor.
Hotel Waldorf-Astoria Corporation, New York City, publisher 11 3/8 x 9 inches (29.0 x 23.0 centimeters).
The Wolfsonian – Florida International University, Miami Beach, Florida, The Mitchell Wolfson, Jr. Collection
87.1459.2.1
Published with the permission of The Wolfsonian – Florida International University (Miami, Florida).
Photo: Lynton Gardiner
Printed in Germany
Print-ISBN 978-3-8376-3781-6
PDF-ISBN 978-3-8394-3781-0

Table of Content

Acknowledgments | 7

Introduction | 9

Research Object and Status of Research | 10
Methodological Considerations | 21
Hotel History | 41

1. Hotel Waldorf-Astoria – American Grand Hotel Par Excellence | 57

1.1. The Hotel as the Stage for the Wealthy | 63
1.2. The Hotel as The Palace of the People | 80
1.3. The Hotel as a City within a City | 97

2. Hotel Algonquin – Birthplace and Home of New York Sophistication | 111

2.1. The Hotel as the Hotelman's Tool | 119
2.2. The Hotel as Childhood Home | 127
2.3. The Hotel as Home and Salon of the Artist | 139
2.4. The Hotel and its Literary Circle | 147

3. Hotel Chelsea – New York's Bohemian Mecca | 163

3.1. The Hotel as the Artist's Refuge | 178
3.2. The Hotel as the Artist's Place of Initiation | 191
3.3. The Hotel as Source of Inspiration | 196

4. Hotel Theresa – Harlem's Center of African-American Self-Manifestation | 213

4.1. The Hotel as Center of the African-American Community | 225
4.2. The Hotel as Stage for Black Pride and as Symbol of
    Black Achievement | 234
4.3. The Hotel as Platform for Politics and as Victim of Desegregation | 240
4.3. The Hotel as Training Ground for an African-American Leader | 252

5. Grossinger's Hotel and Country Club – Acculturation in Style | 259

5.1. The Hotel as Point of Entry to American Culture | 273
5.2. The Hotel as Place of Female Empowerment | 287
5.3. The Hotel as Site of Identity Struggle | 297

Conclusion | 313

Works Cited and Illustrations | 321

Acknowledgements

Just like a hotel manager in a big hotel, I had to rely on the support of a number of people to accomplish this study. First and foremost, I want to thank my supervisor Prof. Dr. Jochen Achilles for allowing me to focus on a quite unusual topic and for guiding me along the way. I am also grateful for the support of PD Dr. Ina Bergmann and Prof. Heike Raphael-Hernandez. My deepest gratitude I want to extend to Dr. Juliane Braun and Dr. Andrea Stiebritz, who listened to my musings and whose belief in the topic helped me to pull through.

The success of this study also relied very much on the help of the people I have met during my research trips to New York, supported with grants by the University of Wuerzburg and the Cusanuswerk. Prof. Dr. Gordon Whatley from the City University of New York provided me with a workplace and entry to libraries and the academic network. Moreover, he and his wife Mary showed me endless hospitality and friendship for which I am most grateful. For my research on the case studies I was supported by Erin Allsop from the Waldorf-Astoria Archive and Alice de Almeida from the Hotel Algonquin, who provided me with material from the two establishments. Dr. David Coppen, Head of Special Collections of the Sibley Library at the Eastman School of Music, enabled me to view the papers of Alec Wilder and answered all my questions about these texts. Prof. Dr. David Demsey from the William Paterson University, Co-Executor of the Alec Wilder Estate, gave me permission to use quotes from Wilder's unpublished papers. Prof. Dr. Phil Brown from the North Eastern University, who takes care of the archive of the Catskill Institute, advised me and provided me with material on this hotel region and especially on Grossinger's Hotel and Country Club. The staff of the Manuscript Division of the New York Public Library, of the New-York Historical Society as well as the YIVO Institute for Jewish Research helped me with their advice and services. Thank you all very much for your help!

I need to thank Madonna Hill, Mary Keane, and Johannes Schinagl who read through this manuscript and helped me to get it into the right shape. I am also grateful for the moral support of Christl Ney, Elke Demant, Stefan Hippler, and Sonja

Bonneß, who pushed me when it was necessary. Furthermore, I want to thank the Cusanuswerk, especially Dr. Manuel Ganser and Liane Neubert, who supported me not only financially but also ideationally.

Most of all I want to thank my wonderful sisters Alex and Theresa and my parents. They believed in my ability to accomplish this dissertation project at times when I did not believe in myself and were always there for me. They are the hotel people that have inspired me. I am blessed to call them my family!

Introduction

> "The story of Greece is in its temples, that of America is in its hotels."
> GENE FOWLER/QTD. IN MCGINTY 2

With this quote by American journalist and author Gene Fowler Brian McGinty starts his history of American *Palace Inns* (1978). At first glance this statement sounds like a gross exaggeration of the hotel's position in American culture. Mentioning Greece immediately invokes the image of the cradle of human civilization. Greek temples are still admired as lasting evidence of Ancient Greece's contribution to the human world heritage. And yet, Fowler is not alone in stating the importance of the institution of the hotel for America. The first historian to publish a book on hotel history in America, Jefferson Williamson, champions Fowler's view, writing: "Our hotels have been …'the thermometers and barometers of our national civilization," (Williamson 4) and continues: "Tinsel and all, our ornate hotels symbolize and typify the spirit of America. They have been, perhaps, the most distinctively American of all our institutions, for they were nourished and brought to flower solely in American soils and borrowed practically nothing from abroad" (Williamson 4). Hotel space offers its users to live a life of a certain rootlessness, to give in to their inner drive of restless mobility and to fulfill the wish to see and be seen by the community. These traits are often perceived as typically American as they combine the Puritans' concept of a tightly knit, observing and controlling community and Turner's often invoked frontier spirit. Thus the hotel is the ideal space for American people. Since the early nineteenth century, the hotel presents a new kind of spatial entity to Americans. Especially the accessible American hotel lobby was a place of exchange and shaped the development of the nation, helping it to become a united country. The hotel is a product of capitalism, it made possible to enable and control modern life. Yet, according to Caroline Levander, "[h]otels … are not passive sites but bring a power of their own to the resident experience, real or imagined" (Levander 6).

The hotel is a most complex construction. It can be home, meeting place, work place, place of leisure, and entertainment.[1] Hotel scholar Molly Berger writes, it "is unlike any other institution because it is all these things at once" (Berger, *Hotel Dreams* 10). Henry James, the famous novelist and social critic, even went so far as to call the hotel a synonym for American civilization (James 105). Even though the hotel touches all parts of human life and challenges people's relationship with place more than any other institution in modern American society, the hotel has been neglected as research object in American Studies for quite some time. Thus, the research object of my thesis is the cultural phenomenon hotel.

RESEARCH OBJECT AND STATUS OF RESEARCH

While the hotel is often only perceived as a stopping place for the night, for a number of people it is their permanent home, work place, and a stage or platform to re-invent themselves. It is a place of intense human interaction, a reservoir of memories and experiences, a safe, yet liberating shelter, and a social laboratory for new ways of living. Its importance for modern societies can hardly be overestimated as the hotel has played "a powerful role in the constitution of the modern self" (Levander 3). My focus lies on the experiences people make in the hotel and how they preserve these in their writings. I argue that the special kind of hotel experience both enables and inspires the production of culture and provides the ground for social change. Influenced, manipulated, united, and liberated by the hotel atmosphere, a number of people from all walks of life decided to put their hotel experiences to paper. They recorded them in their autobiographies, memoirs, essays, and authorized biographies. In this thesis I will analyze these accounts together with several other texts, to support my claim of the considerable agency of hotel space for American society and culture. The entity hotel has been used in many ways, as an abstract image or concept, a setting and plot line for narratives, and it exists as an actual place in our everyday world. A hotel's nature is multifaceted. I am interested in the hotel as a physically existing and literary structure that has played a significant role in the development of New York urban society and culture over the last two hundred years. My focus thereby lies between the 1890s and the early 2000s. There seem to be endless possibilities to play with the idea of the hotel and many ways to use it for individuals and whole communities. German writer Leo Koszella stated:

---

1   See also Levander 14. She ascribes the undertheorization of the hotel to the unique malleability of its space, which makes it so hard to grasp for scholars.

Heut, wo das Hotel für eine Unmenge von Menschen geradezu die zweite Heimat darstellt, wo sich infolgedessen auch diese wichtige Kulturinstitution darauf eingestellt hat und – in Amerika noch stärker als auf unserem Kontinent – eine Welt für sich, ein Kosmos im kleinen bildet, heut ist der Begriff Hotel trotzdem oder gerade deswegen für die meisten eine Art Neuland, Märchenland, eine Art exterritorialen Gebietes. (Koszella 662)

With this study I will help explain the seemingly "extraterritorial space" of the hotel and put it at the center of scholarly discussion.

This study focuses on hotel experience in New York. What does hotel experience mean in this context? With hotel experience I describe the impact the institution has on the people that interact in it and with it. There are three main levels that have to be considered: the insider/hotel relationship of owners, staff, and hotel children; the liminal, more temporary guest/hotel relationship; and the outsider/hotel relationship, which includes broader New York society and the American public. They discuss the hotel from a 'once-removed' point of view, their hotel experience can be described as vicarious, meaning it is mediated through the eyes of others, e.g. in artistic products (Relph 52).

The selected New York hotels of this study are to a certain extent unlike the 'typical' hotel one might have in mind. They are special cases and the texts created around them have been created by an uncommon clientele. But they remain hotels with all the functions, codes, social practices, and chronotopic quality that we connect with the word. The term hotel experience covers the dynamic mutuality between people and place, how the actors shape the hotel according to their ideas and are themselves changed and positioned by their surrounding. This reminds one of Churchill's statement "We shape our buildings; thereafter they shape us" (Churchill in Sandoval-Strausz 229). The hotel is a liminal space that is open for many different uses (Pritchard and Morgan 763). Seemingly as a consequence, this highly emotionally and meaning-charged space became the favorite place of producers of culture, such as writers, actors, directors, musicians, and painters (Krebs 39; Sandoval-Strausz and Wilk 175). Hotels provided them with a space to work in and liberated them from social conventions, which often led to a close identification with these places. Each of the hotels discussed here inspired texts, which are set in these institutions. They caused and enabled the creation of culture. These hotels have also become platforms for social and cultural developments in their communities because hotel experience is not limited to individuals but affects whole groups. I agree with Daniel Boorstin that it is the institution's multi-facetedness and its multilateral impact on human life that makes hotels "both creatures and creators of communities" (143), real "microcosm[s] of American life" (147). Thus, I am also interested in the reactions of the surrounding communities.

Hotel experience has been captured in a variety of texts. Because experience is a phenomenon difficult to pin down, the material for my study covers a number of different genres, from novels and films, historiographies, essays and magazine articles to functional texts such as speeches, hotel brochures, advertisements, and reviews.[2] Most important for this study, however, are life-writing accounts. More than any other text form, both autobiographical and biographical texts convey the experience of people and disclose the hotels' deeper (and more philosophical) meaning combined with their actual, physical dimension. The texts I use in this thesis reflect the different roles hotels play in the personal life of people, as well as in their communities, and the larger city surrounding them. They have been written by hotel owners, staff members, guests and also hotel children, who can be considered as a special American phenomenon. Hotel children take on a unique position in the discussion of hotel agency.

Spatial awareness and the expression of spatial experience are most apparent and graspable in life writing texts.[3] It is, therefore, surprising that the importance of space and place has been largely neglected in the discussion of life writing texts as Julia Watson, one of the leading scholars in the field of autobiographies, states: "space has not been theorized in Anglo-American autobiography in a systematic way" (Watson 13). Watson is one of the few scholars who consider space and place in autobiographies. She writes on the issue of place and identity in American autobiographies: "For some autobiographers, place is a problem to be solved; for others, it is the basis (or 'ground') for a claim of authenticity" (13). I argue that in my case studies we can see the latter. The life writing texts of hotel people all show an uncanny awareness of the peculiar space that surrounds them. They feel a close link to their hotel environment and derive a large part of their identity from it,

---

2 Caroline Levander uses a similar approach in her book Hotel Life. She writes: "for it is through this unorthodox mix of various kinds of materials that we can begin to delineate the ways in which the hotel, not merely as bricks and mortar or physical site but as imaginative location and shelter, comes to enable the creation, design, and curation of the modern self over time" (Levander 3).

3 I am aware that it is difficult to categorize these texts as non-fiction or fiction, as an autobiographical text consists of a specific selection of elements of the past, which is shaped into a certain narrative that represents only one facet of the 'truth' (McLennan 10f). For my purpose, however, it would be wrong to completely overlook the factuality of these accounts, which can often also be cross verified with other, scholarly researched texts. Furthermore, while I accept to a certain degree Lejeune's classic definition of autobiography as "a retrospective prose narrative written by a real person concerning his own existence, where the focus is his individual life, in particular the story of his personality" (Lejeune qtd. in Eakin 4), I also acknowledge the criticism wielded against his too simplified definition, e.g. by Linda Anderson who comments on the inherent "slipperiness of autobiography" (2). See also Rachel McLennan, American Autobiography.

which can be seen in the titles of their life writing texts: *Be My Guest* (Conrad Hilton, Waldorf), "Hotel Pilgrim" (Elsa Maxwell, Waldorf), *Tales of a Wayward Inn* (Frank Case, Algonquin), *Growing Up at Grossinger's* (Tania Grossinger, Grossinger's) or "The Chelsea Affect" (Arthur Miller, Chelsea).

Although place has not been discussed in a systematic fashion in scholarly texts on autobiographies, many have perceived a link between this genre and American national identity. Jay Parini writes that autobiography "could easily be called the essential American genre, a form of writing closely allied to our national self-consciousness" (11). This claim seems too essentialist and exceptionalist. However, it conveys the feelings of many that this genre is indeed of great and historical importance for Americans. Life writing has been part of the national experiment since the beginning of British colonization of America, starting with the Puritans, blossoming with statesmen like Benjamin Franklin, leading public thinkers like Henry David Thoreau and Henry Adams, and writers like Mark Twain and Walt Whitman. It has also been a genre in which female writers and minorities could express themselves, most notably in captivity narratives and slave narratives. Today, the medium is still a popular outlet for a great variety of people, including immigrants and people with disabilities, to tell their story and take their place in the discourse of Americanness. It is therefore only fitting that American hotel people, too, express their special experiences in life writing texts. Together with the other text sources, this mix of material will present a more diversified analysis of the historical, social, and cultural dimension of the hotel and will fill the existing gap in the scholarly discourse on the hotel.

It is in the nature of the topic that the life writing texts I analyze here come from a specific group of people. These people are directly connected to the hotels as managers, staff members and their families, as well as regular and longterm guests, often artists who are familiar with a creative outlet for their thoughts. Furthermore, several texts also come from communities that have close ties to the respective hotels and that perceive them as an essential part of their social and cultural sphere. This means that my study will not represent the point of view of transient hotel guests who check-in for a short time and use the hotel as stopping place on their journey. While their attitudes toward hotels are also interesting, discussing them would go beyond the scope of the work at hand. I will also not consider two interesting fields of hotel study, the chain hotel and hotels in Las Vegas as this would explode the capacity of this work. Concerning hotel experience, chain hotels rarely create enough deep relations with their guests to have a literary repercussion. I do not attempt to present here a complete overview over all types of hotel experience. With this study I want to present a specific and fascinating slice of New York's urban culture and show how certain hotels played an important role in its development.

New York lends itself as the obvious choice when it comes to researching hotel experience. Historically, the first structure worthy of the name, the City Hotel, was opened in New York in 1794. Over the next two centuries, New York developed into "the greatest hotel city in the world" (Williamson 76), leading hotel development in almost every aspect. Today, New York has more hotels per square mile than any other city in America. It is also the most international city in the country and therefore more affected and more reacting to new developments that cross the Atlantic. New York is perceived as *City of Cities*, as one can see for example in E.B. White's famous article "Here is New York" (1949). People see New York as a mirror of the whole of American society. Many of the leading hotel groups in the world have a flagship house in New York because no other city in the world is seen as so prestigious and economically relevant. For a hotel chain, it is a must-have to have a location in New York. New York is, furthermore, sufficiently diversified to harbor hotels that address specific groups, for example African-Americans and Jewish Americans. It is at once an outstanding and generalizing example for the analysis of hotel experience.

By focusing on the geographical region of New York I am also taking up a suggestion by Martina Krebs. At the end of her dissertation *Hotel Stories: Representations of Escapes and Encounters in Fiction and Film* (2009), she considers it to be "worthwhile to analyze hotels more closely from a cultural-geographic perspective, locating hotels in their geographic contexts, examining their ensuing cultural meanings" (Krebs 165). I agree. Analyzing the close links between this particular city and its hotels in my thesis I will show what the institution hotel has done and still does for New York City and how hotel experience continues to shape our perception of this city.

Concerning the time span of my work, I have decided to focus on the twentieth century. This decision is connected to the status of research on the American hotel as well as to the nature of the hotels which I have selected. Even though one currently perceives a growing interest in the topic hotel in several academic fields, the number of texts existing on the topic remains still quite small. This neglect, especially by American Cultural Studies, is somewhat surprising since Jefferson Williamson's *The American Hotel: An Anecdotal History* (1930) and Norman S. Hayner's *Hotel Life* (1936) were already published in the 1930s. With the exception of Boorstin's enlightening chapter "Palaces of the Public" in *The Americans: The National Experiment* (1967), not much has been published in academia on the hotel's importance for American society until the 1990s.[4]

---

4 There are a few publications containing the history of specific hotels, many of them belonging to the group of grand hotels. However, most of these books belong in the category of coffee-table books, beautifully illustrated but only with a limited number of essays on the topic included, for example David Watkin's *Grand Hotels: the Golden Age*

With Paul Groth's *Living Downtown: The History of Residential Hotels in the United States* (1999) the hotel as research object has again stepped out of the shadows. Writing from a sociological point of view Groth's social and cultural history explains the centrality of the hotel in people's urban living experience, especially for San Francisco and New York. In the 2000s two publications followed which have been of great importance for my study: Andrew K. Sandoval-Strausz's *Hotel: An American History* (2009) and Molly Berger's *Hotel Dreams: Luxury, Technology, and Urban Ambition in America, 1829-1929* (2011).[5] These two texts make a powerful case for the importance of the hotel as a research object, especially concerning its impact on American society. They have greatly inspired my work and have provided a large portion of the historical information of my study.

Since the year 2000, the topic hotel has also been increasingly discussed from a European perspective. These books, however, concentrate more on the institution's presentation in literature. There are two very interesting German studies on the use of the hotel as setting by Bettina Matthias and Cordula Seger. In *The Hotel as Setting in Early Twentieth-Century German and Austrian Literature: Checking in to Tell a Story* (2006), Bettina Matthias provides us with a good entry point into the nature of hotels in modernist literature by highlighting the cultural and theoretical context in which the institution developed. Cordula Seger's *Grand Hotel – Schauplatz der Literatur* (2005) goes further time-wise, by also considering the hotel's position after the war and its development at the end of the century, finishing her study with a look at the fantastic buildings of Las Vegas. Both authors, however, focus mostly on German-speaking texts by e.g Thomas Mann, Stefan Zweig, and Vicki Baum and except for Seger's outlook on Las Vegas hotels their studies remain concentrated on European culture.

Different from these two scholars, Martina Krebs centers her study around English-speaking texts of hotel literature. In *Hotel Stories: Representations of Escapes and Encounters in Fiction and Film* (2009) she discusses the hotel's function in literature by using Michael Bakthin's concept of the chronotope. Beyond considering the hotel chronotopes of escape, encounter, crime, and desire she also discusses the impact of the hotel on the identity of the characters in literary

---

of Palace Hotels (1984), Catherine Donzel's *Grand American Hotels* (1990) and Carol Berens *Hotel Lobbies and Bars* (1996).

5 Another scholarly 'hotel text' which belongs in the same period is Wayne Koestenbaum's book *Hotel Theory/Hotel Women* (2008). This text is partly a philosophical discussion of hotel theories, concepts, and personal ideas about the place and a pulp-fiction novel set in a hotel. Koestenbaum has created an interesting compilation of information on hotels and their significance for people, yet the text remains on a very abstract level and therefore does not lend itself so much for my study. Still, I have used some of his ideas and recommend it as a fascinating reading on hotels on two different levels.

texts, even including the impact the hotel has on the authors of the books she discusses. Although she uses some American examples, the main corpus of her study is made up of British and Irish texts. And while she also considers the historical institution hotel she remains focused on its use in literature throughout her book.

Both Joanne Pready and Holly Prescott have worked on specific functions of the hotel in English-speaking literature in their online-published PhD-theses. In her study *The Power of Place: Re-Negotiating Identity in Hotel Fiction* (2009), Pready focuses on identity constructions in hotel texts while Holly Prescott is interested in the *Rethinking of Urban Space in Contemporary British Writing* (2011). Both scholars provide interesting theoretical insights into the possible use of hotel space in literature and beyond, and have been inspirations for my work. However, they, too, mostly remain in the realm of British literature in their studies and, except for marginal comments, do not further consider the historical and social impact of the hotel on American society.[6]

Betsy Klimasmith is one of very few scholars who have written about the historical context of American hotel literature. In her book *At Home in the City: Urban Domesticity in American Literature and Culture, 1850-1930* (2005), she has included an interesting chapter on the use of the hotel setting in Edith Wharton's *The Custom of the Country*. Klimasmith convincingly embeds the novel's hotel setting in its socio-historical context and provides useful inspirations on hotel life in the Gilded Age for my study. There are only two books currently available on the history of New York hotels: Jeff Hirsch's *Manhattan Hotels, 1880-1920* (1997) and Ward Morehouse III's *Life At The Top: Inside New York's Grand Hotels* (2005). However, the first one is strictly speaking an illustrated book and contains only short texts on the hotels depicted and the second one is a quite subjective and anecdotal account. Still, at the moment they are the most extensive books existing on the topic of New York hotels. A handful of scholarly books on hotels will be published in the next years, among them Caroline Levander's *Hotel Life* (2015), the book *The Rise and Fall of the Grand Hotel* by Laura Kolbe et al., containing the proceedings of the conference "Grand Hotels at the Fin de Siécle" (CMS, Humboldt

---

6   Besides these books there are a number of articles from different scholarly fields such as sociology, architectural history, hospitality studies, and cultural studies that deal with the hotel. Among them are Karl Raitz and John Paul Jones's article "The City Hotel as Landscape Artifact and Community Symbol" (1988); Roy Wood's "The Image of the Hotel in Popular Literature: a Preliminary Statement" (1990); Carolyn Brucken, "In the Public Eye: Women and the American Luxury Hotel" (1996); Charlotte Bates "Hotel Histories: Modern Tourists, Modern Nomads and the Culture of Hotel-Consciousness" (2003); Donald McNeill's "The Hotel and the City" (2008); Olga Garcia's "Das Hotel im Spiegel der deutschsprachigen Literatur – Motiv, Kulisse, Bühne und Schauplatz" (2011).

University, Berlin 2013), and *Inns and Hotels in Britain and the United States in the Long Nineteenth Century* (forthcoming 2017) edited by Monika Elbert and Susanne Schmid.

With my study I hope to bring together findings from literary studies, cultural studies, human geography, and history to present a more rounded picture of the impact which hotels have on American society and culture through the hotel experience of people. This study intends to function as a bridge between already existing research and new concepts concerning the importance of places on people's identity.

Working with the texts listed above, it surprised me that many of them, especially the American studies by Berger and Sandoval-Strausz, close with the decade of the 1930s. They declare the era of great hotel development in America closed with the opening of the second Waldorf-Astoria in 1931, the last grand hotel project of this size in America for decades. In this decision they are not alone. Other publications like Arthur White's *The Palaces of the People* (1968)[7] and Elaine Denby's *Grand Hotels: Reality and Illusion* (1998) also agree with them. During my research, however, I repeatedly encountered hotels in contemporary American novels, as well as in other text types that I needed for context.[8] For me, the history of American hotels and their importance for American society and culture does not end with the year 1930. Most of the hotels that I will discuss continue to be relevant in the second half of the twentieth century. As my study will show, the institution hotel has lived on to play an important role in New York society and can still be seen as inspiration and as enabler of cultural and social change. Thus, as the American hotel has already been well researched for the nineteenth and early twentieth century (see chapter 1.3), my study will focus on the twentieth century. While I accept that the institution hotel had its greatest impact on American culture nationwide in the nineteenth century, I still consider its continuous influence after 1900 as crucial, for the city of New York as well as beyond. For example, the Jewish resort hotels in the Catskills, which I will discuss in chapter 6, can be considered as forerunners of Las Vegas casino hotels and by this sparked one of the best known hotel types of the twentieth century.

In addition, this time frame is necessary because I focus on the importance of hotel experience for the production of culture and social change. For hotels to have a significant impact, a large and stable middle-class is needed along with a well-developed infrastructure, modern media, and an approximation of life styles,

---

7   White's book offers interesting insights into the history of hotels in Europe and America, yet it is too anecdotal and unfocused to function as scholarly source.
8   See for example Arthur Hailey's *Hotel* (1965), John Irving's *Hotel New Hampshire* (1981); Paul Theroux's *Hotel Honolulu* (2002); Laurence Geller's *Do Not Disturb* (2005); Karen Tei Yamashita's *I Hotel* (2010).

education and values. Moreover, two of the hotels that I discuss in my study did not exist in the nineteenth century the way they did in the twentieth century. Neither Jewish-Americans nor African Americans were yet fully accepted in American society. Hotels like the Hotel Theresa and the Hotel Grossinger's would not have been viable and even if smaller equivalents started in the nineteenth century, they did not have the marked impact on society that the two institutions developed in the middle of the twentieth century.

To approach the topic of hotel experience and its influence on New York society and culture I will present five case studies, each focusing on one distinctive hotel. I have selected these five hotels to show the different types of hotels existing in New York, as well as the use of the institution by different social groups, taking into consideration the categories of class, lifestyle, race, gender, and religion. All five establishments are situated in New York City or, in one case, nearby. The hotel experience described in this thesis is quite specific and is not representative for all American hotels. Yet, I argue that the five institutions present a very unique and important slice of New York culture that becomes visible through examining hotel experience.

I have arranged the five case studies chronologically, considering the time when the respective hotels were at their peak. I will start with three established New York hotel institutions, the Hotel Waldorf-Astoria, the Hotel Algonquin and the Hotel Chelsea. The focus with them is on their function as stages for society and for personal achievements, work places, and as homes. I will then examine the Hotel Theresa in Harlem and the Hotel Grossinger's in the Catskills and I will analyze their important roles as platforms for their respective communities and social laboratories for change and cultural self-manifestation. By using this structure, basic notions of hotel experience will already have been established and can then be put to effective use in the more complex cases of the last two hotels.

Each case study is structured by the main narratives of hotel experience that surround the respective hotel. This will help to clarify each hotel's particular importance and its special position in New York. I have filtered these narratives from the life writing texts as well as other text sources mentioned above. They present the hotel's different functions and examine which role took precedence in the respective hotel. Using these narratives also establishes a red thread, which runs through all five case studies and enables us to see the parallels but also the specific differences that occur when a hotel is adopted by a special group or community.

The Waldorf-Astoria, the grand hotel par excellence, functions as a kind of prototype and point of entry for the discussion of New York hotels. This does not mean that all American hotels operate on such grand a scale as the Waldorf, yet, for good reasons (see chapter 1) this institution has been repeatedly called "the mother of modern hotels" (McCarthy 107). Due to its particular history, the Waldorf is also the bridge between the well-researched hotel period of the nineteenth century and this work's focus on the twentieth century. When speaking of the Waldorf-Astoria we are actually talking about two different hotel structures. The first Waldorf was erected in 1893, marking the beginning of the boom of hotel building in the Gilded Age. After its demolition in 1929, a second structure of the same name was erected in 1931 on Park Avenue and 49th Street, covering a whole city block.[9] As the leading hotel of the city, the Waldorf-Astoria played a crucial role in New York's history and the development of the city's society. As I will show in this case study, the hotel experience made in this establishment helped on the one hand to democratize New York and on the other hand confirmed society's position. The hotel performed both the role of a stage as well as a microcosm of the larger city. In the case of the Waldorf we can perceive the hotel in its prime function as a stage for society.

My second case study focuses on the Algonquin Hotel. This comparatively small city hotel on 44th Street between Sixth and Seventh Avenue became the birthplace of New York's sophistication in the 1920s and 30s and continued to house literati, artists of reputation, and members of the intelligentsia throughout the twentieth century (Mordden 24). The hotel was the home of the Algonquin Round Table, a literary circle, and inspired the creation of the quintessential urbane magazine, *The New Yorker* (1925). With the Algonquin, the uncommonly close relationship between hotel people and the hotel is apparent. In this case study we have a number of life writing texts and first person accounts, telling us in detail how owner, family, and guests came to identify with this city hotel and how it has received its reputation. The Algonquin functioned as a workplace and as a home in the texts I am analyzing. It was also New York's literary salon.

The Chelsea Hotel will be discussed in the third case study. It is probably the most iconic New York hotel. Famous as the mecca for bohemians it has housed free spirits and convention-defying artists since the late nineteenth century, even before it was turned into a hotel in 1905. However, the heyday of this hotel undoubtably lies in the 1950s and 60s, when the world's alternative culture scene looked upon the hotel for new impulses and "listened" to its walls for inspiration. Because of its peculiar nature, the Chelsea Hotel is the ideal example to study the hotel experience of artists, a quintessential clientele of hotels worldwide. Their life accounts show how the place inspired the residents in their creative process. With the Chelsea, a special kind of hotel/people relationship can be observed, which had an equally large influence on New York culture as the Algonquin, yet was more unconventional. The Chelsea, too, was a work place and stage, but here the emphasis is on the hotel's function as artist's home and source of inspiration.

---

9 These two buildings are not only connected by the same name but also by the people that work in them and the guests that stay there. Therefore, I will treat the Waldorf-Astoria as one hotel phenomenon in my thesis.

With the Hotel Theresa in Harlem, the focus shifts from the hotel's impact on creative people to the socio-political impact the institution can have. Opened as a whites-only establishment in 1913, the Theresa was desegregated in 1940 and run by black management. By that time Harlem had already become New York's dominantly black neighborhood. As the best black hotel of its time in America, probably in the world, the Theresa became the center of Harlem's community and African American society beyond. On the one hand, the hotel was perceived by its guests as a secure haven from the discrimination of midtown hotels. On the other hand, it was the stage for a new black self-confidence and a platform for politicians who wanted to better the situation of African Americans and made the hotel their stomping ground. In this case study we can see the intricate links between a hotel and its surrounding community, which is quite visible here. The Theresa Hotel is a prime example to see how the institution hotel is successfully adapted by a minority group and how race plays out in hotel experience.

In the last case study of my thesis I will discuss not only one hotel, but a whole hotel region, the Jewish Catskills. This area, about 90 miles Northwest of New York City, performed a crucial role in the acculturation of Jewish immigrants in American culture. A significant number of New York Jews went for vacation to the Catskills and here they came into their own as Jewish-Americans for the first time. For a certain comparability I will use the example of Grossinger's Hotel and Country Club to point out the most important narratives of Jewish-American hotel experience. Grossinger's was called the "Queen of the Mountains" (T. Grossinger 178), the leading hotel of the Borscht Belt. In this fifth case study, the categories gender and religion will be the main focus. It will also be of interest how a resort hotel interacts with identity formation and how hotel experience in the country differs from its city counterparts. This resort presents an especially interesting case of hotel experience because three different members of the Grossinger family have written about their lives at the hotel.

The aim of my five case studies is to better understand the hotels' influence on New York's urban society and the creation of culture. In his seminal text "Traveling Cultures" the anthropologist James Clifford realizes that an understanding of the dynamic relationship between dwelling and traveling is crucial to read our modern-day world. He comes to the conclusion that it is necessary to take travel knowledge seriously and to rethink cultures "as sites of dwelling *and* travel": "Thus the ambivalent setting of the hotel suggest[s] itself as a supplement to the field... It frame[s], at least, encounters between people to some degree away from home" (104).

The hotel is the ideal place in this dwelling/traveling approach to culture as it indeed provides for both states. In New York, more than in any other American or European city, hotels have been homes for permanent residents as well as for transient travelers. Seen through the hotel, our understanding of New York's society and culture can open up in new ways. In the following I will present the methods I will apply in my study.

METHODOLOGICAL CONSIDERATIONS

To examine the hotel experience presented in the five case studies of this book, space-oriented approaches and theories are necessary. My argument is that hotel experience results from the interaction between people and the place hotel, both sides having a certain agency. Therefore, an analysis of both the individual practices creating the social space of the hotel as well as the influence of the actual materiality of the institution on people is necessary. Seen together, they create people-place relationship that enables the production of culture in hotels and the creation of new social conventions.[10]

Since the 1980s, the Spatial Turn has created a great momentum in the Humanities, starting a new discussion about space and place. In various fields of social and cultural sciences, scholars reinforced their work on theories that explain the creation and function of space and place and make it a workable research subject. In the first part of this introduction to my methods I will present some key spatial theories that informed this work. The first part contains the foundations of spatial theory in humanities as conceived by Henri Lefebvre, Michel de Certeau, and Edward Soja. As Morgan and Pritchard write, it is important to understand the hotel as a "phenomenon which is much more than simply an operational entity, but a cultural construction which exists in lived, perceived and conceived as well as physical space" (771). While these ideas will inform the main part, their use is implicit here. In the second part of this subchapter on methodology, I will present those concepts that are directly used in the case studies and that I will refer to repeatedly throughout the main part. Embedded in a phenomenological approach these are atmosphere and spatial agency, place-identity and social centrality, and the consideration of hotels as microcosms.

The first important step for the Humanities was to go beyond the Euclidean idea of space and the concept of space as an empty container that can be used in various

---

10 I have not conducted empirical surveys using questionnaires and I will not discuss hotel statistics here. While this kind of sociological material might present interesting information on the institution hotel, it would not work as well for the analysis of hotel experience. Accordingly, it is not the aim of this study to work on a sociological and empirical basis.

kinds of ways and can be filled without further consequences.[11] Henri Lefebvre most successfully achieved this in his study *The Production of Space* (1991, original *La Production de l'espace*, 1974). The French Marxist scholar was one of the first thinkers to understand that space is socially produced and that social relations are produced and reproduced through space (Aitken 148). In his work, Lefebvre made clear that space is not only a mere container for human activity but that "space is never empty: it always embodies a meaning" (Lefebvre 154). For Lefebvre, space is a social product that is used as a tool for thought and action. By deciphering social space we are able to understand the mechanisms behind a given society and learn about its hierarchies and power structures. According to Lefebvre, each society produces its own space (59). Only if it does so, it can be successful. When we consider this in relation to the hotel, we can say that Americans created the hotel in the nineteenth century as an important social space that represented their society and provided it with a place in which this society could develop and prosper. Today, hotel space is still important in a number of social practices and functions, e.g. as useful representational spaces for social events such as political conventions and international conferences.

For Lefebvre space consists of three interrelated aspects. These aspects came to be known as Lefebvre's triad. The triad consists of *spatial practice* (perceived space), *representations of space* (conceived space) and *representational space* (lived space). All of our lived experiences of the world are comprised of these three aspects (Watkins 209). *Spatial practices* refer to how people concretely relate to the outside world and what they do in space, e.g. "journeys to work, to home, to sites of leisure..." (Thacker 19f). One can think of it as physical place. *Representations of space* refer to the spaces as conceived by planners, architects and governments. By creating maps and drawing up plans the production of space is connected to the political. This aspect can be described as mental space. According to Lefebvre, the third aspect, *representational space,* is "directly lived through its associated images and symbols" (39). This space results in symbolic and artistic productions. In contrast to representations of space, representational space for Lefebvre is alive and "it speaks" (42). It can be thought of as social space. All three aspects are interrelated with each other and cannot be thought of separately. While Lefebvre is almost frustratingly vague in his application of his triad, it becomes clear that for the French scholar "social space is inherently composite, mingling heterogenous spaces together in one physical location" (18).

The hotel space is a social product. Therefore, Lefebvre's triad can help in deciphering hotel experience and its meanings. The geographical location and floor

---

11 In a Euclidean understanding "place is basically understood as location definable by sets of coordinates" (Relph 24). It does not consider the human interaction connected to places and place-making.

plans of the hotels discussed in my study, these representations of space, tell us about the function of these social spaces for society and the intentions of their planners. The social practices occurring in the hotels show us how the respective institutions are perceived and how they are made part of the daily life of people. By analyzing what kind of social practices happen in each of the five case studies, one can learn how each of these buildings contributes to their particular community and their role in the hotel network of New York. Finally, by reading the life writing accounts of 'hotel people', the representational space of the hotel, we can understand the symbolic meanings which the hotels take on for the people who interact with them, how these places speak to them and how they reflect this in their lived experience. Lefebvre's triad helps us to examine the hotel experiences that are connected to the five institutions discussed in this study and to comprehend what these experiences mean for the production of culture and social change.

While Lefebvre's approach to space is useful, there is one issue that I have with it. Henri Lefebvre is solely interested in human agency that creates social space, he does not consider the agency of the space created.[12] This focus is too limited for my understanding of hotel space. In the second part of this introduction, I will show how we can open up the discussion of space by including also the idea of spatial agency.

Lefebvre does not discuss the distinction of the words space and place in depth in his text. For him: "Place is ultimately...only one form, though with its own ideology and politics, of the many existing discourses of social space" (19). The distinction of space and place, however, plays a significant role in Michel de Certeau's works. In his seminal work *The Practice of Everyday Life* (1984, original *L'invention du quotidien,* 1980) de Certeau defines place as "the order (of whatever kind) in accord with which elements are distributed in relationships of coexistence" and space as "composed of intersections of mobile elements" (de Certeau 117). For de Certeau "space is practiced place" (de Certeau 117). Through human actions place is transformed into space, like a street that comes alive through the actions of walkers. It is important to de Certeau that one does not make an absolute distinction between space and place, as "there are passages back and forth" (de Certeau 118; see also Thacker 32).

Michel de Certeau writes of the "identification of places" and "actualization of spaces" (de Certeau 118). Place is considered to be more fixed while space is more mobile, flexible and abstract. De Certeau adds two new concepts to the discussion of space and place, *tour* and *map*. In his work, the identification of place relies on a mode of discourse termed the *map*. *Maps* describe a more distant, objective view of

---

12 See Prescott 193. For Prescott, Lefebvre's understanding of space is also too much focused on the actions of humans. He does not consider the dynamic mutuality between people and places, that people are also influenced by the space that surrounds them.

place, as if seen from a great height.[13] *Tour*, on the other hand, describes a more direct, intimate contact with space. It is the experiential discourse associated with the actualization of space (Thacker 31). The *tour* is the pedestrian's experience of space, less graspable, less ordered but more alive and showing the changing nature of space. These two concepts, *map* and *tour*, add new dimensions to the spatial discussion. For my work they are indirectly important. In the life writing accounts as well as in the other text forms, an intermingling of both concepts can be found. Very often the autobiographies and memories start with a map of the hotel, describing its layout, contents, and location and then move on to fill the building with life by touring it. Here, then, the hotel experience takes place. In their life writing texts hotel people describe how they are affected by the hotel space, what functions it has for their lives and how the people/place relationship can be perceived as a mutual and dynamic. The place of the hotel becomes an actualized space through the interaction of people with it. De Certeau's concepts help us see this identification of place and actualization of space in hotel texts and get us closer to understanding hotel experience and its effects.

Both interrelated concepts are needed. I argue that without the *map*, the uninitiated reader is not able to follow the narrator in the texts. In addition, the mapping parts contain important information that influences the touring parts. Together, the hotel experience can be conveyed in a rounded way. Taking both *map* and *tour* into consideration the reader in turn can grasp and examine the described place.

De Certeau and Lefebvre's concepts are fruitful for an understanding of hotel space and to a certain extent hotel experience. Both highlight the relationship between people and their environment. The two scholars focus strongly on human agency as generating space and place. However, the strong focus on human agency of both scholars is also what I find problematic. Reading the life accounts of the people discussed in my study, it emerges that it is not enough to explain space only as a social construct created through human agency. While some of the people, whose life accounts I analyze in this study, are actively involved in the production of the social space in the hotels and even in the material creation of the place, there is still a spatial element recognizable in the texts that goes beyond human agency. To explain this, additional theoretical concepts are needed.

As a connection point between a Lefebvrian understanding of space and that of human geographers belonging to the school of phenomenology, one can look to Edward Soja's writing. Soja has been strongly inspired by Lefebvre and has expanded Lefebvre's concepts with his own, called "Thirdspace." For him, "[e]verything comes together in the Thirdspace: subjectivity and objectivity, the

---

13 De Certeau uses the examples of standing on a skyscraper in New York and viewing the city which lies immobilized and readable in front of the viewer.

abstract and the concrete, the real and imagined, the knowable and the unimaginable, the repetitive and the differential, structure and agency, mind and body, consciousness and unconsciousness, the disciplined and the transdisciplinary, everyday life and unending history" (Soja 56). Using Lefebvre's triad as foil, Soja loosely links his Firstspace to representations of space and social practices, and the Secondspace to the imagined, representational space. In Thirdspace then all come together in the lived experience. Thirdspace is "a distinct mode of critical spatial awareness that is appropriate to the new scope and significance being brought about in the rebalanced trialectics of spatiality-historicality-sociality" (Soja 57). This threeness allows him to see beyond binary structures and to challenge conventions. While his text is criticized for trying to encompass too much, it nevertheless inspired many to think about space and place in a new way. The emphasis in his work to combine imagined space with actual places allows also for a combinational treatment of the two the way I attempt it in this study. Andrew Thacker writes that for Soja "society shapes spaces according to its needs, but, equally, space plays a formative role in the construction of social life" (17). Soja himself calls this the "socio-spatial dialectic" (78).

Ray Oldenburg was inspired by Soja's work for his own concept of the *third place* in *The Great Good Place* (1989). He makes a strong case for the preservation of places like the barbershop or the pub, which are neither home nor work-place and fulfill important social functions for communities: "Most needed are those 'third places' which lend a public balance to the increased privatization of home life. Third places are nothing more than informal public gathering places. The phrase 'third places' derives from considering our homes to be the 'first' places in our lives, and our work places as the 'second'" (Oldenburg, "Our Vanishing 'Third Places'"). Among other places like parks and cafés, hotels and their lobbies fulfill this function in a city like New York, where hotels have a long tradition of offering privatized public space. An example is the importance of the Hotel Algonquin for the original Algonquin Round Table. The regulars met in its dining room each day to lunch together and exchange ideas. For the members of the circle, it fulfilled the role of a third place. It was open and inexpensive.

Third places like hotel lobbies are especially important in American cities because America historically lacks the variety of public places that developed in Europe and that Habermas described in his seminal book *The Structural Transformation of the Public Sphere* (1962, transl. 1989). The openness of the hotel lobby is a crucial spatial feature, which was "invented" in America and sets it apart from European hotels. About the importance of lobbies Carol Berens writes: "Lobbies are where our public and private worlds meet. …This sense of place is critical in present day America where locations for public life are disappearing fast" (xiii). She continues: "One of the defining characteristics of urban life is that it is lived in public. There are times, however, when rampant urbanism must be tamed.

The best respite from frenzied streets is the well-designed, well-tendered hotel lobby. Here one can find an attitude fast disappearing in the public realm – courtesy is respected and one's comfort is important" (xv).

Soja and Oldenburg see a mutuality between people and places. This leads us to the understanding of place by phenomenologists, which will allow us to see hotel experience as a combination of human *and* spatial agency. Repeatedly, the life writing texts discussed in this thesis speak of an influence of the physical surrounding that is not a mere projection of people's actions but that emanates from the structures themselves. To explain this, a phenomenological approach is necessary as well as the concepts of atmosphere and spatial agency, place-identity and social centrality, and the idea of the microcosm. Combined with the understanding of space and place outlined above, this will allow us a deeper understanding of the phenomenon hotel experience as expressed in the writings examined in this study.

Phenomenology explicitly deals with "those direct experiences of the world" (Relph, PaP 4) which presupposes all formal knowledge. It is, so to say, the science of experience. The special people-place dynamic and the mutuality of it have been championed by a number of scholars who affiliate themselves with the field of phenomenology. The 'trailblazers' of this approach are Yi-Fu Tuan, Edward Relph, and Maurice Merleau-Ponty. For them, place is of crucial importance for human life because human beings are always already embedded in place. As humans we live in places and experience them. According to Cresswell, "[w]hat experience does is transform a scientific notion of space into a relatively lived and meaningful notion of place" ("Place" 171). While space is abstract, place, for me, is concrete and experiential. The main interest of this work is a place's meaning for humans and the interrelationship between people and place as expressed in a variety of texts, but foremost in life writing accounts.

One of the most useful place studies is Edward Relph's seminal text *Place and Placelessness* (PaP, 1976). It had a large impact on the humanities and is still considered an important source for the discussion of the experience of place. Relph makes clear that place is "not a bit of space, nor another word for landscape or environment, it is not a figment of individual experience, nor a social construct... It is, instead, the foundation of being both human and nonhuman; experience, actions, and life itself begin and end with place" (Relph, "A Pragmatic Sense of Place" 36). Place is of crucial import for human existence because people have to organize their experiences of the world. Living in this world one has to know, distinguish, and react to the different places in which one works, relaxes, and sleeps (Relph, PaP 1). For Relph, places are the combinations of the human and natural order and are "the significant centers of our immediate experiences of the world" (Relph, PaP 141).

Places are filled with real objects, activities, and meanings, they are constituted by all three. A phenomenology of place is interested in lived space, as it is experienced by people and communities, concerning its functions for them as well the intentions apparent in the place-making. Consequentially, places are important sources for individual as well as community identity.

Place is a multifaceted phenomenon of experience, therefore Relph distinguishes different levels of involvement, to show how the experience of a place can differ according to the level of involvement. He starts with existential outsideness, which is a strong feeling of not belonging somewhere, of being condemned to the position of a mere observer.[14] Relph also lists different levels of insideness, which are of importance concerning hotel experience in the present texts. Emphatic insideness, for example, means to understand the place as "rich in meaning" (54). People who experience emphatic insideness are very aware of the place and its special identity. They are, however, not unconsciously part of it as it is the case in existential insideness. Here, one is part of the place and the place is part of oneself (55).

There is one more level of insideness, which is quite complex, but important for this study. Relph calls it 'vicarious insideness.' It means the experience of places through artistic products such as novels, photographs and other kinds of media (50). Even though this is a second-hand experience of place, it allows us to feel a deep involvement with a place without having actually been there. According to Relph "[t]he degree to which we are transported and the identity of those places to which we are transported depends presumably both on the artist's skills of description and on our own imaginative and emphatic inclinations" (53). The five hotels in this study have all been written about in articles and fictional texts. The respective hotel's identity is therefore not only founded on the first-hand experience of hotel people, but also on the vicarious insideness transported in the texts of journalists and authors. I will present the influence of some of these texts and discuss how successfully this insideness is transported and what the impact on people outside of New York is.

These different levels of involvement in the respective hotels are important for the analysis of the selected texts, especially the life writing accounts. Depending on how much the writer is involved in the hotel, different shades of hotel experiences are described and different facets of the hotel's identity become apparent. As a sense of place is necessary for people's sense of reality (63), the reading of the hotel space that surrounds them and with which they often intensively identify themselves tells us also much about the writers.

It is also important to mention here is that while Relph's distinction into insider and outsider experiences can appear exclusionary, insideness and outsideness in the case of hotels is much less fixed than in 'normal', unifunctional places. Almost

---

14 In the case of Jewish Americans and African Americans, both groups have been forced to take this position toward mainstream hotels until the mid of the twentieth century.

everyone can become a hotel insider. Looking at the special institution hotel in this study allows us to challenge some classic concepts connected to place such as inside and outside, private and public, owner and guest, home and away from home. These challenging notions run through my whole study, breaking up some fixed ideas about places to connect them to the changing reality of our mobile world.[15]

Place-identity and the Hotel

Edward Relph's work has inspired David Seamon, a fellow phenomenologist, whose approach to place and his use of the concept place-identity has informed my understanding of place for this thesis. For David Seamon one of the central concerns of phenomenology "is identifying foundational structures through which human life is given coherence and continuity" ("Place, Place Identity and Phenomenology" 3). As with Relph, the focus of Seamon's understanding of place centers on the experience of place by people in their "lifeworld" (8). According to Seamon, it is important to see place in relation to people, and also to see people in relation to the place which surrounds them: "researchers need to understand place as incorporating a lived engagement and process whereby human beings afford and are afforded by the world of places in which they find themselves" (Seamon 3).[16] By approaching place with the concept of place-identity, David Seamon sees a way of getting closer to the nature of place and its role in human life.[17]

To discuss human/place relations on a deeper level, Seamon uses a triadic approach like Lefebvre and Soja, yet he specifically adds a relationship-level.

---

15 To look at the hotel as a more open place also supports Doreen Massey's invitation to consider the character of a place as extroverted, "which includes a consciousness of its links with the wider world" (Massey, "A Global Sense of Place" 155). She asks us to see places as "articulated moments in networks of social relations and understandings" (154). In my study I want to show the network that exists among the five hotels which strengthens their own character but also shows that this character depends on their relation with the city surrounding them and the connections they strike up with the larger world.

16 Seamon refers also to Jeff Malpas, for whom the mutuality between place and human is fundamental for his work. Malpas writes: "It is through our engagement with place that our own human being is made real, but it is also through our engagement that place takes on a sense and a significance of its own" (Malpas 23).

17 Seamon approaches place with a more body-centered focus. His best known contribution to the discussion of place is the 'body-ballet'. To a certain extent his definition of place-identity is connected to this. For more about this concept, see David Seamon, "Body-subject, time-space routines, and place-ballets" in A. Buttimer & D. Seamon (ed.), *The Human Experience of Space and Place* (1980).

Seamon distinguishes the geographic ensemble, people-in-place and the spirit of place as the three elements of the triad of place (Seamon 10).[18] Out of this triad develops *place identity*. This mutuality between people and places is described as the way "how people living in a place take up that place as their world; how they unself-consciously and self-consciously accept and recognize that place as part of their personal and communal identity" (Seamon 12f). For Seamon, place-identity is an essential dimension for understanding place experience and the making of places. For place identity to develop, places need identifiable, singular, obvious elements, which people can identify with.

Using Seamon's concepts I will bring together the physical nature of the respective New York hotel, the way people write about their interaction with it, and I will carve out the spirit, or atmosphere, that people perceive in the place and which we can discover in their texts. The hotels selected for this study all have a specific style, something unique to them, which does not only come out of their structure or their location, but out of a mélange of the three elements presented above. They have a certain physical legibility to them that hotel people translate into their writings and which I will examine. This close identification can be seen already in the circumstance that these people label themselves as Waldorf Crowd, Algonquinites, Chelseaites etc. It also shows itself in how they describe their spatial experiences in the hotels. The intense way in which they experience security at the hotel and a sense of belonging is a sign for a strong place-identity, which involves "positively valenced cognitions of one or some combination of these settings which outweigh" (Proshansky 76) more negative aspects.[19]

It might seem surprising that place-identity develops in the institution hotel, a place that due to its temporary nature appears unlikely to develop place-identity. Hotels are often only conceived as what Augé terms "non-places," spaces that "cannot be defined as relational, or historical or concerned with identity" (Augé

---

18 Seamon mirrors with this Relph's idea of place-identity being made up of physical setting, activity, and meaning.

19 Up until the 1970s, place was largely ignored as an important factor in people's self-perception. By the 1970s, human geographers and environmental psychologists realized that not only social roles, but "the places and spaces a child grows up in, those that he or she comes to know, prefer, and seek out or avoid also contribute significantly to self-identity" (Proshansky et al. 74). Proshansky et al. outline that place-identity has a similar conceptual structure as social roles for self-identity and that physical settings are directly relevant to the successful performance of these social roles and the definition of who we are (Proshansky et al. 74). Seamon expands Proshansky's approach to focus more on the physical place involved in the creation of place-identity.

78).[20] Yet, the institution hotel has been an important part of American culture for more than two hundred years and is said to fit the American restless, mobile nature better than most other environments. Another explanation has to do with the kind of people frequenting hotels. Most of them are used to a mobile lifestyle, several of them are artists. For them, the nature of the hotel, its simultaneous public and private quality, the liberating spirit of not being tied to domestic obligations paired with the opportunity of social interaction in the public parts of the house, is a seemingly perfect fit, not exclusively in America, but especially here (see also Garcia 25; Peters 76; Zeveloff).[21] Place-identity and the triad of place complement Elisabeth Bowen's understanding of the hotel as an entity consisting of historic, social, and organic aspects. In the life writing accounts that I discuss the question of place-identity will come up repeatedly.

Social Centrality of Hotels

Connected to the issue of place-identity is another concept that is also useful for my study, the concept of *social centrality* as conceived by Rob Shields and extended by Kevin Hetherington. It goes beyond the place-identity of individuals and considers the identity-shaping power of certain places for whole communities. Edward Relph writes about place and its importance for the identity of a community: "The relationship between community and place is indeed a very powerful one in which each reinforces the identity of the other, and in which the landscape is very much an expression of communally held beliefs and values and of interpersonal involvements" (PaP 34). Kevin Hetherington thinks along the same lines when he takes up Rob Shields's concept of social centrality and shows its impact on identity formation processes of groups, in his example of those at the margins of society.

---

20 In his book *Non-Place: An Introduction to An Anthropology of Supermodernity* (1996) Augé focuses mostly on contemporary transient places like airport terminals, highways, and chain hotels. He does not see the term non-place as necessarily negative but as a mere description of its nature. Even Edward Relph, who started the discussion in *Place and Placelessness* (1976), concedes that placelessness can also mean freedom from place (140), freedom from conventions and obligations. In some cases non-places can also feel secure or liberating. They are useful in a mobile world and a part of everyday life. As the hotels discussed in this study were all originally non-chain hotels, they are not non-places. Thus, Augé's central term is not applicable to them.

21 To pay for a temporary home alienates us from it, but as Georg Simmel writes: "[t]he desirable party for financial transactions – in which, as it has been said quite correctly, business is business – is the person completely indifferent to us, engaged neither for us nor against us" (Simmel 227). We feel no obligations to the hotel clerk and therefore are freed from personal obligations.

Hetherington defines social centrality as the property of a place that "provides a focus for the articulation of identity and a sense of belonging" (34). This also necessitates the identification of key sites (Hetherington 34). In his essay Kevin Hetherington focuses especially on outsider groups like New Age Travelers. For them, places that are marginal or outside of the norms of society can act like shrines; coming together in these places creates a feeling of community and gives the participants group identity (34). The concept can also be applied to other groups that come together in one specific place and draw their identity from this meeting place, like longterm hotel guests.

Hetherington is especially interested in heterotopic spaces as for him they not only provide the symbolic properties of social centrality for a group, they also provide, through their alternate ordering, a distinctive place for being different and a shared sense of belonging expressed through that difference that takes the form of a *communitas* of intensely affectual forms of sociality among the initiands (39).[22]

One example of a heterotopia, as Foucault defined it, is the hotel. The concept of social centrality can thus be applied to hotels and their communities.[23] They are part of their cities, but for guests, hotels are often only stopping places or places they use at a time of crisis. Hotels project permanence and transience at the same time. According to Hetherington, it is "this key ambivalence, which gives it its heterotopic significance" (47). For regulars of the Waldorf, the Algonquin and the Chelsea Hotel in particular, the respective hotel can take on a deeper, more spiritual meaning. In the life writing texts on these two institutions one finds statements describing them as "temples," "meccas," and centers of the city's nerve system. Algonquinites and Chelseaites actively derive their communal identity from their connection to these hotels. The spirit of community that develops in hotels among the guests and staff has been often observed and is surprisingly strong. The concept of communitas can be applied to the guests' relationship to hotels, while employees may share such feelings. However, they are also bound by a contract and are paid for being part of the operation. All five hotels described in my thesis show this strong sense of community feeling, of social centrality. For the people frequenting these hotels regularly, staff, guests, and hotel family members, this communal

---

22 The term communitas goes back to Victor Turner and suggests the spontaneous development of a community as opposed to its institutionalization (Achilles and Bergmann 9). Hetherington defines communitas here as "an intense, if fleeting, condition of affectual solidarity and bonding that produces its own forms of sociation through which an identification and shared sense of belonging is formed" (39f).

23 The community identity described in this text does not counter Doreen Massey's statement concerning the misidentification of communities with places. It just shows that communities can be connected to places, they just do not necessarily have to be.

identity is not a coincidental occurrence but a decisive element in their lives and in the way they perceive themselves.

Atmosphere and the Hotel

To get closer to what causes the uniqueness of places, especially hotels, so that they become a part of one's identity or a community's identity, one has to consider the concept of *atmosphere*. Edward Relph calls it the *genius loci* of a place, this quality that a place exudes which is hard to grasp, but often powerful. People usually circumscribe it with the term atmosphere. Atmosphere, one of the "central tenets of spatial theory" (Pready 76), is an important concept for this study because it expresses that part of the hotel experience not originating solely in human agency. It comes up in almost all the texts analyzed in this work and is of great importance for the understanding of hotel experience.

There is an ongoing debate what constitutes atmosphere.[24] Some scholars believe that atmosphere is wholly a projection of people's feelings and emotions on a place. For Seamon, atmosphere is something that arises in the in-between or, as he puts it: it "has its own phenomenal reality and integrity that human beings can know and engage with" (11). While sociologist Martina Löw acknowledges a certain "generability" (Löw 44) in atmosphere, she sees more to it.[25] For Löw, atmosphere is "an external effect, instantiated in perception, of social goods and human beings in their situated spatial order/ing" (25). Another term that she uses for atmosphere is the *potentiality of space*, which underlines again the spatial character of atmosphere. Löw stresses the point that it is important to realize that the perception of atmosphere is socially pre-structured (46). In the examples of this study, the groups connected to the hotels discussed, and a large portion of New Yorkers, experience the atmosphere, the spirit of place, of the selected institutions in a similar way.

I agree with the findings of Seamon and Löw on atmosphere as my research on the five selected hotels shows that the selected hotels draw people to them because they exude some kind of inherent attraction. Guests describe that coming to these hotels, their mood can change, they feel different, empowered, inspired.[26] While the

---

24 Among the most recent studies is Andreas Rauh's *Die besondere Atmosphäre: Ästhetische Feldforschungen* (2012). Rauh perceives atmosphere as one of the basic phenomena of our lifeworld and, despite the vagueness of the concept, as crucial part of our everyday experience.

25 People work hard to achieve a certain kind of atmosphere, as can be seen in the case of hotels.

26 This mood change is seen by scholars as the most significant proof for the claim that atmosphere is something external (Löw 44).

hotels' atmosphere originates partly in the aura of their guests and staff, the institutions themselves bring something into this equation, they have spirit of place. Seamon puts it in the following way: "Just by being one way rather than another, [place] can affect human life because of its particular physical, spatial, and environmental qualities" (12). The specific spatial and social nature of a hotel, with its ordering, code, hierarchy, and its economical need to attract guests shows this even clearer than any other institution. Edward Relph writes: "just as the individuality and distinctiveness of the appearance of any one person endures from childhood to old age, so the identity of a particular place can persist through many external changes because there is some inner, hidden force - 'a god within'" (31).

Hotel and Spatial Agency

The examination of the potentiality of space leads us to the concept of spatial agency, which will help us further to understand the hotels' role in New York culture and people's hotel experience in them. Spatial agency in hotel literature has already been discussed in two dissertations in the last years, Joanne Pready's *The Power of Place: Re-Negotating Identity in Hotel Fiction* (2009), and Holly Prescott's *Rethinking of Urban Space in Contemporary British Writing* (2011). While Pready uses spatial agency of the hotel more abstractly in her work, Prescott makes a strong case for it by using and adapting Bruno Latour's concept of 'material agency' to the discussion of space.[27] In her dissertation, Prescott works on developing new ways of reading urban spaces in literature, especially spaces on the margin of society like ruins, underground spaces, and transient spaces like the hotel. This new way is necessary, according to Prescott, because too many literary scholars have used Lefebvre's framework of reading space in literature, by this neglecting and even rejecting the notion of non-human agency of spaces, reducing spaces completely to a man-made, socially produced entity.[28] I support Prescott's claim for more openness to a spatial, material agency, especially when it comes to analyzing the hotel in texts.[29]

---

27 Latour is one of the scholars developing the actor-network theory.
28 According to Prescott, in a Lefebvrian framework of reading space, the notion of spatial agency "would be seen as theoretically dangerous, further fetishising space and concealing the social relations from which this agency 'really' arises" (58). I agree with Prescott that to allow for the existence of spatial agency does not necessarily mean that one shuts one's eyes to other agencies at work.
29 In her texts, Prescott moves away from the Lefebvrian framework of reading space in literature and instead uses the concepts of Walter Benjamin and Siegfried Kracauer, who both allow for the particular power of space to shape narratives and human experience and who are both also interested in more marginal spaces of society, including the

Bruno Latour defines non-human agency in the following way: "In addition to 'determining' and serving as a 'backdrop of human action' things might authorize, allow, afford, encourage, permit, suggest, influence, block, render possible, forbid, and so on... ." Thus, "we should be ready to inquire about the agency of all sorts of objects" (76).[30] He questions the sole supremacy of human agency. For Latour objects do influence human actions and therefore one can speak of a certain agency, even if this effect is not as intentional as it is with humans: "anything that does modify a state of affairs by making a difference is an actor – or, if it has no figuration yet, an actant" (Latour 71).

For her redefinition of the theory of space in literature, which allows a use of it in a wider context, Holly Prescott expands Bruno Latour's concept to also utilize it for space, which is a convincing consideration. Prescott claim spatial agency especially for hotel space because a "hotel [is] a space with an irresistible ability to arrest human agency" (28). The hotel space itself influences the people acting in it. Like their surrounding cities, the microcosmic space of hotels is a "field[] of movements ... bringing into relation all kinds of actors, human and non-human, in all manners of combinations of agency" (Amin & Thrift 83).[31]

The influence of hotel space on fictional stories has already been examined. As an example, Prescott introduces Virginia Woolf's use of the hotel in her texts and shows that "the ways in which taking the hotel space as one's literary subject matter may indeed have necessary and profound implications for the ultimate narrative structure of the resulting work" (Prescott 29). From Woolf's texts as well as from ur-texts of the hotel genre like Vicki Baum's *Menschen im Hotel* (1929), a plot type has been derived which can be called *hotel plot*. In the hotel plot a number of unrelated plot lines are united and become credible only because of their setting in the hotel (Matthias 174). Here, the hotel is not only backdrop but the structural reason why the plot works for the reader. Alexa Weik von Mossner describes this kind of dynamic of the fictional space as 'mithandelnder Schauplatz', "a diegetic space that is not so much the setting for the action as it is an *active agent* and thus *part* of the action" (Weik von Mossner). The hotel plot shows how a specific urban space and its agency can have "profound influence on literary form as well as content" (Prescott 29). First related to modernism and reworked and used by

---

transient space of the hotel. Kracauer emphasizes "how a space refers beyond itself, points to past as well as distant associations" (John Allen 31). He recognizes and accentuates the importance of hotel spaces in his seminal essay "The Hotel Lobby".

30 Note the word choice "backdrop of human action." This already evokes more of a spatial consideration.

31 Armin and Thrift are cultural geographers and follow the non-representational theory, which is related to the actor-network theory of Latour and the concept of material agency.

postmodernists, it allows for a fragmentary structure to make sense and capture more authentically the urban experience of modern individuals.

I will show this spatial agency at work in life writing texts and a number of other text forms, which allows us to consider the impact of space on the fictional creations of people and their understanding of place in their artistic work. All the hotel people whose texts I am analyzing are deeply influenced by their respective hotel. They express in their works the spatial agency of the hotel surrounding them. Furthermore, inspired by their hotel experience, the writers are able to 'jump' in their narration between topics and introduce people and events without a long pretext. In that, their writings are quite similar to Vicki Baum's *Menschen im Hotel*, where this kind of nonlinear combination of different plot lines was successfully used for the first time. The same can be said for cultural products created at the hotel such as books of hotel photographies which present a seemingly wild mixture of subjects and angles, but which are all connected by the topos hotel.

I argue that due to their peculiar heterotopic quality and their openness hotels exceed their original uses similar to the underground spaces Prescott analyzes. The strong dynamic mutuality between people and the hotel space allows it to be used more creatively, becoming a powerful and empowering place. I will present one example. James Donald writes: "No longer can you assume that people's experience of space will be determined by your plan for that space" (140). In his biography, Oscar Tschirky, the maître d' hotel of the Waldorf, remembers: "When the architect designed the Waldorf his only purpose in including the corridor [Peacock Alley] was to have a spacious entrance to the Palm Room, which was destined to be New York's most exclusive restaurant. The natural vanity of man and woman turned the dead-end alley into the hotel's greatest asset" (Schriftgiesser 71). The materiality of the space together with the social practice of the people give this place, Peacock Alley, its meaning as New York's foremost parading ground. In my case studies we see this "interdependence of human agency and a distinct kind of spatial agency" (55), as Prescott puts it, repeatedly. It becomes most obvious when the place is not just fulfilling the role that it has been planned for, but when it encourages a kind of behavior that goes beyond this use, that shows dynamics that we can describe as spatial agency.

Hotel As Microcosm

As we saw above, the hotel, like its surrounding environment the city, is a place that brings together all kinds of human and non-human actors. Due to this it can function as a condensed version of the city. This is the reason why the hotel has been repeatedly called a microcosm of the city. In my study I will treat the hotels discussed in the five case studies as microcosms of certain parts of New York society, sometimes more inclusive, sometimes more limited. The *Oxford English*

Dictionary defines microcosm as "[a]ny complex entity, esp. a community, regarded as forming a self-contained or self-regulating world or universe. ...More generally: a place, situation, etc. regarded as encapsulating in miniature the characteristic qualities or features *of* something much larger" (OED). Many scholars working on the hotel repeatedly use the term microcosm to express the nature of the institution and its function and position for the community that surrounds it (Raitz 32; McNeill 384; Krebs 43). For Daniel Boorstin, "American hotels were a microcosm of American life" (Boorstin 147). I argue that the reason for the constant use of this word is that it comes closest to the complex nature of a hotel. We can treat hotels as miniatures of the larger society because in their complex spatial ordering and hierarchy almost all groups of society can be found. The hotel functions as home, workplace, place of leisure, meeting place, information exchange, and in this mirrors the human activities occurring in the larger urban society.

Different functions create different kind of hotels, such as the city, railroad or resort hotel, different identities of hotel people, and consequentially different hotel experiences. What causes and allows these various uses of space to occur in the same place is the heterotopic and liminal nature of the hotel, already mentioned shortly in the discussion of social centrality. Pritchard and Morgan write: "The hotel is a similarly betwixt transitory space, outside the ordinary of most people's everyday social life, distinct from our normal place of home" (764). The term heterotopia is a concept made popular by French philosopher and social critic Michel Foucault. A heterotopia is defined as "all the other sites that can be found within [a] culture [which] are simultaneously represented, contested, and inverted" (Foucault 24). In contrast to utopia and dystopia, a heterotopia is an actual place in modern society and is often used in times of crisis or for rites of passage (such as the hospital or the honeymoon suite) and for the social ordering of people defying the norm (such as prisoners, but also artists like Udo Lindenberg who decided to live permanently in the Hotel Atlantic). A heterotopia is "capable of juxtaposing in a single real place several spaces, several sites that are in themselves incompatible" (Foucault 25). This is the case in the hotel. Because it is private and public at the same time, open to all but limited by certain rites and norms like the check-in, hotel space is heterotopic and multi-functional.[32] Over the decades it has been used as workplace, stage, and home. I argue that the heterotopic nature of the hotel allows it to play such a focal role in American society and imbues it with so much creative energy. I want to end my methodological considerations by discussing these

---

32 The hotel, of course, has also an economic function. The hotelkeeper earns his or her livelihood with the hotel, he pays the employees with the money guests pay for using the rooms. This should not be overlooked and will be considered in the main part.

seemingly contradictory functions, which will be of importance in the five case studies.

Basically, a hotel is a place of shelter and refreshment, which is provided by the innkeeper and the hotel staff. Someone of the hotel staff needs to be on-site 24/7. Several scholars and writers have commented on the fact that people working in hotels often identify themselves to a large degree with these hotels. In classic hotel novels such as the *Grand Babylon Hotel* by Arnold Bennett, *Work of Art* by Sinclair Lewis, and *Martin Dressler* by Steven Millhauser, the hotel people depicted see themselves as part of their hotels, they derive their own self-identity from their work place.[33] In my thesis, several of the autobiographies and life writing accounts have been written by managers and staff members. Their texts are often as much a biography of the hotel in which they work as their own life stories. The accounts of hotel children, often depicting the diverse obligations and long work hours of their parents, also stress the uniqueness of the hotel as workplace. Hotels are open 24/7 and hotel work never becomes routine due to the circumstance that the guests are constantly changing. Pritchard and Morgan add: "as workplaces, hotels also traverse many different social positionings and the boundaries between staff and guests are often crossed" (768). In this study, it is often the case that long-term guests perceive the hotel staff no longer only as service-providers but as part of the family. They are considered as friends and intimates even though or probably because they are paid employees and the relationship between guests and staff follows clearer, less messy lines than among normal friends, which especially artistic guests like e.g. Alec Wilder prefer.

On the other side of the front desk, the guests use the hotel as place of rest on their business trips, but sometimes also as actual workplace, as for example the writers Joseph Roth and Maya Angelou. Joseph Roth developed such a close relationship with hotels that he called himself a "Hotelpatriot" (Roth 6). Maya Angelou once stated in an interview that she needed the liberating, neutral atmosphere of a hotel to write. So she reserved herself a hotel room for months at a time in which she would not sleep but only come to work each morning and leave each afternoon (Zeveloff). Thus, hotels can be workplaces for owners and employees as well as guests.

Hotels are not only workplaces, but they often perform as stages for society and politics (Matthias 28f), a side of the hotel which is often neglected in analyses. Places like lobbies, hotel restaurants, lavish hallways, and ballrooms have performed as the background to many bigger and smaller human dramas. It is the function of the hotel as stage, which allows us, for a moment, to consider the paradoxical nature of the hotel as an elitist and a leveling place. For me, this is a

---

33 Martina Krebs as well as Joanne Pready have dedicated whole chapters to the staff-hotel relationship in their studies.

consequence of the heterotopic condition of the hotel. The phrase 'palace of the public' is a condensation of this tension existing in the American hotel. The American grand hotel developed as a counterpart to European aristocratic residences, so an elitist character was part of the hotel experience from the beginning. A hotel was a prestige object for a community, representing the town at its best (see the development of grand hotels in 1.3). Accordingly, it was decorated pompously. On the other hand, many hotels made their real profit not with their hotel rooms but instead with their bars, restaurants and event business (Sandoval-Strausz 168). The essayist N.P. Williams remarks: "The going to the Astor and dining with two hundred well-dressed people, and sitting in full dress in a splendid drawing room with plenty of company – is the charm of going to the city" (qtd. in Sandoval-Strausz 169). Hotels needed the larger public as customers, those who could not pay two dollars for a room, but could pay for food, barber shop service, and a drink. The money made from selling alcoholic drinks balanced out losses at times of low occupancy. Accordingly, in the public places of the hotel, a very heterogeneous mix of people existed. As long as everyone adhered to the basic hotel rules, one did not even need to purchase anything. So-called hotel loungers are probably the most famous result of the public nature of American hotels. This was a term for usually white men, who dressed respectably and used the lobby as their extended living rooms but never actually consumed anything there.[34] It is true that these white middle class men do not represent the whole of American society. Yet, their behavior created the impression that hotel lobbies were places where everyone was welcome. This was underlined by the circumstance that hotels also functioned as stages for politicians and were the places where one could see the actual workings of the democratic process. As we will see in the following case studies, the hotel as stage can have a powerful impact on society, so much as to even alter society's behavior. It can become a social laboratory for change.

Besides being a stage the hotel's most often discussed function is that of a temporary, or even permanent, home. Most of the writers of autobiographies and memoirs in my study experienced the hotel to some degree as home. The home is the place which arguably has the strongest impact on us. The word 'home' is recurrent when it comes to any discussion of hotels and hotel space. The best-known description of the hotel is that of a "home away from home," a kind of substitute home when people, for whatever reason, have to leave their own home and take up accommodation in a hotel. For most hotels it is their ultimate goal to succeed in giving people this feeling of being at home, of offering privacy and

---

34 The most famous description of this type can be found in the character Hurstwood in Theodore Dreiser's novel *Sister Carrie* (1901). After Hurstwood elopes with Carrie to New York and is unable to find a suitable job, he joins the brotherhood of lounge lizards, who were an everyday occurrence in New York hotels at the turn of the century.

security, a nurturing place in a hectic world. Yet, this image of the hotel as "home away from home" is also the starting point for most criticism wielded against the hotel. Critics of the hotel state that it is only a commercial institution, which fakes being a real home. For them, it does neither have the necessary foundation nor the true spirit of a home. With increasing standardization hotels have come to resemble much more a well-oiled machine than a 'home.' Thus, the relationship between the terms *home* and *hotel* is tense.

What, then, is the definition of home? Many scholars have concerned themselves with attempts to try to define 'home.'[35] Human geographer Tim Cresswell writes that "[h]ome is an exemplary kind of place where people feel a sense of attachment and rootedness" (*Place* 24). For him, it is a "center of meaning and a field of care" (24). For David Seamon, the home is a place which lends people a feeling of security, a place where they can control what happens to some degree (*A Geography of the Lifeworld* 78f). Home is often considered the place where people can be themselves without needing to hide behind a social mask. For philosopher and phenomenologist Gaston Bachelard, home is "our corner of the world. ...[I]t is our first universe, a real cosmos in every sense of the word" (Bachelard 4). It is an intimate space where experience is particularly intense, the starting point from which most people understand the wider world.[36]

What do we make of these considerations of 'home' in relation to the hotel? In my opinion, the criticism directed against the hotel as a fake and empty "home away from home" is too short-sighted. Although I know of instances where hotels are indeed despised by people who have to be away from their private homes too often and stay in too many hotels, there are an equally large number of people who are very grateful for the institution hotel as a "home away from home" and gladly seek shelter there. Considering my findings, hotels can indeed become homes, and for some, even better fitting homes than the classic private residence. In the anonymity of hotels, they are freed from expectations of their family or their jobs. My case studies show that this is especially true for people connected to the arts. Hotels can develop into places where people experience rootedness (see e.g. Alec

---

35 Recently, Klaus Stierstorfer has published a collection of essays on the topic, *Constructions of Home: Interdisciplinary Studies in Architecture, Law, and Literature* (2010).

36 According to Cresswell, the concept 'home' has seen much criticism in the last years from the side of feminists who take an issue with the over-positive, nostalgic depiction of home. For them this view is a male-dominated understanding of the place. For women, home is often less a nurturing place, but a place of oppression, of exploitation and isolation (Rose 53). While other female scholars do not view home as negatively, they ask at least for a more cautious and open definition of what home means and how this meaning was attached to the place in the first place.

Wilder and the Algonquin Hotel), where they can be more themselves than at home where they would have to fulfill preexisting role models (see e.g. Elsa Maxwell at the Waldorf, and Edgar Lee Masters at the Chelsea). After going through the rituals of checking-in they are liberated by the hotel from domestic duties and conventions. For them the anonymity of hotel life is what allows them to be themselves or to play with different identities. While guests in hotels have not the same amount of control over the place as they would have in their private residence, they are often quite happy to let go of this control temporarily. In the case of hotel children, who are less free in their choice of location, they themselves find ways to undermine the classic hotel order and create places of their own, because the complex character of hotel space allows for it.

I do not want to claim that a hotel can be a comfortable home for everyone. But I argue for a more open-minded approach to hotels as "homes away from home." Architectural critic Ian Nairn writes about modern nomadism and the increasing mobility of the twentieth century world: "People put down roots... in a terribly short time; ... I would even argue paradoxically, that that mobility increases the sense of place" (Nairn 10). Looking at the autobiographical texts of this study, I agree with him. I think that in a world, which has become more mobile than ever, alternative homes like hotels are needed to make this mobile lifestyle safe and comfortable. In addition, for people who cherish mobility and a certain lack of bourgeois convention, hotels remain open and open-minded places to find shelter. Each of the hotels discussed here will fulfill all three functions discussed above to some degree. It is often impossible to make a clear distinction between them, as the three functions often merge.

Hotels are microcosms of society. Confronted with this microcosmic perception of the hotel, some critics point out that not the whole of society is represented in hotels, that often marginal figures are left out, especially the unemployed and poor, and that hotels are places out of the ordinary and not part of the normal life. I do not disregard this criticism. I am aware that in the case studies here not all groups existing in American society are represented. It is also true that grand hotels like the Waldorf-Astoria are places were 'regular' people are only able to stay as part of a once-in-a-lifetime experience. However, a grand hotel, as any other hotel, still consists of people of all classes, from wealthy residents, rich guests, white-collar workers, people celebrating special anniversaries or rites of passages like proms and weddings, to visitors from the street, blue collar-workers, and freshly arrived immigrants who often work in menial jobs.

I also want to point out again that the American hotel, in contrast to the European hotel, is thought of as inherently more public, more open for visitors and more part of the local community. When I speak of the microcosmic nature of the Hotel Algonquin, I do not mean to imply that all hotels are like this particular institution and that always all of society is represented at once in this place. But for an artist residing there or regularly meeting friends for lunch, it contains at that moment everything that her or his world is meant to contain. It fulfills that person's needs and expectations and represents a self-contained society, which she or he defines as relevant.

Finally, due to the legitimate criticism of social selection and class bias I felt it to be especially important to examine how different ethnic groups make use of the institution hotel. I want to demonstrate that the institution hotel has been successfully adapted to different environments and functions. The hotel is not exclusively for the rich white establishment. In the case study of the Hotel Theresa in Harlem and Grossinger's Hotel and Country Resort in the Catskills I will show that for African Americans and Jewish-Americans the hotel, too, is a useful entity that fits their needs and can be used as a tool to achieve their goal of integration, acculturation, and acceptance.[37] Over more than two centuries, the American hotel has become an important institution for the inspiration, production, and distribution of culture and social change. Its history shows that the hotel has been and still can be used and adapted to a wide range of different groups and communities, a microcosm of America.

HOTEL HISTORY

At the beginning of this introductory chapter I have already alluded to the close historical connection between America and the institution hotel. The special hotel experience described in the five case studies and the great significance of these hotels for New York society and culture can only be understood against the hotel's historical background. To round off this introduction, thus, I will now present a condensed historical overview.

Hotels became essential institutions in American society at a time when America was experiencing the greatest changes since its foundation. In the nineteenth century, America changed from a more agricultural country to an industrial nation. This caused change in the social make-up, creating new kinds of classes and social structures. This era also saw an explosion of urbanization, a huge influx of immigrants, a revolution in the transportation system, and a greater mixture of cultures than ever before. For these developments, new institutions were needed. According to Williamson, these new places became reality in "the modern

---

37 People know that there are certain ways to behave in public, like not running naked in the streets. These rules seem to be dictated to us by commonsense. However, according to Cresswell "[i]t is this very commonsense nature of place-based norms that make them so powerful and ideological tool" ("Place" 174).

hotel, an institution that is perhaps the most representative and expressive example of those changes that we have had" (Williamson 3). For the historian, "the modern first-class hotel was an invention, with the old-style inn merely furnishing the root idea – just as ... Stephenson's locomotive, based on Watt's condensing steam-engine" (Williamson 3). Williamson was writing this in 1930. More than seventy years later, Andrew Sandoval-Strausz still comes to the same conclusion: "[t]he hotel was part of the project of American nationhood" (Sandoval-Strausz 39).

The most common critical reaction to these claims is that places for the accommodation of strangers have existed since before the Roman Empire. Accordingly, freely quoting Anne Bradstreet, they have not just sprung up lately in America. Moreover, the word 'hotel' itself is not American, but of French origin, meaning a noble man's house. Both points of criticism are valid. Yet, looking at the findings by Williamson, Sandoval-Strausz, Berger, and other scholars America's leading role is nevertheless correct.

Hospitality is one of the most necessary and basic rites of human society. According to anthropologist Julian Pitt-Rivers: "hospitality is a 'rite of incorporation'" (Julian Pitt-Rivers qtd. in Sandoval-Strausz 137). Strangers are accepted into a community, are cared for and protected. Thus, the exchange of information and traditions can take place. Already 12,000 years ago, tribes provided a special hut or cottage for foreigners seeking temporary shelter, usually suited for one person. According to Williamson the history of the commercial inn starts in the 6th century B.C., with the invention of money. At the beginning of the Modern Age, inns provided rooms for up to thirty travelers and basic services like food, drinks, and stables for the animals. Concerning the built structure, the services, and the cleanliness of the place, there were no great differences to the inns of the Roman Empire. With the stagecoach, travel increased on the European continent and the British Isles but the comfort in the accommodations stayed largely the same, with common dining and common sleeping, often three or four guests in the same bed.

Indeed, a really new change in hospitality businesses occurred for the first time in hundreds of years on the American continent at the end of the 18th century. Up until then, British America was covered with inns and taverns very closely resembling the British role models and of the same standard. This, however, began to change. Berger writes: "Toward the end of the eighteenth century, the word *hotel* came into use in America to describe the elite group of taverns and inns that catered to upper-class patrons" (Berger, *Hotel Dreams* 14). One of the great changes was a superior service that justified this new word 'hotel.'[38] Yet, it was not only the type

---

38 The new meaning of the word 'hotel' is defined by the *Oxford English Dictionary* in the following way: "A building or establishment where travellers or tourists are provided with overnight accommodation, meals, and other services. Hotels may be distinguished from other forms of temporary lodging for travellers by their larger size and range of

of service that changed, but for the first time buildings for the explicit use of hotels were erected to accommodate larger numbers of people.

Image 1: The First American Hotel, "The City Hotel," New York

City Hotel, Trinity & Grace Churches, Broadway, 1831. From the New York Public Library

Most historians agree that the first place worthy of the name 'hotel' was The City Hotel, New York, which opened in 1794. In a city of 30,000 inhabitants it offered 73 rooms, "a ballroom, public parlors, bar, stores, offices, and a circulating library" (Sandoval-Strausz 24). It quickly developed into the "chief social center" (Williamson 10) of the town. As can be seen in the print above, the hotel creates traffic, is a hub in early New York (Image 1). While it still largely resembled an overgrown inn, it was erected expressively for hotel purposes (10). In contrast to other early establishments, The City Hotel in New York was financed by a stock company, a joint group of citizens that wanted to improve the town's accommodation for visitors and that raised the money together to realize this enterprise.[39] With this type of financing, the early American hotel becomes part of

---

facilities, now often being equipped with a restaurant, bar, conference rooms and leisure facilities, though the term is also widely used to refer to smaller establishments" (OED).
39 According to Sandoval-Strausz, the erection of the first hotels at this particular time can also be linked to the first Presidential Tour of George Washington. During this journey, Washington refused to stay with leading citizens of the towns he visited to avoid

big business (10), a player in the early capitalist system. After the City Hotel, hotels started to open across America. New constructions followed in Boston, Baltimore and Philadelphia. These buildings were larger and improved on the role model of the City Hotel. Yet, none of them presented a full break away from the original inn.

A real innovation came with the opening of the Tremont House in Boston, finished in 1829. It is widely regarded as the first urban luxury hotel of the world.[40] Built by architect Isaiah Rogers in the Greek Revival style the hotel set standards for all modern hotels to come.[41] The reason why this hotel is seen as the trailblazer for the modern hotel is found on the ground floor of the new structure. For the first time a hotel offered services like a barber-shop, a post office, a ticket and a law office, as well as bathing rooms: "The concentration of service on the ground floor was the first step toward the goal to satisfy every traveler's anticipated needs, eventually leading to the hotel's designation as a 'city within a city'" (Berger, *Hotel Dreams* 19). The Tremont is the first structure were the later famous metaphor for the hotel, being "a city within a city," was indeed justified.

In addition to these services, the Tremont also had several other innovations to vouch for its uniqueness. It was notably the first structure to possess a separate, impressive lobby (Williamson 16).[42] Before, the entry point to a hotel was usually the barroom. The importance of a real lobby should not be underestimated as it put the enterprise on a new professional level. It enabled greater exchange among locals and foreigners than the bar. While the early hotels still had ladies' entrances, lobbies did not exclude women in the same way as barrooms did. Furthermore, this elevated the position of the hotel clerk, who was now in a more visible place.

---

accusations of favoritism. Instead, he opted for the existing inns. However, as his own writings show, these accommodations often were of the lowest order, uncomfortable and filthy. As a reaction, several of the larger cities in the recently founded United States made it their task to build better and more comfortable establishments, out of civic pride and a sense of business (Sandoval-Strausz 15). The former colonies realized that they needed to work closely together now that they were a common nation. This caused an increase of travel, in addition to the constant influx of immigrants.

40 According to Berger the urban luxury hotel has to be treated as the starting point of modern hostelry because it performed as showcase of domestic progress. If innovations at palace hotels proved successfully they were copied by commercial and family hotels.

41 Isaiah Rogers became the foremost architect of American hotels, building, amongst others, the famous Astor House, New York's first luxury hotel and the Tremont's most serious rival. The choice of the Neo-classical style was not a coincidence but deliberately selected to marry the concepts of democracy and commerce (Berger, *Hotel Dreams* 26).

42 The lobby was still called 'the office' back then, the term 'lobby' only became common usage in the 1850s.

With its 170 rooms, the Tremont became the standard against which other houses were judged. It was the first hotel that provided each guest with a pitcher and a bowl, and a piece of soap, something that was unheard of before. It had eight water closets and eight bathrooms on the first floor. At that time plumbing was still in its early days, so indoor bathrooms were seen as a great step forward in personal hygiene. The Tremont House also set standards by having mostly single and double rooms, ending the habit of putting up several people in one bedroom. In addition, for the first time each door had its own lock and guests were now handed a separate key to their room, establishing the separation of public and private space in hotels.

Throughout the nineteenth century, hotels in America were seen as showcases for inventions in domestic technologies. The logic behind this was simple, as often people first came into contact with new amenities at hotels and then decided to order them for their private homes. Among the innovations for the home that became popular through the hotel were modern bathrooms, starting in the 1840s and 50s (Europeans would later call Americans 'bathroom crazy;' by the 1890s most of the larger hotels had bathrooms in each room). The Fifth Avenue Hotel in New York famously introduced the first 'vertical railroad', the original name for elevators introduced in 1859 (Williamson 64). Elevators made rooms higher up attractive and profitable. In 1882 the first hotels in New York introduced electric lighting (66). The first telephone exchange in New York started in 1879 (70) and the phone was shortly after installed in hotels (e.g. the Netherland Hotel was the first hotel with its own telephones and switchboard in 1894). These innovations were further proof that hotels were the leading institution of the country and justified its fame as a progressive place.

Similar to the City Hotel, the Tremont House, too, was financed by a corporation of citizens of Boston. Berger writes: "The hotel became important, not just as an investment and a city necessity but also as a public representation of the personal, business, and civic ethos of a class of men" (Berger, *Hotel Dreams* 35). The hotel became a symbol for the city's aspirations, embodying the hopes already aired during the opening that it would be an expression of the city's public spirit (49). According to Edward Relph, a cityscape is a "medium of communication in which all the elements may have messages – buildings, streets, parades ... all serve not only to unite communities but also to make them explicit" (34). The Boston Tremont House is a fitting example. It sent out the message to Bostonians and visitors that the city was welcoming, open-minded and ready for business. The first luxury hotel of Boston was perceived as the expression of the values of its city and its leading citizens (Sandoval-Strausz 314). Charles Dickens, a visitor from across the Atlantic, acknowledged in his *American Notes* (1842) that with the Tremont House a new kind of comfort was established (Williamson 16).

It is important to mention once more that an urban luxury hotel like the Tremont House was not only catering to foreign visitors but, by being a new kind of public institution, was linking these people to the local community. The new public spaces, like the lobby, "created a sense of community among guests, residents, and locals, imbuing hotels with a resolutely public culture" (Sandoval-Strausz 143). It is important, too, that in contrast to other kinds of public institutions, such as the theater, community halls, and parks, hotels brought different people together not only for minutes or a couple of hours but often for days. This kind of contact did not only take place in the public sphere but in intimate places like the parlor or the bedroom (143). It should not be underestimated how important this kind of contact was, especially for a nation so large and loosely connected as the United States. Daniel Boorstin writes in 1965: "Hotels were among the earliest transient facilities that bound the nation together. They were ... symptoms of the frenetic quest for community" (Boorstin 143). Boorstin is joined in this assessment by other scholars, among them Paul Goldberger, the famous architectural critic. He sees hotels as the only places "in which Americans have been comfortable living the public life, and admitting to urbanity" (Goldberger 8).

As Boorstin mentioned, hotels helped bind the nation together. They also played an important role in the development of America's political culture: "The principle of deliberative democracy on the basis of geographic representation required by its very nature that individuals from across a large territory gather at a single location in order to discuss and resolve matters of public importance" (Sandoval-Strausz 42). Due to the vastness of the American landscape, candidates needed to tour extensively to reach voters and encourage their following. They needed hotels for their accommodation, but also as semi-private places for strategic meetings, and as public stages for their speeches.[43] Since the early nineteenth century, political parties held their conventions at hotels, a practice that is being continued. Because they offered public as well as private space and were centers of their communities, hotels played a decisive role in the democratization of America, offering the political network a strong partner.

The connection between hotels and democracy was first made in an editorial in the *National Intelligencer* on June 18, 1827, in which the modern American hotels were dubbed 'palaces of the public' (Berger, *Hotel Dreams* 5). However, despite the high praise for the public spirit of the first grand hotels in America, there is also criticism in how far these often blatantly elitist structures could be called democratic. Berger describes the luxury hotel as "one of the most important institutions through which American urban elites forged a highly unified identity

---

43 *Harper's Weekly* printed a number of political speeches and cartoons with drawings of politicians standing on a hotel balcony or on pedestals in front of a hotel. This can also be seen in many Civil War images, where President Lincoln and the Confederacy leader Jefferson Davis are shown in front of hotels speaking to the crowds (see Sandoval-Strausz 254).

that was both local and specific to place and, at the same time, representative of national ideas" (4). For several years, until the American middle-class developed into the leading force in American culture, the possibility to live in these palatial edifices was limited to people who could afford the relatively high prices.[44] Therefore, Paul Goldberger writes that "[t]here is something fundamentally un-American about the idea of the grand hotel: it is not democratic, it is not fair-minded, it is not for everyone" (8). Goldberg, however, continues: "But it is an altogether wonderful paradox of the American grand hotel that it is, in fact, for everyone: if it is not for everyone to spend a night in, then it is for everyone to visit, to fantasize about, to celebrate in" (8). Because of the peculiar publicness of the modern American hotel it became one of the "most leveling of all American 'institutions'" (Sandoval-Strausz 185). And while, according to Berger, the hotel "presented a class-defined, idealized version of life outside its walls" (Berger, *Hotel Dreams* 6) the hotel space was too complex and open to keep life so neatly segregated as elitist groups wished it to be. Instead, hotels represented the city outside realistically, with its achievements and failures.[45]

Visitors from abroad agreed with this assessment. In the 1930s, Leo Koszella writes that hotels are different in America: "wo gerade in den großen und größten Hotels alle Welt ein und aus geht, wo man sich in den Hotelhallen trifft, ganz gleich zu welchem Zweck und ganz gleich, ob man dort wohnt oder nicht und ohne Rücksicht auf äußere Eleganz. Dort sind eben das demokratische Prinzip und der Servicegedanke bedeutend entwickelter" (662). European visitors often reported their shock over the social heterogeneity seen at American hotels, writing in detail about "a promiscuous mixing of social classes that characterized the growth of the American bourgeoisie" (Berger, *Hotel Dreams* 58).[46] Hotels in America, especially

---

44 In her introduction, Molly Berger describes a visit with her family to New York, including a short stop at the Essex House. From a contemporary perspective she muses: "This was an American palace. What did it take to belong? Our American birthright supported our presumption that we could claim equal access to any public space. This particular public space, however, asked for a certain level of economic achievement or, alternatively, a convincing performance that – through dress and manners – would convey the affect of that achievement" (Berger, *Hotel Dreams* 2). The quote tells us that the atmosphere at luxury hotels in America is still paradoxical, while Berger's story confirms that the lobby of a grand hotel is indeed public.

45 Caroline Levander writes on the question whether the hotel is a site of freedom or coercion: "The hotel is never just one thing. It is always a site of power and resistance, authority and self-fashioning, dominance and subversion" (Levander 5).

46 Carol Berens describes the difference to hotels across the Atlantic in the following way: "While American and European hotel forms often resemble each other, their substance indeed differs. There are dramatic contrasts in heritage and pedigree between European

of the luxurious class, were seen as the counterpart to European palaces, yet more open and more penetrable for social mobility. Lacking a court as social center

Americans created their counterpart in the community hotel. ...In the period of most rapid growth, it was not by churches or government buildings but by hotels that cities judged themselves and expected others to judge them. ...The hotel lobby, like the outer rooms of a royal palace, became a loitering place, a headquarter of gossip, a vantage point for a glimpse of the great, the rich, the powerful. (Boorstin 135)

The special nature of American hotels made them at the same time leveling *and* elitist, democratic *and* palatial. It lies in the heterotopic, stage-like nature of the hotel as well as in the accepting nature of the heterogeneous American society that the institution is able to overcome this apparent paradox and to function for all at the same time.

Anthony Trollope's *North America* (1862) may serve as an eyewitness account of the most striking features of mid-nineteenth century American hotels. Trollope's depiction of the American nation shortly before and during the Civil War is fascinating. He even includes a chapter solely focusing on the modern American hotel, the facility which vexed and occupied him probably the most. Written after traveling the non-seceding states, except for California, his estimation of the situation of hotels in America is a very enlightening one, despite his statement that he does not like the American hotel at all.

Trollope starts his chapter by writing:

I find it impossible to resist the subject of inns. As I have gone on with my journey, I have gone on with my book, and have spoken here and there of American hotels as I have encountered them. But in the States the hotels are so large an institution, having so much closer and wider a bearing on social life than they do in any other country, that I feel myself bound to treat them in a separate chapter as a great national feature in themselves. They are quite as much thought of in the nation as the legislature, or judicature, or literature of the country. (Trollope 480)

Trollope acknowledges right away that the Americans have a special connection to the institution hotel. He also makes clear that in America the hotel has more impact on daily life than in any other nation that he encountered. Comparing the American establishment with hostelries in the different countries of Europe he finds that the American hotel is "altogether an institution apart, and a thing of itself" (483).

hotels and their American counterparts. In Europe, the phrase 'fit for a king' constitutes not hyperbole because, in contrast to American hotels, which were built as palaces for the people, continental hotels were designed as palaces for royalty" (Berens 145).

Trollope is surprised by the wasteful way space is used in the hotel. In contrast to Europe, where the crowdedness of the old cities would not allow for such lavish use of space, in America "[e]verything about them [the hotels] must be on a large scale. ...They are always built on a plan which to a European seems to be most unnecessarily extravagant in space" (485). The writer also confirms that, in contrast to European establishments, American hotels always have an office, or lobby, allowing the public to use the building. This democratic publicness highly irritates Trollope: "In those other more congenial chambers is always gathered together a crowd, apparently belonging in no way to the hotel. It would seem that a great portion of an American inn is as open to the public as an Exchange, or as the wayside of the street" (491). Trollope also dislikes the fashion of public eating or mass-feeding as he sees it: "Certain feeding hours are named, which generally include nearly all the day. ...When the guest presents himself at any of these hours he is marshalled to a seat, and a bill is put into his hand containing the names of all the eatables then offered for his choice. The list is incredibly and most unnecessarily long" (490).[47] While Americans saw this generous food plan as a sign of hospitality, foreign visitors were often aghast at the amount of food eaten and wasted. Moreover, they were often shocked that people of all classes were sitting together at one table, and that there was no possibility of private dining.[48] From the American perspective this was just seen as one more proof of the egalitarian atmosphere of the hotel.

One of the most interesting parts of Trollope's text is his estimation of the importance of the institution hotel for the project of westward expansion. He writes that even in the most remote frontier town "the first sign of an incipient settlement is an [sic] hotel five stories high, with an office, a bar, a cloak-room, three gentlemen's parlours, two ladies' parlours, a ladies' entrance, and two hundred bedrooms" (Trollope 483). He adds in a mocking way: "When the new hotel rises up in the wilderness, it is presumed that people will come there with the express object of inhabiting it. The hotel itself will create a population, – as the railways

---

47 What the writer describes here is the so-called American Plan, which was introduced very early in the development of the modern American hotel. This plan included all mealtimes, usually four, and allowed people to eat as much as they wanted.

48 On the difference of American and European manners see for contemporary accounts Fanny Trollope, *Domestic Manners of the American's* (1832) and Henry Lunettes, *The American Gentleman's Guide to Politeness and Fashion* (1858); academic sources are Dietmar Schloss, *Civilizing America: Manners and Civility in American Literature and Culture* (2009); Aurelian Craiutu and Jeffrey C. Isaac, *America Through European Eyes: British and French Reflections on the New World From the Eighteenth Century to the Present* (2009); Kenneth D. Rose, *Unspeakable Awfulness: America Through the Eyes of European Travelers, 1865-1900* (2014).

do" (484).[49] It is very interesting that the writer describes here that pioneer hotels attract a following of their own, that they become active players in the expansion of America. Reading the development correctly, Trollope draws a direct connection between the growth of the railroad network and the spread of hotels across the country.[50] The first commercial railroad routes were established in the 1820s and rapidly increased until the Civil War. In 1862 Trollope can declare: "The railways and the hotels have between them so churned up the people [in America] that an untravelled man or woman is a rare animal. We are apt to suppose that travellers make roads, and that guests create hotels; but the cause and effect run exactly in the other way" (485). Again Trollope comments on the great agency of the institution hotel, which is more than a passive construction. The hotel is not only reacting to but it causes these developments. This comment shows that spatial agency of hotels has a long history in America. It existed from the beginning of hotels and found its entry early into literature and life writing

Besides commenting on the appearance of the place, the behavior of the staff, and the rates, Trollope also describes the people residing in the hotels, noting an important difference between Europeans and Americans. According to the British traveler, many young couples start their life together in hotels, and actually seem to prefer it there to founding their own household: "I think I may allege that the mode of life found in these hotels is liked by the people who frequent them. It is to their

---

49 Many hotel historians agree with Trollope on the importance of the institution hotel for westward expansion. Sandoval-Strausz writes: "Hotels would anchor new cities along an advancing western frontier, extending settlement across the continent" (Sandoval-Strausz 44). See for this function of the hotel also Boorstin (145f) and Raitz and Jones, who call hotels in their text "cornerstones of urban development on America's settlement frontier" (17). According to them, a town with a hotel was perceived by settlers as a "place of permanence and potential, a bit of civilization in the wilderness" (19). The most famous hotel on the west coast in the nineteenth century was the Palace Hotel in San Francisco with 755 rooms, opened in 1875 (Williamson 91). For hotel development in the West see Richard A. Van Orman, *A Room For the Night: Hotels of the Old West* (1966). In the South hotel building lagged behind the rest of the country until the late twentieth century. An important exception is the St. Charles in New Orleans: "It used to be said of the St. Charles that 'half of the history of Louisiana' was written in it" (Williamson 98).

50 According to Groth and Sandoval-Strausz, one important type of the hotel was the railroad hotel, built for the railroad workers as well as being a shelter for travelers and first accommodation for settlers. Sandoval-Strausz lists all together seven different hotel types. These are the luxury hotel, the commercial hotel, the middle-class hotel, marginal hotels, resort hotels, railroad hotels, and settlement hotels. It can be debated if all these types can be clearly distinguished from each other, but this categorization provides us with a useful tool to discuss the different ways hotels cater to people in America.

taste. They are happy, or at any rate contented, at these hotels, and do not wish for household cares" (Trollope 484). What Trollope describes here is a condition particular to the American hotel. In contrast to European hotels, which in the nineteenth century mostly catered to transient guests, American hotels often housed permanent residents (Gregory 4). Hotel living was already very popular in the middle of the nineteenth century and continued to draw people for many decades. Williamson confirms this by stating that the second major difference between the American and the European hotel, besides the egalitarian atmosphere, is "the American habit of permanent living in hotels" (9).

Hotel living was seen as problematic by many social critics. According to them, the more public life in hotels interfered with the normal family life: "the husband is but half a husband, the wife but half a wife, the child but half a child, when all three reside in some huge caravanserai in common with some hundreds of other persons" (qtd. in Sandoval-Strausz 271).[51] The comparatively large percentage of Americans residing in hotels permanently caused Europeans to believe "that home life in a house was almost unknown on this side of the Atlantic" (Williamson 48).[52] It is clear that Trollope was intrigued by the institution of the modern American hotel, yet at the same time he was also disgusted by it. It remains unclear if this disgust is really caused by the conceived faults of the institution or if it is a result of the

---

51 While it is true that cases of disrupted family life were reported in newspapers, often caused by neglect or adultery, hotel living was also seen as liberating by women of the nineteenth century. Charlotte Perkins Gilman spoke out for communal living to liberate women from household chores in *Women and Economics* (1898). It would allow them to enter the public sphere, thereby become active members of society: "From the most primitive caravansary up to the square miles of floor space in the Grand Hotels, ...the public house has met the needs of social evolution as no private house could have done" (Gilman 187). For many families, permanent residence in hotels was also cheaper than keeping a traditional household. For young couples, it allowed them to start private living without the interference of their parents.

52 Edith Wharton takes up this prejudice in her novel *The Custom of the Country* (1913). Here, the French relatives of Udine Spragg, the American protagonist, criticize her for her lifestyle: "It was natural that the Americans, who had no homes, who were born and died in hotels, should have contracted nomadic habits" (Wharton 512). Later in the text the hotel is used again as a symbol for the erratic behavior of Americans, when Udine's third husband, Comte Raymond de Chelles, exclaims: "you come from hotels as big as towns, and from towns as flimsy as paper, where the streets haven't had time to be named, and the buildings are demolished before they're dry, and the people are as proud of changing as we are of holding to what we have" (Wharton 545). For an analysis of the use of the hotel in *The Custom of the Country* see Betsy Klimasmith, *At Home in the City* (2005).

writer's patriotism in the face of what he felt to be American superiority. Anthony Trollope ends his chapter fittingly with an ambiguous comment: "I do not like the American hotels; but I must say in their favour that they afford an immense amount of accommodation" (Trollope 491).

Overall, Trollope's chapter on American hotels in *North America* is a most fascinating glimpse into the early era of this institution and the depiction of hotel experience in literary travelogues. In addition, it is a very useful testimony of the importance of hotels for American society. Trollope realizes the relevance of the hotel for America's westward expansion. He understands the close ties between the railroad and the hotel network and sees that the two together actively shape the mobile character of Americans. Furthermore, for the European readers he establishes the American hotel as an institution set apart from its European counterpart. In America it is a place where people come together on a mostly equal standing and share their meal with a large number of strangers. Americans freely decide to live permanently in hotels, defying the Victorian conventions still dominating Western life. In addition, Trollope grants the hotel an agency that scholars would only rediscover more than a century later.

As can be read from Trollope's chapter, hotel building in Europe, despite its long history in inns, lagged behind. George Augustus Sala, another well-experienced British traveler writes: "the American hotel is to an English hotel what an elephant is to a periwinkle... as roomy as Buckingham Palace and not much inferior in its internal fittings" (Sala qtd. in Gregory 20). While Trollope rightly criticized the lack in style and training among the hotel staff in the 1860s, by the last third of the century Europeans concede that "American dominance in hotel architecture had been matched by leadership in the provision of hospitality" (Sandoval-Strausz 185). It was finally accepted that America had become the trendsetter in the hostelry business and the modern hotel became one of the most successful American exports of the nineteenth century.

By the end of the nineteenth century the hotel had become an essential institution of American cities and small towns. It represented to visitors the community's self-perception and functioned as an important center of social exchange (Raitz 28). Hotels were workplaces for a large amount of people. Some of the grand hotels at the end of the century employed up to 1,000 staff members, small cities in themselves. They were permanent homes for a surprisingly large number of guests and staff members, as well as temporary accommodations for thousands of strangers. In addition, over the century hotels had become important places for leisure and social activities. During the Gilded Age, grand hotels were some of the preferred showcases to confirm one's status. They functioned as stages for "conspicuous consumption" to quote Thorstein Veblen's *The Theory of the Leisure Class* (1899). Hotels had become so defining in the urban life of Americans that Henry James stated in his travelogue *The American Scene* (1907): "one is verily tempted to ask if the hotel-spirit may not just *be* the American spirit most seeking and most finding itself" (102).

By the beginning of the twentieth century, hotels on both sides of the Atlantic could claim relatively similar standards. Still, America continued to lead the way in hotel development. Following the national trend of time-saving and homogenization of the work process, first attempts of standardization were made. Early in the century, E.M. Statler created one of the first hotel chains. Between 1907 and 1927 he built seven hotels throughout the North East. With his slogan "A bed and a bath for a dollar and a half" Statler revolutionized the hotel business, making hotels even more affordable and accessible to a now large American middle class. Other hoteliers followed his example, most famously Conrad N. Hilton, J. Willard Marriott, and Kemmon Wilson, the founder of Holiday Inn.[53] While the expansion of their hotels around the globe was criticized as a form of American imperialism, they provided travelers, especially Americans, with predictable and reassuring standards.[54]

Travel culture in America changed in the twentieth century. After 1930, almost no new grand hotels were built for many years. Hotel scholars see the opening of the second Waldorf-Astoria in 1931 as the terminus of the influential period of hotels – a consideration that I want to challenge in this thesis. Since the 1920s three more global hotel booms have been registered by hospitality researchers. In the 1950s, a new type of hotel transformed the desert of Nevada, the casino resort hotels in Las Vegas. The first successful casino hotel was The Flamingo, which opened its doors in 1947. Over the next decades, the casino hotel industry turned Las Vegas into the "world's largest multifaceted resort" (Rutes, Penner & Adams 179) with over 145,000 hotel rooms. More than any hotel type before the casino resort hotel focuses on the elements of illusion and escapism and tries to present its

---

53 Motels were another important development in the hospitality industry in the twentieth century. This very American type of accommodation, where the important asset is that one has a parking space directly in front of one's room, was a reaction to the huge success of the car in American society in the 1920s. It revolutionized America's mode of traveling. By 1928, more than 3,000 motels had been built and in the 1940s more motels than hotels existed in America. They were cheaper, smaller and often located on the outskirts of towns or on the road, which made the running of motels less expensive. They also importantly lacked a lobby. Due to this they were not fulfilling a role in the local community. Therefore, I disregard motels in my study. While some economists predicted the end of hotels with the coming of motels, hotels continued to exist.

54 According to hotel anecdotes, in Spain, a country which took to the idea of the modern hotel very late, people believed for some time that the word Hilton is synonymous with the word hotel, as Hilton hotels were the first large group of hostelry establishments to open in the country.

guests with a complete dream world of its own. This combination of hotel, theme parks, shopping malls, and convention centers is also called "integrated resort" development and has been copied all around the world, particularly in Asia, here especially in Macau (180).

The 1980s saw a boom of holiday villages, specialized hotels like boutique hotels, as well as convention hotels, which helped the hospitality industry out of a period of stagnation and economic depression. Boutique hotels were especially important for New York. The first boutique hotel was The Morgans, created by Ian Schrager and Steve Rubell. They wanted to "[d]e-emphasiz[e] the traditional vocabulary of hotel space" of functionality and pompous luxury, and instead tried to fulfill the "societal desire for *experience*, ... a mise en scène for contemporary life" (Volland 26). This hotel type presented a move away from so-called 'monster hotels' toward a more individualistic kind of enterprise. The last significant period of new hotel construction has been registered around the year 2000 with the erection of very luxurious hotels in the Arabian world, so-called seven star hotels, and a revitalization of the cruise ship industry (Rutes, Penner & Adams 10f). Although these last developments show that the American hospitality industry is no longer the only force behind new hotel types, one can still state that "[t]oday, an international American style is all-pervasive" (Gregory 17).

To summarize this overview of the history of the American hotel one can see that since their 'invention' in the early nineteenth century, hotels have become symbols for the nation's aspiration and self-perception. Over the decades, they functioned as stages of society, workplaces, and permanent homes, enabling American society to deal with the challenges of immigration, urbanization, and industrialization. Hotels made social change possible and at the same time stabilized existing social hierarchies. They were crucial meeting places for politicians and businessmen and helped unite the vast American nation in a time before telecommunication and air travel. Hotels were as much a product of market society as part of the mechanism behind it (Berger, *Hotel Dreams* 28). I want to stress once more that since the early nineteenth century hotels have actively helped to shape the urban cultural landscape in America (Berger, *Hotel Dreams* 6; Williamson 4). While Sandoval-Strausz is cautious with using the word agency in connection with the built structure of the hotel, it is still important to put on record that "the spatial arrangements and social behaviors specific to hotels led to or at least favored particular historical outcomes" (Sandoval-Strausz 229).[55] All in all, the history of the American hotel is full of proof for the existence of a close people-place relationship. The experience of Americans in the cultural phenomenon hotel is one of the most obvious examples of the power of place in people's lives.

---

55 He considers intentionality problematic with regard to an inanimate object.

Molly Berger writes that every person has a hotel story, which translates into: everyone already has a preconceived notion of what a hotel is and what it means to her or him. The following examples will support some convictions, but often they will challenge our understanding of what the hotel can mean for society and culture. Hotel experience is a powerful, inspiring, sometimes life-changing phenomenon. It has played an important role in New York's development for more than two hundred years. By examining hotel experience, we will learn more about America's leading city and understand better the complex mechanism and structures which made New York what it is today and which will shape it in the future.

1. Hotel Waldorf-Astoria – American Grand Hotel Par Excellence

> "The Waldorf is so complex and many-sided an institution, and ministers to so great a variety of social needs, that it seemed best to think of it – much as a diamond-cutter might – as a phenomenon of sixteen facets, each presenting a new surface to the beholder."
>
> CROWNINSHIELD VII FF

Frank Crowninshield was not the first, nor the last person to comment on the uniqueness of the Waldorf-Astoria and its importance for New York and its people. Stressing the multi-facetedness of this famous grand hotel, he sets the tone of the following chapter. The Hotel Waldorf-Astoria is the most famous and most written about grand hotel in the United States, if not the world.[1] No other hotel in New

---

1 At the moment there are at least ten titles focusing on the history of the Waldorf-Astoria alone: *The Waldorf-Astoria* (1903) by George Boldt; *The Story of the Waldorf-Astoria* (1925) by Edward Hungerford; *Peacock Alley: The Romance of the Waldorf Astoria* (1931) by James Remington McCarthy; *Peacock on Parade: A Narrative of a Unique Period in American Social History and Its Most Colorful Figures* (1931) by Albert Stevens Crockett; *The Waldorf-Astoria: a Brief Chronicle of a Unique Institution Now Entering Its Fifth Decade* (1934) by Henry B. Lent; *The Unofficial Palace of New York: A Tribute to the Waldorf-Astoria* (1939) by Frank Crowninshield; *Confessions of a Grand Hotel: the Waldorf-Astoria* (1953) by Horace Sutton; *The Greatest of the All* (1982) by Frank Farrell; *The Elegant Inn* (1986) by Albin Pasteur Dearing; *The Waldorf-Astoria: America's Gilded Dream* (1991) by Ward III. Morehouse. Furthermore, there are more books on American Grand Hotels, the Gilded Age, New York City landmarks etc. which have whole chapters on the Waldorf-Astoria, for example, *The Palace Inns: A Connoisseur's Guide to Historic American Hotels* by Brian McGinty (1978) and *Grand American Hotels* (1990) by Catherine Donzel.

York has such a close relationship with the city and embodies the concept of a city within a city as much as the Waldorf. Conrad Hilton, the hotel chain mogul who owned all of the most famous hotels of America at some point,[2] called it "the greatest of them all" (Hilton 230). The Waldorf has been perceived as the stage for New York's society, a microcosm of the great city on the Hudson and its "unofficial palace" (Crowninshield 1). In my study I will use the case study of the Waldorf-Astoria as the entry point to hotel experience in New York. I will focus on the hotel experience that is embedded in the discussed texts and expressed in the discourse that has been created around this institution. The Waldorf-Astoria is the only classic grand hotel in this study. For most of its past it has functioned as a platform for social distinction and public display. This first case study will focus on texts written by Waldorf insiders as well as scholars, newspaper people, advertising companies and writers. Their comments will add to hotel experience expressed in autobiographical writings. As Kurt Schriftgiesser writes: "[The Waldorf's] fame spread all over the world, for cosmopolitans met there, lecturers talked of it, authors wrote of it, humorists kidded it, the newspapers could not leave it alone" (71).

The Waldorf-Astoria has a more universal clientele than the other four hotels. This is why I will discuss generic narratives of hotel experience here that also fit other grand hotels: the Hotel as 'Stage of the Wealthy,' as 'Palace of the People,' and as 'City Within a City.' Yet, like the other four institutions examined here, the Waldorf is also a specific example for New York's hotel world. The people and social groups living and working in this grand hotel defined New York culture to a certain extent. I argue that they did this through the Waldorf-Astoria. At the same time, they themselves were influenced and positioned by the Waldorf-Astoria. Today, the hotel has lost its outstanding position in New York. Yet, it is still considered to be a focal point in the urban structure of the city, especially when the General Assembly of the United Nations celebrates the big opening gala in the Waldorf's opulent public rooms.

The Waldorf-Astoria was seen as the prototypical American grand hotel, the one against which all others had to measure up. A typical grand or palace hotel is large and impressive on the outside and provides its guests with state of the art amenities and excellent service on the inside (Sandoval-Strausz 81). The guest-staff ratio is high, so that the patron's every wish is quickly fulfilled. Besides restaurants, bars and public parlors, palace hotels also usually contain other facilities that might be needed by the hotel's elite clientele such as barbershops and beauty parlors, medical offices, florists, ticket offices, and shoe cleaners.[3] What proved useful and

---

2 Among others the Palmer House in Chicago, the Drake in San Francisco, and the Plaza in New York.

3 The Waldorf-Astoria, for example, also boasted its own photographer complete with studio.

financially viable in a grand hotel was later copied in commercial and middle-class hotels. Because they were trailblazers and showcases for domestic innovations and fashions, grand hotels were said to be the forerunner of all other hotel types (Berger, *Dream Hotels* 9). Accordingly, starting with this hotel type provides a good insight into the way hotels work. The microcosmic nature of hotels allows the Waldorf to be a testing ground for new developments in society which would later affect the whole of New York and even America. The first Waldorf is said to have been the first 'modern' hotel. It was one of the first hotels in America which were no longer thought of as mere stopping places but as destinations. It offered some of the most recent innovations and technologies.[4] Thus, the Waldorf-Astoria was a social laboratory and stage for New York culture.

The current Waldorf-Astoria between 49th and 50th Streets, Park Avenue and Lexington Avenue was opened in 1931. However, historians and the hotel's public relations department usually use the opening in 1893 of the first hotel of this name, located on 33rd and 34th Streets, as the birth hour of this institution. This fact has to be mentioned at the beginning of my analysis of the Waldorf-Astoria. When one speaks of the Waldorf-Astoria one has to be aware of the existence of two structures, which are not physically connected to each other or even in the same location. Instead, it is connected by the name, the hotel's historiographies, advertisement material, urban legend, and most of all by the people working and spending time in it. For my study this presents an interesting case as the hotel not only fulfilled important functions for New York in its first incarnation at the beginning of the twentieth century, but also in its second version during the so-called American century. That the Waldorf kept its outstanding position and could convincingly bridge its move across Manhattan shows how powerful its narrative of continuity is.

In the following, I will examine the hotel experience of Waldorf-Astoria insiders and the specific narratives that have been created about this institution. This will be done by analyzing the life accounts of Oscar Tschirky, Elsa Maxwell, and Conrad Hilton in connection with historiographical and journalistic texts available on the hotel. I will also use the writings of Henry James, Willa Cather, and Langston Hughes and the movie *Week-end at the Waldorf* to show how "outsiders" critically discussed the narratives surrounding the hotel. Led by the spatial theories of Edward Relph, Martina Löw, and Michel Foucault I will read this built space as a text, a cultural product whose analysis tells us more about people's place identity, urban life, and the culture of New York.

To start, I will position this grand hotel in its historical and urban context and then move on to examine its first important narrative: The Waldorf as 'Stage for the

---

4   The Waldorf-Astoria had one of the most advanced generators in America which powered its elevators, central heating, electrical light, telephones, modern plumbing etc.

Wealthy.' Because of the hotel's close connection to New York's high society, this narrative highlights the hotel's functions as a platform for the city's expanded Four Hundred, the leading families of New York.[5] Following this, the Waldorf's function as 'Palace of the People' and 'City Within a City' will be examined. These three narratives are the most often invoked ones when it comes to this New York grand hotel.

The Biography of the Waldorf-Astoria[6]

The Waldorf Hotel was owned and built by William Waldorf Astor, great-grandson of John Jacob Astor, and managed by George Boldt, a German immigrant from Ruegen. The architect employed was Henry J. Hardenbergh, who had already made himself a name with the construction of the apartment building, Dakota.[7] The exterior was designed in German-renaissance style, evoking the roots of the Astor family. The hotel was opened to great acclaim in March 1893, its pompous opening celebration already establishing it as New York's chicest new venue. The event was widely written about across the country and abroad and was seen as a sign of dawn for a new kind of American hotel (Hungerford 67f). The Astoria Hotel was added in November 1897, owned and built by William Waldorf's cousin John Jacob Astor IV and again designed by Hardenbergh. Together, the Waldorf-Astoria Hotel was the biggest hotel in the world.[8] With its amount of decorative elements and its height of thirteen, respectively, seventeen floors, it commanded the view of any onlooker as can be seen in the postcard below, a destination in itself (Image 2). The

---

5   Allegedly the term "Four Hundred" derived from the fact that exactly four hundred socially acceptable people fit in Mrs. Astor's ballroom, at least according to her social arbiter, Ward McAllister. Today, this origin is disputed, yet it is still widely used as explanation for this specific number. This story fits the reasoning that the much larger ballroom of the Waldorf allowed more people to be invited and considered included in the upper echelons of society. In a hotel, the upper-class was also more approachable than at the private functions taking place in the Armory, the only other big event place outside of private households.

6   According to Molly Berger, "a building's 'biography' enables us not only to 'know' the building descriptively but, more importantly, to delve into the personalities, conflicts and context that help us understand the culture that produced it" (Berger, *Hotel Dreams* 8).

7   From the Waldorf Hotel onwards, Hardenbergh made himself a name in building hotels, among them the Willard Hotel in Washington D.C., and the second Plaza Hotel in New York.

8   The first part of the hotel was named after the hometown of the Astor family in Baden-Wuerttemberg, Germany. The second part was named after the trading town that the first Jacob Astor founded in Oregon.

structure dominated the former residential area.[9] It expressed through its impressive exterior and interior and the trailblazing location the claim to the leading position among New York's hotels.

Image 2: The First Waldorf-Astoria on 33rd and 34th Street and Fifth Avenue

The Waldorf-Astoria. From the New York Public Library.

---

9   The first Waldorf-Astoria, covering a block between 33rd and 34th Streets and 5th Avenue was erected on the private homes of William Waldorf and his aunt Carol Webster Schermerhorn. This was once the most sought after residential area of the city, covered by mansions of the wealthiest members of New York. Building a commercial structure in the form of a hotel here caused some criticism. However, it was overcome by the success of the enterprise (Hungerford 21). Carol Webster Schermerhorn was known as "the Mrs. Astor," who defined New York's society for years. It was her ballroom that limited the number of the cream of New York to this specific number (Mordden 2). She was the wife of William Backhouse Astor, Jr. This marriage brought together Caroline Schermerhorn's Knickerbocker heritage with the fabulous money of the Astor family, a combination that was destined to "rule New York society" (Mordden 2).

The Waldorf-Astoria was a place for leisure and for doing business, a meeting place for local groups as well as for foreign dignitaries. Edward Hungerford writes: "Its very coming seemed to mark a distinctive change in the urban civilization of America" (130).[10] The hotel not only catered to transient guests, but a large number of rooms, especially in the Astoria, were rented permanently, making it semi-residential. The parts of the hotel not accessible for guests were almost of the same size as the public rooms, consisting of offices for the clerks, the kitchen, staff rooms, repair shops, storage rooms etc. According to Michel Foucault, a place like the Waldorf can be described as a heterotopia, a place that contains "all the other sites that can be found within [a] culture [which] are simultaneously represented, contested, and inverted" (Foucault 24). The Waldorf-Astoria was an almost self-sufficient structure mirroring the outside city, an illusionary version of it.

The first Waldorf-Astoria was razed in 1929 to make way for the Empire State Building. In 1931, a new hotel structure of the same name opened, erected above the railroad tracks of the Grand Central Terminal, with the hotel covering a whole block. This area was just becoming a vibrant business district in the 1930s.[11] The size of this second Waldorf overshadowed any contemporary hotel structure. Compared to the old building on 34th street, it was several times larger and higher, with 47 floors and 81,337 square feet. It offered approximately 2,000 rooms and employed around 1,600 people in its early years (Sutton 51; Farrel 4). The second Waldorf's architecture was more massive and less ornamental, a prime example of the 1930s Art Deco-style. The style expressed the management's wish to project to the world the hotel's modernity. In addition, the design of the hotel by Lloyd Morgan, of the architectural company of Schultze and Weaver, symbolically nodded to its predecessor by incorporating two towers at the top, one representing

---

10 Edward Hungerford's book *The Story of the Waldorf-Astoria* (1925) is the oldest historiography of the institution. The account is written in a personal, embroidered style. It is not an academic book. Still, it provides a good chronological overview of the development of the hotel and gives an insight into the way people saw it. The book offers an interesting kind of hotel biography that reminds one, in style, more of a human biography than that of a building.

11 When the old hotel was sold, Lucius Boomer, the last hotel manager of the first Waldorf-Astoria, retained the rights to the famous name for the symbolic amount of a dollar. According to the hotel's legend, he believed in a second Waldorf-Astoria. The second hotel was no longer built by individuals but, as is traditionally the case in America, by a joint-venture, the Hotel Waldorf-Astoria Corporation (comprised of several banks and railroad companies), with Lucius Boomer as its president (Sutton 37f; Lent 16).

the Waldorf and one the Astoria.[12] Since 1993, the hotel has been named a New York City Landmark, after a decade-long, 150 million dollar renovation to restore the original grandeur of the place (Morehouse 57).

1.1 THE HOTEL AS THE STAGE FOR THE WEALTHY

The hotel experience of the Waldorf-Astoria as 'Stage for the Wealthy' marks it as a public place, which also provides space for conflict and class tension. The hotel displays the progressive side of New York's society, and yet it is also a symbol for the first capitalist climax in New York, promoting a wasteful lifestyle and reckless Social Darwinism.[13] While Grand Hotels have been showcases for conspicuous consumption the world over, the Waldorf-Astoria has been most exemplary among them and has played a more important role for the Gilded Age society than any other hotel in New York. According to Oscar of the Waldorf, its maître d'hotel for fifty years, it was part of the management's plan to attract and re-shape society: "After all, the Waldorf was not to be just another hotel. It was designed to attract the wealthy, the elite of the country; without the 'socially elect' traipsing through its corridors the very purpose for which the hotel had been planned would be defeated" (Schriftgiesser 56).

When the Waldorf Hotel opened its doors in March 1893, it was the highest, most elegant hotel in the world, containing state-of-the-art technology and a very professional staff under its manager George Boldt. This newspaper quote of the opening conveys the astonishment and almost sublime spatial experience that the building aroused in New Yorkers:

To American enterprise is due most of the movement abroad in the world today toward luxurious hotels. But heretofore even American enterprise has not dreamed of such splendors as those through which the fashionable throngs moved last night. In few palaces of the Old World can such costly and artistic surroundings be found. ... All the refinements of all the

---

12 Here the narrative of continuation is written into the building itself. This is another way of strengthening the ties between the former and the current hotel structure, expressing the connection in stone.

13 The most conclusive scholarly article on the symbolic quality of the Waldorf-Astoria for New York society has been written by Annabel Wharton, "Two Waldorf-Astorias: Spatial Economies as Totem and Fetish" (2003). In her essay, she portrays the hotel as totem for the Gilded Age society and fetish for New York society during the Great Depression. Her text covers a wide range of examples and sources and paints a very convincing picture, yet overall her depiction of the hotel's symbolism appears too one-sided and negative. I will make use of her reasoning and expand on it in places.

various civilizations had been drawn upon and the artists who had the work in charge had so blended, that nowhere was there incongruity. ... Louis XIV could not have got the like of the first suite of apartments set apart for the most distinguished guests of the hotel. There is a canopied bed upon a dais, such as a king's bed should be. Upon this couch shall repose the greatnesses and, looking about them, see many thousands of dollars in fineries. Think of the joy of being great! One sees throughout the hotel a mingling of foreign and American customs. There are baths, elevators and electric lights, recognizable as American improvements. ... The owner has made the hotel the natural abode of transient and houseless fashion and wealth. ("The Most Splendid of Hotels" 2)

The impression the reader gets from the quote is one of almost impossible grandeur and worldliness. It also offers a kind of composite style, typical of America since James Fenimore Cooper's *The Pioneers* (1823). The hotel presents its guests not only with the perfect stage for their wealth, but also with a journey through time and space.

The Waldorf's Peacock Alley, the lavishly decorated hallway between the Palm Garden and the restaurant, became the main spot for people of leisure.[14] Here, they could be seen and admired by the public. Kurt Schriftgiesser writes in his biography of Oscar Tschirky: "During the era that was invariably referred to as the Gay Nineties, when the nation was still expanding and its people still expansive, Peacock Alley set the pace. A now forgotten journalist of the time once wrote that in that fabulous corridor every day was Easter Sunday and every moment was a promenade" (71). Originally located in the Waldorf part of the hotel, the term was later applied to the newer and even more luxuriously furnished hallway between the café and the restaurant of the Astoria. Unintended as a parade ground it quickly developed into *the* place to display one's newest fashion purchases.[15] The liminal

---

14 The origin of the name Peacock Alley is unclear. Allegedly a journalist called it Peacock Alley in his article, referring to the proud display of one's attire. However, neither the name of the journalist nor of the article are known today.

15 Some accounts claim that the existence of Peacock Alley is owed to a family conflict that gained legendary fame in New York history. After several unsuccessful runs for a political career and allegedly due to hurt pride William Waldorf Astor wanted to cut all ties to America and left for Great Britain. Before he did, he had a hotel built on the plot of his family's residence, which was located right next to his aunt's home. This insulted his cousin John Jacob IV and his mother, *the* Mrs Astor, neé Schermerhorn. As revenge for having a commercial building erected next to his mother's home, John Jacob Astor allegedly first considered building a stable on their home, to spite his cousin and damage his enterprise. Yet, convinced by the Waldorf's success, John Jacob decided to erect his own hotel. This building would be three stories higher, more elaborately decorated and called after his mother. This last part, however, was never realized, as the difficult

quality of the hotel caused this development. While not as public as a market square, this corridor was also not private and the hotel implicitly encouraged locals and visitors, who did not live at the hotel, to observe the daily parade of fashion. Through the large windows of the hallways one could look at the wealthy patrons inside the Palm Garden dining room and, seated in the corridor, one could gaze at the hotel's patrons free of charge. Schriftgiesser writes of the routine: "Daily and nightly Peacock Alley was jammed with people. Most of them had neither the intention nor the where-withal to dine under Oscar's grand supervision: they came to see the parade of fashion, beauty and importance, to bask in reflected finery" (Schriftgiesser 71). The wealthy seemed to accept and enjoy this kind of performance in front of an audience, as they did not push the management to stop it. Instead they continued to bask in their role as admired spectacle until the beginning of World War I.

The tension between living in an exclusive environment and inviting the public masses to partake in this exclusiveness is characteristic for the Waldorf. It was the focal meeting place of the city. *Pall Mall* journalist Stephenson writes: "it was perfectly fair to affirm that nearly every adult resident of Manhattan, male or female, excluding the laboring and poor classes, visited the Waldorf once a week" (Stephenson 253). The account of journalist William Marion Reedy is more critical and elaborate concerning the clashing cultures and conflicting ideas about the hotel. He observes in his article "A Westerner in the Waldorf":

The place is like Port Said as Kipling described it in the phrase that if you stopped long enough there everybody in the world that is worth knowing would eventually happen along. You meet the 'magnets' from everywhere in the provinces. You bump into adventurers, pikers, chevaliers d'industrie. ... There are the mashers who ogle women along Rubber Neck lane or Peacock Alley walk. ... But it's all a whirl. There is a certain splendor in it, of course, but the splendor doesn't conceal the sordidness of it All. You look into the faces of these men

---

pronunciation of the name would have hampered its recognizability. He, too, employed George Boldt to manage his hotel, which in the end caused the strategic merging of the two structures, symbolized in the famous hyphen among the two names. However, in case of another family feud, the two separate structures could be easily closed off from each other. According to this story, Peacock Alley was the bridging element between the two structures. While this narrative is widely known and even considered "canonical" (Wharton, "The Two Waldorf-Astorias" 525), there are strong doubts as to its accuracy. Too much speaks for a joined effort: the same street level, employing the same architect and manager and adding several facilities with the Astoria that the Waldorf lacked (Wharton, "Two Waldorf-Astorias" 526). Peacock Alley did not run between the buildings but ran the length of the Astoria side of the hotel. Yet, this little misrepresentation of architecture did not take away from the hallway's success.

and there's no joy therein. ... Peacock Alley seems to be a sort of sample of Paradise for women. It is the Mecca of dowagers, dames and damsels of the outlying districts. (Reedy 8f)[16]

It is impossible to overestimate the impact that the Waldorf and its Peacock Alley had on New York society and the people's perception of New York. A mere corridor became the essential space to define oneself and to project to the world one's self-esteem. The excerpt describes the tensions present in this place of conspicuous consumption as Thorstein Veblen famously called it. It is a women's paradise, yet at the same time it is perceived as sordid and joyless.[17] The author's experience of Peacock Alley is certainly different from the one intended by Boldt and Tschirky. He sees the pomp and its popularity, but is at the same time disgusted by it. However, he accepts the Waldorf as a symbol for the Gilded Age and a leader of society.

Praise and rejection are a constant theme in the reaction to the Waldorf. The hotel is not only a place; it is also a myth, a story told about New York all across America. A historian once commented: "so many and so appealing were the luxuries offered, and so widely were these read about and talked about, that in time, if a man wished to be of any importance when he came to New York, he simply had to stop at the Waldorf" (Kaplan 77). People wanted to see the hotel, this important sight in their tour of New York, for themselves.[18] Described in detail in newspaper

---

16 That Peacock Alley is compared to Port Said adds an interesting dimension. Kipling's quote at once brings up connotations of imperialism and colonialism. It marks the hotel more as a national public space, a thoroughfare that is recognized as an essential hub for New York and American life. Considering the time of the article, comparing the hotel with Port Said is also a critical commentary on the hotel's promiscuous variety of people, disregarding class and heritage, allowing 'everyone' in.

17 The Waldorf-Astoria was not only a place for women. Its bar was also known as the uptown branch of the Wall Street. Many important business deals that were negotiated in the Financial District were sealed after hours in the bar of the Waldorf-Astoria. This was especially the case when 'Betcha-a-Million' John W. Gates took up residence at the hotel at the turn of the century (Williamson 274).

18 It is interesting that Kaplan specifically comments on the circumstance that people outside of New York read so much about the hotel and develop their own ideas about the place. This second-hand experience of place can be described with Edward Relph's concept of vicarious insideness (Relph 52). According to Relph this insideness is created out of the successful depiction of a place by an artist and the reader's capacity for imagination. Without having been there oneself, one can feel deep involvement with a certain place.

articles the Waldorf was not only a physically existing thing but an abstract idea that people aspired to.

Henry James and the Universal Waldorf-Astoria

Before the Waldorf, New York's Four Hundred only entertained in their private homes. After the precedent set by Mrs Vanderbilt on the opening of the grand hotel, however, hotels became *the* venue for 'doing' social events.[19] It brought high society out of their salons and into the public eye. Yet, this gregarious method of display of wealth at the hotel and the extreme wielding of financial and political power was not universally approved of. The best known account reflecting the tensions caused by the Waldorf's role as stage of the wealthy is Henry James's travelogue *The American Scene*, published in 1907. Even though he visited the Waldorf-Astoria Hotel only once, for a short duration of time, James's hotel experience is one of the most telling ones of the early phase of the hotel.

In his account James conveys his impression of returning to his native country, especially of his birthplace, New York City.[20] Bewildered by the many changes, he is very critical of the developments. He sees the contemporary American comportment in an unfavorable light in comparison to Europe. Describing New York, James focuses on the Waldorf-Astoria, using the hotel as representative for all the changes he perceives: "New York told me more of her story [in the Waldorf-Astoria] than she was again and elsewhere to tell" (James 103). The author elaborates:

This one caravansary makes the American case vivid, gives it, you feel, that quantity of illustration, which renders the place a new thing under the sun. It is an expression of the gregarious state breaking down every barrier but two – one of which, the barrier consisting of the high pecuniary tax, is the immediately obvious. The other, the rather more subtle, is the condition, for any member of the flock, that he or she – in other words especially she – be presumably "respectable," be, that is, not discoverably anything else. (104)

---

19 Mrs. Vanderbilt held a charity event for a children's hospital at the opening of the Waldorf-Astoria. The most famous society event given at the old Waldorf-Astoria was the Bradley-Martin costume ball in 1897, which was the most reported costume party of the Gilded Age. It cemented the Waldorf-Astoria's reputation as the stage for social functions, but also as a place of conflict where the decadence of wealthy patrons clashed with the reality of the city (see also Dearing 135f; Hungerford 101f; McCarthy 125f).

20 Henry James has had a close relationship to hotels. They accompanied him his whole life. In his autobiography, *A Small Boy and Others* (1913) he writes: "I feel that I must not only to this but to a still further extent face the historic truth that we were for considerable periods, during our earliest time, nothing less than hotel children" (James 30).

For him, the Waldorf-Astoria is emblematic for the many new ways the Americans have acquired in his absence. What irritates James most is the American need to live one's life in public. The author recognizes that the hotel is the quintessential place to fulfill this need: it "had found there, in its prodigious public setting, so exactly what it wanted. One was in presence, as never before, of a realized ideal ... which one was so repeatedly to recognize, in America, as the note of the supremely gregarious state" (105).[21] The Waldorf-Astoria becomes the natural habitat for the new American society. It not only caters to the need to live publicly, but also allows displaying one's wealth in a gregarious fashion. James conceives of this as the promiscuity of the Waldorf-Astoria on which he elaborates:

It [promiscuity] sat there, it walked and talked, ... and came and went there, all on its own splendid terms and with an encompassing material splendour, a wealth and variety of constituted picture and background, that might well feed it with the finest illusions about itself. It paraded through halls and saloons in which art and history, in masquerading dress, muffled almost to suffocation as in the gold brocade of their pretended majesties and their conciliatory graces, stood smirking on its passage with the last cynicism of hypocrisy. (104f)

The Waldorf-Astoria with its pomp and ornaments is the perfect stage to show off one's own wealth and achievements. Yet, in contrast to a European palace, this 'public palace' retains for the writer an inauthenticity that the hotel can never really get rid of. He speaks of "masquerading" and "pretended majesty," pointing out the facade-like appearance of this kind of performance. James expresses his dislike for the newly rich, gregarious Americans. Like the hotel, he finds modern society inauthentic and lacking real depth. Joseph A. Ward writes, for the nouveaux-riches the Waldorf-Astoria is "a grandiose arena" in which they can "exercise their very public conceptions of their identities" (Ward 151). This arena enables and creates a society that comes into existence in New York at the turn of the twentieth century. I argue that in his travelogue James understands and acknowledges the hotel's agency, the power of place, that brings forth a new type of society in New York.

James, furthermore, describes the hotel as an entity that transcends everyday life. He elevates the Waldorf-Astoria, with its paradoxical, stage-like nature, from a public institution to a semi-sacred entity:

For that is how the place speaks, as great constructed and achieved harmonies mostly speak – as a temple builded, with clustering chapels and shrines, to an idea. The hundreds and hundreds of people in circulation, the innumerable huge-hatted ladies in especial [sic], with their air of finding in the gilded and storied labyrinth the very firesides and pathways of

---

21 Ward calls this James's "contention that hotels reflect the compulsion of Americans to live their lives in public" (Ward 153).

home, became thus the serene faithful, whose rites one would no more have sceptically brushed than one would doff one's disguise in a Mohammedan mosque. The question of who they all might be, seated under palms and by fountains ... such questions as that, interesting in other societies and at other times, insisted on yielding here to the mere eloquence of the general truth. Here was a social order in positively stable equilibrium. (James 106)

The comparison of the Waldorf to a temple likens this grand hotel to a space of spiritual significance.[22] Temples, churches, and shrines are sacred places in human culture, enriched with meanings, rituals, and special behavioral codes. They are peopled by a community that understands those rules, and shares the values and norms that are part of its belief (Kracauer 175f). By comparing the hotel with a temple James makes the Waldorf-Astoria a totem for New York culture (Wharton, "The Two Waldorf-Astorias" 541). The comparison between the hotel and a sacred place is not exclusive to James.[23] Most famously the idea has been used in the essay "Die Hotelhalle" (English title "The Hotel Lobby") by Siegfried Kracauer, in which he shows the parallels and differences between the space of a church and of a hotel lobby and its influence and meaning for people using these spaces. Kracauer reads the hotel space in the context of Weimar, Germany. In his essay he understands the lobby as a waiting room, empty of meaning and lacking any real essence. For him, people are waiting for nothing in the lobby, wearing masks, hiding their identities and remaining in almost complete isolation. By contrast, in a church Kracauer sees a community with a meaningful purpose, united by a greater idea. Foreshadowing Kracauer's reading, James does not accept the Waldorf as a truly spiritual place. To him, it is just an empty stage for displaying one's wealth, more akin to the golden calf in the Bible than to a New Jerusalem.

As the text shows, New York society does not share James's and Kracauer's impression of hotel lobbies as isolating and alienating. Instead, the Waldorf's public places are used by people to mix and mingle, to exchange and to celebrate an idea they all share: living a public life and displaying conspicuous consumption. The sheer size of the building, its elaborate furnishing, and the great public rooms, which are used for social display, turn the hotel into a temple for the leisure class.[24]

---

22 It is not the same as a department store, which is only built for the tendering of goods, but a hotel does mean more for a community, e.g. as a surrogate home.
23 See for example the biography *Crooks of the Waldorf* (1929) about the Waldorf's first hotel detective Joe Smith, written by Horace Smith. Here, Smith writes: "The Waldorf was his church and any violation of its sanctity was a desecration" (7).
24 In an essay on the wrecking of the old Waldorf in 1929, Bernard L. Jim sees the transcendental quality of the Waldorf confirmed in the reactions of the people to the destruction of the old structure: "New Yorkers ... viewed [the Waldorf-Astoria] as nearly sacred icon[s], constructed of personal and collective memories" (289).

While this publicness and materialism might appear empty, and rightly so, it captures the spirit of the Gilded Age. As James puts it, he perceives the Waldorf-Astoria for this moment as "a social order in positively stable equilibrium" (106).

Upon reading James's experience of the Waldorf, it becomes clear that he is overwhelmed by the imposing structure, the maze-like interior, and the conflicting impressions. Try as he might he cannot fully escape the lure of the place. The writer perceives the shallowness of society's actions here; he sees the tension between the outside world and the illusionary one that the hotel creates for its followers; and yet he cannot rid himself of being awed by this. He confesses: "I am now carried back to it, I confess, in musing hours, as to one of my few glimpses of perfect human felicity" (105) and further "[s]uch was my impression of the perfection of the concert that, for fear of its being spoiled by some chance false note, I never went into the place again" (108). Although he does not approve of the public display of wealth, James accepts the "universal Waldorf-Astoria" (441) as *the* foremost institution for New York's society and its visitors.

Henry James is critical of the building, but his awe leaves his remarks ambiguous. James's travelogue became one of the best known texts on the first Waldorf and is an important source for the grand hotel's narrative as stage for the wealthy. No other writer is quoted more often in books about American hotels, and especially the Waldorf. In his travelogue Henry James "establishes the importance of the old Waldorf-Astoria" as "the preeminent space of social definition in the United States at the beginning of the twentieth century" (Wharton, "The Two Waldorf-Astorias" 523).

Willa Cather's Critique of the Waldorf-Astoria

Willa Cather's short story "Paul's Case" (1906), written around the same time as *The American Scene,* also comments on the narrative of the Waldorf-Astoria as a stage for conspicuous consumption. The short story, published in *McClure's Magazine,* is Cather's most anthologized work and is said to be "a testimony to the reality of youthful dissatisfactions and the common failure of families to understand and of schools to be helpful" (Sirridge). I argue that the tale shows us how accepted the first Waldorf-Astoria had become as an important third place for New York's society. Cather presents the hotel as signifier for a new kind of American society.[25] The Waldorf fits people like Paul, the protagonist, who searches for an alternative identity outside of his conservative background. However, the story also shows that he is not yet able to understand this new environment and the temptations it brings.

---

25 Theodore Dreiser uses the hotel in a similar way in his novel *Sister Carrie.* It confirms Carrie's status as a successful actress and her affiliation to this new kind of American society.

In the text, a young high school student named Paul is unsatisfied with his life in Pittsburgh and the mundane plans his family has for his future. When the opportunity arises he steals money from his employer and spends it on a weeklong stay at the Waldorf-Astoria, a place he has dreamt about. Here he lives out the fantasy of finally taking part in "the life" and enjoys all the luxuries and the rarified atmosphere on offer. When his deed is discovered and it becomes clear that he cannot keep up this charade forever and has to return home as, he commits suicide.

Places are very important in this short story and the reader learns through the third person narrative perspective how they affect the protagonist.[26] While his school, home, and neighborhood are unacceptable surroundings for Paul due to their dreariness and lack of beauty, the theaters and the big hotels of his home town Pittsburgh fascinate the young man and give him a feeling of belonging: "Over yonder the Schenley [Hotel], in its vacant stretch, loomed big and square through the fine rain, the windows of its twelve stories glowing like those of a lighted cardboard house under a Christmas tree. ... Paul had often hung about the hotel, watching the people go in and out, longing to enter and leave school-masters and dull care behind him forever" (Cather 77). He fantasizes about a life in which he would be part of this "tropical world of shiny, glistening surfaces and basking ease" (Cather 77) only to be brought back to reality by his position in the cold street outside the hotel.[27] This illusionary hotel world works as a foil against which Paul perceives his own neighborhood, which is respectable but common (78). Paul rejects "the monotony in which they lived" and craves for a more glittering, if artificial surrounding. In his world, "the natural nearly always wore the guise of ugliness" so that an "element of artificiality seemed to him necessary in beauty" (79). The protagonist in Cather's story feels alienated from his familiar surroundings and is drawn to the glamour of hotels. The thought of forever living in the "ugly sleeping chamber, the cold bath-room, with the grimy zinc tub, the cracked mirror, the dripping spigots" (78) becomes so unbearable that it drives him to go through with his plan to escape from this world and enter the one he dreams about, New York's hotel world.

---

26 This short story is often analyzed with a focus on the inner turmoil (and probably gender-conflict) of the main protagonist, see Eve Kosofsky Sedgwick, "Across Gender, Across Sexuality: Willa Cather and Others" (1989) and Jonathan Goldberg, "Willa Cather and Sexuality" (2005). Sedgwick treats Paul in his hotel surroundings quite positively, seeing it as one of the rare examples when a protagonist actually gets what he dreamt of. While this approach to the story is certainly legitimate, I focus instead on the power of place and the issue of Paul's place-identity in my reading, as this has been largely neglected.

27 It is interesting to note the semblance between James's and Cather's descriptions of the inside/outside contrast between the street life and the hotel.

Indeed, he fits naturally into the world of the Waldorf, a hotel that he purposefully selected before his escape by researching the newspapers.[28] At the grand hotel, he encounters no trouble because Paul knows the social practices of the hotel and is able to merge with his chosen surroundings.[29] His subsequent settling down in the hotel room is a reversal of the beginning of the story: in the hotel he completely identifies with his surrounding (81). Paul is no longer the one standing outside looking in, but he is a guest of the Waldorf-Astoria and takes full advantage of his position on the inside. By having stolen more than two thousand dollars from his employers Paul holds the key to the Waldorf's hotel world. Money is the one condition one has to fulfill to enter this 'unofficial palace' of New York.[30]

The description of Paul's hotel experience can be read as a criticism of the hotel's capitalist nature. Through Paul's eyes the reader sees "on every side of him ... the glaring affirmation of the omnipotence of wealth" (82). To choose "glaring" as adjective here expresses a negative attitude to this stage-like world. The following description of the protagonist's dinner complements this impression, calling to mind James's description of the Waldorf:

When Paul went down to dinner, the music of the orchestra came floating up the elevator shaft to greet him. His head whirled as he stepped into the thronged corridor, and he sank back into one of the chairs against the wall to get his breath. The lights, the chatter, the perfumes, the bewildering medley of color – he had for a moment the feeling of not being able to stand it. But only for a moment; these were his own people, he told himself. He went slowly about the corridors, through the writing-rooms, smoking-rooms, reception-rooms, as though he were exploring the chambers of an enchanted palace, built and peopled for him alone. (82)

Similar to James, Cather's main character experiences moments of disorientation and dizziness while navigating through the hotel. The route through the hotel brings

---

28 I disagree in this with Marilyn Arnold, for whom the Waldorf in "Paul's Case" is only a metaphor for the world of art and illusion. For me, there is also something very concrete about the hotel; it is a real physical environment that grants Paul spatial insideness for the moment (Marilyn Arnold, "Two of the Lost").

29 The reader learns that Paul planned his arrival in detail: "Not once, but a hundred times, Paul had planned his entry into New York" (81). As a hotel is a social space, created by people, the right conduct and knowledge of the institution's code is essential for acceptance and for a smooth procedure.

30 About the dynamics between money, space and time at the hotel see Matthias 25f. Also interesting here is Marc Augé's definition of entry qualification to non-places. In the case of the hotel these are today most often fulfilled by the handing over of a credit card (Augé 100) which allows for even more anonymity and possibilities of opaque social behavior.

the maze-like comment of *The American Scene* to mind. Yet, Paul wants to fit into this place with all his might. He recalls to himself that he is now allowed to feel existential insideness as the people around him "were his own people." Paul, in contrast to Henry James, is willing to overcome the flood of impressions that the hotel throws at him. In entering the dining room, he seems to have arrived inside the place, not only physically but also mentally:

> The flowers, the white linen, the many-colored wine glasses, the gay toilettes of the women, the low popping of corks, the undulating repetitions of the "Blue Danube" from the orchestra, all flooded Paul's dream with bewildering radiance. When the rosy tinge of his champagne was added – that cold, precious, bubbling stuff that creamed and foamed in his glass – Paul wondered that there were honest men in the world at all. (Cather 82)

The last sentence comments on Paul's position in the hotel. The reader is reminded that he only gained entrance to the hotel by theft. Paul remains a kind of unauthorized observer. However, this is a position that he enjoys and prefers: "He was not in the least abashed or lonely. He had no especial desire to meet or to know any of these people; all he demanded was the right to look on and conjecture, to watch the pageant" (82). We can deduce from this statement that Paul remains in an in-between place, or a 'non-place' as Augé puts it, where he meets people but does not really interact. He symbolizes the tensions present in a grand hotel like the Waldorf. It is not his home, but "a home away from home." It is open to all, but only with the necessary funds. To become a part of the hotel world, guests need to play their role and behave in a certain way, which Paul does successfully.

When Paul reads in the newspapers that his crime has been discovered and that his father searches for him, he knows that "his golden days" have come to an end. He once more takes in "the glare and glitter about him" and the "scenic accessories had again, and for the last time, their old potency. ... He looked affectionately about the dining-room, now gilded with a soft mist. Ah, it had paid indeed!" (83). The stage-like quality of the Waldorf is once more apparent. While the disclosure of his crime alone might not have stopped him from leading the good life somewhere else, the end of his funds allows Paul no other way of escape. After getting to know this environment from the inside and feeling a belongingness, even if it was just temporarily and artificially, the main protagonist does not see any other solution than to kill himself by jumping in front of a train in Newark. The idea of living in the "wrong" surrounding again is unbearable for Paul.

Willa Cather's use of the Waldorf-Astoria is deliberate. The hotel had achieved such a great reputation by the beginning of the twentieth century that the name alone implied everything luxurious and decadent. To use a hotel for Paul's dream escape seems a natural choice, as grand hotels have always been a mixture of illusion and reality (Denby 289). From the many similarities between James's and

Cather's texts we can derive that the hotel experience of the Waldorf-Astoria as stage for society is generic for this grand hotel.[31]

As Löw states, an institution is a place that works through routine and repetitive actions beyond our own personal involvement. The act of synthesizing[32] by Cather and James achieves the same result here. The particular surrounding of the Waldorf-Astoria can influence a person's identity and in Paul's case can create an identity from nothing, allowing him to play his dream role in the fantasy world of the hotel. Cather's text can be seen as biting comment on the first Waldorf and its function as a stage for the wealthy. She acknowledges the hotel's leading position for New York society, but she also sees the artificial and materialistic side of this structure. While a grand hotel can take on a greater meaning for society, it remains a business venture and only the wealthy really belong here.

Langston Hughes and the African-American Impression of the Waldorf-Astoria

The tensions created by the hotel's function as a stage for the wealthy were not only part of the first Waldorf-Astoria. In the following, I will examine how conflicting experiences worked themselves out in the second incarnation of the hotel. For this I will discuss the poem "Advertisement for the Waldorf-Astoria" (1931) written by Langston Hughes. There are several similarities with James's and Cather's writings, but Hughes's text also adds new isues. It provides us with insights into the position of the second Waldorf-Astoria in New York's society.

The new Waldorf, opened in 1931, is a huge structure, covering a whole block between 49th and 50th Streets and Park Avenue and Lexington. From the day the papers were signed, one day before Black Thursday in 1929, to its opening in 1931, it took only two years to build the 47-stories-high hotel. It was the largest hotel

---

31 From an interview in 1943 we know that Willa Cather used her own experience of the Waldorf-Astoria as inspiration for the story. Willa Cather lived in New York for more than forty years and enjoyed treating herself to dining-out at the old Waldorf-Astoria. Loretta Wasserman explains: "The story rose, she [Willa Cather] says, from her memory of a troubled boy in her Latin class and from her own feelings about the old New York Waldorf-Astoria" (Wasserman). The quote is part of *The Selected Letters of Willa Cather* (2013), edited by Andrew Jewell and Janis Stout. Although we would usually be careful not to over-interpret the writer's biography when analyzing a text, the author herself states that her own hotel experience influenced her writing. In the letter she also makes clear that while she enjoyed frequenting the old Waldorf, she thinks the new one is a "horrid structure."

32 This means the connection of goods and people to form spaces "through processes of perception, ideation, or recall" (Löw, "The Constitution" 35).

structure of its time and opened into the hardest years of economic struggle. Yet, due to its massiveness and height, the building seemed to stand above the problems of its time and apart from the nation's financial troubles. However, the second Waldorf-Astoria did not make a profit during the first twelve years of its existence and had to file for bankruptcy under special New Deal measures in the mid-1930s.

This new Waldorf, too, was a stage for the wealthy and a place of tensions. The hotel's opening was warmly praised by the local and national press and by celebrities who were guests of the old institution.[33] In contrast to these odes, a sharp criticism wielded against the second Waldorf-Astoria is the poem "Advertisement for the Waldorf-Astoria" by Langston Hughes, published in late fall 1931 in *New Masses*.[34] Hughes at that time was already a celebrated figure of the Harlem Renaissance and well known for his social criticism and leftist views. In his autobiography, *The Big Sea: An Autobiography by Langston Hughes* (1940), Hughes describes his feelings concerning the opening of new grand hotel:

In the midst of that depression, the Waldorf-Astoria opened. On the way to my friend's home on Park Avenue I frequently passed it, a mighty towering structure looming proud above the street, in a city where thousands were poor and unemployed. So I wrote a poem about it called "Advertisement for the Waldorf-Astoria," modeled after an ad in *Vanity Fair* announcing the opening of New York's greatest hotel. (Where no Negroes worked and none were admitted as guests.)
The hotel opened at the very time when people were sleeping on newspapers in doorways, because they had no place to go. But suites in the Waldorf ran into thousands a year, and dinner in the Sert Room was ten dollars! (Negroes, even if they had the money, couldn't eat there. So naturally, I didn't care much for the Waldorf-Astoria.). (Hughes 320f)

The statement presents several interesting consideration for my examination. Hughes is very aware of the physical structure, the architecture of the building, describing it as "towering" and "looming proud above the street." The architecture of hotels often plays an important role in the building's success. It carries symbolic

---

33 See the books on the new Waldorf-Astoria by Crowninshield and Lent.
34 The poem "Advertisement for the Waldorf-Astoria" is not the only cultural treatment of the relationship between the hotel and African-Americans. In the musical revue *Ain't Misbehavin* (1978) the song "Lounging at the Waldorf" also picks up the topic of the exclusionary policy of the hotel. Similar to Hughes's poem, the song is about the all-white policy of the hotel while enjoying black culture as entertainment: "Don't rock they like jazz but in small doses / No shock Bop! and you could cause thrombosis / Don't sing loud when you sing at the Waldorf / Or find somewhere else to play." The Waldorf is seen as "the swellest hotel of them all," yet it is not open for blacks. The hotel is presented as a place of tensions.

meaning for the prospective guests. For people who resented this display of wealth, the timing of the opening seemed to be a provocation by the white American upper class that used the difficult times to reach their goals more quickly and to exploit their workers even more. Another aspect is very apparent, too. The hotel offers a blatant display of wealth in a city that is hard hit by financial depression. In addition, it is also a symbol for racial discrimination. Until the 1950s, most hotels in New York did not allow African-Americans as their customers. When Lena Horne sang in the Waldorf-Astoria's Empire Room this was celebrated as a first sign for abolishing the color bar. However, she allegedly still needed to stay at the Hotel Theresa for the night because the Waldorf would not accommodate her (Wilson 77). While the hotel on Park Avenue was leading in several sectors it was not a trailblazer when it came to racial equality. In this it also mirrored the city that, until the end of the 1950s, was still accepting *de facto* segregation.

In Hughes's poem, which is a "stinging social commentary on the 'fruits' of capitalism" (Zadra), the tensions of wealth versus poverty, beautiful suites versus homelessness, and white upper-class entertainment versus black struggle for survival lie at the core of his text. "Advertisement for the Waldorf-Astoria" is a biting parody modeled on a real two-page advertisement in *Vanity Fair*, one of the most fashionable magazines of America. It has to be understood as an "angry response to the opening of the obscenely opulent new Waldorf-Astoria" (Wharton, "The Two Waldorf-Astorias" 523). While the original ad is divided in headlines that spell "PRIVACY," "FREEDOM FROM RESPONSIBILITY," "MODERN CONVENIENCES," Langston Hughes contrasts this with his own subdivisions: "LISTEN, HUNGRY ONES," "EVICTED FAMILIES," and "NEGROES."

The poem is divided into six stanzas. The first three are addressed to a universal working-class audience "that was proscribed from the experience of the hotel's space" (Wharton 523). The fourth stanza directly addresses African-Americans and is the only part in which the lyrical-I appears and the lyrical-thou is changed to "we." Here, the language shifts from the prose of left social protest to black vernacular, which was very different from the register spoken in the Waldorf or used in *Vanity Fair*.[35] The second but last stanza addresses, as the headline says, "Everybody" while the last stanza, fitting the season when the poem was published, is headed with "Christmas Card." This part displays most clearly the communist ideology of the poem and contains the harshest criticism expressed in the poem. It is excluded in some versions.

The poem starts with the invitation from the advertisement of the *Vanity Fair*, here addressed to the working-class people of Depression-hit America:

---

35 Smethurst clarifies: "poems during this period often feature a racially ambiguous generically 'hard-boiled' working-class speaker whose diction derives as much from pulp fiction and the movies as from any actually spoken English" (Smethurst 110).

Fine living . . . à la carte??
Come to the Waldorf-Astoria!
LISTEN HUNGRY ONES!
Look! See what Vanity Fair says about the
new Waldorf-Astoria (Hughes l. 1-5)

The biting satire of this invitation becomes clear in the following lines: "Now, won't that be charming when the last flop-house/ has turned you down this winter?" (l. 7-8). The biting tone of the poem is established, created out of incongruity of phrases taken from the *Vanity Fair* ad and contrasted with the actual situation of the poor, the homeless, the working-class, and the community of African-Americans. By this, Hughes makes the reader aware of the great gap between the upper-class frequenting the new hotel and the current situation of depression-hit Americans (Shulman 266). The irony created by this linguistic gap increases the impact of the criticism. The conflicting nature of this symbolic display of wealth is further supported by the naming of facts and details of the new hotel. Oscar Tschirky, the famous maître d' hotel and Alexandre Gastaud, the first chef of the new Waldorf, are mentioned, as well as the cost of 28 million dollars for the construction of the establishment. This will guarantee that the hotel "will be a distinguished ... background for society" (l. 13-14).

Clearly, one of the biggest grievances aired is that this staging of wealth at the Waldorf happens at a time of the worst economic downturn in the history of the United States. While people on the street only have a coffee all day, the newly opened hotel serves a "swell board" offering "GUMBO CREOLE/ CRABMEAT IN CASSEROLE" and "PEACH MELBA" (l. 25-30). Those obviously American dishes are unreachable for the masses as they cannot just

Dine with some of the men and women who got rich off of
your labor, who clip coupons with clean white fingers
because your hands dug coal, drilled stone, sewed gar-
ments, poured steel to let other people draw dividends
and live easy. (l. 33-37)

The rhythm of this stanza, created out of the alliterations and the combination of hard-sounding consonants such as "clip coupons with clean" with dark vowels in "dug coal, drilled stone," is haunting. It drives home the message of social inequality with force. Promenading down Peacock Alley, which James R. McCarthy earlier described as the new "Main Street of America" (McCarthy 59), is not open to the poor even as they have "nothing else to do" (l. 41). The required funds are not available to them. While the poem addresses working-class people, the harsh criticism is of course also meant to be read by the upper crust, which lives from exploiting them.

Hughes repeatedly quotes real amenities like "(Special siding for private cars from the railroad yards)" (l. 88) from the ad to present the absurdity of luxury offered. Looking closer at this, the reader can see how the poet uses parts of the spatial structure as symbols for the ostentatious display of wealth. Space is not innocent here. The comment on special siding for private cars from railroad yards,[36] which is even put in brackets as an almost dismissed aside, expresses the fury that the writer feels. Seen through Hughes's eyes, the narrative of the Waldorf as a stage for the wealthy is presented as a proof of the white man's moral bankruptcy.

Up to this point the poem speaks to a general working class audience. All people of this class are affected in the same way. The addressee changes in the part headed "NEGROES." Here, Hughes's writes of his second great grievance in the poem, the problem of the color line and the hypocritical way in which the white upper-class treats African-American culture:

You know, downtown folks are just
crazy about Paul Robeson! Maybe they'll like you, too,
black mob from Harlem. Drop in at the Waldorf this
afternoon for tea. Stay to dinner. Give Park Avenue a
lot of darkie color – free for nothing! Ask the Junior
Leaguers to sing a spiritual for you. They probably
know 'em better than you do – and their lips won't be
so chapped with cold after they step out of their closed
cars in the undercover driveways.
Hallelujah! Undercover driveways! (l. 61-70)

The style of the poem changes to African-American vernacular from Harlem. This part is a satirical comment on the white upper-class's consumption of African-American culture. Consumption is the main issue in this poem, not only of material goods but also of culture. Hughes uses the fourth stanza to "subvert the upper-class fascination with things Negro" (Shulman 267), a fascination that many artists of the Harlem Renaissance experienced as very problematic, yet could hardly escape if they wanted to continue to create art.[37]

---

36 A short historical note: The private siding was rarely used, yet, became important during the presidency of Franklin D. Roosevelt, who arrived with his private car in the basement to avoid people seeing his leg braces.

37 Langston Hughes himself depended on white mentorship until the 1930s when he broke with them for the ethical reasons he describes here.

In the last stanza of the poem Hughes encourages the working-class members to end the unfair conditions by rising against them, led by a savior figure that he models, fitting the season, on the nativity scene: "Listen, Mary, Mother of God, wrap your new born babe in/ the red flag of Revolution: the Waldorf-Astoria's the best manger we've got" (l. 107-109). This last part shows Hughes's leftist convictions and his hope for a future, in which communism becomes the new religion of America. The lines put the grand hotel cynically at the center of Christian ideology: "Hughes vividly connects depression hunger and poverty and that of the Holy Family. He does so with a blasphemy – Mary as whore – that he compounds in relating the immaculateness of the Immaculate Conception to the clean bed Mary needs and the manger of the Waldorf can supply" (Shulman 269). Going back to Luke's scripture in the Bible, where the holy couple cannot find a bed for the night at an inn for pregnant Mary, Hughes connects this well-known topos with the Waldorf's discriminatory and excluding practices.

"Advertisement for the Waldorf-Astoria" is modeled on a real ad for the hotel. According to Shulman, Hughes was one of the pioneers amongst poets who combined elements from media and pop-culture with their writings (Shulman 269). This collage element is taken into account in the poem's display in the *New Masses*. The text is surrounded by drawings mimicking the pictures of the original ad. The impressive imagery of the *Vanity Fair*'s two-pager shows the hotel's massive exterior as well as its richly furnished bedrooms. In contrast to this, Hughes's text is surrounded by illustrations from Walter Steinhüber. Steinhüber visualizes the conflict by offering of a voyeuristic look through windows that actually do not exist, showing the decadent going-ons in the hotel (see for this Wharton, "The Two Waldorf-Astorias" 523). The hotel is sketched resting on the down-trodden figures of the masses that are drawn on the lower margin of the page, functioning as the road material on which the rich people's cars are rolling. The drawings add to the powerful impression with which the poem leaves the reader. This visual level very literally represents the narrative of the Waldorf as stage of the wealthy. I agree with Annabel Wharton who reads Hughes's poem as "an expression for those on the outside of the not-to-be-lived experience of the inside of the new Waldorf" (Wharton, "The Two Waldorf-Astorias" 523). More than James's, Hughes's experience of the space of the Waldorf is that of existential outsideness. Hughes's position is a forced one. One could argue that his poem creates of vicarious outsideness. He allows African-Americans all across America to experience the same out-of-place feeling that he had when passing the building. Including Langston Hughes's text in my examination of the Waldorf-Astoria functions not only as an interesting addition to how the hotel as stage of the wealthy is perceived and portrayed, it also allows me to consider the neglected position of black Americans in the narratives of the Waldorf-Astoria's hotel experience.

1.2 THE HOTEL AS THE PALACE OF THE PEOPLE

With Hughes's criticism in mind, it sounds ironic that the second Waldorf-Astoria only became profitable by the end of the Second World War. When the new Waldorf opened in 1931, the hotel was only sparsely occupied due to the Great Depression.[38] Yet, as a commercial enterprise with a staff of more than 1,500 people, a sizable village, the management needed to come up with solutions to fill the almost 2,000 rooms. Lucius Boomer's plan to fill the hotel and keep its name in the tabloids was to allow guest with great names but small purses to live in the hotel for free or for a minimal fee. One case in point is Elsa Maxwell, a celebrity during the middle of the twentieth century, who understood better than anyone else how to make the most out of difficult circumstances. Elsa Maxwell contributed to the Waldorf fame with her column "The Party-Line" and with essays, and made it a well-known institution. It became her platform for teaching New York society how to entertain and celebrate. On the other hand, the Waldorf helped to cement her name as the most successful hostess of the city.

Elsa Maxwell – The Atypical Waldorf-Astoria Guest

Maxwell's hotel experience can be attributed to the narratives of the Waldorf as stage of the wealthy as well as a palace of the public. The wealthy are her clientele and she organizes parties for them in the hotel. At the same time, the hotel is her public palace as it provides her with the necessary tools to pursue her American Dream. By mingling with the rich she reaches her goals, even though she herself is not part of the upper class. Her recollections function here as a bridge between the two narratives. Furthermore, Elsa Maxwell's account adds the guest's perspective to my discussion of the Waldorf's hotel experience.

The Waldorf-Astoria, old and new, certainly was and is a stage for the wealthy, which creates experiences of conflict. Yet, as one of the greatest hotels in New York it is not just that. The Waldorf as a palace of the public is also an accessible, almost democratizing institution that shaped urban life in New York and changed how people thought about society. A grand hotel can also be a liberating institution. A number of people highlight the grand hotel's potential for inclusiveness and unification. The hotel experience at the Waldorf-Astoria positions people; it can appear inclusive and excluding; it can turn people into critics or admirers. In the following I will show how the experience of the Waldorf as a palace of the public is

---

38 It was only able to remain open due to New Deal aid programs. The hotel had a very strong connection to the US government, which was sometimes seen critically by outsiders.

described by Elsa Maxwell, Oscar Tschirky, Herbert Hoover, and Conrad Hilton and how it reflects back again on New York City.

Image 3: The Second Waldorf-Astoria from Park Avenue

The Second Waldorf-Astoria. Private.

Elsa Maxwell was born in 1883 in Keokuk, Iowa, into a middle class family.[39] She grew up in San Francisco, witnessed the earthquake of 1906, and by twists and turns, became the most sought after hostess of the middle of the twentieth century

---

39 As Maxwell constantly created new stories about her past, usually playing down her background and opportunities, a true account of her past is difficult to get. Sam Staggs probably got farthest in his biography of Elsa Maxwell, *Inventing Elsa Maxwell* (2012). Amongst other things, he gives her real birth year as 1881. As the dates are not so important for my analysis, I will keep mostly with Elsa Maxwell's own account as presented in her autobiography *R.S.V.P.: Elsa Maxwell's Own Story* (1954) and the authorized biography by Bernd Ruhland, *Elsa Maxwell: Mein verrücktes Leben* (1964).

through her natural talent for music and entertaining. She gave parties for royalty in Monaco and on the Riviera, made Hollywood stars famous, and brought together well-known celebrity couples. She achieved all this with a minimal amount of formal education, very plain looks, and almost no money.

Shortly after its opening, Elsa Maxwell allegedly accepted Boomer's invitation to live in a suite on the 41st floor of the Towers, understanding fully that his intention was to draw in other, more financially viable guests. Maxwell writes about this agreement:

The nearest approach to a home I've had since leaving San Francisco in 1907 is The Waldorf-Astoria Hotel in New York, where I have been living from October through April, on and off, since 1931. I moved into the Waldorf for the very good reason that I was given a rent-free suite. The Waldorf opened in October 1931, in the depths of the Depression, and Lucius Boomer, the president, made the offer thinking my presence in the hotel might bring other, more desireable guests. Boomer was right; the Towers filled with friends. (Maxwell qtd in Morehouse 96)[40]

Elsa Maxwell contributes to the grand hotel's reputation as a glamour castle, even though she herself does not fit the expectations or requirements of a Waldorf guest. Her presence at the Waldorf makes high society appear more accessible. Maxwell was one of the first hostesses to include guests that were not rich but interesting, their capital being their talents and skills and not their checkbooks. Maxwell was even accused of having killed society by the liberal mixture of people invited to her famous parties (Mordden 199). With her love for spectacles, her restlessness, and her bedazzling personality, she appears to be the perfect candidate for hotel life: "I have always lived in hotels during my gay, gregarious life. For me, a nomad by nature, homeless and unregenerate by pathological urge, hotels have usurped the place of a family fireside" (Maxwell, "Hotel Pilgrim" 127). Maxwell's word choice here reminds us of James's description of the Waldorf. He explicitly referred to the gregariousness and publicness of this hotel. At the Waldorf, Elsa Maxwell is constantly 'on-stage,' yet also liberated from social conventions and expectations.

Most interesting is her essay "Hotel Pilgrim," which she wrote for the souvenir-record book *The Unofficial Palace of New York* (1939) by Frank Crowninshield. Here, Maxwell describes her personal relationship with the Waldorf-Astoria. Remarkable is her depiction of her entry into the hotel:

---

40 The tactic of inviting famous guests to live at a hotel, a form of living advertisement, had already been used before Boomer. This practice has even found its entry into literature. Carrie Meeber is famously offered to live at the Waldorf at the end of the novel *Sister Carrie* by Theodore Dreiser.

Finally I moved into The Waldorf-Astoria Towers, the year it opened, 1931, just after the debut of the depression. The Waldorf-Astoria had packed up its prewar antimacassars, its gilt chairs and lace-curtains, its Peacock Alley and red plush portieres, and had moved up to 50th Street and Park Avenue. The only things it brought with it intact were the great and only Oscar and Mr. Bagby's Monday-morning concerts. Its towers glistened high in the skies, whitely, like a twentieth-century Taj Mahal, and I viewed its glistening ramparts in mild alarm as I drove up to the portals of my future spiritual home. (131)

Maxwell accepts the hotel's narrative of continuation. Yet, her description of the transformation from the old Waldorf to the new one contains critical elements, for example, when she declares Oscar and Mr. Bagby's music sessions were the only elements intact after the move. By mentioning the former symbols of decadence of the old grand hotel, the "gilt chairs and lace-curtains," she evokes the impression of an era and a way of doing society that is already passé. The hotel is still a stage for society with its "glistening ramparts," however, she perceives this with "mild alarm," probably already planning how to change the impression.

The Waldorf has been called many things in its past. It has been compared to a temple, a public court, a maze, and paradise. The multitude of metaphors used to describe the Waldorf can be seen as attempts to grasp the seemingly ungraspable atmosphere of the hotel. Maxwell's impression of the hotel as "a twentieth-century Taj Mahal" is an interesting, ambiguous addition. Maxwell leaves it open if the connotation is meant positively. The original Taj Mahal is a white marble mausoleum built for the third wife of Mughal emperor Shah Jahan in the middle of the seventeenth century. It has been called "crown jewel" of Muslim architecture in India. The Taj Mahal is a supreme symbol of power and wealth. It is also a structure loaded with emotions, as according to legend it was meant to embody the shah's eternal love for his favorite wife. The impressive size of the New York grand hotel, its whitish color, and its twin towers appear to recall the famous mausoleum as can be seen in the picture above (Image 3). It, too, is a symbol of power and wealth and according to its builders was meant as a "monument to the courage and faith of those who believed that it was an institution to be maintained" (Lent 16). Moreover, Maxwell's title of her essay, "Hotel Pilgrim," seems to fit well her comparison of the Waldorf with the Taj Mahal. Yet, a mausoleum is not a very nice sobriquet for a hotel. Probably Maxwell meant to highlight its emptiness during the early days of depression, which she set out to change.

Elsa Maxwell has found her home in the Waldorf-Astoria. She describes the fellow hotel guests and the hotel staff as part of her circle of friends that made her forget feelings of loneliness: "Though I do not see some of them very often, when I turn on my reading light at night at the head of my bed, the warm feeling of friends about me [in the Waldorf] is more comforting than my comforter" (Maxwell "Hotel Pilgrim" 137). The Waldorf indeed is her preferred shelter, a home in the classic sense of the word. Elsa Maxwell's statement confirms that the Waldorf management indeed managed to create a home-like atmosphere in this monstrous structure.[41] She remained there for several decades. Calling the Waldorf her "future spiritual home" shows that Maxwell not only sees this place as mere living space but as the right surrounding where she can fulfill her calling. The Waldorf provides her with everything she needs to become the famous hostess she is now remembered for. Maxwell became a kind of live-in event planner, organizing New York's biggest parties in the Waldorf, like the "April in Paris" ball. She also introduced unconventional themes to its ballrooms like a barn party, including livestock and hay, by this slightly mocking the extravagantly rich who did not have contact with this world anymore. Maxwell's life at the Waldorf was to the advantage of both sides. Besides attracting rich friends by her presence in the hotel and repaying some of her debts by organizing and hosting parties for the Waldorf, Elsa also functioned as chronicler for the place. Her famous entertainment column, "The Party Line," gave the public outside an image of the hotel's glamour. It also made the Waldorf appear more accessible. Through the column, people from across America had the possibility of taking part in the going-ons of the great hotel and learned what living in a grand hotel could mean. Elsa Maxwell's role as a kind of house reporter was used in the movie *Week-end at the Waldorf* (1945), which is loosely based on the novel *Grand Hotel* (1929) by Vicki Baum.[42]

Elsa Maxwell's position at the hotel is located between that of a guest and a staff member. She lives in a hotel suite, but as a kind of public relation manageress she also earns her place there. Her recollections show how the relationship between institution and person can be a reciprocal one, especially in a hotel that needs publicity. Listing the names of all her famous friends and acquaintances, she writes: "these are the friendly spirits that make up the glittering milieu of The Waldorf-Astoria Towers" (Maxwell, "Hotel Pilgrim" 138). While she enjoys living in this dreamlike atmosphere she is still aware of its illusionary quality. Maxwell writes of her benefactor, Lucius Boomer: "How all this [the smooth operation of the hotel] is done I never question, but I suspect that Lucius Boomer of The Waldorf-Astoria is really the reincarnation of the great Houdini, master of necromancy and Black magic" (138). Elsa Maxwell is not a regular Waldorf Tower guest. Like the hotel, her life as society hostess has an illusionary quality to it. Yet, she shows that while

---

41 This was the expressed wish of the hotel owners: "The entire physical design of the building as well as its furnishings, is influenced by the thought that here shall be a home in which to *live* – not merely a hotel at which to stay" (Lent 24).

42 She worked as an adviser for the movie (Staggs 186). Actor and theater critic Robert Benchley plays an Elsa Maxwell-like role. As the narrator he shapes the impression the audience gets of the hotel. The character is clearly modeled on Elsa, which confirms her special position in the Waldorf, her long-time home (Sanders 293).

not everyone can stay in a grand hotel, people can make use of its public spaces as creative background. At least, it enables a meeting of different worlds.

The Waldorf-Astoria has a democratic quality to it, even though it is also elitist. In that, it invokes the democratic understanding of early America, which also differentiated between land-owning gentry and the mob, yet allowing via natural aristocracy for a certain permeability. Many scholars agree that the first Waldorf-Astoria was the place that brought high society out of their private residences and made public entertaining fashionable (see also Denby 224; McGinty 173). Mrs. Vanderbilt was the first society lady who had her charity event at this hotel (Schriftgiesser 58; Farrell 26). The consequence of its success was that many society ladies copied Mrs. Vanderbilt's example and had their events at the Waldorf. By now it has become quite common to have family functions, business conventions, and prize ceremonies in hotels. One no longer has to have a big house to be able to entertain a large group of people. Although this might not seem to be a great change, by this the Waldorf-Astoria helped to transform how people thought about private and public spheres. It brought on a striking change for New York's society. Democratization here starts with a greater visibility of the upper classes, a first step toward expanding it. The liminal space that the hotel offered, not quite as public as a railroad station but certainly less private than the family's drawing room, allowed to physically and socially expand New York's Four Hundred. The Waldorf was therefore perceived as "a public court for the island of Manhattan, a palace of midtown hospitality" (McGinty 174).

The Waldorf contributed to transforming New York society. In addition to influencing society ladies, the grand hotel also started to play a major role for the city's business world. Known as the "Waldorf Crowd," bankers and business men like J.P. Morgan, 'Betcha-a-Million' Gates and Charles Schwab continued their business meetings after hours at the Men's Bar of the Waldorf-Astoria. Here they made some world changing business decisions, such as preparing the merger that produced the United States Steel Corporation (McCarthy 89; Williamson 273). By doing this in the public space of the Men's Café, the business leaders were visible and more approachable than in their offices on Wall Street. This did not cause an outright social revolution, yet it made the business world more permeable.

In *The American Scene*, Henry James describes the hotel as a symbol for American society. Referring to the Waldorf-Astoria, he stated:

The moral in question, the high interest of the tale, is that you are in presence of a revelation of the possibilities of the hotel – for which the American spirit has found so unprecedented a use and a value; leading it on to express so a social, indeed positively an aesthetic ideal, and making it so, at this supreme pitch, a synonym for civilization, for the capture of conceived manners themselves, that one is verily tempted to ask if the hotel-spirit may not just *be* the American spirit most seeking and most finding itself. (103)

This hotel spirit goes beyond the physical space hotel. It describes a mindset that came into being at the turn of the century and dominated the twentieth century. America broke away from the confining Victorian ideals and created a new American class structure that was based more on financial means than pedigree and heritage. It strains our modern definition of the word to call the result democratic, but the power of the liminal hotel space, which brought forth James's so-called hotel spirit, helped American society to develop into the more inclusive, more equal society that we know today. Fittingly, the hotel has been used by American writers repeatedly in their texts, most famously by Edith Wharton and Theodore Dreiser, to depict this changed state of mind.[43]

The hotel's chronicler Hungerford writes of the change that the Waldorf brought to New York: over the years the Waldorf-Astoria "was to become slightly less a hotel for the mere feeding and housing of travelers, and considerably more a semi-public institution" (Hungerford 130). Carol Berens examines this development in her book *Hotel Lobbies and Bars*. She writes that hotels are the "grand public spaces that permit us to live like royalty. Sumptuous palaces were once the stuff of royal privilege, open to only an invited few. But now they are public, and their dazzling splendor is available by appointment or whim" (Berens, Foreword xi). Berens describes the important public spaces of the Waldorf-Astoria. Although Peacock Alley was an important location to show off one's wealth, for Berens it was also a public place that invited middle-class onlookers to take part in the presentation: "Located in the first Waldorf-Astoria Hotel ... this hall capture[s] New York society's imagination, becoming the setting of its dynamic social urban scene" (23). So, while this hallway was a place of spectacle, it was also dynamic and urban, a place where people of different strata came into contact with each other. According to Molly Berger, some journalists actually complained in their writings that there was a too great mix of people allowed in the old Waldorf. She states that "the hotel was a place where social and cultural events could and would be expanded to include different sets of people" (Berger, "Rich Man's City" 63).

The idea of the Waldorf-Astoria as an institution that brings different classes into contact with each other is echoed in Oscar's biography. Oscar is quoted, saying: "We have entertained a prince of royal blood whose quarters were the entire

---

43 Wharton has used the hotel as a meaning-filled, symbolic space in many of her stories, most notably in *The House of Mirth* (1905) and *The Custom of the Country* (1913). Dreiser has not only repeatedly used the hotel as an important place and agent in his texts, such as *Jennie Gerhardt* (1911) and *An American Tragedy* (1925), but has made direct use of the Waldorf-Astoria as for example in *Sister Carrie* (1900) and *The Titan* (1914).

third floor. We have entertained a prince of good fellows in a single room under the roof on the thirteenth floor. And we have had the thanks of both" (Schriftgiesser 67). To run an enterprise as large as the Waldorf, one needs the money of wealthy aristocrats and of traveling salesmen. Although the old Waldorf-Astoria certainly was designed as a place for the upper-class, its manager George Boldt, also became famous for bringing "exclusiveness to the masses" (Schriftgiesser 82), as Oliver Herford quipped. The most poignant way of showing the openness of the hotel to the general public is the existence of tour guides:

The astute Mr. Boldt realized the value of the visit to his establishment of the less privileged and welcomed them as cordially as he did the now swollen Four Hundreds. As the managers of Rockefeller Center and the Empire State Building were to do in later years, he engaged a staff of bright, glib young men whose duty was to dress impeccably, talk smoothly, as guides for the unspending through the glories of the hotels. This was the first time in history of hotels that professional guides were a part of the staff. It places the Waldorf on par with such other wonders of sightseeing as the Aquarium and the Statue of Liberty. (Schriftgiesser 63)

It is interesting that people were actively encouraged to visit the hotel as a touristic sight of New York City. Furthermore, the comment concerning the "now swollen Four Hundreds" is another indicator that the Waldorf made high society more accessible. While under the old Mrs. Astor and her favorite social arbiter, Ward McAllister New York, society consisted of exactly 400 members, the hotel's public space allowed this number to increase and enabled people to be included that would not have been formerly considered good enough.

Oscar of the Waldorf

There is one man who is more connected to the institution Waldorf-Astoria than anyone else in its history. Although Oscar Tschirky, the maître d' of the hotel for 50 years, did not written an autobiography, he has worked closely with Kurt Schriftgiesser on his biography, *Oscar of the* Waldorf (1943). The maître d'hotel also wrote several articles on the Waldorf for magazines in New York that present his attitude toward the hotel.[44] Except for the first chapters on Oscar's early life, Schriftengiesser's book is as much about the hotel as it is about the man. His point of view is that of an insider. This causes a lack of critical distance, yet the hotel

---

44 In the Waldorf-Astoria Archive there exists part of a manuscript for what seems to have been planned as another biography of Oscar, this time by the author James McCarthy who had already published on the Waldorf-Astoria. However, the project remained unfinished for unknown reasons. The Archive does not have further material on this manuscript.

experience of Oscar allows us a deeper insight into the mechanisms and the agency of the hotel, which to him is a palace for the public.

Image 4: The Waldorf's own song, "Meet Me at the Hyphen"

Cover of "Meet Me at the Hyphen". From the New York Public Library.

Oscar started working for the Waldorf Hotel three months before it officially opened in 1893 and continued to do so until 1943. As Frank Crowninshield, the publisher of *Vanity Fair*, once stated, "He stands as a bridge between the fragrant and romantic Nineties ... and the present, war-swept Forties" (Crowninshield qtd in Schriftgiesser 9). Oscar Tschirky fills a prominent position in all texts on the Waldorf (see Maxwell and Hughes). By working for the Waldorf, Oscar became a "national figure. He was almost as inseparable from the Waldorf-Astoria as the hyphen itself" (127). As the maître d'hotel he was the face of the Waldorf, acting as Mine Host. The style of the text is very anecdotal and the amount that is dedicated to the hotel and its manager George Boldt seems to sometimes eclipse Oscar in his life account. It becomes clear that the man Oscar is very closely connected to the institution Waldorf-Astoria, so much so as to almost leave no space for anything else.

The pride Oscar took in being part of the grand hotel is expressed in his 'title,' a peerage he proudly earned from guests and visitors of the hotel:

I was just 'Oscar of the Waldorf.' I felt it was title enough, and I was proud of it. It sounded good, too – substantial, as if I were really a part of the Waldorf. Oscar of the Waldorf! A very good title indeed. I couldn't have hoped for a better one if I had named myself. And the best part of it was, I didn't. The public gave me my name. (Schriftgiesser 66)

It is interesting to note that he cherishes the act of being named by the public. His peerage is not one of aristocratic origin, but a title of honor awarded to him by the hotel's citizenry. In his function as the host of the Waldorf, welcoming each and every guest, no matter if he or she was famous or not, Oscar became an icon of popular culture. He is even mentioned in the lyrics of a popular song around the turn of the century, "Meet Me at the Hyphen" (1898, Image 4).

The relationship between Oscar and the hotel is extremely close and very complex. He took part in the making of the hotel together with its first manager George Boldt; he designed parts of it, furnished it, and fulfilled Boldt's visions in the service department. He actively created atmosphere by positioning goods and by his social practices. Seen through his eyes, the hotel is an institution of modernity, a leader of its kind and a palace of the public in New York. For Oscar, the public spaces of the hotel are meant to attract rich guests, but they also allow for a society that "was expanding and less exclusive" (Schriftgiesser 86). For all its luxury, the Waldorf-Astoria is a commercial enterprise, which needs to fill hundreds of beds each day to remain financially viable. According to Oscar, the hotel functioned as an open meeting space, combining peacefully all nationalities, types of people, men and women. Almost from the beginning the Waldorf's management allowed single women, who were excluded from most respectable hotels until the 1920s to live and dine at the Waldorf unattended. The hotel claims for itself to be the first one to end the tradition of the Lady's Parlor and to open (most) of its public rooms for women,[45] a point which Oscar stresses in his biography. The Waldorf was also a leader in employing women in important positions, granting them entry into the city's public sphere.[46]

Oscar Tschirky's biography shows that his relationship with the Waldorf-Astoria was uncommonly close. The enormous amount of time Oscar spent at the Waldorf and the strong identification he had with the hotel made it his home, even though he only moved in after the death of his wife in 1939. Oscar perceives the hotel as a pivotal space for himself as well as for New York's society. In conclusion, one can say that Oscar's view of the hotel is a privileged one and subjective. He acknowledged in the biography that he lacked a healthy distance to the place as it had so much grown on him. Yet, through Oscar's eyes we are also

---

45 All were open to women except for the Men's Cafe.
46 It is debatable whether the Waldorf can be seen as a democratic place. African-Americans were barred from the hotel until the late 50s and early 60s. Poor people do not have the chance to stay in one of its rooms. Yet, this is not atypical for American democracy. The phrase "all men are created equal" from the Declaration of Independence was at first not considered to include black people, women and the poor, non-land owning people. The redefinition took more than a hundred years and was only fully achieved with the Voting Rights Act of 1965.

able to get an insight into New York life and the influence the Waldorf-Astoria has on the city between the late 1890s and the 1940s. Frank Crowninshield, editor of the *Vogue*, stresses that Oscar's "long and intimate connection with the Waldorf-Astoria" helped it to become "a hotel which, more than any other in history, managed to influence manners, even the pattern of life of a goodly proportion of an entire people" (Crowninshield qtd. in Schriftgiesser 9). It made New York's upper class more permeable, it made entertaining outside of the private home fashionable and it provided an entry for women into the public sphere.

President Herbert Hoover's Waldorf Speech

Hotels are embodiments of their respective communities. The Waldorf-Astoria fulfilled this function for New York City. This also continued with the second hotel of the name. It was designed as an improved successor of the first version, thoroughly modernized and once more the last word in hotel business. At its opening gala in 1931 President Herbert Hoover gave a speech, which was broadcast from the White House to the Waldorf-Astoria by the NBC. In it he elevated the hotel's status beyond the borders of New York and turned it into a symbol of national progress. The hotel fit ideally into Hoover's strategy for economic recovery as it was a private enterprise that created jobs and tax revenue.

In his text, President Hoover first establishes the importance of hotels for American society: "Our hotels have become community institutions. They are the center points of civic hospitality. They are the meeting place of a thousand community and national activities. They have come to be conducted in far larger vision than mere profit earning" (Hoover). Hoover connects the Waldorf-Astoria to the larger history of hotels in America and makes the audience aware of their civic function, beyond their commercial nature.[47] To the president, the developments in the hotel sector also mark "the measure of the Nation's growth in power, in comfort, and in artistry" (Hoover). Hoover sets the Waldorf-Astoria apart from other hotels, telling the listeners that this opening is "an event in the development of hotels even in New York City" (Hoover). In the main part of the speech Hoover invokes the historical context in which this opening takes place and formulates the dreams and expectations that he connects with its future:

---

47 Interestingly, at this point in time, historical studies of American hotels did not yet exist. The first well-known scholarly text is Jefferson Williamson's *The American Hotel: An Anecdotal History* (1930). Still, Hoover's comments remind one very strongly of Williamson's and Boorstin's text. I argue that this shows us that the American public was already aware of the great potential that hotels had for their nation and understood their importance for their communities.

The erection of this great structure at this time has been a contribution to the maintenance of employment and is an exhibition of courage and confidence to the whole Nation. This occasion is really but the moving day of an old institution with all its traditions of hospitality and service into a new and better structure. I have faith that in another 50 years the growth of America in wealth, science, and art will necessitate the institution's moving again to an even finer and more magnificent place and equipment. (Hoover)

Hoover acknowledges the Waldorf as an important contributor to the nation's economy and society. He sees the institution as a symbol for the country's prosperity, connecting its success with that of the nation. It is interesting that, indeed, the Waldorf-Astoria, just like American economy, was not financially viable until the end of World War II.[48]

The speech functions as a counterpoint to Hughes's poem, white establishment versus the marginal status of African-Americans at the time. The two texts show the potential for ambiguity of the Waldorf Hotel. It can be perceived as a screen on which people can project their expectations and against which they can hurl their frustrations. Still, it remains a commercial enterprise that needs the public to fill its rooms. As a stage for the wealthy alone it would not have survived the Great Depression, it had to become also a palace of the people to foot the bill. As we will see in the discussion of Hilton's autobiography, the hotel also had to draw the masses.

Many Americans became dissatisfied with Hoover's performance as a president during the financial crisis. Yet, his comments on the Waldorf still struck a cord with the people. Not only the public relations office of the hotel, but countless articles, hotel histories, and scholarly articles have taken up Hoover's statements and used them to debate the hotel's aura and its special position in New York. Because of this speech, it became an almost patriotic act to frequent the hotel. Embodied by the Waldorf, we can see the tension very clearly that underlies urban life in New York: while rugged individualism is celebrated, voices are raised to support the weaker

---

48 Hoover's relationship to the hotel became very close after his presidency ended. He made the Waldorf Towers his permanent home. Hoover's four-room suite, 31-A, was his home and office, where he "conducted the largest and, arguably, the most productive ex-presidency in U. S. history" ("Galler Nine"). The homepage of the Herbert Hoover Library and Museum calls the Waldorf-Astoria his "comfortable monastery" ("Gallery Nine"). While Hoover could certainly have lived in a sumptuous house of his own, the central location of the hotel, the stimulating "neighborhood," and the service made the hotel an ideal retirement residence. Hoover died in the hotel on October 20, 1964. Here the hotel took on another heterotopic function as, "[f]or five days the Waldorf became a virtual hospital annex as doctors administered two hundred blood transfusions" ("Gallery Nine"). Hotel spaces literally encompass all parts of life including birth and death.

members of society. The liminal, public and private hotel space of the Waldorf makes it an arena for vibrant discussions, which is the basis of a democracy.

Conrad Hilton and "The Greatest of Them All"

Probably no one was more inspired by Hoover's speech than Conrad N. Hilton, who made it the goal of his career to become "The Man Who Bought The Waldorf."[49] In the following, I will examine Hilton's Waldorf experience as expressed in his autobiography *Be My Guest* (1957). Hilton's account of his life is a unique example for showing how a hotel executive views the institution hotel as a tool in the hands of a knowing person. It is not only a passive, physical structure. A hotel can develop a certain kind of agency. With his autobiography Hilton sets himself and his favorite hotel a monument. The book is a rich source for understanding Hilton's relationship with the Waldorf and his belief in the democratizing potential of hotels. As the defining achievement in the life of America's foremost hotelman, the Waldorf-Astoria gains an outstanding place among the city's and the nation's hotels.

The autobiography of Conrad N. Hilton, who was born in 1887 in San Antonio, Territory of New Mexico, and died in 1979 in Santa Monica, California, reads like an Alger-esque rags-to-riches story. In *Be My Guest* (1957), Hilton presents himself as the quintessential American.[50] He is a Christian, an active citizen, and a capitalist fighting communism. In his book, Hilton describes how he uses the institution of the modern hotel as a tool to achieve success in life, as well as enable change. Born into the modest circumstances of a family living on the frontier, he found his calling as a hotelkeeper at thirty years of age and went broke in the 1930s before becoming the founder of the best known hotel chain in America, with today more than 4,300 hotels in 93 countries (*Hilton Worldwide*).

In his text, which is written in a very anecdotal and approachable style, Hilton presents a humble image of himself as a rugged individualist with one major goal in life: to become the world's foremost hotelier and to establish hotels as "little

---

49 This is the title of one of the biographies of Conrad N. Hilton, *The Man Who Bought The Waldorf: the Life of Conrad N. Hilton* (1950) by Thomas Ewing Dabney. The book title needed to change quickly as it originally read: *The Man Who Bought the Plaza*. When Hilton managed to sign the papers for the Waldorf, however, this was seen as an even greater feat and the publishing house decided on the new title. Strictly speaking, it was Barron Hilton, Conrad Hilton's son, who bought the Waldorf. Conrad Hilton only bought the rights to manage the hotel. The building and its grounds were purchased in the 1970s by Barron Hilton in memory of his father.

50 See also Annabella Fick, "Conrad Hilton, *Be My Guest* and American Popular Culture" (2013).

Americas," in other words little American palaces of the public, to spread the American way of life throughout the world.[51] Hilton's life account presents an especially interesting example for the instrumentalization of hotels for spreading ideology. In the early 1940s, having recovered from his financial problems, Hilton started to build a hotel chain, first across Texas, then spreading across the United States. Finally, at the end of the decade, he exported his hotels to foreign countries. In the years that followed, Hilton made it his goal to build hotels internationally, using the buildings and their staff as "ambassadors of good will" (237), especially in countries close to the Iron Curtain. As he proclaimed in his autobiography, he wanted to display the fruits of capitalism in the backyard of communism by opening hotels in Istanbul and West Berlin. Through his hotels, he wanted to convert communists to American capitalism (Hilton 237).[52]

Reading *Be My Guest*, one realizes that Hilton is very aware of the potential that the institution of the hotel offers. The multi-functionality of hotel space, the architectural symbolism, the progress displayed in modern technology, and the interaction with well-trained staff members made it an ideal place to influence people and the communities in which the hotels were located. They were meant to encourage exchange among guests and, beyond that, also to enable contact between visitors and locals, residents and transient guests as palaces for the public.[53] The Waldorf-Astoria was the embodiment of all this for Hilton.

Conrad Hilton describes the purchase of the lease for the Waldorf-Astoria as the all-defining achievement of his life. The speech by Herbert Hoover on the Waldorf was a major inspiration for him during the time of the Depression and while building up his hotel chain. He quotes parts of the speech in his autobiography and states that he carried a newspaper clipping of the hotel with him for years, on which

---

51 It is interesting that he furthered this goal by having his autobiography placed in every hotel room of his company, right next to the Gideon Bible. This unconventional form of distribution provided the book with an uncommonly large readership. The practice is still continued. The only similar situation that I am aware of is that the Marriott Hotel company distributes the Book of Mormon in their hotels, as the founding family are Mormons. This placing of books is an interesting and often overlooked way of spreading an ideology, as a hotel room is a special space as home away from home and, one could argue, people are more easily affected when they are in an unfamiliar surrounding.

52 A very interesting analysis of Hilton's expansion methods and his utilization of hotels in his fight against communism can be found in Annabel Jane Wharton's book *Building the Cold War: Hilton International Hotels and Modern Architecture* (2007).

53 The Hilton in Istanbul is a very good example for this, as it became a trailblazer in the Turkish hotel industry. It was the first big project financed by an international company after the war and helped the economy of the metropolis to recover, opening it to foreign investments and interactions.

was written: "the Greatest of Them All" (189). Hilton did not visit the hotel during the years of building his chain and did not have a personal experience of the place before the negotiations started. Yet, the newspaper articles and Hoover's speech, together with the histories that he read of the famous hotel spurred him on his quest.[54] Even though he also acquired the Palmer House and the Stevens, as well as the "other" New York grand hotel, the Plaza,[55] Hilton shapes his life's narrative around getting the Waldorf. It becomes the node of his personal journey: "it is a central point around which I focus my life. Events happened 'before the Waldorf.' 'After the Waldorf.' Or 'during the Waldorf negotiations'" (230). From this perspective Hilton's life account can easily be read as his quest for the Waldorf-Astoria. It is during the silver-anniversary of the new Waldorf that he allegedly had the inspiration for writing *Be My Guest* (23). When he finally acquires the management rights of the hotel his phrasing makes clear that he reaches the climax of his story: "That day, October 12, 1949, I became 'the Man Who Bought the Waldorf'. ...I couldn't get used to it. ... It sounded fine! It felt good, too." (240).[56] This accomplishment defines him as a hotel man.[57] The Waldorf-Astoria is the fulfillment of his American Dream. While he would sell some of the prestigious

---

54 When Hilton bought the Plaza and later the Waldorf, guests and New Yorkers raised the question if a man from the South West would be able to understand the special codes working in those hotels and their refined way of living there. In both cases, Hilton won his critics over with a surprising amount of discretion and huge amounts of money to restore the grand establishments to their former beauty.

55 The debate over which is the greatest of the New York hotels, the Plaza or the Waldorf-Astoria, has been going on for more than a century. Hilton decided for the Waldorf. Real estate mogul Donald Trump later decided for the Plaza Hotel. When Trump bought the grand hotel in 1988 he published an open letter in *The New York Times*, stating: "I haven't purchased a building, I have purchased a masterpiece — the Mona Lisa. For the first time in my life, I have knowingly made a deal that was not economic — for I can never justify the price I paid, no matter how successful the Plaza becomes" (Ghigliotty).

56 The word choice here is similar to Oscar Tschirky's (Schriftgiesser 66). Both men closely identified with the hotel. Both were majorly involved in making it the pinnacle of hotel living in New York. Both could see the hotel's potential also as a place bringing people together and celebrating American values.

57 The hotel mogul's unique personality and his special connection with the hotel on Park Avenue was so inspiring that the makers of the hit show *Mad Men* decided to use it as a story line for the third season of the show. Here the main protagonist, Don Draper, meets Hilton in a suite in the Waldorf where they come to a business agreement and show a celebratory function at the hotel to which Hilton invites Draper. Even though these scenes are short, it is nevertheless noteworthy that the connection between Hilton and his prime hotel, the Waldorf-Astoria, was so powerful as to be transported into a current TV show.

buildings again, the Waldorf remained part of the Hilton group even after Conrad Hilton's death.

Throughout the text, the reader gets the impression that Hilton wishes to position the Waldorf as a public place, a palace of the public. He wants to make it accessible to more people, fitting his ideal of American free market system. This approach makes the hotel finally profitable. When Hilton purchased the Waldorf's right of lease it became a chain hotel on paper, something that many New Yorkers saw with anxiety. Yet, despite being a chain hotel man, Conrad Hilton keeps the unique spirit of the institution (Sutton 236). About Hilton's relationship to the hotel Horace Sutton, a Waldorf historian, writes:

Boldt's idea of bringing 'exclusivity to the masses,' and Boomer's efforts to bring society into a public hotel have been altered by Hilton to fit the economic structures of another day. But there is nothing to say that either of the first two operators held the Waldorf in deeper reverence, and it is certain to say that the Waldorf is held in more loving hands by it present owner than by its first. (237)

Hilton was a firm supporter of American style capitalism with all its problematic connotations and ideological burdens. But he was also a philanthropist and idealist who wished to improve social interactions globally with his hotels and especially with his flagship, the Waldorf-Astoria.

Through his people oriented personality and his celebrity status, Conrad Hilton brought much attention to the Waldorf-Astoria in the 1950s and 60s. In those years the Waldorf became the retreat for New York's café society, catering to the rich, the famous, and even to royals. However, the Waldorf continued to fulfill the tradition of the earlier grand hotels by also being an accessible meeting place for locals and by providing space for the activities of civic groups and charity organizations.

For the United Nations and the United States of America State Department the Waldorf-Astoria's fulfilled its role as "unofficial palace of New York" (Crowninshield viii).[58] In texts about the second Waldorf, it is repeatedly mentioned

---

58 Since its opening the Waldorf is the official residence of the American representative to the United Nations and houses most of the state guests that attend meetings at the UN. Over the years, "numerous studies conducted during both Republican and Democratic administrations have concluded that it is cost effective and convenient" ("Feds Take Close Look At Sale of Waldorf Astoria to Chinese Company"). Fulfilling a long list of requirements the grand hotel has proven to be the most fitting place for the mission in New York City. The Waldorf is also the site of the annual gala at the opening of the United Nations General Assembly. It is the State Department's 'guest house' in New York and the choice for many foreign administrations. The Waldorf is also the city's

that the Waldorf is a place for meetings of the highest diplomatic importance as a kind of neutral ground (see also Farrell 79f; Morehouse 148; 183). Because it is a privately owned space and works under the rules of the free market, the hotel is seen as unbiased. The hotel's head of the International Department once stated:

> Another thing that this hotel has that is very special is that we can house, on one floor, the Prime Minister of Israel or the Foreign Minister of Israel, and on another floor we will have Saudi Arabia. ... And sometimes when they don't talk to each other in the United Nations, they will talk to each other in the hotel. Sometimes they do get together to discuss things behind closed doors that they would not discuss otherwise. (Sutton 148)

The best-known political event that has taken place at the hotel is the meeting of the "Big Four" after the Second World War to discuss the reorganization of Europe and the foundation of the United Nations. Here the Waldorf played host to heads of states and diplomats from America, Great Britain, France, and Russia alike, witnessing and to a certain degree enabling the development of a more peaceful world (see Sutton 73f; Farrell 78f). The Waldorf's appearance of neutrality was supported by the fact that the talks took place in Suite 37A, which was then the home of Lucius Boomer, the president of the company owning the hotel. By using the owner's suite, combined with the equal number of rooms and equal service of the hotel to all four powers, a selection of food that was balanced so to not over-represent one dining-culture, and even drinks that were typical of each represented country, a common ground was achieved (Sutton 77). The most apparent element of neutrality in the hotel's procedure was the presenting of the bill, which charged all participants the same amount. The economic transaction makes the whole affair a relatively unbiased one. That the State Department paid the tab for the jointly used conference facilities makes the U.S. the official host of the conference without overstressing the fact that all procedures took place on American soil. Morehouse states that for the mid-twentieth century: "the U.S. was the center of the world, New York was its heart, the Waldorf was the center of the heart" (Morehouse 122).

Besides this representative function for the United Nations, the country and the city, the Waldorf has also played host to events undertaken by smaller national associations, private companies, and welfare organizations. To avoid the accusation of being a place strictly for those on the top of the capitalist food chain, the Waldorf-Astoria, for example, offered space for a yearly "Bake-Off", in which all kinds of people competed for winning the title of best baker and with that the first prize of $25,000. Oscar's successor Philippe said about this event: "The Waldorf-Astoria ... has a greater responsibility to the country than most hotels. Although it

---

preferred event location. As New York City does not have representative space of their own, the hotel has taken on the role as substitute host for the city's guests.

is interested in princes and shahs it is conscious of the democratic process" (Philippe qtd. in Sutton 153). This deliberate openness to the wider public was further supported by the prize for the second winner, which was a four-day stay at the Waldorf. With such an event, the Waldorf management tried to diminish critical voices that accused the hotel of elitism. It is a form of compensation, to further legitimize the image of the hotel as palace of the public.

To conclude, the first Waldorf brought high society out of the private parlors into the public. The second one stressed its role as a meeting place for New Yorkers and the world. The hotel's leading men Oscar Tschirky and Conrad Hilton tried to imbue the hotel with an open atmosphere, which did not take away from its glamour. Instead, it allowed the hotel's guests to experience the Waldorf as a accessible American palace, with its public spaces open to all. Over the years meetings of groups, institutions, and businesses became one of the Waldorf's most important and financially viable sectors. The hotel became the convention place of choice in New York, which can be seen when using the search engine of the CUNY library. Entering "Waldorf-Astoria" in the search banner brings up more than 2,800 results, most of them concerning events and conventions by a myriad of societies that have taken place at the Waldorf, cementing its position as representative venue number one.

1.3 THE HOTEL AS A CITY WITHIN A CITY

The big modern American hotels of the nineteenth and twentieth centuries have often been described as mirrors of their communities, microcosms of their cities. Both incarnations of the Waldorf can be called a 'city within a city,' considering size, staff number and facilities (Morehouse 58; Sutton 52). This is the narrative most often used in connection to the Waldorf-Astoria. Albert Dearing writes: "As a symbol the Waldorf-Astoria ... epitomized both the opulent power as well as the inexhaustible vitality of New York. ... Like New York itself, the Waldorf-Astoria crystalized the improbably and fabulous" (69). It was not the first New York grand hotel, yet the Waldorf's size dwarfed the others when it opened in 1893. With more than 1000 employees and the same amount of guest rooms, the structure had more inhabitants than an average village. Furthermore, the hotel not only provided bedrooms, but also offered dining rooms, a café and bar, newspaper stands, shops, a library, meeting rooms, offices, and many more amenities to its guests.

The metaphor of 'a city within a city,' however, encompasses more than the mere material aspect. According to Molly Berger: "Hotels are extremely complicated buildings – materially, socially, and culturally" ("Rich Man's City" 50). The Waldorf-Astoria also mirrors the city in its social structure. It is, as Matlock calls it "a doppelgänger of the city" (Matlock 78). The people who visit, work and live at hotels come from all walks of life and create a microcosmic version of the larger society outside the hotel. Henry James called the Waldorf "a synonym for civilization" and for Ward the grand hotel becomes a metaphor for America itself (Ward 152).

Since its opening the Waldorf has attracted a loyal workforce, with a number of people working for the hotel for twenty, thirty, or even more years. Frank Case, the owner and manager of the Algonquin Hotel, commented on the staff situation in the Waldorf-Astoria in 1938: "There are waiters in the new Waldorf that were transplanted from bulbs at 34th Street and Fifth Avenue" (156).[59] The staff did not always work for the hotel without conflicts, as the Hackman Strike of 1893 shows. No unions existed for hotel people during the time of the first Waldorf, so the work environment was not yet controlled and could be difficult.[60]

Hotels are also first ports of call for immigrants searching for work (Krebs 146). The Waldorf being one of the largest ones offers many opportunities due to the wide variety of positions available from highly visible white-collar work to invisible back-of-the-house work, which does not require any language proficiency. As a commercial enterprise a hotel should be interested in avoiding clashes among its different groups, it has to consider its reputation. The second Waldorf, the preferred address for the United Nations and leading institution of hospitality, also has a very diverse group of guests, so tensions among guests and staff might arise due to different national and ideological backgrounds (Morehouse 153, 186). In a hotel that provides space for important political and social meetings there is an additional responsibility to keep the code of hospitality and to put the professional work attitude above personal inclinations.

The Waldorf did not always succeed with this. While the hotel was progressive in some service sectors and in its history has employed different members of minorities, e.g. Irish room maids, like the rest of the city it lagged behind in the

---

59 The diverse social structure of the employees is an important element in all hotels. Together with the large number of facilities contained under one roof it is the most obvious reason for calling a hotel a microcosm of the city. For many employees their position in these institutions is identity-shaping (Krebs 131).

60 The Hackman strike was an infamous incident in the employment history of the institution (Dearing 87). Boldt demanded of the drivers working for the hotel to come on duty only with clean-shaven faces, as in his understanding it mirrored the professionalism of his hotel. This demand, however, was interpreted as trespassing into the private life of a worker, regulating an intimate element of a person's body. The reaction was, as expected, harsh and caused a public outcry that made necessary the action of the governor of New York who called Boldt's demand "undemocratic and un-American'" (Hungerford 90). Boldt won out in the end because with changing fashion, clean-shaven faces became the standard in the early twentieth century.

employment of colored workers. Being 'a city within a city' not only mirrors the positive trends of a community but often also the negative, exclusionary ones: "Like all cultural contexts, hotel life is governed and structured by certain regulations, by markers of difference, ritualized behavioral codes and processes of negotiation and identification" (Krebs 120).

On the positive side, the Waldorf functioned as a trailblazer for women's work. The grand hotel was seen as a highly attractive working space for young women. It was one of the first larger institutions in New York that employed a great number of female staff, even outside of the 'typically female' departments like housekeeping and laundry. Boldt was the first manager to recruit female cashiers and clerks, positions that demand training and responsibility and were very visible. This employment practice was discussed in the media and contributed to the modern image of the hotel (Hungerford 145). The practice of leading in the field of gender equality was also continued in the second Waldorf which is said to have been the first hotel to put a woman into a chief managing position.

Maître d'hotel Oscar Tschirky, who experienced the Waldorf first hand, perceived the institution as a world in itself. He writes: it was "my home and my world" (Schriftgiesser 2). The hotel and its complex social and technological mechanism eclipsed for Oscar the rest of the world. He hardly needed to go outside as everything that concerned him, his work, his friends, and to a certain degree his family, could be found or could take place inside the building. To what extent the hotel had taken over his life only became apparent on the rare occasions when he left the Waldorf. Returning in 1924 from his first vacation in thirty years, he recalls: "How different, indeed, was New York. I had lost a great perspective, remaining so close to the Waldorf-Astoria. I had not seen the forest, for the sight of the trees. I had never seen the famous skyline of Manhattan, for sight of the buildings" (Schriftgiesser 209). Visitors who came to the Waldorf-Astoria got the impression that if they only remained long enough in Peacock Alley or in any other public part of the building, like in Port Said at some point "everybody in the world worth knowing [would] eventually happen along" (Reedy 8).

The close ties between the city and its doppelgänger became very apparent, when the first Waldorf was torn down in 1929. In his article "'Wrecking the Joint': The Razing of City Hotels in the First Half of the Twentieth Century," Bernard Jim describes the strong reaction of the public to the demolition of the Waldorf. The event had a strong impact on New Yorkers, reflected in the number of articles and books written about it. In April 1929, shortly before the closing of the building, Virginia Pope wrote for the *New York Times* that the life of the Waldorf Hotel "has touched the history of New York and of the Nation" (Pope 7). Its closing was paramount with the passing of an era. Most New Yorkers could not imagine that anyone would want to raze the old grand hotel, despite it having become outdated.[61] After learning of considerations to close the hotel, Oscar recalls thinking: "Why, New York would no more think of tearing down the Waldorf-Astoria than of throwing over the Statue of Liberty in the harbor! I fretted and worried, especially when away from the hotel. The Waldorf-Astoria was my life. I had never even thought about going elsewhere" (Schriftgiesser 214). For many New Yorkers, the old hotel was a symbol for their way of life. The company in charge of building the Empire State Building on the hotel's site needed to take these reactions into consideration and made them part of their advertisement campaign. They created a narrative that connected the new enterprise with the iconic hotel. Through this, they wanted to transport the glamor of this place to their new structure. In the campaign the iconic position of the Waldorf was closely linked to the new skyscraper, giving it an almost mythical status by describing the Empire State Building as "worthy follower of its historic predecessors" (Jim 299).

According to Kopytoff the reason for the strong emotional reaction to the hotel's demolition can be explained with the concept of "singularization." This term describes people's interaction with an object or a building. Their memories and experiences with it "work to remove [it] from the commodity sphere, protecting it from being exchanged and put up for sale" (qtd in Jim 297). The singularization of the Waldorf did not prevent its demolition. Yet, as a reaction, many of the texts about the Waldorf date from the period of its destruction. They were meant to preserve the cultural significance of the institution for future generations.

For the famous architect Rem Koolhaas, the demolition and rebuilding of the Waldorf-Astoria can be seen as the fulfillment of its fate for Manhattan:

The Waldorf is the first full realization of the conscious Manhattan. In any other culture the demolition of the old Waldorf would have been a Philistine act of destruction, but in the ideology of Manhattanism it constitutes a double liberation: while the site is freed to meet its evolutionary destiny, the idea of the Waldorf is released to be redesigned as the example of an explicit Culture of Congestion. (Koolhaas 138)

Koolhaas grants the Waldorf-Astoria a special position in New York culture. As a condensed version of New York it functions as a testing ground for developments that are of importance for the larger city surrounding the hotel.

---

61 The fading of the first Waldorf is captured in Gloria Vanderbilt's and Thelma Lady Furness's autobiography *Double Exposure, a Twin Autobiography* (1958). Here they write: "The old Waldorf must have been magnificent in its day; but in the summer of 1917 it had the quality of a flower pressed too long between the pages of a book. ...Could it have spoken to us I am sure it would have said, 'Youth, be wary. Don't look at me with such disdain; I, too, have had my day'" (qtd. in Donzel 54).

Many of the spaces and functions of the old hotel were included in the second Waldorf-Astoria. As mentioned above, it is several times larger than its predecessor and justifies even more the description of a 'city within a city.' The new building even offered a private railroad track for guests arriving in their private trains. In addition, the second Waldorf contained one of New York's largest signal networks and even more restaurants, shops, and event space than the first one. A cutaway image of the new Waldorf-Astoria used in an advertisement shows the combination of private, semi-private, and public hotel space next to each other. It underlines the hotel's claim as a 'city within a city.' The depiction allows the curious public an uncommon look inside the workings of this "monster hotel," also including the basement space with its back-of-the-house facilities like the laundry, kitchen, and storage. That the public relations office of the hotel decided on this kind of presentation shows that they were aware of the great interest the public has in the anatomy of a grand hotel. It demystifies the hotel at the same time as it awes people with the actual multi-functionality of the structure.

When Conrad Hilton took over the Waldorf-Astoria in 1949, *Time Magazine* dedicated its lead article to him, asking him about his visions for and ideas about hotels. The article states: "In the U.S., more than in any other country, the big hotel has become a city in itself. There, says Hilton, 'you could live out a full life without ever going out of doors. …You can park your car, eat your head off and sleep till noon. Home was never like that!'" ("Hotels: The Key Man" 89). As could be seen above, this particular kind of hotel experience is part of the Waldorf-Astoria's fabric. The grand hotel gives its guests the impression of living in a perfected version of the city. In its American Art-Deco appearance the institution mirrors New York today more than it did a century ago. The Waldorf-Astoria is as fast paced, wasteful, arrogant, liberal, open and brash as the people and the city in which it is located. It is microcosmic New York.

The Hotel and Its Film – *Week-end at the Waldorf*

The movie *Week-end at the Waldorf* (1945) by Robert Z. Leonard most conclusively captures the hotel experience of the Waldorf-Astoria as a 'city within a city'.[62] This adaptation of Vicki Baum's *Grand Hotel* (*Menschen im Hotel*, 1929)[63]

---

62 Unlike in the analysis of a written text, I also take the visual level and the camera technique into consideration to examine this movie so far as it is of use for the discussion.

63 Vicki Baum's novel can be considered to be the ur-hotel novel. Hotels have been used in fiction before, in American literature e.g. in "The Blue Hotel" (1898) by Stephen Crane. Yet, Baum creates a new type, as here the plot is only possible because of its unique setting. The so-called hotel plot is defined as a plot that brings together very different kinds of narratives that are only connected by the characters' position in the hotel. It is

uses the eponymous hotel as its main and only setting, incorporating elements from the original book, yet focusing less on the development of the characters than on the glamour of the building and its inhabitants and the vast size of the place. For the movie the hotel management worked together with the producers, considering the movie to be a useful advertisement for the hotel. As the historiographies and the homepage of the hotel proudly state, it is the only hotel that has its own movie about it (Morehouse 253).[64] The whole plot takes place on the premises of the Waldorf-Astoria. The screenwriters Sam and Bella Spewack have been criticized for not thinking up "anything particularly original or intriguing" ("'Week-end at the Waldorf'"). It is a rather flat version of the *Grand Hotel* plot. However, in this adaptation from 1945, the film was not supposed to show the complex character types of Baum's book. Instead, the focus was on the possibilities and adventures that could be experienced in such 'a city within a city,' a little escapism after World War II.[65]

The focus on hotel experience becomes clearest in the in-between scenes, which separate the different plot lines of the story. In these scenes the going-ons of a grand hotel are depicted, mostly in long shots to convey the number of workers and the size of the building: the telephone operator girls that function as symbols for the interconnectedness of the Waldorf with the city and the world at large, the cleaning staff that shows off the huge size of the space they have to clean and the professional reaction of the staff towards unconventional requests of their guests, such as modeling a hospital for the top of a wedding cake or walking the guests' dogs in the Poodle Parade. These hotel operation scenes are repeatedly underlined by the jocular comments of the movie's narrator Randy Morton, who is based on Elsa Maxwell (Sanders 293). The movie review commented positively on these scenes, as they are an unusual element among the very conventional plot lines

---

the agency of the hotel that makes these stories credible. It is a 'mithandelnder Schauplatz.'

64 This last statement demands closer attention as it does reveal interesting elements about the Waldorf and its potential as a place for identification. To make it reasonable for a movie company to add the name of the hotel to the title the hotel must command a certain position in American society. It has to be well known enough to draw attention to the movie. Hotels have used the name "Waldorf" across the globe to convey the impression of luxury and top-level hospitality. Even in New York State several hotels gained or encouraged the use of the nickname "Waldorf" to present their important position for their particular communities. Notably here are the Hotel Theresa and the Grossinger's. The Theresa was called "the Waldorf of Harlem" while Taub's history of the Hotel Grossinger has been titled *Waldorf-of-the-Catskills* (1952).

65 See also Annabel Wharton, "Two Waldorf-Astorias: Spatial Economies as Totem and Fetish" (2003).

("'Week-end at the Waldorf'"). They allow special glimpses into hotel life. In the movie the staff is always smiling, efficient, helpful, and professional and (with exception of Bunny, the stenographer) they merge with the background. Yet, these scenes with the staff are necessary to turn the built structure from a huge block of rooms into a hotel. The employees' tasks fulfill the expectations of the viewer to see a space that resembles the city but in a perfected way. The fascination lies in the fact that this place, the Waldorf, exists in reality, as a heterotopia where work and leisure, moments of crisis, and everyday happenings exist in the same space; better still, a place that the viewer can actually visit when he or she comes to New York.

As the metaphor 'a city within a city' implies, the hotel is a complex entity. It is actually so large and anonymous that one can assume any identity one wishes to have.[66] This is another important element that is also at the forefront of this fictionalized account of life at the Waldorf. According to Sanders a grand hotel is a plausible setting for assuming identities as it is "no less than the waterfront or train station, a natural home for strangers, a zone of transience" (Sanders 292). Playing with identity is an important element in the novel by Vicki Baum.[67] In *Week-end at the Waldorf* the mix-up of identities is used in a comic way when war correspondent Chip Collyer surprises famous actress Irene Malvern "Baron Geiger"-like in her suite. This reflects positively on the hotel because the scene presents the hotel as a place where one has the chance to meet attractive and interesting people. This playing with identity is a plot line, which is only conceivable and acceptable in the surrounding of a hotel. In his book *Delirious New York: A Retroactive Manifesto of Manhattan* the architect Rem Koolhaas describes specifically the Waldorf-Astoria when he claims that a hotel

is a plot, a cybernetic universe with its own laws generating random but fortuitous collisions between human beings who would never have met elsewhere. It offers a fertile cross-section through the population, a richly textured interface between social castes, a field for comedy of clashing manners and a neutral background of routine operations to give every incident dramatic relief. (Koolhaas 148)

In contrast to the original film version of *Menschen im Hotel, Week-end at the Waldorf* is not cut off from its surrounding but is very much embedded in the city of

---

66 About the topic of hotel stories and the play of identities see Matlock 80 and Matthias 4.
67 Here Kringelein and Baron Gaiger make use of the anonymity and coincidental nature of the hotel to either experience life in a new way or to use their unstable hotel identity for criminal acts.

New York and its historic context, the Second World War (Sanders 293).[68] In the American adaptation of 1945, the Waldorf does not just refer to itself, but also beyond, to the city of New York: "The Waldorf of *Week-end* ... is linked inextricably to its larger context; it is a 'city within a city.' In this interplay between inward and outward, focus can be found the special urban significance of the grand hotel" (Sanders 293). This is shown clearest in the exposition and in the final part where the hotel is visibly placed in the city context. The aerial shots of the grand hotel at the beginning and at the end powerfully present its position in New York, even for the uninitiated viewer. As the camera eye circles the building, the hotel gains a symbolic dimension and appears to be the pinnacle of the city, its palace of the public, dominating yet all-including.[69] The Waldorf, due to its size, its heterogeneous mix of people and its location, fits this statement more than any other places. This echoes the final words of the movie by the narrator that sum up the two hours of the movie: "Anything can happen, in a weekend at the Waldorf" (*Week-end at the Waldorf*, quoted in Sanders 294).

Overall, one can state that the movie is not a very deep text and not a very faithful adaptation of the original novel. It is a quite blatant, visual advertisement for the hotel, as Wharton writes: "In *Week-end at the Waldorf*, spectacle is unproblematically sufficient" (Wharton, "The Two Waldorf-Astorias" 540). The movie shows the hotel's attractive features, rooms and services in a most positive light. This is underlined by comments of minor and major characters that directly point out certain attractive hotel amenities. Accordingly, the movie review states: "In any event, Mr. Lucius Boomer's elegant boarding house sure has hit the publicity jackpot, thanks to Metro" ("'Week-end at the Waldorf'"). Still, besides its lack of literary depth the movie fittingly depicts the Waldorf's hotel experience as 'a city within a city.'

Grand Hotels like the Waldorf-Astoria have inspired many writers and filmmakers over the years. In their works the hotel is often more than a mere backdrop but acquires a certain agency. This kind of agency of non-human objects can be described as "material agency" (Knappett and Malafouris xii). The physical surrounding not only influences the story as a kind of stage but becomes an active part of the story, the German term for this being a 'mithandelnder Schauplatz' (Weik von Mossner). The setting can create a certain mood, allows for a certain diegesis, and it can be a hint or key to interpreting the scene in a deeper way. The presented space can influence the plot line and make it more credible or more

---

68 In the famous film adaptation of 1932, the surrounding city is only shown in very few glimpses through windows, but is otherwise excluded from the going-ons. For a more in-depth analysis of the depiction of hotel space in Grand Hotel see Matlock and Matthias.

69 In these shots the Waldorf-Astoria indeed looks somewhat like a modern day Taj Mahal as Maxwell noted.

ambiguous. A real place like the Waldorf already implies certain ideas and meanings, it creates in the audience specific dreams and expectations. Due to its multi-functional and heterotopic nature, a grand hotel like the Waldorf inspires the creation of cultural products.

Week-end at the Waldorf is not the only instance in which the Waldorf has been used in movies. Among the best known appearances of the Waldorf in film are the movies *The Out-of-towners* (1978) starring Jack Lemmon, *Serendipity* (2001) starring John Cusack and Kate Beckinsale, and *Maid in Manhattan* starring Jennifer Lopez (2002). There is a natural affinity between the institution and the silver screen. According to Rem Koolhaas the reason for this circumstance is that

With the Waldorf, - the Hotel itself becomes ... a movie, featuring the guests as stars and the personnel as a discreet coat-tailed chorus of extras. By taking a room in the hotel, a guest buys his way into an ever-expanding script, acquiring the right to use all the decors and to exploit the prefabricated opportunities to interact with all the other "stars." ... Only the territory of the block frames all stories and lends them coherence. (Koolhaas 148f)

The variety of plots the grand hotel offers, the simple solution for throwing together different characters and manufacturing meetings among unlikely acquaintances, and the escape from the everyday are factors that explain the fascination of creatives and regular guests with the Waldorf. The 'city within the city' narrative that so fittingly describes the Waldorf-Astoria experience in New York is one key to understand the hotel's influence on the city's culture and society.

The Waldorf in a Children's Book

I want to end my analysis of the three main narratives of the hotel experience at the Waldorf-Astoria with the unusual yet very revealing glimpse into life at the Waldorf presented in the children's book *The Dog Who Lives at the Waldorf* (1964) by James Brough.[70] Children books and (real) hotels go together quite well. The most famous example is the children book series *Eloise* by Kay Thompson from 1955, which takes place in the Plaza.[71] The Waldorf has its own variety on the

---

70 Not much secondary literature exists on the book *The Dog Who Lives At The Waldorf*. It is known that the book is based on an actual resident, Rosalind Cole, and her dog (Gross). She was a long-term resident of the hotel and published a Waldorf cookbook. Some parts of the texts are also said to have been produced with the help of Hedda Hopper, another famous resident of the hotel. Thus, the text provides an insider's point of view that might have been compromising had it been told from any other perspective than that of a dog.
71 The little girl who lives at the Plaza Hotel is a well-known and beloved children's book. It is republished on a regular basis. The character became the synonym for all hotel kids.

topic. In contrast to Kay Thompson's book, here a dog called Jingabo is the protagonist. The advantage is that an animal narrator can air all kinds of impressions and ideas without the danger appearing too nosey or direct. He is able to enter places that would be off-limits for human residents.

From the beginning, the reader learns that the dog shares his home, the Waldorf-Towers, with luminaries like the Windsors, Herbert Hoover, Gina Lollobrigida, and many others.[72] The encounters, mostly in the elevator, are narrated with obvious nonchalance, mentioning the famous people *en passant*. For the reader this namedropping confirms the status of the narrator and his mistress. It confirms the hotel as a stage of the wealthy. The Waldorf's function for society is implied through the guests that the dog encounters during the week he narrates in the story. Furthermore, the reader learns of the different events that are held at the hotel and which are displayed on the black board in the main lobby: "a pie-baking contest in the Grand Ballroom, the American Iron and Steel Institute in the Sert, Kozy-Tozy Knitwear in the Empire Room and a fashion luncheon in Peacock Alley" (Brough 29). This diverse mix reflects the narratives of the Waldorf as 'a city within a city' and palace of the people. The lobby is the meeting place of the house, where something or the other is always going on.

As in most hotel texts, the staff plays an important role. Not only are they everywhere the dog goes, but they clearly are what keeps the whole structure functioning. The protagonist makes this clear by listing all of the employees participating in the great charity ball at the end of the book. As is quite typical for most hotel texts, there is one staff member that the main character feels most

---

For example, historians at the Waldorf call the son of Lucius Boomer, the second general manager of the Waldorf, a male-Eloise as he lived a life as described in the eponymous children's book. *Eloise* presents an interesting insight into the workings of the hotel. She presents the leisure class's life in a palace hotel. Eloise is mostly raised by her nanny and the different employees in the hotel. The hotel child is a test for the place. She terrorizes room service, she constantly produces additional work for the staff, she is seldom satisfied with what she gets and talks down to others from her relatively small height. The hotel, however, is shown in a positive light as it functions as the child's surrogate family, taking care of her *in loco parentis*.

72 In one scene the text mentions Conrad N. Hilton, then the owner of the Waldorf-Astoria. In just a short remark to the dog, his typical Westerner character traits are convincingly recreated, using one of his favorite expressions "by golly" (Brough 35). For the adult reader, the short remark on the encounter between the dog and the hotel mogul is enough to call up all connotations of the name Hilton, the history of the Waldorf-Astoria, and probably also his rags-to-riches story.

attached to, in this case the maid Rose.[73] While maids are often negatively depicted as sloppy and lazy, Rose is efficient and pleasant. She is the dog's friend. Rose is also the key for Jingabo to see all parts of the building, even bringing him up to the suite of the American ambassador.[74]

The building is described in detail from the perspective of the dog. He narrates the correct entryways of the hotel, including a comment on which entry is used by which social group.[75] Jingabo's description of the lobby, including the famous clock from the World Columbian Exposition, resembles Michel de Certeau's concept of a *tour*. The reader experiences the hotel through the eyes of an animal *flaneur*. The dog mentions the different facilities and services that the hotel has to offer and even knows the twin towers of the hotel by name. The narration makes clear that the Waldorf-Astoria is as a city within a city, a place no one really has to leave to get everything one wants or needs. The reader even learns that in bad weather, Jingabo can get all the exercise he needs by strolling along the covered driveway beneath the main lobby.

The text ends with the narration of a charity ball, a huge undertaking in which the wealthy guests and all members of the staff are involved. It is based on real events. The dog for example mentions that an elephant is part of the evening. This is a direct allusion to the famous "Paris in April" balls organized by Philippe and Elsa Maxwell, where elephants were the main attraction of the evening. The dog's unexpected appearance in the ballroom causes quite a disruption. However, as this is the famous Waldorf-Astoria, which has the best-trained and most professional staff, both the dog and the event remain unharmed. That his misstep is without consequence for the perpetrator, Jingabo, is testimony to Boldt's first rule, "the guest is always right." Overall, the text is a very interesting addition to the literature inspired by and written on the Waldorf-Astoria.[76]

---

73 Maids have become stock characters over the long history of hotels and texts about hotels in America (see Sandoval-Strausz and Wilk 165ff).

74 While guests are free to move in the public parts of a hotel, the staff has the necessary spatial knowledge of and entry power to all parts of the building, including the back-of-the-house and guest rooms.

75 The Lexington Ave door, according to Jingabo is used by business "Brains" while the Park Avenue entrance is used by "Society" (Brough 8).

76 James Brough was aware of the larger hotel literature. The reader learns that the dog and his mistress watched the movie Grand Hotel in their room. In just a few sentences the author is able to acknowledge the film, without giving the name, commenting on its content and connecting it with the actual situation of his book's protagonists. The quotes given from the film contain the gist of the story, including Garbo's famous line "I want to be alone" (Brough 25). This element of intertextuality is interesting on two accounts. First, *Grand Hotel* by Vicki Baum is the ur-text of hotel literature, establishing its own

The reason for setting a children's book in a real life hotel remains ambiguous. I suggest that it is a way of influencing future guests and create in the young reader the desire to visit the place for him- or herself. It creates in them the wish for their own Waldorf hotel experience. One could say that it is a starting point for people to enter the Waldorf discourse and win a positive impression of it before even going there. *The Dog Who Lives At The Waldorf* provides an intimate look inside the hotel. As a children's book, it offers some interesting perspectives on the narratives surrounding the Waldorf. It reflects many of the above described ideas, concerning the hotel's function for society, its position in New York and its heterotopic character as 'a city within a city.' Sometimes children's books provide us with richer insights than many history books do.[77]

Today, the influence of the Waldorf-Astoria on New York is still there. It is no longer the all-defining grand dame among grand hotels. There are fewer publications on the Waldorf-Astoria.[78] In fall 2014, the hotel has been sold to the Chinese Anbang Insurance Group for $1.95 billion (Bagli). Yet, there are more and more webpages and blogs dedicated to the hotel, its history, and its legendary connection with New York's high society. The hotel encourages this fascination in the hotel's past by making their hotel archive searchable on the internet. *The Waldorf-Astoria Archive* is a interesting collection of hotel memorabilia, media texts, photographs, personal recollections, and more. The hotel's archivist creates exhibitions on facets of the hotel's history. Parts of the collection are always on view in the new Peacock Alley next to the Waldorf's main lobby and Harry's Bar. With the permanent collection, plus special exhibitions, e.g. for the New York Archive Day, the hotel successfully reminds its patrons of its glorious past, presenting them with the opportunity to become part of the legend themselves. The display of the hotel's story fosters feelings of place-identity even in guests who only stop there once or twice and heightens their hotel experience.

---

genre, to which this children's book also could be counted. Second, it hints at the movie *Week-end at the Waldorf* (1945). This neatly ties hotel literature to the Waldorf discourse, and its history overall.

77 Another children's book that incorporates the Waldorf hotel in its story is the mystery *City of Orphans* (2011) by Avi. Here the hotel is the site of a burglary, of which the main protagonist's sister, a maid at the hotel, is accused. The showdown of the story happens in the lobby of the Waldorf. The story, set at the turn of the century, uses the hotel as stage for the wealthy, but it is also a symbol for modernity, an employment opportunity for young immigrants. While it is not high literature, it shows us how the hotel is still seen as an essential part of New York culture and influences the imagination of writers even today.

78 The last monograph dedicated to the Waldorf-Astoria has just been published by William Morrison, *Waldorf-Astoria* (2014) in the series *Images of America* by Arcadia Publishing.

The combination of memorabilia of the Waldorf, names like Peacock Alley and Empire Room, and the by now again successfully recreated Art Deco style create an atmosphere which makes guests come back. If one lacks the necessary funds one can attend the public tours offered by the hotel for guests and visitors. With these guided tours the hotel extends parts of the grand hotel experience to people who do not stay at the hotel. These bi-weekly tours enable visitors to learn about the hotel's history in an anecdotal way. More importantly, it allows them a peak into facilities and even suites that, due to the price tag, are usually above the visitors' financial means.[79] While the tours offer historical information, their main draw certainly is of a more voyeuristic kind. As with the guides employed by Boldt in the early days, these tours are meant to show the luxury and amenities of the hotel to those not yet able or willing to pay for a stay. It might persuade them to become patrons themselves in the future. That the tours are still a success and take place on a regular basis, shows that the standing of the Waldorf-Astoria as a New York sight is still secure.

The three key narratives of the Waldorf-Astoria discussed above show the different kinds of hotel experience surrounding this grand hotel and establish its role as platform for society and leader in New York's hospitality world. As mentioned before, some of the statements that I have made about the function of the Waldorf in and for New York, especially concerning the hotel as 'a city within the city,' are also true for other hotels, including the ones discussed later in this study. Yet, I agree with those observers who see this hotel as "the Mother, the Father, the Model of every modern hotel in the world" (James Wood qtd in Lent 39). The discourse surrounding the hotel, the recollections of people interacting with it, together with the impressive physicality of the building or, as James Donald calls it, its "thinginess" (8) make the Waldorf-Astoria the outstanding example of a grand hotel in New York.

The Waldorf-Astoria functions as an entry-point to my study of the diverse hotel experiences in New York and the institution's function as platforms for specific communities and their cultures. The Waldorf's reputation rests on its importance for New York society as a great public center. The next hotel has a very different reputation and feel to it. Here intimacy and a home-like feeling are of great importance, and instead of catering to a huge diversity of people from all walks of life, at the Algonquin we have a very specific kind of clientele and a specific impact on New York culture.

---

79 Another special attraction of the tour is visiting the hotel's own beehives which are part of a roof garden. The clue is that these can only be seen during the tour. The tour ends with a lunch at one of the hotel's restaurant, where classic Waldorf recipes are part of the menu, such as the Waldorf Salad and Eggs Benedict.

2. Hotel Algonquin – Birthplace and Home of New York Sophistication

> "The Algonquin Hotel, of which mention is made here and there in these pages, is not the whole of New York. There are other spots of interest and some distinction. The Algonquin is only the heart from which goes out warmth and light sufficient to make these other places possible for human habitation."
>
> FRANK CASE/ THE WAYWARD INN 263

The movie *Rich and Famous* (1981) by George Cukor, starring Candice Bergen and Jacqueline Bizet, is about two old friends who both pursue a career in writing. Their difference in style and success is expressed in their choice of accommodation. Merry Noel Blake, who develops into a bestseller writer of shallow fiction, resides in the Waldorf-Astoria, while Merry's friend, Liz Hamilton, described as a serious writer, lives at the Algonquin Hotel on 44th Street. This movie fittingly connects the first two hotels in this study. It presents their particular positions in New York and for New York culture. Both hotels function as symbols for the two authors' cultural standing: huge luxury hotel vs. distinguished boutique hotel; stage of the wealthy vs. New York's salon of the literati. The moviemakers are aware of the Algonquin's well-known reputation. Protagonist Liz tells a friend: "There's only room here for me, and the ghost of Dorothy Parker" (Cukor 1981).[1]

Like Parker and her colleagues of the Algonquin Circle, Liz does not only stay at the hotel, but lives and works here. She identifies herself with the place and its

---

1 This statement, interestingly, is not much further discussed in the movie. This leads to the assumption that viewers are aware of the hotel's literary history and that they are able to understand the implication. The hotel is the location of the famous Algonquin Round Table, the literary circle of New York journalist, writers and artists who are said to have brought sophistication to New York in the 1920s (see Mordden, *The Guest List*).

aura. The movie *Rich and Famous* brings two of the most well-known hotels of New York together, using both places as status-confirming institutions. It displays the importance of these establishments not only as temporary accommodations, but also as a necessary third place for writers, artists, journalists and others.

Like the Waldorf-Astoria, the Algonquin Hotel is part of New York's closely-knit hotel network. However, it is very different in atmosphere and clientele from the famous grand hotel and has an identity and position in New York that stands for itself. The Algonquin shows another important phase and facet of New York's hotel life. It became a platform for writers and artists who developed a unique urbane style in and thinking about literature and the theater. The Algonquin started to be successful at the moment when the attraction of the first Waldorf started to wane in the 1910s. The hotel had its heyday when the Vicious Circle, another nickname of the Algonquin Round Table, was *in situ* in the 1920s, and it experienced a revival starting in the 1950s. Today the Algonquin is still famous as *the* hotel for people serious about writing.

The hotel stands out not only because of its artistic clientele, but because of the special people/place relationship presented in the texts surrounding the theater hotel. The life accounts discussed here display a particular sense of place that is felt by the former owners, Frank Case and Ben and Mary Bodne, Case's daughter Margaret, the Bodne's grandson Michael, and some of its most loyal residents. Their identification with the place was so strong that they wrote about it in their autobiographies, memoirs, and letters. They have created rich material for an analysis of the close relationship between people and their surroundings, described as *place-identity* by Harold Proshansky and David Seamon. The texts show that these hotel people formed the hotel, while they themselves were influenced and inspired by it. With his writings Frank Case created a kind of early "branding" for the hotel as an artists' salon. He also made use of the channels of early advertising by providing newspapers and magazines with anecdotes of his hotel. By this he distinguished the Algonquin from the rest and attracted his preferred clientele. Case makes use of the modern day consumer culture as described by Baudrillard. Isabelle de Solier explains:

[b]ecause we are no longer afforded the comfort (or restriction) of being defined by tradition, ... the burden of creating identity and meaning in life has shifted onto the individual. ... most understanding of this process emphasize the seminal role played by commodities, suggesting that it's through consumption that we make ourselves today ... . We make our selections from the array of goods on offer and combine them to shape who we are or who we want to be: selves, then, are made through things. (de Solier 1)

The Algonquin functions as such an identity-shaping commodity. It transfers to its guests (and the managers and staff) a certain aura. By staying here, 'consuming' the 'commodity' hotel, the guests create their identity. At the same time through its artistic clientele the hotel's identity is made. In my discussion of the Algonquin Round Table this will become most apparent.

In addition, I argue that the particular use of the Algonquin's hotel space offers an interesting discussion of the multi-functionality and heterotopic character of hotels. The Algonquin is permanent home, work place, and third place. Overall, the text material of this chapter shows a more intimate, direct, and personal kind of hotel experience. Analyzing the Algonquin hotel experience, I will focus on people/place relationships. I will start with the makers of this hotel: famous 'mine host' Frank Case, and his successors, Ben and Mary Bodne. Examining the hotel experience of 'mine host' will, on the one hand, tell us more about the process of making a complex hotel space and the dynamics of atmosphere. It will help us understand how Case and the Bodnes managed to turn the Algonquin into the cultural center it became famous for in the 1920s. On the other hand, it also shows the spatial agency of the Algonquin and its influence on the hotel's insiders. I will discuss the classic figure of the 'hotel child,' which is represented here by Margaret Case Harriman and Michael Colby. They experience the multi-functional, transient space of the hotel as their childhood home. The 'hotel child' is a stereotype that has been discussed in relation with the hotel since the late nineteenth century and became somewhat of a staple in the hotel discourse. Following this, the focus will move to the perspective of long-term guest, a hotel resident, and his experience of the hotel as 'Home and Salon of the Artist.' By studying the memoirs of composer Alec Wilder, which cover his fifty years-stay at the hotel, I will discuss the importance that Wilder grants the hotel in his creative life and shaped his self-perception. I will end my examination of the Algonquin experience by having a closer look at the relationship between the hotel and its literary circle, the famous Algonquin Round Table. This group is the major reason for the hotel's continuing reputation. I will analyze how the Algonquin continues to play a role in the creation of culture through this group of literati.

While the Waldorf is the prime example of an American grand hotel, the Algonquin fulfills a different function for its regulars: it is a cross of a country inn and a literary salon in the heart of Manhattan, a more liberal successor of the English gentlemen's club.[2] It caused a strong community spirit among people of the arts, across national borders (most note-worthy British artists) and artistic fields, a good example for Keith Hetherington's concept of *social centrality*. Before

---

2 Norman T. Simpson, writer and founder of Select Registry, calls the Algonquin "the closest thing to a country inn I'd found yet in Fun City" (Simpson qtd. in Ehrlich). Ehrlich adds in his article that this "venerable American hotel" is "still run like an English club" (Ehrlich). The curious New York twist on the English club is that the hotel allowed single women travelers from the beginning.

discussing the four main aspects of Algonquin hotel experience, I will present the hotel's biography. This will help to geographically and culturally locate the hotel for the reader.

The Biography of the Hotel Algonquin

The Algonquin Hotel became a historical landmark in 1987. Part of the usual procedure is a survey by the commission containing the history, neighborhood, architecture, and individual importance of a site. Unlike the Waldorf, which has been widely covered by scholars and writers, there is not much material on the history of the Algonquin Hotel.[3] Thus, the commission's report functions as the foundation for my discussion of the hotel's history together with the books by Frank Case.

The Hotel Algonquin opened its doors on November 22, 1902 as a family and apartment hotel, focusing on long-term residents ("Algonquin Wit," Winter 1995).[4] The first manager and owner was Albert T. Foster. The building was designed by the well-known Chicagoan architect Goldwin Starrett, who was also involved in the building of the Union Station in Washington, D.C., and the Woolworth Building in New York (Geoschel 3). The Neo-Renaissance style of the building was inspired by the Beaux-Arts movement, executed in red brick and limestone, as can be seen in the photography below (Image 5). The ground plan followed a modified version of the 'dumbbell' arrangement with recessed courtyards on the east and west elevations ("Algonquin Wit," Winter 1995). The building is twelve stories high with a three-story annex later added on the west side of the building, which

---

3 Francisca Matteoli dedicated a chapter to the hotel in her book *Hotel Stories: Legendary Hideaways of the World* (2002, 6-11), where she writes "The Algonquin is everything a literary hotel should be. Snug, discreet, cozily retro, the perfect rendezvous for the crème de la crème of the literary and publishing worlds" (8). Ward Morehouse III, who also wrote about the Waldorf-Astoria, published a book titled *Life at the Top: Inside New York's Grand Hotels* (2005), with a chapter on the Algonquin. Kevin Fitzpatrick describes the Algonquin Hotel in his books *A Journey into Dorothy Parker's New York* (2005) and *The Algonquin Round Table New York: A Historical Guide* (2015). Additionally, there are magazine articles by Quentin Reynolds and Brendan Gill as well as newspaper articles on the hotel's opening and renovations and on the history of the Algonquin Round Table. Furthermore, the hotel's newsletter, "The Algonquin Wit" (published in the 1990s), is useful for the history of the hotel. However, the most quoted sources remain the two autobiographical books by Frank Case, *Tales of a Wayward Inn* (*TWI*, 1938), and *Do Not Disturb* (*DND*, 1940).

4 The first hotel brochure sets the date as October 15, 1902. Seemingly, there was a delay of more than a month as the newspapers record the opening date as November 22, 1902.

formerly held a stable. The appearance fit well into the row of the already established buildings of the New York Yacht Club (1899) and the Harvard Club (1894), complementing them and thus creating an ensemble worthwhile for landmark protection.

Image 5: The Hotel Algonquin on 44th Street

Hotel Algonquin. Private.

The neighborhood underwent large changes in the years between the 1870s and the start of the twentieth century. The block was originally home to a slaughterhouse and several stables, some of them used for the carriages of the Vanderbilts. By the late 1890s the block had transformed into a "decidedly smart neighborhood" (Case 47), due to the aforementioned clubs as well as New York's most famous restaurants of the time, the Sherry and the Delmonico. Around the same time, the theater district moved uptown to where it is now situated, around 42nd Street and

Sixth and Seventh Avenue. Thus, the hotel was right next to the new entertainment quarter of New York. This was the reason why the manager decided to open the hotel also for transients, as the location brought many short-term visitors to this part of town, making a semi-residential hotel more profitable than a full residential one. In his text, Case states that he was grateful that the hotel became a "regular" hotel: "Fortunately ... we were forced into making it a regular hotel, with the attendant excitement and fun of having crowds of people coming and going as they pleased and furnishing us with entertainment fresh every hour" (*TWI* 39).[5]

At the time of its opening, the *New York Daily Tribune* described the hotel in the following way: "The Algonquin presents in claim for public consideration an unexcelled location, a superb design, modern fireproof construction and a house and table equal to the demands of the most fastidious" (*NY Daily Tribune*). While the hotel was not extraordinary from its built-structure and size, it allowed for a certain amount of elegance and comfort for middle-class American travelers. The interior design was Edwardian in style, reminding its guests of a British country inn or a gentlemen's club. The lobby was tastefully furnished, yet in comparison with the lobby of the Waldorf-Astoria, it looked almost sparse. The Algonquin's appearance was markedly different from grand hotels of its time, yet well-fitted to its middle-class customer base.[6]

The name of the hotel was originally meant to be 'The Puritan,' which its future manager and owner Frank Case found "too strait-laced" (Goeschel 3).[7] Instead of following the "more prevalent European allusion of contemporary New York hotel nomenclature" (Goeschel 3), which favored Anglo-American historical figures and events, Case opted for the name of "Algonquin," after the Native American tribe that was said to have resided on this part of the land.[8] The choice of name can be seen as a signal to move toward a more open and liberal-minded establishment.

---

5   Case is aware of the chronotopic character of the place, the close time/place relationship as coined by Michael Bakhtin. He understands the opportunities that come to him through the transience of the place, enabling a constant exchange of people and their ideas.
6   For more information on middle-class hotels in America see Sandoval-Strausz 83f. The Hotel Theresa, described in chapter 4, is also a middle-class hotel.
7   Frank Case started to work as a clerk for the hotel during its construction, becoming its manager in 1907.
8   According to Case, he found the name of the Algonquin tribe while researching the history of the neighborhood in the New York Public Library and the nearby Iroquois Hotel borrowed the idea from his hotel. However, Anspach, the Bodnes' manager, states that the Iroquois already existed before the Algonquin opened its door, which would mean that Case himself adopted the idea from their neighboring hotel. Still, it is a fact that during its construction the Algonquin was called The Puritan, built by Foster and his Puritan Realty Company, and that Frank Case renamed it. Overall, this anecdote shows

During the first years the Algonquin did not show much of a profit, almost going bankrupt at one point and becoming a pawn in the divorce suit of the first owner.[9] Frank Case, already employed as a clerk, took over management in 1907. About the importance of this change the Landmark Commission writes: "The particular cultural character of the Algonquin was nurtured by its devoted and congenial proprietor, Frank Case" (Goeschel 2). By the 1910s, the hotel had acquired a substantial following of members of the world of theater and literature, such as Booth Tarkington, Douglas Fairbanks, John and Ethel Barrymore, and Sinclair Lewis. Essential for drawing in guests to the hotel, especially in a location close to the theater district, was the existence of a well-run restaurant.[10] The Rose Room, the hotel's dining room, was one of the most important features of the hotel: "According to tradition his [Frank Case's] kitchen and accommodating service were what first attracted the Round Table group to the hotel" (Goeschel 2). In the 1920s, the Algonquin Hotel gained international fame as *the* meeting place of the Algonquin Round Table for their regular lunch during the week.

Due to the joint hits of Prohibition and the Great Depression the hotel was in need of repair when Frank Case died in 1946. The hotel's legendary tradition continued under Ben Bodne, a former guest. Bodne, according to an interview given to Quentin Reynolds, had promised his wife on their honeymoon to buy the hotel (Reynolds 25). By 1946, South Carolinian Bodne had made a fortune in oil, thus being able to afford the hotel after it came on the market with Case's death. The new owner continued to favor guests from the literary and theater circles. The needed renovations were kept strictly in tone with the original appearance of the hotel's interior, replacing furnishing elements with replicas as closely resembling

---

Case's understanding for marketing. From the beginning, he worked toward a genial atmosphere in his hotel by naming the Algonquin in an untypical way and carefully constructing the reputation of this New York institution. About the importance of a hotel's good name Case wrote: "High on the list of assets of a hotel should be listed 'good name' and how jealously and zealously that name must be guarded, careful what you say or what you do lest it be misunderstood or some flippant meaning attached to it" (*DND* 174).

9   During difficult times, Foster had transferred the management rights to his wife. When they separated, he laid claim to the hotel's management, yet was stopped by his wife's lawsuit ("Fight for Hotel Algonquin" 1904).

10 While hotels were sometimes losing money on their rooms, they usually balanced their losses with the success of their restaurants and bars. In the early 1930s, Case needed to close the rooms of the hotel for two years and continued to run the bar and the restaurant to make ends meet. The Algonquin's Rose Room remained popular and helped the hotel survive the Great Depression.

the old ones as possible.[11] Bodne was supported in this by his son-in-law, Andrew Anspach, who was the manager of the hotel during Bodne's ownership. In the 1980s, the hotel's Oak Room was turned into an exclusive supper club and cabaret, for a second time since the late 1930s, starting the careers of many famous American performers such as Michael Feinstein and Diana Krall. Among Frank Case and the Bodnes the Algonquin was held in private hands for more than eighty years, a unique circumstance in Manhattan.

In 1987, the hotel was for the first time sold to a corporation, the Caesar Park Hotels International Inc., a subsidiary of the Aoki Corporation, a Japanese company ("Algonquin Wit," Winter 1995, 4). Since then the hotel changed hands several times. At the moment the hotel belongs to the Autograph Collection of the Marriott hotel group. This brand calls itself a "Curator of Independent and Extraordinary Hotels" (*Autograph Collection*).[12] The idea is to offer guests a unique hotel experience by keeping the tradition of the hotel intact, not stream-lining it to the corporate identity. According to the *Financial Times of London*, "The Algonquin is one of a fast diminishing breed of hotels – those that still boast personality" (qtd. in "Algonquin Wit," Winter 1995, 4). In a talk with one of the executive staff of the Algonquin it was confirmed that many patrons appreciate the hotel's individualistic style. Yet, there are also those surprised and dismayed that the Algonquin does not offer every standardized service of the Marriott group.

The Algonquin continues to be seen as an institution set apart from other New York hotels. It is understood as an "island of civility just of the hurly-burly of Times Square" which allows its guests to transcend "the confusion of the city" (Stone). Even after several face lifts, its artistic charm and unconventional living-room like lobby are still attracting the type of guests that Frank Case had in mind for the Algonquin. The new owners even continued for a time the hotel's tradition to grant writers a lower room rate, if they present the hotel with one of their books.[13] The Algonquin has been officially named a National Literary Landmark by the *Friends of Libraries USA* in 1996, the first one in New York.

---

11 Bodne was aware of the protective nature of long-term guests like Wilder for the hotel. Therefore, by staying close to the original style he prevented disagreements. Yet, even though the hotel is famous for its nostalgic charm, it was one of the first hotels in New York to have air conditioning in every room and the first one to replace regular keys with electronic key cards in the 1970s.

12 Two other well-known New York hotels, which are part of the Autograph Collection, are the Carleton Hotel, New York, and the Lexington Hotel, New York.

13 This continued until the 1990s. Books of well-known visitors of the Algonquin are, however, still displayed prominently in a book case in the lobby of the hotel.

2.1 THE HOTEL AS THE HOTELMAN'S TOOL

The connection between the Algonquin Hotel and Frank Case, manager and owner of the hotel during its first forty years, can hardly be overstated. Frank Case is largely responsible for the way the hotel was run. He made it a "brand" that attracted his favorite clientele, artists. For him, the hotel functioned as his work place. Yet, as 'mine host' he also lived there and used it as his social meeting place.[14] The mutual identification of Frank Case and the Algonquin is most complex. This hotel is a fitting case of Relph's observation that places are records and expressions of the cultural values and experiences of those who create and live in them (61). Case's hotel experience has been handed down to us in his two auto/biographical[15] accounts *Tales of a Wayward Inn* (1938) and *Do Not Disturb* (1940).[16] Both books are as much about the man as about the hotel. These two texts provide rich material for studying Case's place-identity and the identity of place of the Algonquin. They show a great involvement of Case in his hotel, a level of spatial experience which can only be described as existential insideness (Relph 54). Edna Ferber writes in a letter to Frank Case: Case was the Algonquin and the Algonquin was Frank Case (*TWI* 328).

In the following, I will examine these two accounts to discuss Case's special Algonquin hotel experience and the results of this unique symbiosis. The texts show how intimate the relationship between hotel and hotelman can be. I will present Case's philosophy behind the Algonquin. The Algonquin became his very own social laboratory. Frank Case made it the ideal meeting place for artists because he wanted to be surrounded by them. It also became a platform for literary circles like the Round Table, which Case helped to create and supported. While the texts depict the wide range of functions that a hotel can have, my main interest with his texts lies in the way he created and perceived this institution as the artist's third place. Frank Case embodied his institution. His position here made him an important

---

14 One of the best descriptions of the role and functions of a hotelier can be found in Sinclair Lewis, *Work of Art* (1931), starting with "Hotel-keeping ... Nothing you could do is more important – or interesting – meet all kinds of people, and see 'em with their shirts off, you might say" (70f). Lewis was a friend of Frank Case and might have gotten his inspiration for this text from his discussion with the Algonquin host. According to Case, Lewis even offered to buy a hotel with him and run it together.

15 I use this particular writing of auto/biographical here because the books are both autobiographies of Frank Case and biographies of the Algonquin Hotel.

16 Case also wrote an anecdotal cookbook *Feeding the Lions*, which offers some interesting insights into hotel life. For my discussion, however, I focus on his two life writing texts.

member of society.[17] Because of him, the Algonquin is not only a normal hotel, but a New York monument, a cultural center, and an exchange place for the arts. At the Algonquin, Frank Case is 'mine host' of culture and sophistication.

American hotel history is rich with rags-to-riches stories.[18] Frank Case has also been described as an example of this when he bought the hotel in 1927, finally owning the hotel after managing it for twenty years.[19] Case's reason for writing books about the Algonquin is to present his side of the story. Surrounded by artists, his life's dream was to become a published writer himself. Case's narrations do not follow any clear chronology and he deliberately uses breaks in the narration. He explains this style of writing with the hotel setting: "There is no continuity in the life of a hotel man, there is continuousness but no continuity" (*DND* 1).[20] His texts are caleidoscopes of Algonquin experiences, offering insights into the hotel's position in New York.

From his early training at the Hotel Taylor in Jersey City onward Frank Case had an individualistic and guest-oriented approach to hotel business. His employer taught him to provide "a happy home for a lot of lovely people" (*TWI* 15). Throughout his accounts it is clear that the hotel man has a deep interest in the arts. When asked why so many famous literary and theater people stopped at his place, Case answered that his love for these guests, more than anything else, draws people

---

17 Since hotels were considered to be an important asset of a town in nineteenth-century America, the manager of a hotel was an honored member of society. This was surprising for early European travelers because in Europe an innkeeper was often considered morally dubious. The American hotelkeeper instead was considered an important person, fulfilling the necessary role of taking care of guests, protecting the community by monitoring visitors and representing the town to foreigners as their first contact person (Sandoval-Strausz 11).

18 Case himself comments on his Alger-esque nature. He writes: "In 1927 there appeared in the New York papers a story telling how a former hotel employee had bought the hotel he worked in, paying a million dollars for it. A million dollars is always good for a story and the Horatio Alger inference, from Rags to Riches, still has its appeal" (*TWI* 189). The circumstance that he was able to buy his own hotel fits the pattern and Case indeed seems to take a certain pride in this. Many of Alger's story feature hotels as signs of achievement, e.g. the Astor House, where Ragged Dick meets his mentor.

19 See for example "Frank Case Buys Algonquin for $1,000,000; Hotel Long Home of Writers and Stage Folk," 1927.

20 One might conclude from this statement that the parameters of time are less important than those of space; the life of a hotelman appears more spatially concerned than time-wise.

to the hotel.[21] Case uses the hotel as his tool to provide his protégés with the basic foundations for the creative process (*TWI* 65). With mouth-to-mouth advertising, the Algonquin naturally turned into an artist's abode.

Case is aware that the greatest asset of his house is its reputation. As the Waldorf drew society out of their salons and residences, the Algonquin achieved to bring artists together, creating a community of creative people. This can be described as Case's mission: with the right kind of tutelage the hotel became a center of culture. In the Algonquin Hotel the spirit of the place is partly made up out of the modest, but elegant architecture and comfortable interior, as well as the human element, its distinguishing feature. Throughout the two books Case describes himself as a hotelkeeper of passion. Case's attitude appears to be that of a gentleman of leisure, who keeps the hotel as a pleasurable pastime. This hits the right notes for his clientele.[22]

Case places himself in the long line of hosts who fulfilled the ancient obligations of hospitality, which were deemed sacred. He invokes in his texts similar guidelines as Conrad Hilton does in *Be My Guest*, yet, he is more directly involved in running his hotel and more aware of the complex duties that the position 'mine host' brings with it. The Algonquin differs from Hilton's as it is smaller and more intimate, and operated on a more personal level.[23] For Case, it is the keeping of his hotel and not the expanding that fulfills him. Thus, Case remarks on the pleasure of being a hotelman: "One advantage in hotelkeeping not enjoyed by other commercial endeavors is that there are always first-class minds around the place" (*DWD* 254).

Case is convinced of the importance of his establishment for the city of New York even though he hides his pride behind ironical remarks. He perceives the city through the lens of the Algonquin. For him, the Algonquin is a kind of microcosm, one imbued with artistic spirit and personality. He elevates the Algonquin to an almost sacred place when he writes: "I leave the Algonquin and visit 21, El Morocco, the Stork and some of the larger hotels, returning to the Algonquin to be purified" (*DWD* 263). Usually we understand the term purifying in connection to

---

21 Case states in his book that a hotelman who has a heart for bricklayer might have the same attraction for them as he seems to have for artists.

22 Case's definition of what the profession hotelman means is encompassing all areas of classic innkeeping (*DWD* 58). He might have been inspired by the famous literary description of the tasks of a hotelkeeper in Sinclair Lewis's *Work of Art* (1931).

23 In *Do Not Disturb* this is also underlined by a comment from Leo Molony, manager of the Hotel New Yorker, who says of Case: "Oh, Frank doesn't really keep hotel, he just plays at it" (*TWI* 134). While Case admits this to certain degree, he adds: "But the spirit of hotelkeeping does not change. ... It is the same in a house of 2,000 rooms as it is in one of only 200" (134).

rites at churches, temples or shrines. The hotel is for the proprietor a spiritual place that, seemingly, cleans the visitor from the staining influences of New York life. Despite its singularity, the hotel remains a part of its surrounding city. It influences its culture and is influenced by it. Case writes that he and his hotel are a link in the larger network of New York hotels.[24] What sets the Algonquin apart is its special atmosphere which fosters the patronage of men and women of the arts. Frank Case makes the reader repeatedly aware of the close ties between the hotel world and the literary world, strengthening its "branding" power.[25]

For its regulars, who call themselves Algonquinites, the Algonquin is not just a stopping place, but it functions as a muse. According to Case, many writers, composers, and actors have directly profited from the spirit of the hotel: "I am pretty proud, as any one might well be, that the Muse, starting twenty-five or thirty years ago, has continued through the years and is still as alive and as young to-day in the Algonquin as she was then, for it is an everyday occurrence ... to have five or six or seven well-known writers in the house all at one time" (*TWI* 71f). Case lists many writers and their works, which have been written fully or partly at the hotel, such as Eugen Walter's *The Easiest Way*, Hendrik van Loon's *The Arts*, and Paul Armstrong's play *Alias Jimmy Valentine*.[26] Besides texts written in the hotel, Case also lists those written about the hotel or in which the hotel was prominently

---

24 He narrates meetings and conversations with hotelmen from the Waldorf, the Biltmore, and the Commodore. The New York hotel network is a very interesting aspect that presented itself to me during my studies. There is not much research on this underlying structure of the city that appears repeatedly in hotel histories. All five hotels in my studies are in some ways connected to each other by the people who work there, live there, or frequent them as third places.

25 Case knows that hotel life fascinates readers and provides good material for a story, which is still true. In the last years several autobiographies by members of the hotel world have been published, e.g. Jacob Tomsky's *Heads in Beds* (2013) and Anna K.'s *Total Bedient* (2012). The possibility for readers to have a look behind the hotel facade, into the hidden life of the hotel satisfies a certain voyeuristic urge. Case mentions the authors and titles of two of the most famous fictional books that belong to the genre of hotel literature: Arnold Bennett's *Imperial Palace* and Sinclair Lewis's *Work of Art*. He describes them as being almost 'shockingly' precise accounts of hotel life. About the literariness of hotels see also Roy Wood, "The image of the hotel in popular literature: a preliminary statement" (1990).

26 That writers like to write while staying at hotels or in their lobbies has often been commented upon. Writers perceive the atmosphere of hotels as liberating. It provides them with the kind of isolation that enables a continuous flow of writing. Additionally, the mix of people at hotels provides enough needed inspiration without becoming disturbing (Peters 78; see also Zeveloff on Maya Angelou).

mentioned, among them Joseph Hergesheimer's *Linda Condon*[27] and Gertrude Athertone's *Black Oxen* (*TWI* 205). Overall, Case calculates the success of his hotel in typewriters being at use in his hotel (*TWI* 72). He loves his writer guests and they love him. In contrast to other hotelkeepers of his time, he has a marked disregard for the social register, and allows a liberal air in his institution.[28]

The author's relationship with his guests is uncommonly close. While I use the terms guests and patrons in an interchangeable way, Case dedicates the matter of the right denomination extensive thought. He writes that in his eyes Noah Webster has not offered a fitting term

to describe or designate the person who eats, and/or sleeps at a hotel. 'Guest' carries the connotation of free entertainment, which is far from true – I hope. 'Patron' suggests the Arts and no one except Sinclair Lewis has thus honored hotelkeeping ... . 'Customer.' A trifle commercial. Besides making Georges, our headwaiter, a customer's man. 'Inmate.' Well, you can see why this wouldn't do. 'Habitué.' Stuffy. And dangerous if applied to second generation. 'Client.' Not descriptive although some hotels claim 'a smart clientèle.' ... Perhaps some kind reader has a thought and will send it in. (*DND* 317)

This quote shows how much Case thinks about his Algonquinites. Their loyalty is living testimony that he succeeds in creating a positive atmosphere for his clientele. Frank Case tells of a circle of friends who dined at the hotel's restaurant almost every day during the Great Depression. When the hotel is back in the black again they approach him, saying: "For the last couple of years, we have felt that you needed us and we could not very well go anywhere else for dinner, but now that your business appears to be all right again, we are serving notice on you that we

---

27 *Linda Condon* is not set in the Algonquin. Yet, Hergesheimer confirmed that he used Margaret Case Harriman as the role model for his hotel child Linda.

28 Frank Case repeatedly remarks that his own writing is inspired by the literary atmosphere of his hotel. He is very conscious of the process of writing a book. In contrast to his guests who come to the hotel to have the freedom to write, for a hotel man this freedom is, naturally, not granted: "Another interruption. It's the plumber. If this keeps on, it looks as if I might have to close the hotel in order to get the book finished. No hasty decisions, though. The hotel has been good to me and the book" (*TWI* 282). The paradoxical element here is, of course, that without the hotel, there would not be a book to write. The hotel proprietor does not only support art and artists in his hotel, but by writing a book on the Algonquin he himself becomes a part of its literary world. Case proudly announces that his son and daughter also entered the field of literature as journalists and critics. Case's books and those by his daughter have been positively reviewed in *The New York Times*.

feel free to go anywhere we please" (*DND* 287). Selecting this anecdote shows the reader how connected people felt to the Algonquin and its manager.[29]

It becomes clear that the right kind of 'atmosphere' is crucial for the commercial enterprise hotel, especially when it functions as a salon and home for artists. In his life accounts Case philosophizes at length on the meaning of the word 'atmosphere' and the importance of the concept for his hotel. Martina Löw's reading of atmosphere is most useful to analyze Case's ideas. According to Löw, atmosphere arises "through the perception of interactions between people and/or from the external effect of social goods in their arrangement" (Löw "Constitution of Space" 44). Frank Case is aware that some guests come to the hotel because the place transfers to them a certain glamor and imbues them with a certain mood and attitude which allows them to achieve things. He narrates the case of a young man who comes to the hotel for lunch, even though he cannot afford it. The young man tells Case that he wants to

try to catch this fever of confidence and assurance. I have an appointment at three and I was sunk in doubt this morning, so I decided to come in and absorb the atmosphere. ... I shall sit here until ten to three feeling strong and important. I hope the feeling will last when I get into this guy's office. (*DND* 197)

Similar to the writers who see in the hotel a muse for their inspirations, for this young man the hotel's atmosphere does something: it boosts his self-confidence. His hotel experience allows him to think of himself in a new way. Visitors and guests come to the Algonquin not only because it provides the essential services, but because this place offers something more. This experience is captured in the elusive term 'atmosphere.' Similar to Martina Löw, Case writes:

Atmosphere. Atmosphere. This place or that place has atmosphere. What does this word mean, atmosphere? What is atmosphere? Is it a quality possessed by a room, by inanimate walls and furniture and bestowed on animate creatures, men and women, or is it the other way round, an aura, a nimbus, an exhalation brought to the place day after day by the animate ones and left behind when they part, like the scent of lilacs in a room long after the lilacs are gone...? (*DND* 195f)

---

29 I am aware that many of Case's story have been written with a humorous undertone and cannot always be taken literally. Yet, the selection of examples that he presents in his texts are meant to present a quirky picture of the hotel. By themselves they tell us much about the place's atmosphere and the hotel experience that people make there. In addition, the letters of regulars found at the end of *Tales of a Wayward Inn* confirm Case's anecdotes.

He continues by asking the big question that continues to fluster scholars: "Does the place give its atmosphere to the people or do the regular visitors, the habitués, give atmosphere to the place?" (196). Case decides "in favor of the habitués," (196) yet he explains that this is "not one of those inflexible decisions, ... but a nice and comfortable decision ... , for all at once I think of those people who depend almost entirely upon their surroundings, their associates, to hold them erect and make them walk like a man" (196).[30] So, while he seems to be sure that the atmosphere of a place lies with and is created by people, he at the same time realizes that there is some kind of spatial agency.[31] This consideration also supports Case's statement that the hotel harbors the Muse and that people achieve surprising success with their artistic works because they have created them inside the walls of the Algonquin. Walls, according to the hotelman "that have heard many discussions and plans, walls that have listened at the birth of a new play, a new book, sometimes, alas, been present at the funeral and burial of same" (DND 197).[32]

Concluding, the proprietor is not able to solve the question of atmosphere for himself. For Case, as for Löw, atmosphere is created by the dynamic interplay of human and spatial agency. Case ends his discussion of the topic by writing: "So 'atmosphere' is composed of many things – ingredients, facts, and truths, half-truths or less, conceptions, misconceptions, wisdom and absurdity, but through it all, lively thinking" (198). By his own acts and decisions Case has created a special place with the Algonquin that has a spatial power for of its guests which is impossible to grasp, but still felt.[33] The Algonquin is imbued with a unique *genius*

---

30 This reminds one of Willa Cather's "Paul's Case."

31 He also mentions that in *Tales of A Wayward Inn*: "[A]ny story of the Algonquin would be incomplete without mention of people who add so much to the atmosphere and importance of the place." (289). Notice here he writes "adds" and not that they bring it all with them.

32 In the case of the Chelsea Hotel, the walls are also granted inspirational power (see chapter 3).

33 In his books Case claims that he is unable to answer the question why his hotel had such great success with artists. Andrew Anspach, the Bodnes' manager, has the following explanation: The Algonquin was not designed as a transient hotel but as an apartment hotel catering for residents only. Accordingly, it did not have the standardized functionality of a modern hotel with large service departments, a full kitchen, and several dining rooms. This information, that the "building wasn't built to be a hotel" (Anspach qtd. in Wilder 122) comes as a relief to many architects and designers because this helps explain why the lobby and also the other public parts of the hotel feel more like a private living-room and home. In addition, Anspach states: "The things we've been talking about – the physical and the human things above all – are sensed by those kindred spirits who respond to this kind of human environment" (126).

loci. Case's mission to make his hotel a cultural center and haven for creative people is successful.

Perhaps the greatest pleasure for Case was that his texts were received positively by his writer friends and were kindly remarked upon in book reviews.[34] As one reviewer wrote:

> The Algonquin occupies a special place in our life and times. Some people go there, of course, to see the folks who pass as celebrities, or to put on a bit of affectation, but most of the customers go there simply because they like it. It is a comfortable place, and much of its distinction comes from the simple fact that its keeper is neither bandit nor tycoon, but a gentleman. (Walker)

Some of the regulars even came together for the publication of the book to share this special moment with him, as, for example, Dorothy Parker and Marc Connelly. Others wrote letters to Frank Case about their appreciation of the Algonquin's qualities, which he proudly added to *Tales of a Wayward Inn*.[35] Probably the most famous guest remark about the Algonquin comes from H.L. Mencken, often considered to be the best known Algonquinite of his time: "You keep, by my specifications, the most comfortable hotel that I have ever found in America – and God knows I have seen a lot of them" (*TWI* 351).[36] To include remarks of the hotel's regulars at the end of the book functions as proof for some of Case's claims. Cleverly, the praise of the hotel comes from people who have experienced the hotel, not from Case himself. It gives credibility to the Algonquin's reputation as artists' hotel and does not smell of blatant advertisement (which it is to a certain degree).

The close host/hotel relationship did not only happen to Frank Case, but with the Algonquin, this special bonding between host and hotel occurred twice. After Case's death in 1946, Ben Bodne and his wife ran the hotel for 41 years, almost as

---

34 The book review of *Tales of A Wayward Inn* in the *New York Herald Tribune* stated that his style "is as light as a good souffle," and that "Case has finally proved that he can write better than most of his customers" (Walker).

35 The close relationship between hotels and artists is not surprising, as artists have felt comfortable at hotels for more than a century (Krebs 39). Yet, it is interesting that modernist writers, who often described hotel space as alienating and isolating, write so positively about this particular "unpretentious side-street hotel." J.P. McEvoy, writer and famous comic strip creator, goes so far as to state: "I would rather live in the waste basket on the back stairs of the old Algonquin than lead a life of hollow splendor in a tower suite of a great caravanserai in whose lobbies and endless corridors thousands daily perish in frightful agony trying vainly to find the washroom" (*TWI* 346).

36 This quote is given in several of the Algonquin publications and advertising materials and is also mentioned in Morehouse's *Life on the Top* and Matteoli's *Hotel Stories*.

long as its first owner did. Most New Yorkers expected that the Algonquin would die with its late owner. Instead, however, it was saved and returned to former glory by the Charlestonian oilman, who bought the hotel in 1946 for $1,000,000 dollars.

The Bodne family came from a very different background than the urbane Frank Case. The Bodnes belonged to Russian Jewish families that had emigrated to the American South around the turn of the century. They were neither hotel trained nor familiar with New York and its social scene. Yet, as they had fallen in love with the Algonquin during their honeymoon, they wanted to save the old 'theater hotel' and preserve it as a haven for actors and writers. They, too, liked having contact with the creative Algonquin crowd. Ben Bodne did not write about his experience at the Algonquin, yet, he was interviewed by Quentin Reynolds for an *Esquire* article, by Alec Wilder for his memoirs and is quoted in the texts of his grandson Michael Colby. From these accounts and from reactions of guests we know that under Ben Bodne's management the character of the Algonquin did not change much, it remained the favorite watering hole for artists from all walks of life.[37] On this continuity of identity of place Edward Relph writes: "just as the individuality and distinctiveness of the appearance of any one person endures from childhood to old age, so the identity of a particular place can persist through many external changes" (31).

The host perspective is not the only significant one when it comes to the Hotel Algonquin. The Algonquin was also an important place for the hotel children Margaret Case Harriman and Michael Colby who both grew up at the hotel and committed their experiences at the hotel and with the hotel to paper. In the following I will discuss the special experience of the Algonquin 'hotel children,' and examine their relation with the hotel and their reaction to it.

2.2 THE HOTEL AS CHILDHOOD HOME

As mentioned above, hotel children have become a staple in the hotel discourse, a special group of residents that concerned both social critics and writers. In the late nineteenth and the first half of the twentieth century, scholars from different fields wrote repeatedly about the 'hotel child.' It was seen as a result of changing American living habits. Due to housing shortage and rising costs for domestic staff, more and more city dwellers made their homes in hotels instead of keeping a private household. In his book *Hotel Life* (1936) sociologist Norman S. Hayner dedicates a whole chapter to hotel children.[38] He writes at length on the negative

---

37 I will discuss the Bodnes' hotel experience when I examine the life accounts of their grandson, Michael Colby, and long-term guest Alec Wilder.
38 The book is one of the earliest comprehensive social studies on hotels in America.

consequences that a childhood at a hotel has for the child. Those children were said to become precocious, unrestrained, and spoiled or neglected.[39] Allegedly, they ran wild in the hotel, where the staff needed to take care of them, since most of the time the mothers would abandon them in pursuit of their own pleasures. This is a simplification and overgeneralization of family hotel life. Still, a special childhood environment like a hotel does influence the child to a great degree (Proshansky 62).

There are several autobiographies and memoirs written by hotel children, e.g. *Hotel Kid* (2002) by Stephen Lewis and *The Ender's Hotel* (2008) by Brandon R. Schrand. They try to come to terms with their uncommon childhood surroundings as the unique growing-up environment of the hotel distinguished them from their peers. These texts show that hotel children are more aware of their surrounding and often more comfortable with adults than with children. Yet, in almost none of these accounts has the experience been described as especially problematic for their development.[40] There are also several fictional texts in which hotel children play a certain role, for example, in Kay Thompson's *Eloise*, Edith Wharton's *The Custom of the Country*, Joseph Hergesheimer's *Linda Condon* and the short story "The Hotel Child" by F. Scott Fitzgerald. There is, however, a marked difference between those depictions and the life writing texts. In most of the literary examples the hotel children are the children of hotel guests and often described as being neglected. In contrast, most of the memoirs and autobiographies are written by the children of the owner or staff members, where the experience is described as positive and enriching. While these hotel children can be as spoiled as the children of hotel guests, they do not perceive themselves as guests in their parents' hotel, but they get to know the behind-the-scenes life of the respective establishment, the economic factors contributing to a hotel's success and the hardships connected to running one. They are more rooted and better behaved. The accounts by former hotel children show the hotel from a unique perspective. In contrast to adults in a hotel, they are able to ignore the unwritten hotel code and transgress existing boundaries (physical and symbolic ones) in the hotel. At the same time, they lack the power that adult actors have and are more influenced and positioned by the surrounding space.

---

39 See Wayne Koestenbaum: "Hotel children are virtually orphans; spawned and raised by the hotel, they qualify as furniture. A hotel child opens a new chapter in the history of immaturity" (34). Betsy Klimasmith also discusses the issue of hotel children critically in her study *At Home in the City: Urban Domesticity in American Literature and Culture, 1850-1930* (see 170f).

40 Even Henry James, despite his ambiguities concerning the institution hotel, preferred being a hotel child to being "'any small person more privately bred'" (James qtd. in Koestenbaum 34).

Growing up in a hotel that functions as a center for the arts like the Algonquin, produces a special type of hotel children. About the normalcy of having children at his hotel Frank Case wrote: "I can't remember all the children who lived in my house, and when I say 'lived' I don't mean that they dropped in for a day or a week but that they lived there" (*DND* 233). He refers to the children of his long-term guests like the Fairbanks family, whose son, Douglas Fairbanks jr., played with Case's daughter and grew up next to her at the hotel. His daughter, Margaret Case Harriman collected her experience as hotel child at the Algonquin in her autobiography *Blessed Are the Debonair* (*Blessed*, 1956), which I will analyze in the following. In addition, I will also discuss the blog "The Algonquin Kid" (2013/14), written by Bodne's grandson Michael Colby.

Margaret Case Harriman – The Innkeeper's Daughter

Margaret Case Harriman's book focus on her close relationship with her father. It is almost an apotheosis of Case. Due to Frank Case's extremely close identification with his hotel, the book is, therefore, "mainly about the Algonquin" (*Blessed* 203). Frank Case started working at the Algonquin in 1902, four years before Margaret's birth. Accordingly, the hotel was her childhood home. This distinguished Margaret from other children, as "every survivor of New York's Nineteen Twenties should know, Margaret Case Harriman is the only person to have been born in the famed Hotel Algonquin" ("Casing the Algonquin").[41] Nostalgia for the good old times is very apparent in the text. Margaret presents her father and the hotel in a positive light. Still, despite her subjectivity, the text provides valuable insights into the Algonquin hotel experience.

The first part of the book deals with Margaret's growing-up at the 'theater hotel.' Case Harriman makes clear that she "was not only a hotel child, but a motherless hotel child" (*Blessed* 16). Her mother died in childbed at the birth of her brother Carroll when Margaret was still very young. She tells the reader that "I suppose no two children ever had a nursery so crowded with beautiful actresses tucking them in bed as my brother Carroll and I did" (*Blessed* 24). As the size of the Algonquin is comparatively small, with about 250 beds, the relationship between guests and the hotel manager's family is quite close. Additionally, Frank Case was actively pursuing friendly relations with his artistic clientele and so these guests became surrogate family members to the two children. This situation remains the same even after Frank Case marries Bertha Walden, nicknamed "Hebe" from Case's memoirs and Margaret's friendly stepmother.

Hotel children often perceive the staff as additional family members. About the close connection between the Algonquin staff and herself the author writes: "All of

---

[41] This is not absolutely true as her brother Carroll was also born at the hotel.

the employees seemed just like a part of my own family" (*Blessed* 46). They educate her, they show her how to roller skate, bring her to school if need be and teach her about their own culture. Georges, the legendary Greek headwaiter of the Algonquin, tells her everything important about ancient Greek myths and legends (46). As most of the staff remained with the hotel for many years, the author reports for a visit in 1956: "so many of the old crew are still at the Algonk that my every entrance there nowadays is something of a social occasion" (46). A hotel is said to be the American equivalent of a European palace. Margaret is indeed treated like a princess by the employees. Closest to her family were the African-American pastry chef Sarah Victor, who is also mentioned in Case's texts and Germaine, the French maid to Bertha and Frank Case. Margaret calls them "[t]he retainers in our immediate family" (47). While the hotel hierarchy remains in place at the Algonquin, the author views her relationship with the employees as familiar and important for her development. It has a shaping influences on her life.

Despite the positive elements of hotel life, Margaret Case Harriman does perceive the differences between a hotel and a private home in the recounting of her childhood. At the Algonquin she has a large menu to choose from every day, yet she misses out on the experience of having something cooked just for her. She writes that her favorite treat as a child was the malted milk prepared for her by a long-term guest in the guest's hotel room: "And that is strange, because, as the innkeeper's daughter, I could order practically anything I wanted from the hotel menu. Every day, I could have any kind of five soups, any kind of meat ... , and all the ice cream and cake I could hold." Yet, with the malted milk "it was the first time I had ever seen anyone cook something especially for me" (Blessed 16). Even though Case Harriman writes in the most positive terms of the Algonquin throughout the book, the question remains in how far the hotel is a rival to her father's affection and takes his time away from his children. In texts of hotel kids, this is often a critical issue.[42] Her status as a half-orphan combined with her father's job caused loneliness. Nevertheless, writing from her mature point of view as a mother and grandmother of two, Margaret Case Harriman hotel experience remains mainly positive in *Blessed are the Debonair*. The Algonquin is more to her than a hotel, more than a meeting place in Mid-Manhattan and more than a childhood home.

Throughout the book Margaret Case Harriman stresses that being raised at the Algonquin was an advantage and set her apart from the rest. The impressive reputation of the hotel is established by the author in the short "Prologue" that she inserts before the main narration. In the prologue Margaret writes of meeting a foreigner during a journey through Spain who, learning of her background,

---

42 See for example *The Hotel Kid* and *The Enders Hotel*, as well as Tania Grossinger's autobiography *Growing up at Grossinger's*.

exclaims: "Frank Case of the Algonquin! I say! Was he really your father? ... Everybody knows about Frank Case of the Algonquin. I say!" Case Harriman comments on this: "Well, there it was again. It happens all the time, in one way or another ... 'But of course I know all about Frank Case of the Algonquin!'" (*Blessed* 10). Throughout her life she is defined by her childhood home and recognized by her father's friends and former guests.[43] This influence of the hotel reaches far beyond the city limits of New York. The Algonquin continues to shape her self-perception and personality during her adult life.[44]

The atmosphere of the hotel influences Margaret's self-perception to a large degree: "I moved in a kind of benign haze, sparked only by the fact that I was continually surrounded by bright people. Away from the Algonk – on a farm, or in a Midwestern town – I might have been considered plain stoopid [sic]" (*Blessed* 132). While there is a certain amount of irony in this passage, it still shows that Case Harriman is very aware that her surrounding made her the person she is. The constant contact with people from around the world, the temporality of these encounters, and the great mixture of characters shape her person and her ideas. While she might be overemphasizing the case for the sake of the book, it is still remarkable. Her description fits other hotel children's experiences concerning the lasting influence of the hotel's special environment.[45]

Growing-up in the Algonquin, Margaret writes that she did not consider famous guests as special anymore but just took their existence there for granted: "As the innkeeper's daughter I grew up among famous people so gradually that I came to take them with a great, and perhaps regrettable, calm" (*Vicious Circle* 22f). As a child Case Harriman was playing with the children of the Barrymore and Fairbanks families, two of the foremost actor families of the first half of the twentieth century in America. As an adult she gets to know important editors and writers such as Frank Crowninshield of *Vanity Fair* and Joseph Hergesheimer, whom Margaret Case Harriman describes as her best friend. Influenced by the literary crowd of the hotel, Case's daughter becomes a writer, working mostly for magazines like *Vanity Fair*, *The New Yorker*, and the *Saturday Evening Post*. The space surrounding the hotel and its neighboring publishing houses is perceived by the innkeeper's

---

43 "[I]t is a fact that you could not visit any city in the United States or Europe without running into friends of Father's" (*Blessed* 87).
44 It should be noted that hotel children remain hotel children even when they have become adults. It is not a term that refers to a certain age. The reason is that their growing-up experience continues to influence them for the rest of their lives.
45 Another lasting influence in Margaret Case Harriman's life is her relationship to the two magazines, *Vanity Fair* and *The New Yorker*, where she started her career. *The New Yorker* has been actually conceived at the Round Table in the Rose Room of the hotel, making it, metaphorically, a kind of sibling of Margaret.

daughter as perfectly sufficient for her needs: "For a couple of years after returning from France I lived a full life while scarcely ever leaving one city block – Forty-fourth Street, between Fifth and Sixth Avenues. My home was at the Algonquin (59 West 44 Street) and I worked at *Vanity Fair*, which was then at 19 West 44 Street" (*Blessed* 117). While her life is not as closely connected to the Algonquin as her father's (she writes that he hardly ever leaves the hotel during the week), she nevertheless feels content to remain inside the immediate block that the hotel occupies, a microcosm which provides for all her needs. After moving into a small apartment with her son, writing for the two magazines meant for her to be still able to visit the Algonquin regularly. Her identity is rooted to this particular spot on 44th Street. She writes: "Although we [Margaret and her son] had our own home, our headquarters pretty much remained with Father and Bud – at Sag Harbor in the summer and the Algonquin in winter" (224). The term headquarter conveys that the Algonquin is the spatial node of Margaret's existence.

Margaret Case Harriman's awareness of her relationship with the Algonquin might not have been as obvious to her had it not been tested in her adult life and threatened by outside influences. This challenging event was the marriage to her first husband: "My own safe world of actors and writers, of the Algonquin and *Vanity Fair*, rocked slightly when, in the nineteen-twenties, I became engaged to marry Morgan Morgan, a stockbroker who, with his parents, tended to stiffen up in the presence of the lively arts. ... 'No actress is decent,' he [Morgan] proclaimed, 'and all writers are bums'" (*Blessed* 169).[46] This implied criticism of her home makes her aware that there are others in New York who do not accept the kind of life led in the Hotel Algonquin. Her fiancé refuses to get married at the hotel, saying: "'It's just that the Algonquin is a theatrical hotel,' he explained, 'and you know how the family feels about that. Not that your father isn't a gentleman, of course ... . But, well ... it isn't as though he were the manager of the Ritz!'" (*Blessed* 169).[47] This passage is the only moment in the book where Margaret allows the reader to see the hotel from the perspective of a critical outsider. It also

---

46 This question of morals in a hotel that caters to theater people was repeatedly a problem in the early part of the twentieth century. Artists and actors belonged to a sizable minority of people who preferred hotel living, not only because of their necessary mobility, but also because many regular landlords refused them. Even some hotels refused to cater to actors and artists, which made the Algonquin and also the Chelsea Hotel important stopping places for them (Groth 60).

47 Getting married at a hotel is one of the rites of passage that is a typical part of a hotel's everyday routine. For Margaret, the Algonquin would not just be the venue of her wedding but it is her childhood home. This would have heightened the experience. Margaret knows that it is important for her father "to have me married from the Algonquin he was so proud of" (170) and that it pains him not being able to do so.

shows the position of the Algonquin in relation to other hotels in New York in the eyes of the city's more conservative inhabitants. The Morgan family would accept the connection to a high-class address like the Ritz Hotel, yet not to a hotel of a more flamboyant reputation. Seen through the eyes of the Morgans the Algonquin is an unconventional hotel, different from grand hotels like the Ritz and the Waldorf-Astoria. It is known as a place for writers and actors and for its liberal influence on New York society. Case Harriman's reaction to her future husband's remark tells the reader not only about the connections between New York hotels but also about her own evaluation of her father's position and the status of the Algonquin:

'Listen,' I said. 'My father is no manager of any hotel, he owns his own hotel. It is a famous hotel, where illiterates like you are not tolerated. And furthermore, for your information,' I intoned, 'when my father walks into the Ritz, the manager of the Ritz KNEELS!' I am sure that Mr. Albert Keller, who was then manager of the Ritz and a good friend of Father's, would have forgiven this exaggeration if he had heard it. (*Blessed* 170)

In the end, the difficult beginning already foreshadows that the marriage between Harriman Case and Morgan is doomed. They get divorced four years later. The hotel child Margaret, now an adult, continues to feel a very close connection to the place. It is a security net in her life, especially at times when she moves through emotional crisis.

Being a hotel frequented by actors and writers, the Algonquin had a more tolerant policy towards minority groups otherwise excluded from midtown hotels. Case Harriman writes that it was important to her father (as well as to herself) to make the hotel an open place for all members of the arts, including African-American performers. Earlier than many other Manhattan hotels, the Algonquin catered to African-American artists, for example, the classical singer Marian Anderson. In the time of segregation this was still a difficult issue (*Blessed* 39). Anderson was a regular at the hotel, yet she never visited the dining room of the hotel despite being specifically invited by Case. Anderson was very aware that some of the guests present in the dining room might take issue with having an African-American woman dining next to them while segregation was a still widely accepted practice.[48] Frank Case could make his own rules for his hotel, but he could not change society. Yet, he set an example. Thus, the Algonquin was perceived as a safe haven for all kinds of artists. For Margaret Case Harriman it is important to

---

48 Marian Anderson later became a leading force in the Civil Rights Movement and received high honors for her efforts in the fight for African-American equality. The Algonquin is still favored by African-American guests. For example, it counted Maya Angelou among its regular guests.

highlight this part of her father's legacy. This open-mindedness toward all people is also a consequence of being an Algonquin hotel child.

Case Harriman does not only focus on the atmosphere and reputation of the hotel. She understands that the physical hotel space also plays a role in the experience of the hotel. In her description of the Algonquin Margaret Case Harriman's focuses especially on the lobby. She writes about the one dominating feature of the living-room-like lounge, the grandfather's clock, and describes its impact on the hotel's creative crowd: "Playwrights, hating to go back to work after lunch at the Algonquin Round Table, have been stirred to action by its warning bong" (*Blessed* 14). The other remarkable contraption in the lobby is the elevator, which she sees as a microcosmic place inside the Algonquin, representing the spirit of the hotel in condensed form:

Its one passenger elevator generally had four or five people waiting for it, and they were often such a mixed bag as H. L. Mencken, Fannie Brice, Marilyn Miller and Commander Evangeline Booth from the Salvation Army. Waiting for the Algonquin elevator was a special occupation, like skin-diving or being tattooed; you had to have been through it before you could develop any aptitude, indulgence, or affection for it. But its veterans carried a kind of accolade. (*Blessed* 41f)

In hotel literature, elevators are often used as special places inside the hotel where dramatic changes occur in the plot or where surprise meetings take place.[49] Case Harriman describes the action of waiting for the elevator as a moment of initiation into the Algonquin's hotel experience. With this machine she is able to introduce the impressions of other regulars of the hotel. Case Harriman recalls an interview with H.L. Mencken in the Algonquin's lobby where the interviewer asked him where he got all the good ideas from for his book. Mencken answers:

You forget that I belong to the company of deep thinkers who daily congregate and wait for the Algonquin elevator. The Algonquin elevator is the muezzin of Forty-fourth Street. Like the Mohammedan, it climbs to its tower and makes strange noises and we below can only wait and pray. When it comes down again we go about our business as usual. There is ... plenty of time for contemplations in between. (*Blessed* 42)

The statement could be understood as a criticism of the place's lack of innovation. However, Mencken points at something else: The Algonquin Hotel allows its guests to get into contact with each other and to actually think 'deep thoughts.' It is an essential third place that many creative people need for their inspiration. The result,

---

49 See Matthias 59f for the function of elevators in hotel literature. A hotel novel in which the elevator plays a decisive role is *Hotel* (1965) by Arthur Hailey.

according to Mencken, is that the elevator reminds them that they have returned to their favorite place, a surrogate home and place of artistic exchange.

The hotel is for Margaret Case Harriman an amalgamation of impressions, meanings, memories, chances, and opportunities. Being a public and a private space at the same time, sheltering strangers and acquaintances, and providing work to her family and friends, the Algonquin is the all-encompassing place in her life. The book's review in the *New York Times* states: "[Case Harriman's book] is a love letter to the past, sparkling, good-humoredly shrewd, candid and evocative of the spirit of a time" ("Casing the Algonquin"). For this hotel child the hotel is like a surrogate family member. She grants it an agency that influenced and guided her in her life. It was the Algonquin's experience that inspired her to become a writer and made New York sophistication a part of her identity.[50]

Michael Colby – The Algonquin Kid

For many years, Margaret Case Harriman was the only hotel child of the Algonquin to narrate her hotel experience. In 2013 Michael Colby, the grandson of Ben and Mary Bodne, added his own account of the theater hotel with the blog "The Algonquin Kid", published on *Theaterpizzazz.com*. With it he fills a gap in the Algonquin's history, as until then the only published text existing on the reign of the Bodnes was Quentin Reynolds's "The Hotel That Refused to Die" (1950) for the *Esquire* magazine. Michael Eluhi Colby, a librettist for musicals, partly grew up at the hotel and later made it his home for almost twenty years. Colby's 'hotel child' experience has some similarities to Case Harriman's, yet, there are also marked differences. Although he regularly visited his grandparents' hotel, Colby did not live there on a regular basis during his childhood. Furthermore, it was his grandparents' hotel and not his parents', though his father worked there as a manager for some time. Still, Colby perceived the hotel as an important and lasting influence on his life. It caused him to write about his experience decades after his family sold the hotel to a Japanese corporation.

In his blog, Colby writes that at the Algonquin he grew up on a heady diet of seeing and meeting famous people. Due to his grandparents' ownership of the hotel, he experienced an upbringing very different from his schoolmates. He describes himself as "as a real-life counterpart to Eloise of the Plaza" (Colby Part 1), with all the connotations of a privileged and to a certain degree spoiled childhood. Similar to Case Harriman, for Colby the special atmosphere at the hotel was to a large

---

50 In Hayner's article "Hotel Life and Personality," he argues that hotel life causes the character trait of urbanity and sophistication. He might have had a hotel like the Algonquin in mind while writing this. In his book *The Guest List,* Mordden grants the Algonquin the honor of being the birth place of New York sophistication.

degree a result of one person, his grandmother Mary, who "was someone who made New York feel like home to notables from far and near," despite being at the same time "meddling, bossy, illogical" (Colby Part 6). He calls her "truly the matriarch of the Algonquin ... with a hospitality that transcended just Southern comfort" (Colby Part 6). This information is interesting because during Case's reign, people wrote of his patriarchal influence, describing the hotel as a kind of gentlemen's club. With Mary Bodne a feminine touch enters the Algonquin.[51]

The Bodnes' hospitality, Colby stresses, was open to everyone. Most importantly, his grandparents provided artists a home who were blacklisted under McCarthyism: "As NY theatre continued to employ talents who'd been blackballed elsewhere, my Grandparents made sure blacklist victims were welcome at the Algonquin" (Colby Part 3). They also continued the tradition of making their hotel a welcoming place for African-Americans at a time when segregation still barred many of them from the more sophisticated hotels of Manhattan: "Through the years, their guest list boasted Maya Angelou, Roy Wilkins (head of the N.A.A.C.P.), and jazz greats like Ella Fitzgerald and Oscar Peterson" (Colby Part 3). Colby writes that this was the case even though his grandmother still employed African-American women as kitchen helpers and nannies, a residue from her Southern heritage. Colby therefore grew up in a somewhat topsy-turvy world that he nevertheless saw as a positive element in his life.

Michael Colby felt very close to his grandparents and narrates their history at the hotel in the first issues of the blog. Similar to Case Harriman, his text is as much about his family's relationship with the Algonquin as about his own life. He frequently returns to the achievements of his grandparents and makes clear that under their lead the hotel was still the cultural center of Midtown New York. While Colby's grandmother played hostess, Ben Bodne, his grandfather, "was busy establishing his own version of the Algonquin Roundtable" (Colby Part 4).[52] While this Round Table did not last long, Ben Bodne still became known as "White Knight of the Algonquin Round Table" (Senator Hollings qtd. in Colby Part 4). This shows the continuous interest in the famous tradition of the hotel and the will to keep this tradition alive.[53] It also made sense financially, as it was good advertising material.

---

51 It should be noted that strong matriarchal figures are typical in Jewish families. Mary Bodne belongs to a long line of strong Jewish women leading hotels, manifesting the myth of the nurturing Jewish mother.

52 With notable persons of his time such as David Susskind, Joe DiMaggio, Louis Nizer, Leon Uris, John Hersey, record producer Norman Granz, and an occasional Marx Brother.

53 French film star Simone Signoret states in her biography *Nostalgia Isn't What It Used To Be*: "A few snobbish Americans had laughed at us when we had announced before

Colby writes that Mary Bodne wanted him to train in the hotel business, to take over one day from them. Instead, however, the atmosphere at the Algonquin was the starting point for his interest in the world of theater: "Was it the Algonquin Hotel that sparked my interest in theatre? Not necessarily. It may have been nature as much as nurture" (Colby Part 4). Growing up at the Algonquin had its advantages as well as disadvantages. His grandmother was constantly warning him against theater work and used the example of unsuccessful hotel guests for her argumentation. At the hotel one could see people on the rise of their careers as well as on their way down, e.g. in the case of playwright Brendan Behan.

One of the most interesting passages of Colby's text concerning his life as a 'hotel child' at the Algonquin is the meeting he describes of the two Algonquin Kids, Margaret Case Harriman and himself. He writes:

> One afternoon, [my grandmother] pointed out another Algonquin notable in the corner of the room, an elegant woman whose expression will always haunt me. It was Margaret Case Harriman, who'd written books about the hotel, which her father Frank Case once owned. She looked lost in reverie, gazing at the room, her face both beaming and somewhat sad. Today, as another person who once lived at the Algonquin but who's now just a visitor, I can almost imagine the kaleidoscope of feelings she experienced. (Colby Part 4)

It is interesting that Colby recalls the meeting with Case Harriman and decides to mention it in his memoir blog. For both, the hotel was home and part of their family heritage. While Colby was at the beginning of his 'hotel child' life at the Algonquin, Case Harriman was already an outsider in her former home. Yi-Fu Tuan writes on this phenomenon: "Yet it is possible to be fully aware of our attachment to place only when we have left it and can *see* it as a whole from a distance" (Tuan, "Space and Place" 411). This adds a nostalgic quality to Colby's texts. Although I believe that one can also have a conscious awareness of one's attachment to a place

> leaving Paris that we were going to stay at the Algonquin in New York. The Algonquin! That was the place to go twenty or thirty years ago ... . [W]e'd let them talk, and instead of going to one of those big palaces they suggested, we followed the advice of Uncle Norman; out-of-date provincials that we were, we were going to stay at the Algonquin. The Algonquin is like La Colombe. It belongs to a family, the Bodnes. If we had lived at the Waldorf-Astoria, I doubt very much whether we would ever have met Mr. Waldorf or Miss Astoria. At the Algonquin, the Bodne family awaited us in the lobby" (qtd. in Colby Part 6). Signoret's statement shows several interesting elements of the Algonquin. While the hotel is not as chic as the Waldorf-Astoria, it attracts members of the stage and the arts. The hotel continued to have a strong attraction for European travelers. It reminded them of their own well-established hospitality institutions with a particular kind of New York sophistication added.

before separation, it certainly strengthens the feeling.[54] Considering the findings of Proshansky as well as Relph, this episode is a good example of place-identity. Case Harriman and Colby are united by their relationship with the hotel. While Colby is still an existential insider of the Algonquin at the time of his narration, Case Harriman already moved to a stage once removed. Sitting in the spot that she has occupied during dinners with her father, she is removed from the insider level and remains in an in-between place, "lost in reverie." While it is debatable if Case Harriman actually experienced it in such a way, it seems clear that at least Michael Colby perceives this peculiar in-betweenness at the Algonquin today.

As mentioned before, the hotel is not the regular home of Michael Colby. His time at the Algonquin was mostly limited to weekend visits, during which he was allowed to stay over. The Colby family resided in Hewlett, Long Island, a mostly Jewish community. Colby tells the reader that because of the matrimonial tensions between his parents, the Algonquin became for him a place of refuge. Not unlike many of the artist regulars of the establishment the hotel allowed him to escape his own reality for a moment: a drunken father and an unhappy mother, who were continuously quarreling. At the Algonquin Colby meets the people who later become his mentors. With the support of his grandmother, who decides to accept and even encourage his decision of becoming a librettist, he makes the necessary connections to get started. When he returns after his college graduation, he settles at the Algonquin for the next twenty years, until his family sells the hotel. With his home at the Algonquin he is in the center of the theater district and in the middle of New York's Broadway network. The Algonquin becomes his home, his work place, and most importantly the third place where he exchanges ideas with like-minded people.

Considering the discourse on hotel children, Michael Colby made the best out of his experience in and his connection with the Algonquin, using it as steppingstone as well as spiritual home. Colby is not as deeply connected to the hotel as Margaret Case Harriman was. Yet, he clearly sees himself as an 'Algonquin Hotel Kid,' a native to the place, somebody who is aware of the reciprocal influence which the theater hotel can have on one's identity.

---

54 All accounts of hotel children mentioned above have been written years after they moved out of their hotels. Different from 'normal' homes a hotel can never remain the same and it is always shared by many others. A hotel is a commercial institution that changes ownership and often its character with it. Although the Algonquin Hotel belongs to a small number of hotels which remained in the same hands for many years, both Colby and Case Harriman experienced disorientation when their ownership changed.

2.3 THE HOTEL AS HOME AND SALON OF THE ARTIST

The hotel experiences of Algonquin hosts and hotel children provide the insider-view of this particular institution and tell us about the hotel's ties to the cultural world of New York. These life texts have been written by people who made the Algonquin and were shaped by it. They had the spatial power of ownership and/or a superior knowledge of the surroundings, especially of the inner workings and the behind-the-scene situations. The third type of hotel experience differs from the texts above, as here the writer, Alec Wilder, is in the position of a long-term hotel guest. I will examine his unpublished memoirs, "The Elegant Refuge" (1976),[55] to present how the Algonquin Hotel was perceived as the artist's home and at the same time his salon and place of creative exchange. The accomplished composer and music scholar Alec Wilder lived from 1907 until 1980 (Demsey 919). He stayed at the Algonquin for most of his life, more than fifty years. Similar to Case Harriman and Colby, Wilder describes his relationship with the hotel as being essential for his career as an artist and as a deeply influential factor in his personal life.

Wilder's memoir "The Elegant Refuge" carries a telling title. The hotel is for him a refuge, a safe haven from the world outside. It offers him the necessary liberating atmosphere for the creation of his music and at the same time the important opportunity of exchange with other artists and producers in the hotel's public places, the bar and the restaurant. The Algonquin is part of his lifestyle and his self-definition as an artist. Demsey writes: "The Elegant Refuge" is "a memoir about people Wilder considered family and about a place he knew as home" (921f). In addition to his personal experiences, the composer provides the reader with information on the theater and musical culture of New York, with the theater hotel as its node.

Alec Wilder's long residency at the Algonquin creates in him the strong desire to account for his life there. His biographer, David Demsey describes Wilder as "profoundly literate" (919). To perform his role as a chronicler of the hotel in a satisfactory way, Wilder uses Elizabeth Bowen's approach to hotels as described in

---

55 The manuscript has not been published, even though it is finished and ready for print. According to Demsey the reason is that it did not contain enough gossip about the celebrities at the hotel for the publishers and Wilder refused to turn his memoir into such a tell-all book (Demsey 921). In addition to "The Elegant Refuge" Wilder also wrote an unpublished autobiography, titled "The Search," and published a collection of his letters. "The Elegant Refuge" is one of the most telling texts concerning Wilder's position in the artistic world and his self-perception.

her book *The Shelbourne Hotel* (1951).[56] He takes it as his role model for his own hotel-focused memoirs. Wilder wants to present the Algonquin as "a mine of human experience, into which one could go on delving forever" (Bowen qtd. in Wilder ii). Wilder deems Bowen's three aspects of a hotel, historic, social, and organic, to be very useful for writing about the Algonquin. He is especially interested in the aspect 'organic' which he describes as the "presence" of the hotel. He also follows Bowen's advice of adding some color to his presentation by inserting the experiences and memories of other hotel guests and members of staff. By this, Wilder's life writing text mirrors the microcosmic nature of the hotel, providing room for others, including the Bodne family.[57]

From the beginning on, Alec Wilder makes clear that his hotel experience is a special one (Wilder viii).[58] While he left the hotel occasionally for journeys and also for short stays in Rochester, he always returned "home" to the Algonquin. In earlier writings he claimed to have no home. Yet, in "The Elegant Refuge" he revises this statement and makes clear that the Algonquin is the only home he has ever known (Wilder xv). To qualify this statement, the composer provides the reader with his definition of a home: "a refuge made secure by solicitude and tolerance. [The Algonquin] has been for me a place of nourishment and stimulation" (Wilder x). As discussed in the introduction of my study, the concept of a hotel as a home has been repeatedly criticized. For Wilder, however, a hotel as a home has only advantages, as he can decide to live there and is able to leave it in

---

56 Elisabeth Bowen made herself a name in the genre of hotel literature with her book *The Hotel* (1927). She is seen as an inspiration for many writers who focus on the issue of hotels in their texts. By now her novel is a classic source for those studying hotels in literature (see Krebs, Pready). Her book about the Shelbourne Hotel is a history of the hotel as well as of the city of Dublin.

57 The form of a memoir fits Wilder's purpose of narrating his hotel experience best. He writes: "A memoir is of its nature something different from a formal autobiography: it may often be a mosaic of thoughts, of remembered sensations, of fleeting moments, and a blur of faces" (135). A memoir for him resembles more the experience gained in a hotel lobby. The coming and going of people is what keeps the place alive for Wilder. This is one of the great advantages of hotels, they provide contact and exchange with people of all spheres, backgrounds, and mindsets, even if only fleetingly. It offers the most creative atmosphere in the city.

58 Having lived so long in the Algonquin, Wilder is very well acquainted with every part of the hotel, something that is not normally the case with hotel guests. This makes his position in the hotel even more intriguing as, according to Pready "knowledge of the space is the ultimate means to power" (213). This is especially true in a hotel, where the space is so complex and the ability of successfully navigating it brings many advantages.

"ten minutes" (Wilder, "The Search" 60) time if he wants to. He sees himself in the lucky position to choose his home without being tied down by it (Wilder ix).

Wilder is "the outsider-insider" who was "privy to the daily behind-the-scenes operations that are the heart of the hotel and its complex of small worlds, upstairs and downstairs" (xi).[59] Being longer connected to the hotel than its owners and the oldest staff member, he calls himself a "son of the house" (Wilder x). Because of this, Wilder cautions the reader that he is not able to detach himself from the Algonquin in his text. He acknowledges that he sees it from a very personal point of view: "I am not so much close to my subject as of it" (Wilder x).[60] This statement is especially interesting since Wilder feels this close relatedness from the position of a guest. He has no ownership of the place. His 'professional' relationship with the place still remains the one between hotel and paying guest. Yet, he considers his relationship to the structure so close as to call himself a "son of the house." His life account counteracts the criticism wielded against hotel living which claims that hotels are places devoid of history, personality and 'soul.' There is certainly a difference between the experience of residents and transient guests at hotels. Still, close identification with a hotel as a guest is possible. The specific case of the Algonquin shows that hotels can take on different functions for people than sociologists and social critics often allow for.

To better understand the unusually close relationship between the Algonquin and Alec Wilder it is necessary to shortly consider his personal background. Wilder was born into a wealthy banking family from Rochester, New York. In his text the composer recalls that he realized early that he was not drawn to the conventional life of his family and the banking profession, but was more interested in artistic works, writing and music. Wilder started visiting the Algonquin at the age of four. During those early visits he got his first taste of the artistic flare of this particular hotel: "The Algonquin very soon became to me a symbol of all the glitter and whirl, the romance so sadly missing in my own youth" (Wilder 17).

One of Wilder's goals of the book is to provide an explanation for the question why this theater hotel continues to draw in people from the arts and why, as journalists wrote, it successfully "refuses to die" (Reynolds 25).[61] According to the composer, the first step to approach the question of the special atmosphere of the Algonquin is that "one must go deeper than the cosmetic glamor that attaches to celebrities, of which the hotel has always had a ready supply. One must, it seems to me, enter that what Miss Bowen has called the 'organic' aspect of hotel life – its

---

59 Wilder visited the Hotel Algonquin for the first time with his family in 1911, on the way to their summer house.
60 Wilder is also aware that his text on the hotel can never be really outside of the hotel. It is always part and parcel of it. Wilder has even written the text in the Algonquin.
61 This mirrors Frank Case's attempt to define the special essence of the Algonquin.

presence" (Wilder vi). Although Wilder is aware that the glamor factor of the Algonquin is very high, he nevertheless sees the special character of the institution hotel as the foundation for its success:

A hotel is a home, however briefly it may serve one as such. A home, bedroom and living room alike. But it is also a public gathering place, vulnerable to the whim of all those who come there, the oafish as well as the well-mannered. Ideally, it should accommodate what seem to be conflicting aims and maintain a sense of privacy in a public place. One can lock one's room upstairs, one's bedroom, but one's living room, the lobby, is open to any and all who arrive from the street bringing with them warmth, cheer, meanness, bad taste, intelligence, wit, duplicity, bracing liveliness, or the brash ho-ho-ho of the market place and cavalry charge bonhomie of Madison Avenue. (Wilder vii)

For Wilder, the first answer to the peculiar attraction that the building on 59 West 44th Street has on him is its heterotopic quality as a hotel. He sees the balancing act between private and public space as crucial. It enables the special atmosphere to develop that creates the particular Algonquin hotel experience. Wilder's description of hotel space is a very telling one. The attraction of the hotel lies in the tension between the privacy of the bedroom which liberates him from domestic obligations, and the possibility of chance meetings in the public parts of the hotel. The publicity of the hotel provides inspiration and seemingly endless opportunities that especially an artistic mind craves for (Peters 79). According to Wilder, in the Algonquin this option of getting into contact with creative people is more available than in many other establishments: "Something may happen. ... Looking back I know realize that one of the lures of life at the Algonquin which must have constantly drawn me back was that vague but marvelous sense of expectancy that generates an undercurrent of excitement in its public rooms" (Wilder 68). Not just for the composer, but for many other visitors and locals "[t]he hotel has always been a nerve center of that part of the creative world which has about it a vividness, an immediacy – a quality of inevitability" (68). The term "nerve center" fits Bowen's 'organic' quality of hotels. It is an ideal metaphor to describe the function of the Algonquin. When one sees New York City as a living organ, then the Hotel Algonquin is the place that gives the creative impulses to its social and cultural life.[62]

For the composer Alec Wilder, it is essential for his work to have regular exchange with other artists, not necessarily only with musicians but also with

---

[62] Several writers likened the structure of a hotel to the human body, seeing its facade and public rooms as the outward appearance and skin of the organism, the interaction between guests and staff as the pumping heart, the management as its brain, and the back-of-the-house departments as the bowels and intestines of the structure. See the hotel description in Steven Millhauser's *Martin Dressler,* 170f.

writers and actors: "The Algonquin not only provided me with a creative ambience but it has yielded another stimulating presence, an ever-changing company of actors, and writers, who find there that other stage that most of us need to survive, the hospitable public gathering place" (77). In the Algonquin, the Rose Room and the Blue Bar were the most important of these third places, as Oldenburg calls them. The composer freely admits that without the "good cheer and atmosphere of hope and security in the Algonquin, I might well have given up the whole musical venture" (26). The Hotel Algonquin became Wilder's "creative Mecca" (21).[63] While the Algonquin is not a religious place, it does have a spiritual importance for writers and artists. For them, it is a must to visit the Algonquin when they are in New York because the Algonquin "leaves its mark on the history of the city as well as on those who gather there" (Wilder 2).[64] One could say a mark of artistic distinction.

Going back to his earlier remarks about the special dynamic between private and public sphere at the hotel, Wilder acknowledges that this can exist in every hotel, yet the Algonquin uses it much more successfully than its competitors. One of the strongest criticism that hotels often face is their supposed lack of privacy and their stage-like quality. However, when it comes to the Algonquin, Wilder states: "Privacy in so public a place? It can be done. The Algonquin lobby, one of the prized gathering places for New Yorkers, has achieved this paradox" (Wilder vii).

---

63 As we will also see later in the discussion of the Chelsea, the Theresa, and the Grossinger's, 'Mecca' is a metaphor that appears repeatedly in descriptions of specific New York hotels which provide a platform for particular communities. 'Mecca' from its original meaning describes a sacred city, the end of a long pilgrimage, an important rite of passage in the life of a male Muslim.

64 This is supported by children's book writer Lavinia Russ, another contributor to Wilder's memoirs and regular visitor of the hotel. She states: "[E]very time I was away from New York, when I thought about the city I didn't think of the Empire State Building or anything like that; I thought of the Algonquin. I would get homesick, ... , I would cry and say, 'I want to go back and sit in the lobby of the Algonquin.' It was New York, as far as I was concerned" (Russ qtd. in Wilder 153). During her first visit to New York, she was told by an acquaintance that she was too provincial and should not "come back until you have sat in the lobby of the Algonquin and read a copy of *The New Yorker*" (152). The place has gained a meaning that goes beyond its mere structure of a hotel, it symbolizes New York sophistication. Russ's dream for her future is "to write a best seller so that I could move into the Algonquin for the rest of my life. ...I would like to have a chair in the lobby, known as 'Mrs. Russ's Chair,' so nobody could sit on it but me. ... And I would like to sit there every night and read a detective story and nod off and have one of the bellmen come and tap me on the shoulder and say, 'Mrs. Russ, it's time for you to go to bed'" (Russ 156).

The composer praises the lounge's "Edwardian charm" which, to him, is "similar to 'a venerable London club'" (Wilder vii). The travel writer Stanley Haggart, a contributor to Wilder's memoir, supports Wilder's claim: "At both Brown's and the Algonquin, I can settle-in unobtrusively, exchanging ideas with friends over drinks, a spot of tea, or a good meal. Even though both hotels are commercial establishments, I find them almost womblike as retreats" (Haggart qtd. in Wilder 218).[65]

As the composer stayed at the hotel for more than fifty years, he experienced the era of Frank Case as well as the era of the Bodnes. Through Wilder's account we learn more about the special host/hotel relationship at the Algonquin. He acknowledges Frank Case's role as the creator of the unique atmosphere of the Algonquin: "His presence and manner set a pace and rhythm unique in the annals of American hotels. ... [W]ith the publication of his *Tales of A Wayward Inn*, the Algonquin became a legend" (16f). Case is seen by Wilder as a unique example of a hotel man, a suave, well-versed and well-read man who has created a retreat which draws this mixed crowd of creatives. Yet, despite the appreciation that the composer shows for Case, he criticizes him for his sometimes patronizing air of superiority and for paying low salaries before the hotel was unionized in the early 1930s.[66] In contrast, Wilder's relationship with the second owners, the Bodne family, is one of mutual friendship. He praises them at length and grants both Ben and Mary as well as their son-in-law, Andrew Anspach, space for their own words. Through Wilder's text we learn that the Bodnes drew great pleasure from becoming acquainted with famous writers and actors of their time: Thornton Wilder, for example, "gave [our grandchildren] beautiful references for college" and "Eudora Welty's a sweetheart" (Mary Bodne qtd. in Wilder 118). They confirm to Wilder that "[t]his is what makes life so interesting here" (118). In contrast to Case, they live in awe of the clientele of the hotel and continue to be surprised by the stimulation their hotel provides them with. What started as "a good investment" turns into a labor of love for the Bodne family (Wilder 120). While Frank Case was the perfect urbane New Yorker, the Bodnes were quite provincial: "if someone had told us we were going to live in New York, I would have laughed at him. How can anyone live there?" After years running the Algonquin, however, Ben Bodne

---

65 Brown's is a well-known, long-established hotel in London. Margaret Case Harriman interestingly also compares the Algonquin with Brown's. Both have the same individualistic quality.

66 Concerning the difference between Case and Bodne, Louis Nizer, another long-term resident and member of the second Round Table, writes: "Everyone noticed the tremendous contrast between Frank Case, the old English type of host, the noble who ran the castle – you could almost feel he put a white wig on every morning – and Ben Bodne, a simple man without pretensions of 'cultural background'" (Nizer qtd. in Wilder 207).

confesses: "Now I don't see how anybody could live anywhere else" (Wilder 120). According to Wilder's text, the Bodne family see it as their mission to be the caretakers of the Algonquin. For Anspach, Frank Case had set the pace and created the atmosphere of the hotel and did it right. For the successor the great task is to preserve the *genius loci* of the Algonquin and to keep the place an authentic landmark of New York.

By including the position of the owner family and the impression of other guests, Wilder gives the reader a multi-faceted picture of the hotel. He even includes comments of staff members to present all main actors in the institution hotel. In the recollections of the staff, the writing style of the text changes. The language becomes colloquial and the narrative style is more anecdotal. Tony, the bellman, tells the reader of his special relationship with guests and that, in contrast to what the public might expect, it was not only the guests sharing their problems with the staff but that many of the guests turned out to be good listeners for the staff's problems. It is likely that this is a specialty of the Algonquin, as the hotel code does normally not allow for such familiarity between staff and guests.[67] Wilder also states that a bellman "occasionally becomes exasperated with new guests who either have no style or grace, who have never been in a hotel like the Algonquin" (Wilder 54). In the Algonquin, the staff has certain standards in mind when it comes to the right people to frequent the hotel. They are 'house proud.' People who are only rich, but lack appreciation for the unique atmosphere and culture of the hotel, are seen as intruders and an unpleasant side effect of a transient hotel.

In Wilder's chapters on the hotel staff it becomes clear that all of them, to a larger or smaller degree, are claimed by the composer as surrogate family. They are an important part of his experience of the Algonquin: "I am a very fortunate person. For in the Algonquin I am cared for, loved, tolerated in my eccentricities, cheered up when I'm low, surrounded by jolly men and women. This lovely and loving little world" (215). While we have already encountered this familiarity between guest and staff in Elsa Maxwell's account of the Waldorf, Wilder's relationship with the Algonquin Hotel people goes even deeper.[68] In addition, the special creative

---

67 For typical staff/guest identities in literature see Krebs 147f and Pready 180f.
68 It needs to be mentioned that Wilder did not develop such a close connection to all hotels which he stayed in during his life. He is not a hotel pilgrim per se. While the Algonquin certainly was the place he spent most time in, he travelled quite extensively and resided at other hotels when his purse did not allow for the Algonquin. Wilder calls these other establishments "sad hotels" because they do not provide him with the atmosphere he feels at his 'home' in New York. The composer especially dislikes motels: "there is no time in their mean little lobbies, their warehouse restaurants, or amongst harried, sullen maids for the crumbs of exchange so desperately needed by the lonely" (212). In contrast to the

atmosphere of the hotel and Wilder's profession make them ideal fits for each other. With his residence and writing he continues to spin the artistic myth of the hotel while the hotel provides the composer with inspiration.

In his final chapter Wilder gives Stanley Haggart the honor of writing the epilogue to his hotel memoirs. The travel writer, who has adopted several second homes in his life and who has made extensive hotel experience, writes that beside all changes and metamorphoses

> the bottomless comfort and ease of spirit of the Algonquin endures. It is beyond fads. ... [T]he Algonquin turns out to be a stronger survivor than its guests. The hotel seems to wait patiently for the newest wave which will invade or adopt it, knowing that they, too, in time will be gone – perhaps fading into obscurity or else retreating to write their memoirs. With gentle, compassionate smile, the Algonquin continues on its own course. But quietly. (219)

Wilder does not comment on the last contributor's writing, so we can assume that he agrees with his sentiment. It brings up one more aspect that is important when talking about New York hotels and their influence on the city's society and culture. Haggart writes that the Algonquin is 'beyond fads.' This is interesting as a hotel, which remains a commercial institution and to a certain degree a commodity, is as much dependent on changing fashions and 'fads' as clothes, furniture, and cars. While it might not change each year, the normal life expectancy of a hotel in New York is not much longer than thirty years as could be seen in the first Waldorf-Astoria.[69] Yet, its unique atmosphere, the quality of space in the Algonquin "that you could feel, almost touch, as you walked in" (Wilder 122) protects the hotel from being swallowed by what Rem Koolhaas described as Manhattan's culture of congestion. The block surrounding the Algonquin has changed over the years. Yet, the hotel remains quite unchanged. According to Wilder, it has become a legend with the publication of Case's *Tales of a Wayward Inn*. With his memoirs, the composer takes up Case's work. He continues the myth of the Algonquin by preserving in the text his hotel experience of over fifty years. Unlike Case, Wilder writes from the position of a hotel guest, and by this adds an important perspective

---

Algonquin, where people take care of him and take an interest in his life, those places are soulless and resemble 'warehouses' where bodies are stored for the night: "More than once have I escaped by the skin of my teeth from becoming one more lobby sitter, dozing in a chair after breakfast" (212). Alec Wilder is not a friend of hotels, but a passionate admirer of the Algonquin "because at the Algonquin I feel safe. My refuge... . [I]n none of them [motels] have I known that mysterious compulsion to initiate the mystical process of creation" (213).

69 Indeed, in the 1970s many experts in the hotel field expected for the Algonquin "an honorable burial about twenty-five years ago" (125).

to the Algonquin discourse. He provides us with the hotel experience of an artist for whom the Algonquin is home and salon.

All hotel actors discussed above, host, hotel children, and guest, refer to the others at one time in their texts. Their hotel experiences are interwoven with each other. Together they produce a multi-faceted impression of the Algonquin's position in New York. Through the Algonquin, these four lives are connected with each other as they were influenced in a similar way by their physical proximity and their appreciation for the special Algonquin atmosphere. They can all be described as natives of this hotel. They have, as Yi-Fu Tuan writes, "'a complex attitude derived from [their] immersion in the totality of [their] environment'" (Tuan, *Topophilia* 63). They experienced what Hetherington calls 'social centrality' (34). The Algonquin is a place for them that "provides a focus for the articulation of identity and sense of belonging" (Hetherington 34). They become 'Algonquinites.'

2.4 THE HOTEL AND ITS LITERARY CIRCLE

All texts discussed above mention the Algonquin Round Table, the literary circle which is the crucial part of the Algonquin's legacy. In the following I will examine the reciprocity between the group and the institution and its lasting importance for the hotel. The Algonquin's convenient location and its reputation brought a circle of theater critics, writers, actors and painters together. Their famous daily lunches became the focal point of New York's literary scene in the 1920s. The Round Table's members contributed to making the hotel the birthplace of sophistication. They started to frequent the hotel's restaurant in late 1919 and continued to do so for almost ten years. Today, the Algonquin Round Table, or Vicious Circle as it was also called, has become a cultural icon. It is repeatedly invoked in books and newspaper articles on New York, as well as in movies and exhibitions. With the exception of Dorothy Parker,[70] who stayed for a few years at the hotel, the group

---

70 According to Meade, Parker moved into the Algonquin in 1924, after the second breakup with her husband Eddie Parker. The hotel had already become an important third place for her as her lunch spot. This temporary home had its advantages for Parker because "[a]mong [its] institutional furnishings she felt free and organized" (Meade 123). Writing in the hotel became her "salvation" (123), even though the traffic of friends, staff, and admirers was so frequent that she had problems concentrating at times. For most of her stay, Parker gave the Algonquin IOUs instead of rent, believing that Case was grateful for the publicity she created for his hotel (146). By 1926, she moved out of the Algonquin to live for a time in Europe. In 1927, she briefly went back to the hotel, publishing her first book of verse *Enough Rope*, which became a great success. Edmund Wilson commented that "her wit is the wit of her particular time and place" and Meade adds that the poems

used the hotel mostly as a meeting place and not for accommodation. For them the hotel was what Oldenburg would later define as a third place, a place of informal exchange away from the work place or the home. The importance of the Algonquin Round Table for the reputation of the Hotel Algonquin can hardly be overstated. At the same time, this literary circle is an example, which shows how important the right place is for the creation of culture. It highlights the need for such third places in modern cities. In the following, I will not only focus on the active years of the group, but I will consider the continuous impact of the circle on New York culture and analyze its revival in the last years.

The Historical Algonquin Round Table

In contrast to the nineteenth century, American hotels in the twentieth century offered more individual and less mass-oriented service to its guests.[71] Hotel restaurants were considered to be the place to go to for locals and visitors, not only for patrons, as the menu below shows (Image 6). For the Algonquin Hotel, its dining room, the Rose Room, had a special importance because of the lunch group of literati who called themselves "The Vicious Circle." Through them the reputation of the Algonquin became legendary. Some people called this group the most important gathering of literary minds since the Mermaid Tavern in London during the Elizabethan Age (Gaines 29). As with many great circles, there are several different stories on the founding of the Algonquin Round Table. It was never a formal organization and developed gradually (Case Harriman 4). The two most often told stories are included in the books *The Vicious Circle* (*TVC*, 1951) by Margaret Case Harriman and *Wit's End* (1979) by James R. Gaines. Both authors trace their account back to direct interviews with the circle's members.

"gave off the essence of the Hotel Algonquin" (178). For the next years she returned repeatedly to the hotel, leaving it for good in the early 1930s. By then it contained too many dark memories of failed love affairs and suicide attempts. Later, she made derogatory remarks about the hotel. Asked about this by Andrew Anspach on her only return visit in 1965, she claimed that she had nothing against it, she was just no longer "terribly interested in food I digested forty-five years ago" (403). Despite her criticism, Parker's relationship with the hotel was mutually important. Parker brought publicity to the place while the Algonquin provided her with the liberty she needed for her writing and the status as a serious writer.

71 In her article "The Testimony of the Hotel," Maureen Montgomery writes that many travelers commented on the fact that American hotels were very democratic places where everything was done together and shared without respect for status, including eating dinner. Only in the first half of the twentieth century was the table d'hôte abandoned and much smaller tables for often two to four people were installed.

Margaret Case Harriman was a contemporary of the group. She describes the relationship between the circle and the hotel in the following way: "The Algonquin Round Table came to the Algonquin Hotel the way lightning strikes a tree, by accident and mutual attraction. Actors and writers always enjoyed staying with Father as much as he enjoyed having them..." (*TVC* 21). According to her account the group started with a meeting between the critic Alec Woollcott and writer and publicist John Peter Toohey to taste the highly praised angel cake of Sarah Victor, the African-American pastry chef of the Algonquin. Finding it delicious they decided to return there on a regular basis.

Image 6: Drama Critics Circle Annual Dinner at the Algonquin (May 1945)

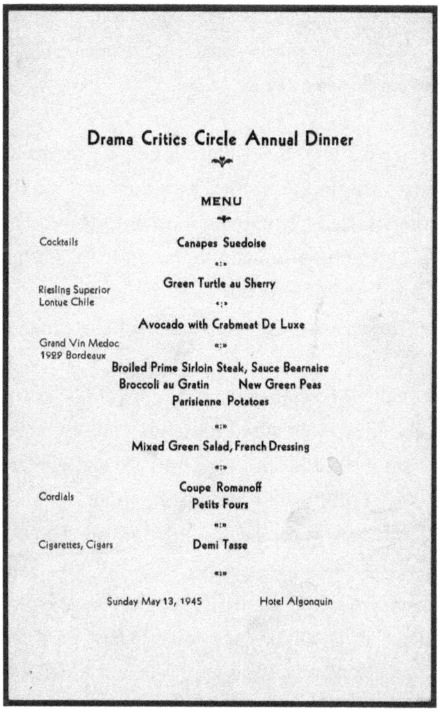

Drama Critics Circle Annual Dinner

MENU

Cocktails	Canapes Suedoise
Riesling Superior Lontue Chile	Green Turtle au Sherry
	Avocado with Crabmeat De Luxe
Grand Vin Medoc 1929 Bordeaux	Broiled Prime Sirloin Steak, Sauce Bearnaise Broccoli au Gratin New Green Peas Parisienne Potatoes
	Mixed Green Salad, French Dressing
Cordials	Coupe Romanoff Petits Fours
Cigarettes, Cigars	Demi Tasse

Sunday May 13, 1945   Hotel Algonquin

Menu of the Hotel Algonquin. From the New York Public Library.

According to Gaines's version, the beginning of the circle goes back to a prank played on Alec Woollcott. Irritated by Woollcott's constant boasting about his time as a newspaper correspondent in the French war theater, several of his war-time colleagues decided to give a fake celebratory luncheon for Woollcott at the

Algonquin to expose his self-importance.[72] Instead of being insulted, however, Woollcott enjoyed himself immensely at the hotel's restaurant and so did the others. They decided to repeat this lunch on a daily basis.[73] Both stories may contain part of the truth.

The founders of the Circle are listed by Case's daughter. She writes:

> The charter members of the Round Table were Franklin P. Adams, Deems Taylor, George S. Kaufman, Marc Connelly, Robert Benchley, Harold Ross, Heywood Broun, Art Samuels, Alexander Woollcoot, John Peter Toohey, the Pembertons, Bill Murray, Robert E. Sherwood, John V.A. Weaver, Laurence Stallings, and a couple of theatrical press agents named David Wallace and Herman J. Mankiewicz; and, on the distaff side, Dorothy Parker, Jane Gran, Ruth Hale, Beatrice Kaufman, Peggy Wood, Peggy Leech, Margalo Gillmore, Edna Ferber, and Neysa McMein. F.P.A. was generally considered the dean of the group, since he was, in 1920, one of its few solvent members. (TVC 11)

Many of them knew each other from their time in France during the First World War. All of them were still young, in their twenties and thirties and most were only just starting their careers, often helping each other with recommendations and space in their respective articles and columns. Due to the strong reciprocity the group was often accused of log-rolling by outsiders and defamed as the "Mutual Admiration Society." In cartoons they were depicted as backslapping each other around the Round Table.

The lunch group at the Algonquin became especially known for their witticisms and sharp retorts which they exchanged amongst each other, and which were retold for the benefit of the larger public in Franklin P. Adams's "The Diary of Our Own Samuel Pepys," his daily column.[74] Through the media people became interested in this group and went to the Algonquin dining room to watch them in action. Frank

---

72 There is also a version in which this prank was played on Woollcott because he refused to grant a fellow editor a favor writing a positive review on a play of an up-and-coming writer called Eugene O'Neill. Woollcott always claimed highest levels of objectivity and did not review plays as favors.

73 The story shows that the emergence of the circle was only possible in a restaurant or hotel, as they needed the service, know-how, and space to make their prank successful. A private home would not have had the same publicity effect. That they selected the Algonquin for their party was due to the fact that many of its 'charter' members already preferred the hotel for their lunches with publishers and friends.

74 Similar to Elsa Maxwell's column "Party-Line" about life at the Waldorf-Astoria, the Algonquin's fame was also spread via a column to all parts of the United States and kindled people's interest in this fashionable location. This is an interesting early form of advertising and building reputation by the creation of networks.

Case quickly realized the appeal of this group and moved them to a large round table in the center of the room (Case Harriman 7). Admiring their talents Case further supported these "young and struggling writers," with free olives, celery and popovers[75]:

> Father's attitude, at first, was no more fulsome than that of any other host who welcomes one more likely looking party to the picnic ground. He didn't expect to make any money out of the Round Table, since nobody there had any and the lunch each member usually ordered consisted of hamburger or ham and eggs, apple pie and coffee. (29)

While they did not spend much money, their presence helped business enough to justify providing their own 'pet waiter' Luigi. The circle grew over the years because the members invited friends to the lunches.[76] In the 1930s, having made their name in New York many of the circle's members left for Hollywood where they were able to secure jobs during the Great Depression. By then the members were also of an age at which many had started a family and could no longer spend much of their time at the hotel. To the surprise of participants and contemporaries the Algonquin Round Table faded away almost unnoticed. Edna Ferber recalls: "I didn't even know that the group had sort of melted away and one day, having finished a long job of work, and wishing to celebrate, I flounced into the Algonquin dining room, sat down at an empty place at the Round Table – and found myself looking into the astonished faces of a family from Newton, Kansas" (Ferber qtd. in Stone 56). Still, Morehouse concludes: "The legend of the Round Table has endured through the decades with a vigor and fascination greater than its individual parts" (*Life at the Top* 23).

The importance of this literary group for and its influence on American culture is difficult to estimate. Already in the 1950s Case Harriman admits that the question "Why was it important?" is "a hard question to answer" (*TVC* 59). According to her: "The Round Table's preoccupation with words, grammar, and accuracy among themselves was the first faint trace of the influence they were to have on American writings as a whole" (55). She adds: "The Round Table symbolized an American Renaissance … . Its influence on American literature, drama, and humor was acute, untiring and permanent" (59). At the same time, the members were interesting personalities, some of the first New York celebrities. The public wanted to read

---

75 This has been preserved in the famous cartoons of the Round Table by Al Hirschfeld.
76 In later years, the group did not only meet at the hotel but also in some of their private homes, in Neysa McMein's studio, in smaller cliques, as well as on a small island in Lake Bomoseen in Vermont, which the group purchased together and used for outings. Throughout the existence of the group the hotel, however, remained their focal meeting point.

more of and about them. In addition, they were "mentally brave" because they did not fear the consequences of their criticism and direct style of writing, even when it was costing them their jobs. For Margaret Case Harriman "[o]ne thing is certain: nothing like the Round Table – for color, interest, and lasting influence – had ever been seen before; and nothing like it has been known since" (*TVC* 79). Marion Meade agrees that the Round Table was perceived as "the country's literary Camelot"(Meade xv). Even president John F. Kennedy once said: "When I was growing up I had three wishes. I wanted to be a Lindbergh-type hero, learn Chinese and become a member of The Algonquin Round Table" (*The Algonquin Wit Newsletter*, Fall 1996, 1).[77]

Case Harriman's account of the group's achievement is certainly more favorable than that of other, later scholars. Throughout her text it becomes clear that she was very close to the group and good friends with some of its members, e.g. Robert Benchley and Marc Connelly. However, despite the lack of critical distance her analysis of the group's influence and its connection to the Algonquin is noteworthy. In Gaines's book *Wit's End* the effect of the group is seen as more limited. He, too, considers the circle an important part of a new, modern type of American literature which emerged after World War I. However, he also writes: "If it [The Algonquin Round Table] was, as the legend goes, the greatest forum of presiding wits since the Mermaid Tavern, it was also a Bronx Zoo of contemporary neurotics, a group so dazzling in its assortment of idiosyncratic personalities that the wonder is simply that they spoke to each other at all, even in epigrams" (29). The Vicious Circle differed from other literary groups of its time. Yet, together with the Lost Generation, they were an important influence on modern American literature.

Probably the most powerful legacy of the Algonquin Round Table and its strongest influence on New York culture is the sophisticated magazine *The New Yorker*, which was founded by Harold Ross and his wife Jane Grant in the Algonquin in 1925. Many of the group's members wrote at one point for the magazine, including the "innkeeper's daughter" Margaret Case Harriman. According to its mission statement, Ross wanted to create with *The New Yorker* a magazine which is

a reflection in word and picture of metropolitan life. ... *The New Yorker* will be the magazine which is not edited for the old lady in Dubuque. It will not be concerned in what she is

---

77 Meads and Kennedy's statement go well together, especially when one considers that Kennedy's presidency is often called 'Camelot.' The Kennedy quote is used widely by the hotel for public relations purposes. Fraser P. Seitel and John Doorley's book *Rethinking Reputation* (2012) on the power of public relations actually uses the Algonquin and their publicity strategy as one of their success examples.

thinking about. This is not meant in disrespect, but *The New Yorker* is a magazine avowedly published for a metropolitan audience and thereby will escape an influence which hampers most national publications. It expects a considerable national circulation, but this will come from persons who have a metropolitan interest. (Ross)[78]

The Algonquin and its suave owner Frank Case expressed this metropolitan flair ideally and are said to have thus influenced the spirit of the magazine.[79] With the exception of a few members like Dorothy Parker, who was a born New Yorker, most of the others came from the Midwest. They became acquainted with the urbane New York spirit through their lunches at the Algonquin. Although the names of the Algonquin Round Table members and their works are no longer familiar to today's readers, in connection with *The New Yorker* and the Algonquin Hotel they are remembered.[80]

Reading Frank Case's and Alec Wilder's life accounts as well as the guests' letters to the host, it becomes clear that not everyone saw the relationship between the group and the hotel as a favorable one for the Algonquin. Case himself, who supported the group at its beginning with free food, later describes his relationship with the Round Table as detached: "Restrain is required to keep from being annoyed by queries as to what has become of the Round Table. What has become of the reservoir at Fifth Avenue and 42nd Street? These things do not last forever. The Round Table lasted longer than any other unorganized gathering that I know of" (*TWI* 60). While he enjoyed it for the time it lasted, he accepts change: "the Round Table faded into a mellow and pleasant memory ... . I never mind seeing the old order change when the new one is just as good" (*TWI* 60f). His comments show that his love for writers made the group interesting for him, and their popularity was certainly a nice advertisement for the hotel, but he did not consider their influence on the hotel and on New York culture as decisive.

Alec Wilder is similarly careful estimating the importance of the Algonquin Round Table. He started living at the hotel during the years of their meetings, and was duly impressed by them at the time, wishing to be part of the vibrant artistic

---

78 Almost from its foundation until today guests get a free copy of *The New Yorker* at the Algonquin. Under Ross's editorship, *The New Yorker* often made mention of the hotel, printing quotes from Case and reporting on the going-ons of the hotel as it was just a few steps from the office of magazine on 44th Street.

79 This supports Norman Hayner's finding that extended hotel living creates a sophisticated, urbane type of personality (Hayner 795).

80 For example, in 1987, Aviva Slesin portrayed the circle in her documentary *The Ten Year Lunch: The Wit and Legend of the Algonquin Round Table* and won the Academy Award for best documentary in 1988. This shows the lasting interest in the group.

banter. Yet, in his memoirs he makes clear that from his point of view of the 1970s he considers their influence on the hotel as limited:

They have generated an enormous amount of publicity for the hotel. But now ... a question remains: What really did they have to do with the long, ongoing success of the Algonquin; with the daily arrival of guests from around the country and abroad, some of whom have returned through four and five decades, and a few of whom are the children and grandchildren of guests now deceased? Probably very little. (Wilder vi)

For him, like for Case, other hotel guests were more impressive such as Thornton Wilder, William Faulkner, and Gertrude Stein. Of the members of the Vicious Circle only Parker is still anthologized. Yet as a group, their influence can still be considered important and through *The New Yorker* their legacy in New York is still very much alive.

In the Algonquin, writers and art critics mixed. While this often worked well and enabled inspirational meetings, the members of the Vicious Circle were not liked by many outside of their exclusive group. Their comments were literally often vicious and hurting. Accordingly, the relationship between the group and other artistic guests was often tense. The letters to Frank Case show this tension amongst guests at the hotel. In Case's appendix, Louis Bromfield wrote of his fear for the Algonquin to come too much under the influence of the Round Table (Case 309). Fannie Hurst is also critical of the group's behavior, stating:

I am not much of a sitter-at-Inns. My Round Table is a long refectory one, and I poo-hoo the boys and gals who like the sound of their own voices rolling and log-rolling along the corridors and among the Columns of the town. Many of them, to be sure, are smart boys and gals all right, who publicly sprout ideas in a world in drought and in need of them. Only I would rather see than be one. (qtd. Case 335)

Even the Round Table members themselves were later cautious and often wary when asked about the impact of their group. Many played down the importance of the circle. For them, their witty and vicious days were a part of their youth. Dorothy Parker later called her former friends "hypocrites" and "show-offs" (Meade 320). Many of them continued to visit the hotel throughout the 30s and 40s, yet they did so individually and because they wanted to see the hotel and Case, not so much their old companions.[81]

---

81 Several Round Tablers came together for the presentation of Case's first book as can be seen in an often printed photograph from 1938. The photography of the book party for the publication of *Tales of a Wayward Inn* shows Case, Dorothy Parker, Woollcott Gibbs, Alan Campbell, and James Thurber (Reprinted in Matteoli 9).

Considering this information, it might seem peculiar that this Jazz Age literary circle is repeatedly invoked in New York magazines and the Algonquin itself continues to use it as a part of its marketing strategy. The reason is that despite all criticism the Algonquin Round Table remains one of the best known literary groups of the Roaring Twenties. They were among the first New York celebrities who were famous for their creative achievements and not for their family names. The circle's name and its decade long lunch tradition kept it connected to the hotel through all these years, something that did not happen with earlier or later groups.

The Algonquin Round Table in Literature

As described above, the Algonquin group was a mixed blessing for the hotel. Yet, its notoriety helped to keep these literati and the Algonquin on everyone's lips. Already during the years of its existence, the Vicious Circle inspired writers to write about them. In these texts the Algonquin is used as a setting, yet it is also a mood cue and becomes a 'mithandelnder Schauplatz.' The two best known contemporary examples are Gertrude Atherton's *Black Oxen* (1923) and Anita Loos's *But Gentlemen Marry Brunettes* (1927), the sequel to *Gentlemen Prefer Blondes*. Their critical stance toward the Algonquin Round Table adds to the Hotel Algonquin discourse.

Gertrude Atherton was a regular visitor at the Algonquin. In contrast to the writers of the Algonquin group she was already of an advanced age when she wrote her bestseller *Black Oxen* in 1923. The question of the importance of youth is at the core of her book which has been described as a thinly disguised autobiographical novel. The main protagonist is a young, successful columnist called Lee Clavering, who heads a group of equally young and illustrious writers dubbed "the Sophisticates", "abandoning 'Intellectuals' and 'Intelligentsia' to the Parlor Socialists" (Atherton 41). Clavering falls in love with a mysterious and beautiful 'young' lady. In the course of the story, however, the lady turns out to be an almost sixty-year-old former actress who appears young due to a revolutionary youth treatment in Europe. The novel ends with the lady's return to Europe, where she is reunited with her husband and does important work, and with Clavering marrying a young flapper more fitting his type.

Clavering's peer group, 'the Sophisticates,' are mentioned repeatedly in the text. They are described as "authors, playwrights, editors and young editors, columnists, dramatic critics, young publishers, the fashionable illustrators and cartoonists, a few actors, artists, sculptors, hostesses of the eminent, and a sprinkling of Greenwich Village to give a touch of old Bohemia" (Atherton 41). For most contemporaries it was immediately clear that Atherton alluded to the Algonquin Round Table members, especially when the protagonist later mentions that he "lunched with friends at the Sign of the Indian Chief, a restaurant where the cleverest of them—and those who were so excitedly sure of their cleverness that for the moment they convinced others as well as themselves—foregathered daily" (148). Atherton does not mention the name Algonquin, yet "Sign of the Indian Chief" is easy to decode, especially since the Algonquin back then indeed had such a sign above its entrance.[82] The narrator's description of the group's mission is quite harsh. While she displays a certain admiration for their sharp wit and intellect, as well as for their passion for vocabulary, her judgment of their behavior is quite negative: "their most solemn causeries were upon the vital theme of The American Reputation in Letters. Past. Present. Future. ... From these judicial pronouncements there was no appeal, and the pleasant spaces of the Sign of the Indian Chief, so innocuous to the uninitiated eye, was a veritable charnel house that stank in the nostrils of the rejected" (148). In this critical statement of the Vicious Circle the only reputation that remains intact is that of the hotel, whose space is described as "pleasant" and "innocuous."[83] Atherton is able to differentiate between the hotel and its literary circle. Even though her book is no longer a well-known title, it should be remembered that *Black Oxen* was the bestseller of 1923 and was even made into a successful silent movie. *Black Oxen* functions as proof for the circle's and the hotel's important position in New York culture.

Anita Loos, unlike Atherton, is said to have been an irregular partaker of the Round Table. She later moved to Hollywood and remained there to write scripts for movies. Loos was personally acquainted with the members of the circle. One could say that she was linked to them through their common fondness for hotels. Already in *Gentlemen Prefer Blondes* (*GPB*), hotels play an outstanding role in the protagonist's life. For Lorelei, the Ritz Hotel in New York is the ultimate expression of everything chic and fashionable. It is the place where she desires to be. When Lorelei travels to Europe, she exclaims that she feels best at the Ritz in

---

82 For readers who did not understand the hints, *Time Magazine* wrote in its review of the book: "Gertrude Atherton writes a novel, *Black Oxen*, dealing with literary New York of today. What is this literary New York? Who are these log-rollers and back-scratchers of whose activities many of us hear, yet whose actuality we are prone to deny? Go into the Algonquin some noon. Anyone can do it. Here you will find the famous 'round table' at which sit the supposedly elect" (J.F.). This statement is followed by the printing of the names of the Round Table members starting with F.P.A. and ending with Robert Sherwood. The little aside "Anyone can do it" refers to the hotel's accessibility. The real identity of the group is also mentioned in Carl Van Vechten's review of the book "A Lady Who Defies Time," published in *The Nation* (Feb 14, 1923). Van Vechten, like Atherton, was an Algonquin regular. He became known as *the* photographer of some of the most famous characters of his time, including Algonquinites.

83 Frank Case was an admirer of Atherton and mentions her book in *Tales of a Wayward Inn*, writing with tongue in cheek: "We are advertised by our loving friends" (*TWI* 205).

London. Surrounded by glamor and fellow-American travelers, who make the hotel for her a surrogate embassy of the United States, she feels at home (Loos, *GPB* 33). Like the rest of the book, this statement is meant at least partly satirically, nevertheless, it expresses an attitude that many traveling Americans had.[84]

In the book's sequel, *But Gentlemen Marry Brunettes*, hotels are again important institutions. This time Lorelei is no longer exclusively interested in the Ritz, but she now focuses her attention on the Algonquin Hotel.[85] She wants to become a writer and finds out "that the most literary environment in New York is the Algonquin Hotel, where all the literary geniuses eat their luncheon. ... So I invited Dorothy to accompany me, and go there at luncheon time" (Loos, *BGMB* 138). From the nonsensical structure of her argument the reader is aware that what now follows should not to be taken too seriously. The night before going to the Algonquin Lorelei already meets established writers like Mencken, Dreiser, Sherwood Anderson, Sinclair Lewis, and Joseph Hergesheimer at a private party. However, because for her it is not so much about really meeting great authors but about following the cliché of being in the place where they exchange their most intellectual remarks, she states: "So the next day I made Dorothy go to luncheon at the Algonquin Hotel, and *that* made up for everything. For they are the *critics* who tell everybody else how to do it, and they know how to act. I mean, after all, they spend practically all their time showing everybody else how literary people ought to act" (Loos *BGMB* 139). Through Lorelei's deliberately naïve kind of voice, the author bitingly criticizes the writers congregating at the hotel for backslapping.[86]

The text excerpts provide a very ambiguous picture of the Algonquin Hotel. In contrast to Atherton's book, here the hotel is directly called by its name. The name is immediately understood by the reader and evokes a certain image of sophistication and pompousness at the same time. By itself, the hotel is not seen negatively, yet the presence of the circle seems to poison its atmosphere: "Well the famous head waiter at the Algonquin is called George, who holds a velvet rope

---

84 By the early twentieth century, the modern hotels in Europe were closely modeled after the American role model and provided all comfort and amenities that Americans had gotten used to. During the Cold War, hotel mogul Conrad Hilton explicitly wanted his international hotels to be little Americas that bring American style and way of life to Europe, functioning as embassies of good will.

85 See also Sandoval-Strauzs and Wilk 175.

86 To authenticate her satire Loos uses real events, e.g. she refers to the circle's journey to Europe which happened in 1922: "So then they all started to tell about a famous trip they took to Europe. And they had a marvelous time, because everywhere they went, they would sit in the hotel, and play cute games and tell reminiscences about the Algonquin. I think it is wonderful to have so many internal resources that you never have to bother to go outside yourself to see anything" (142).

across the doorway of a small exclusive dining room to keep people who do not appreciate genius from going where they do not belong" (Loos, *BGMB* 139). This quote gives the impression that the Algonquin is actively involved in the aggrandizing of the literary group and the staff themselves seem to add to the exclusionary and almost hostile atmosphere that the Vicious Circle creates.

The more open side of the hotel is shown later when Dorothy, Lorelei's friend, returns to the site of the Algonquin. Coming to New York to start a new life, Dorothy needs a place to live. Due to her strange appearance, amongst other things she carries a basket made out of a dead armadillo, several hotels refuse her. However, at the Algonquin she gets a room because they mistake her for a member of a film crew due to her peculiar make-up. Despite the error, she is allowed to continue living there, on the one hand because it is the law and on the other hand because she is the typical kind of Algonquin resident, an aspiring, slightly unconventional actress.

Anita Loos's depiction of the Round Table and the atmosphere they create at the Algonquin is critical and biting. Similar to Atherton she describes the members of the Vicious Circle as being full of themselves while having not much to show for. Nevertheless, it is interesting how both writers deemed the Algonquin Round Table intriguing enough to be represented in their work. If nothing else, the circle is a symbol for its time. The hedonistic Jazz Age was a period in which American society rid itself from overcome conventions, yet still struggled with its newly adopted ideas. One's standing in society did no longer rely on pedigree, but on talent and the ability to promote oneself. The Algonquin functions as a platform for this social reorientation (Mordden 15). It is an early example for "branding." As mentioned earlier, this self-promotion, which happens in and through the Algonquin, reminds one of Baudrillard's thesis that people become what they consume. As we can see with the character Lorelei, people staying at the Algonquin are accepted as artists. The Algonquin as setting makes Loos's and Atherton's plot more credible and allows for certain plot twists and developments to happen.

In conclusion, it is remarkable that the Round Table cannot be mentioned in a text without also alluding to its place of origin, the Algonquin Hotel and the special function and atmosphere the hotel has for artists in New York.[87] Through *The New*

---

[87] The two books described above are not the only texts about the Round Table and the Algonquin. The reputation of the hotel and the eponymous circle also inspired the academy-award winning documentary *The Ten Year Lunch* (1987) by Aviva Slesin. Aviva Slesin did extensive research on the Round Table. Her material can be viewed in the Billy Rose Archive of the Performing Arts Sector of the Public Library in the Lincoln Center, New York. She could win Heywood Hale Broun as narrator for the piece, the son of two original members, Heywood Broun and Ruth Hale. In 1994, the movie *Mrs. Parker and the Vicious Circle* by Alan Rudolph was released. This fictionalized account

Yorker magazine, newspaper columns, and the texts discussed above, the fame and reputation of the Algonquin spread across the American continent. While hotels have attracted writers for decades and have been used as settings for so many stories that the genre 'hotel literature' is a legitimate category of its own (Künzli 9), the Algonquin retains an outstanding position among them. It is not only a convenient location but, as Case put it, it harbors the Muse. It keeps a kind of double connection to the world of arts, not only as a comfortable home to artists but also as a salon and a source of inspiration. The hotel is proud of the fact that William Faulkner wrote his acceptance speech for the Nobel Prize for Literature at the Algonquin and that Maya Angelou regularly came to the hotel to present her new books. Yet, its connection to the Vicious Circle is the longest lasting literary legacy of the hotel, despite its ambiguous record.

A look into recent historical novels shows that the Algonquin Round Table is still remembered for its influence on New York culture, and the hotel as its preferred third place is inseparably tied to it. Several books have been published in the last years which are set in the Algonquin. The books make use of the current revival of the 1920s style. They are examples for the ways in which the Algonquin's history is being used as cultural capital. In J.J. Murphy's three books of *Algonquin Round Table Mysteries*, nominated for the Agatha Award of Best Historical Fiction, Dorothy Parker and her friend Robert Benchley solve mysterious murders in the art scene of Manhattan in the 1920s. Murphy has done extensive research at the New York Public Library and the New-York Historical Society. He even included a historical appendix in his books, which contains a short history of the Algonquin Hotel and its circle. The most recent novel dealing with the hotel's legacy and its prominent residents is *Farewell, Dorothy Parker* (2013) by Ellen Meister. In Meister's book the Algonquin is portrayed as *the* artists' hotel, where creative people go to get inspiration and be emboldened by its confident atmosphere.

Until today, the Algonquin still hands out a little gift brochure of the hotel's literary heritage with information on the history of the hotel and the Round Table, entitled "Quirks and Curiosities: A Hundred or So Years At the Algonquin." Advertisement for the hotel with the help of literature actually goes back to 1931, when the hotel had a series of witty stories published in *The New Yorker*, written by Frank Case. The texts of these advertisements have been reprinted and distributed at the hotel in the 1980s as *Tribal Tales of the Algonquin*, a 25-pages strong collection

---

of the years between 1919 and 1929 won critical acclaim, being an Official Selection at the Cannes Film Festival of 1994. I have already named the movie *Rich and Famous* (1981), in which the director George Cukor can still rely on well-known connection between Dorothy Parker and the Algonquin Hotel. He uses the Algonquin as setting to establish the reputation of Liz Hamilton as a serious writer.

of anecdotes on the hotel. During the 1990s, the owners of the Algonquin published a regular newsletter called "The Algonquin Wit," in which they presented the program of the hotel's cabaret in the Oak Room and information on special events. Each newsletter also included a profile on one of the Algonquin Round Table members and carried an episode of the hotel's literary and cultural history on the front page. The current management of the Algonquin Hotel, the Marriott Autograph Collection, still makes use of the hotel's literary history, especially the legacy of the Round Table. In 2002, the hotel unveiled a new Round Table painting which they had commissioned from Natalie Ascensios. It is now prominently displayed in the dining room above a replica of the old round table. The last page of the brochure, however, is dedicated to Matilda, the hotel cat, immortalized in the children's book, *The Algonquin Cat* (1980) by Val Schaffner with illustrations by Hilary Knight.[88] With this text, I will round up the chapter on the Algonquin.

Like *The Dog Who Lives at the Waldorf*, the cat described in Schaffner's book is based on a real animal, Hamlet, the former house cat of the Algonquin.[89] The children's book is well researched, and presents a detailed image of the Hotel Algonquin and its operative processes. The focalizer of the story is the cat Hamlet. He lives at the Algonquin as the petted and spoiled friend of famous actresses and lonely hotel children. Hamlet is an acute observer of the place. Through his eyes the reader experiences the Algonquin's atmosphere:

After the dazzle of the street, the lounge of the Algonquin seemed to glow in subdued shades of brown and gold, illuminated by antique porcelain lamps that gleamed softly like heraldic shields on the sides of its dark oak pillars, contrasting with the brighter hues and mirrors of the dining room beyond, the Rose Room, which shown like the stage in a darkened theater or, with its white pillars, Hamlet thought, the inner sanctum of an ancient temple. (Schaffner 32)

Like in the *Dog Who Lived At The Waldorf*, having an animal as the main protagonist means that the hotel can be investigated in all its parts. In contrast to the guests or the staff, the cat is not bound by the hotel code, but it can move about

---

88   Knight also did the drawings for *Eloise*, bringing Kay Thompson's character visually to the audience.

89   The Algonquin has a long tradition of house cats. Frank Case describes the arrival of Rusty, the first Algonquin Cat, and its unique behavior in *Do Not Disturb*: "It was as if he [Rusty the cat] had heard there was an opening and came in and applied for it, only he didn't apply, he just took the job" (123). According to Case "his royal catness" (123) actually 'performed a job' by visiting sick guests and keeping them company, out of his own volition. Alec Wilder also refers to the cat, dedicating a whole chapter in his memoirs to it, titled "Chapter VIII: Pause for Cats." Wilder describes the animal as being very indulged and behaving like a substitute host when strolling through the house.

freely, showing all sides of the hotel. It gives the reader the chance to look behind the scenes.

The activities at the hotel, which Hamlet describes, are all in synch with the hotel's reputation. He shows that even the hotel staff is interested in culture: The elevator boy reads *The New Yorker,* and the clerk discusses knowledgably a new play with an arriving guest. Fitting a hotel text, there are several plot lines which are connected through the space of the hotel and made credible by the Algonquin setting: A writer discusses new book projects with his editor; a journalist comes to the hotel to interview a famous theater actor before his opening night; a hotel child stays there awaiting his parents who are touring the country with their show and leave the child in the care of the well-trained staff. After some misunderstandings and surprising twists connected to a missing jewel and a lost manuscript, the book ends with the signing of a new book contract, the granting of new roles for aspiring actresses, and a promising story for a journalist. All of these events fulfill Frank Case's promise of the Algonquin Muse. It remains a place where works of art are created and artistic success is achieved.[90] Like the book *The Dog Who Lives In the Waldorf,* the children's book *The Algonquin Cat* make use of the hotel's reputation. As children slowly develop their sense of space, the depiction of everyday places is a beneficial topic for children's literature. The way space is described for them is also interesting for adults and allows the reader to get a different perspective. It provides surprising insight into the creation of space and its importance for the plot.

The Algonquin Hotel is a platform for the literati and sophisticated artists, and an interesting member of the intricate hotel network of New York City. The institution and its clientele have had a lasting influence on the city's culture and beyond. The way this hotel space was created by owner Frank Case and was preserved by the Bodne family for more than eighty years makes this institution a rare specimen in a city where thousands of hotels exist in close proximity. Furthermore, the interesting coincidence that two hotel children, Case's daughter and Bodne's grandson, wrote about their hotel experience at the Algonquin, underlines the material agency of this New York landmark. The hotel's function as the artist's home and salon has been well capture in the memoir of composer Alec Wilder, the hotel's long-term resident of fifty years. Finally, the hotel's close connection to the Algonquin Round Table made it an icon of Jazz Age New York.

---

90 The book, of course, also mentions the Algonquin Round Table. One of the book concepts that the writer proposes to his editor is an annotated version of the greatest wits of the Algonquin Round Table (Schaffner 40); the journalist is sent to interview an actress but also wants to find out "What happened to the Round Table? Publisher wants to know what they did with it" (29). Finally, there is a well-hidden little reference: at the end of the book a movie producer arrives with a "big blonde" on his arm, an allusion to Dorothy Parker's most often anthologized short story "The Big Blonde" (1930).

It confirmed the important role of the Algonquin Hotel for the development of culture in New York during the twentieth century. By closely examining this hotel's history, the life accounts, and fictional texts connected to it, we learn more about the society and culture of this city, and about the influence this unique stopping place has on it.

Today, the hotel continues to attract business with slogans like "A Living Legend Evolves. The Algonquin" (*Algonquin Homepage*, 2014). With subpages on the hotel's history, the Algonquin Round Table, and interviews of long-time staff members the hotel homepage still nourishes the legendary reputation of the Algonquin. However, with the closing of the Cabaret in the Oak Room in 2012 after 32 years of existence, one of the few classic cabarets left in New York, the hotel became more streamlined to the Marriott company structure and less the unique legend they try to evoke in ads ("The Song Is Over"). However, walking into the Algonquin one can still experience its *genius loci* as described in Newman Levy's poem "Songs of Hotels: The Algonquin", printed in *The New Yorker* in 1928:

The Algonquin
Oh let us bow and genuflect
Before the home of intellect.
Of all that's bright and fair the shrine,
A great important burden's thine,
To feed that rare and flashing horde
That gathers daily at thy board.
....
So feed with care, divine afflatus,
Their rare digestive apparatus.
The fate of Art depends on it,
Algonquintessence, though, of wit.

The "home of intellect" has changed over its more than a hundred years of existence. However, it is still there, despite repeated swan songs and the difficult economic viability of such a small hotel in the huge pond of hotels in Manhattan. The Algonquin continues to refuse to die (Reynolds 25). The hotel is no longer in private hands and is no longer as unique as it once was. It needs to be seen how long the Algonquin will be able to keep its legend alive. For the moment, it still is an icon for one of New York's most important periods, the Jazz Age, and for the influence the city wielded on American culture as a whole.

3. The Chelsea Hotel – New York's Bohemian Mecca

> "You meet people from all over the world on this international bohemian circuit, and they say 'see you at the Chelsea.' It's as if we have a kind of date there."
>
> JAKOV LIND/QTD. IN TURNER 145

It is almost impossible to examine New York hotel experience and to leave out the Chelsea Hotel on 23rd Street. The hotel's reputation has reached far beyond the American borders and attracts artists, activists, and 'normal' guests from all over the world. Together with the other hotels of this thesis, the Chelsea is part of a unique network in New York City, which on looking closely shows the intricate ties amongst each other. As mentioned earlier, in George Cukor's movie *Rich and Famous* the Waldorf and the Algonquin are used as symbolic backgrounds for the two writers playing the lead roles in the film. In addition, a third hotel is shortly mentioned, the Chelsea. The protagonist Liz Hamilton is interviewed by a young reporter for the *Rolling Stone*. He ends the interview with the information that she can reach him in his hotel, the Chelsea. As with the other two institutions, the hotel is used as a mood cue and status-confirmer. The viewer is aware of the Chelsea's reputation as favorite haunt for the young and the creative as well as for radical writers and thinkers. By naming it as his place of accommodation the young reporter gets the 'right' kind of street credentials

The movie is just one instance in which the special connection amongst hotels in New York becomes apparent. The Waldorf-Astoria is the über-Grand Hotel, a continuation of the Gilded Age and at the same time a modern 'city within a city.' The Algonquin represents the sophisticated and civilized hospitality heart of New York. The Chelsea is similar to the Algonquin Hotel, both are hotels for artists, yet it is different in reputation and atmosphere. The two hotels, the Algonquin and the Chelsea, are like two sides of the same medal. Both cater to creative spirits, yet the Chelsea Hotel's patrons are less established, more in-the-making, willing to break rules, and less tied by conventions. Ward Morehouse III describes the difference between the Algonquin and the Chelsea in the following way:

In sheer numbers, they [the artists in the Chelsea] overshadowed those artists associated with The Algonquin, like James Thurber and Robert Benchley. But the Chelsea was and is radically different from the Algonquin. Artists who favor the Chelsea are for the most part employed only by themselves; those at the Algonquin often work for someone else, for newspapers and magazines – that is, they have actual 'jobs'. (18)

Image 7: Hotel Chelsea on 23rd Street

Hotel Chelsea. Private.

While the name Algonquin is used synonymously to denote highbrow magazine culture, Broadway theaters, and sophisticated lifestyle, the Chelsea represents the grittier subculture of the New York art world, which blossomed in the 1950s and dominated pop and punk culture of the metropolis during the 60s, 70s and 80s. One can also say that the Algonquin was the artists' hotel for the first half of the twentieth century in New York and the Chelsea took over by midcentury. Despite their similarities in structure, clientele, and function the Chelsea merits a case study in its own rights. It is more of a residential hotel than the first two hotels. Although the percentage changed over the years, usually more than half of the inhabitants stayed at the Chelsea for an extended time, many for several decades.[1] Due to this, most of the material existing on the Chelsea has been created by its creative residents who made the hotel a watchword in the world of the arts. These artists have searched for different ways of recreating their impressions, memories, and experiences of their time at the Chelsea. Accordingly, in this chapter, the way the guests live in the hotel, shape the place, and are deeply inspired by it lies at the heart of the discussion. I will analyze the functions the hotel fulfills for them as refuge, place of initiation and inspiration, and how their experience at the Chelsea impacts New York culture.

Writers have been attracted to hotels for a long time. As Künzli writes

Es scheint eine Affinität zu bestehen zwischen der schreibenden Zunft und dem Raum, der die Anonymität ebenso zuläßt wie das gesellschaftliche Leben. Das Hotel steht für das Wechselbad zwischen Öffentlichkeit und Zurückgezogenheit am Schreibtisch, mit dem es jeder Schriftsteller berufsbedingt zu tun hat. Für die einen ersetzt es die Heimat, oft notgedrungen ..., die anderen finden im Hotelpersonal eine Wahlfamilie, zu der das Verhältnis genauso herzlich, durch die Höhe des Trinkgeldes manipulierbar, wie verbindlich ist, da es die Freiheit bietet, sie jederzeit 'fluchtartig verlassen zu können.' (Künzli 9)

In the texts on the Chelsea we will find this affinity between the writers and the hotel repeatedly. After an introduction to the history of the institution and its unique host, Stanley Bard, I will examine the life narratives by poet Edgar Lee Masters and playwright Arthur Miller. Masters can be seen as the starting point of the Chelsea's reputation as an artists' haunt and Miller's stay confirmed the hotel's reputation.[2] For the two writers, the hotel became a hiding place from the world outside. In connection with their texts, I will discuss John O'Neill's novel *Netherland* (2008). I will then continue with Patti Smith's autobiography *Just Kids* (2010). For her, the Chelsea became a place of initiation as an artist. It was her "university," the place which shaped her life in a specific way. As Leve writes: "Like the city itself, it [the

---

1   In 2007, about 60% of the hotel's customers were permanent residents, 40% of the rooms were let to transients (Leve 42).

2   Masters was not the first artist living at the Chelsea, yet, the extended period he stayed at the hotel and his peculiar relationship with it makes him a prototype for the kind of artists living at this hotel.

Chelsea]'s a refuge for reinvention" (Leve 42). Finally, the Chelsea is probably most famous as a place of inspiration. By analyzing the work of Ed Hamilton and Linda Troeller, two photographers living at different phases at the Chelsea, the narrative of the hotel as a source of inspiration will be examined. Their picture books on the Chelsea make the viewer aware of the stage-like quality of this particular hotel space, like a ready-made backdrop for a theater or movie production. Different from the grandeur of the Waldorf or the English club feeling of the Algonquin hotel, the Chelsea always looks like an art work in progress with the careless, democratic mix of good and bad paintings arranged next to each other on the walls, and people constantly reinventing themselves in the lobby. Photographers have helped to make the hotel a cultural icon in New York. Their works show a strong awareness of the physical surrounding by capturing the unique atmosphere of the hotel in their pictures. Complementing the art produced by Chelsea insiders I will also present two examples created by outsiders which have been inspired by the Chelsea. The hotel's spirit is so strong as to influence people who have not experienced its atmosphere for themselves. More than in the first two narratives, here we can get a deep insight into how much the space of the hotel is seen as an essential part of the artistic residents' self-perception and the way they produce art.

In this chapter the focus is on the experience of residents/guests and the hotel. An uncommon variety of people, from different backgrounds and career paths have decided to make the Chelsea Hotel their home. This hotel has traditionally accommodated more long-term guests than transients, yet it is the combination of both that keeps it a vibrant place of artistic exchange. The question which runs through the first three case studies and which is especially relevant here is: what makes people want to live in hotels instead of in private quarters? In his book *Place: A Short Introduction* Tim Cresswell states that home "is an exemplary kind of place where people feel a sense of attachment and rootedness" (Cresswell 24). He concludes that "[h]ome is where you can be yourself" (Cresswell 24). The term 'home' is clearly connected to strong emotions. It has an important function in our lives. Our home helps us to define who we are and provides us with the basis from which we see the world.

Considering these notions, the Chelsea is a veritable home for the bohemians, as I will show here. In their texts, the artists describe the Chelsea as their home and source of inspiration. It is a platform for their way of life. The residents of the Chelsea Hotel agree that here they can be themselves. As Florence Turner states in *At The Chelsea*: "I began to understand the rare quality of the place where we could be ourselves without wariness or the sense of critical eyes" (27). This is exactly what Cresswell says about the prime function of a home: it should be a place where people can live their lives without being criticized for their lifestyle choices. When long-term resident Turner loses her job as theater scout for MGM, her fellow-residents and the staff in the hotel take care of her: "[t]he Chelsea and my friends there became of the utmost importance to me at this point. ... The hotel was a home more than it had ever been" (127). In contrast to the outside world, they were not critical of her failure but sheltered her.

Because of the unconventional and artistic nature of the Chelseaites, a normal home with its domestic obligations and expectations would not fulfill the requirements of what 'home' needs to be. Their lifestyle is often mobile and needs to be flexible. The Chelsea allows for that and provides its inhabitants with the security net of the hotel community, a kind of surrogate family. We know from composer George Kleinsinger that he left his suburban home for the hotel because its ordinary atmosphere was suffocating him. Edgar Lee Masters accepted that his second wife Ellen was leaving him because he was not willing to return to his conventional life in the Midwest. He did not want to move out of the Chelsea, the source of inspiration of his later work and the home of his life's love. Bob Dylan found the needed privacy he wanted for his life with Sara Lownds in the Chelsea, away from the limelights. The Chelsea Hotel was the likeliest structure for all of them. In a hotel, people can play with their identities. They can live hidden desires. It offers the right mix between anonymity and chance meetings, it allows for solitude and at the same time to escape loneliness. For the hotel's first chronicler, Florence Turner, the Chelsea was a "community of friends ... all living under the same roof with our anxieties, our collisions of mood, our general happiness. It worked; it all worked in that old building which was less a hotel than a pulse. Loneliness was a choice you made" (83).[3] For some residents the hotel was only a home for a certain phase in their lives. For others it turned out to be the only place where they could live the way they wanted to. As I will show in this chapter, the Chelsea combined the contradicting concept of home and hotel successfully in its walls without the necessity to be only one of the two, but always both.

From its conception onwards the Chelsea Hotel has been a place of experimental living. It is a space full of conflicts, tensions and contradictions. As

---

3   Florence Turner was a long-term resident at the hotel in its wildest years in the 1960s and 70s. She belongs to the unsung number of guests who resided at the Chelsea without an artistic vision. Ariel Leve writes of them in his article: "but there are no plaques for the people who still arrive, full of hope and despair, to make the Chelsea their home" (20). She wrote the hotel's first history, *At the Chelsea* (1987), by this she became a recognized part of the hotel's fabric. The book is a mix of historiography and personal memoir. Turner writes about the origins of the hotel and the early developments, focusing on the time that she inhabited the hotel from 1964 till 1975. Her account has been the source of many texts on the Chelsea, amongst others the pseudo-novel *God Hates Us All* by Hank Moody and the crime novel *The Chelsea Girl Murders* (2000) by Sparkle Hayter, who herself was a Chelsea resident for several years.

Ariel Leve writes for *The Sunday Times Magazine*, at the Chelsea "[c]ontradictions play out everywhere. It is a place of permanence and transience" (42). After interviews with the residents he comes to the conclusion: "Some who live there enjoy feeling shut off from the world – it is a place where they can disappear from view. Other enjoy feeling part of a community, describing it as a 'vertical village'"(42). This expresses convincingly the betwixt and between character of the Chelsea and its residents, its liminal nature. Despite the many changes which have happened at the Chelsea over its 130-years history, the hotel has been an essential part of New York's culture and history.

The Biography of the Hotel Chelsea

To understand the hotel's special, experimental nature, a short historical overview is necessary. The Chelsea Hotel, like the Algonquin, was not intended to be a classic transient hotel. While there are several contradicting information on the hotel's history the most convincing story of origin is giving by Sherill Tippins in her book *Inside the Dream Palace* (2013). She traces the roots of the later hotel to the ideas of French utopian philosopher Charles Fourier who was the main source of inspiration for the building's architect, Philipe Hubert. Fourier imagined "a self-contained community" (Tippins, *Inside* 8), where all human types would be living together, mingling freely with each other across social classes. Hubert transformed Fourier's philosophy, which also inspired communal experiments like Brook Farm, into a more pragmatic concept by creating some of the first apartment buildings in New York. These buildings were financed by joint-stock corporations, so-called "Home Club Associations" (18). Due to the combined efforts of the building's residents, people of middle class means could afford a comfortable living while keeping the maintenance costs low. Additionally, these houses provided the inhabitants with an interesting mix: people from different professions and social classes lived together under one roof.

With their buildings, Hubert and his partner Pirsson wanted to provide a counter movement to the raging capitalism and strong social Darwinism of the Gilded Age in New York. The building on 23rd Street, a neighborhood known to harbor "the most tolerant, cosmopolitan, and varied social mix to be found anywhere in the United States" (24), was their alleged masterpiece. Hubert and Pirsson bought the plot in 1883 and finished construction in 1884. At the time of its opening the Chelsea Association Building was one of the highest structures in New York, with eleven and a half stories. It had 80 apartments, the "minimum number of households prescribed by Fourier for an experimental phalanx" (26)[4] of which 50

---

4 Fourier's idea of a phalanx describes a self-contained community housing 1,620 people. He determined 810 different psychological types, one woman and one man of each type

apartments were held by members of the association and 30 were offered to outsiders, to provide a diverse circulation. The owners mostly belonged to the builders' community of New York because they were seen as stable members and useful for the building's maintenance. Their artistry could be seen in the hotel's appearance. The structure was praised for its remarkable Victorian Gothic facade mixed with Queen Anne elements.[5] On its completion, the public appreciated especially the wrought-iron balconies, shown in the image above (Image 7), including symbolical American sunflowers. The interior of the building was done by the company of Pottier and Stymus, under the lead of James Ingersoll. Already back in the 1880s the plan of the owners was that the public rooms of the establishment would allow for conviviality among the residents. The soundproof walls provided for privacy in the apartments. The building was built extremely sturdily, a fact that has been commented upon frequently, and it was advertised as especially fireproof, which has been tested regularly by its inhabitants.[6]

Besides the advantage of the Chelsea being fire-proof, it also "boasted every conceivable modern amenity as well: pressurized steam for cooking, speaking tubes for easy communication, a dumbwaiter for room service, eighteen hundred electric lights in addition to traditional gas jets, and even a telephone in the manager's office for residents' use" (5). It housed New York's first duplex apartment, one of the city's first penthouses, and a roof garden, created as a pleasure park for the residents' private use (6). The press commented that the building was "a fundamental change as New Yorkers became 'more capable of organization, more sociable, more gregarious than before'" (David Goodman Croley qtd. in Tippins, *Inside* 31). When the building was opened in 1884 it was at the heart of the theater district in New York, in a lively and well-to-do neighborhood. It had three dining-rooms for the residents, a billiard parlor, a barber shop, and a café on the street level for the public.

---

should be represented (Kreis). The phalanx is furthermore defined as "a type of work unit ... in which work was distributed on a rational and rotating basis" to provide "elegance and luxury" for all. Charles Fourier was described by Marx as a 'utopian socialist' and inspired several phalanxes in the United States, of which, however, none succeeded. Instead, his idea was more successfully used by Zionists in the institution of the kibbutz (Halsall).

5 Queen Anne style refers to picturesque elements such as bay windows and turrets. They create a slight dissymmetry to counter the strict lines of neoclassicism.

6 A typical comment on the Chelsea is that you could put it on its head and no one would notice, which is not only meant as a comment on its unusual residents but also on the stability of the structure. Eddie Sedgwick, Andy Warhol's muse, set fire to her room in one of her drug flushes. Due to the building's sound structure, no other rooms were affected and Sedgwick was only slightly injured.

Despite the high hopes of the first owners, the Chelsea Association Building did not last long in its original make-up of co-operative living. With the uptown move of the theater district and the results of the boom-and-bust circles in the 1890s, the neighborhood deteriorated and the association went bankrupt. The "vast, palatial apartments" were broken up "and no two rooms are alike" (Leve 43). It was sold and reopened as a hotel in 1905. After the transformation, the Chelsea continued to house many permanent residents, yet as a hotel it now also offered space for transients, a condition which was often perceived as problematic in the accounts of the Chelsea's inhabitants.[7] Yet, this change in use helped to continue the creative circulation of people that Hubert and Pirsson had in mind when they erected the Chelsea in 1883. Since the late nineteenth century, the Chelsea is known as home for artists and writers. It has housed painters and writers in its studios on the tenth floor. During its transitional phase, the Chelsea became a temporary home to the writer William Sidney Porter, better known as O. Henry, who has been called the "archetype of the later Chelsea resident" (Hamill qtd. in Edinger 16). He allegedly checked in under a different name each time he visited the Chelsea. William Dean Howells sublet an apartment at the Chelsea and wrote *The Coast of Bohemia* here in 1893, inspired by the hotel's atmosphere.[8] Actress Sarah Bernhardt lived at the hotel when acting in the nearby theaters, Mark Twain held court when touring in New York, and even Eugene O'Neill had signed himself into the hotel's register.[9]

The building was sold in 1921 to the Irish Knott's Company. This was seen as a dramatic shift in the hotel's history as "[t]he Knotts were to devastate the building and wreak havoc on the Chelsea's beauty" (Turner 6). According to Florence Turner they chopped up the suites to make more space for transients and put in a wall between the lobby and the stairwell. The only apartment, which was left intact, was the one of composer Virgil Thomson, who resided in the hotel during these developments and refused entry to his rooms. The building was kept in general disrepair. This was the time when the poet Edgar Lee Masters lived at the Chelsea and complained about the hotel's deterioration. The hotel changed hands again in

---

7 Only after the hotel closed for transients in 2011, the residents realized that these people also contributed to the special spirit of the Chelsea.

8 In her blog for the *Huffington Post,* Sherill Tippins writes about *The Coast of Bohemia*: "With this novel, the seeds were planted for the Chelsea's reputation as a unique enclave – not only drawing more artists to the Chelsea but eventually leading to the founding of the Museum of Modern Art" (Tippins, "12 Famous Writers Who Lived in The Chelsea Hotel").

9 Besides being a preferred address for writers, the Chelsea had a moment in the limelight in 1912, when it housed several of the survivors of the HMS Titanic. Those who were not wealthy enough to reside at the Waldorf-Astoria, where the investigations of the accident were held, resided at the address on 23rd Street for the time being.

1941, after being repossessed by the Bank for Savings at the end of the Great Depression. The Chelsea was bought by the Chelsea Hotel Corporation led by David Bard and his partners Julius Krauss and Joseph Gross. All three were Hungarian emigrants or of Hungarian descent. The hotel remained in their hands for more than seventy years. During the 1940s the hotel was mostly home to British apprentice seamen and European refugees of the Second World War.

In the 1950s, the hotel became again a hub for artistic residents, such as the poets Dylan Thomas, who died in the hotel after drinking 18 whiskeys straight, and Brendan Behan, who had to leave other hotels, including the Algonquin, due to unruly behavior. In addition, the Beat writers William S. Boroughs and Allen Ginsberg worked and lived at the Chelsea. In 1966, the establishment was named a *Historical Landmark of New York* due to its "special character, special historical and aesthetic interest, and value as part of the development, heritage and cultural characteristics of New York City" (Landmark Commission, "Hotel Chelsea").[10]

During the 1960s the Chelsea became a "Hippie Plaza" (Lingeman) and saw a new wave of artists: musicians of all styles and types. The Chelsea became famous for residents like Bob Dylan, Janis Joplin, Jimi Hendrix, and Patti Smith. The musicians appreciated the sturdy, almost sound-proof walls of the hotel and the tolerant leadership of the Chelsea, which allowed them to delay the payment of their rent and sometimes even lent them money when they were down on their luck. This praxis was also extended to writers and painters. Art-fan Stanley Bard, David Bard sr.'s son and the manager of the Chelsea for fifty years, is said to have accepted finished canvases in lieu of a check for the room rate.[11] During his management, the famous staircase and the lobby featured a diverse mix of artwork, among them paintings by Jackson Pollock and Larry Rivers. This practice was a win-win situation for the hotel and the guests, as it brought attention to both.[12] Next to the painters and musicians, writers continued to frequent the hotel. During the 1960s, Arthur Miller lived at the hotel for seven years, as well as the novelist and screenwriter Arthur C. Clarke, who wrote most parts of *2001 – A Space Odyssey* at

---

10 The commission praised the building as one of the pioneer Victorian Gothic apartment houses and confirmed that the Chelsea "has always been noted as the home of famous writers and artists such as Thomas Wolfe and Dylan Thomas" ("Hotel Chelsea").

11 This claim is disputed. In the texts by residents, one finds several remarks on this practice, yet, other articles on Stanley Bard contradict this. Still, the lobby was always hung with artwork of the hotel's residents which allows the conclusion that there is some truth to this statement.

12 Commenting on his own painting displayed in the lobby, the artist Joe Andoe stated: "Twenty-four hours a day, seven days a week in New York City; that painting is on display. You can see it from a car at 60mph. Thousands and thousands of people have seen it. You can't buy that kind of exposure" (Leve 45).

the Chelsea. All these artists found something in the Chelsea that they needed. For the writer and Chelsea resident Pete Hamill the hotel is the ideal spot for artists because it is "a place where solitude is possible within the framework of a larger community" (Hamill qtd. in Edinger 17). The 1960s and 70s can be seen as the most important phase of the Hotel Chelsea.[13]

The hotel was a famous hotspot during these two decades, not least due to Andy Warhol and his art movie *Chelsea Girls*. Still, the building itself continued to deteriorate. At this time, the rents depended on the financial background of the residents, but only a few of them had a regular income. Accordingly, the hotel did not make a profit. To break even, Bard allegedly had a system of renting rooms to pimps charging twice the normal rate, to compensate for blown checks by artists.[14] By the late 1970s the impression of the public was that the Chelsea was a dump and a dangerous place. Although many artists found in the Chelsea a group of like-minded people, something akin to a family, others suffered in silent or not so silent despair. Yearly, suicides and violent attacks among the hotel's guests were reported. Dr. Scheiber, the resident doctor at the Chelsea Hotel, who offered his service for emergencies, is quoted as saying: "The hotel is no substitute for a family" (qtd. in Lingeman). Still, for many it remained "an oasis of friendliness in a city many find baffling and unfriendly" (Lingeman). The deterioration, in a way, contributed to the Chelsea's cult status. The controversial image of the Chelsea lasted into the 1980s. In this decade the residents celebrated the hotel's one-hundred-years anniversary with exhibitions and happenings, leading to an array of book publications, especially by photographers. During these years, punk rock bands stayed at the hotel as well as movie stars like Ethan Hawke, next to common, down-on-their-luck people who profited from the relatively low rent. This mixture can be seen as a darker version of Charles Fourier's utopian phalanx community.

By the 1990s, the Chelsea's appearance was cleaned up. David Bard jr., Stanley Bard's son, joined his father in management and worked with him on renovating the hotel and improving its reputation.[15] They made changes in the guest structure by

---

13   There is a certain chronology to my case studies, mirroring the development of New York and the city's change in character from glamour metropolis, to center of sophistication, and in the 60s and 70s mecca of radical subcultures and unconventional art.

14   As Florence Turner sees it, by this "[t]he pimps, unknowingly, were patrons of the arts" (17).

15   Besides some redecorations in the lobby, from so-called Austrian-bordello style to black and red vinyl-covered furniture, there is no mentioning of larger renovations at the hotel before the 1990s. According to Bard, this was to keep the place authentic. The rooms of the residents were mostly decorated by themselves, often very creatively and telling about the inhabitants' personal style, which made the Chelsea a fascinating object for photographers.

finally turning out some residents, who were long behind with their rent, and bringing in more financially stable residents. The largest change in the Chelsea since the 1940s came in June 2007 when Stanley Bard was ousted from the hotel by the other members of the board of the Chelsea Association, led by Dr. Marlene Krauss and David Elder, the daughter of Julius Krauss and the grandson of Joseph Gross, the original partners of David Bard sr. Bard and his son were replaced by the management company BD Hotels NY. The hotel was sold in 2011 to real estate developer Joseph Chetrit for $80 million and changed hands again in summer 2013, when it became the property of Ed Scheetz. The Chelsea stopped to take reservations from transient guests in 2011, while long-term tenants remained for the time being. After a momentary stop in the construction work, renovations continue since the fall 2014. Currently the information is that the hotel will reopen as a chic boutique hotel, for a wealthier clientele craving for a bohemian lifestyle. As the hotel resident Hamill stated in the 1980s, the place has seen many phases: "radicals in the 30s, British sailors in the 40s, Beats in the 50s, Hippies in the 60s, decadent poseurs in the 70s, and in the 80s... Nobody knows. At the Chelsea, nobody ever knows" (Hamill in Edinger 19) what comes next.

Stanley Bard – the Keeper of the Chelsea's Atmosphere

The material discussed in the following will present the special hotel experience of the Chelsea Hotel and how it is reflected in the works of its residents and their lives. Over the decades, many Chelseaites expressed the hotel's spirit in their writings as well as in music, photography, film, drama, and visual art. Consciously and unconsciously, they described the significance of the hotel space for their creative process and in how far they began to define themselves as Chelseaites. The Chelsea Hotel seems to have created an even stronger 'social centrality' for its inhabitants than it is the case in the Algonquin Hotel.[16]

To understand the *genius loci* of the Chelsea, its almost mythical creative power, a brief analysis of the relationship between hotel manager Stanley Bard and the hotel is necessary. All accounts of guests agree that he was instrumental in making the unique atmosphere of the place. Hotelkeepers are a crucial element in the creation of the specific space of a hotel, its atmosphere and its function as a platform for communities. Unlike Frank Case, Bard did not bring his hotel experience to paper, despite repeated comments that he would do so. Yet, there are

---

16 This might be the case because this 'social centrality' is most pronounced in places that are used by groups which are at the margin of the society (Hetherington 35). The Chelsea has housed radicals, wanna-be artists, down-and-out people, junkies, and those who need the hotel's contradictory atmosphere at the heart of a megacity. They can be considered to be people on the margin of society.

a number of interviews by Stanley Bard as well as statements by residents that give an insight into his relationship with the hotel. This short excursion shall function as a basis for the analysis of the life accounts that will follow. Bard's relationship with the Chelsea is a prime example of place-identity: "There is a collective sentiment that Stanley Bard is the Chelsea Hotel" (Leve 44).[17]

When the Chelsea was turned into a hotel in 1905 it was a makeshift move. Transients were accepted because they brought in the much needed revenue, but the percentage of residents still outweighed them. The Chelsea's large and bright duplex studios, together with the penthouse suites on top of the building, attracted the first artists to the hotel. They proved to be ideal for painters, composers, and film makers. During the early years, the hotel's proprietors did not take a special interest in advertising for this clientele. That changed with the purchase of the hotel by David Bard and his partners in 1941. Bard sr. favored an artistic customer base, he simplified the paying of rents and showed a certain generosity in his treatment of them. This behavior intensified when David's son, Stanley Bard, took over the hotel's management. While there are some parallels between the close host/hotel connection of Frank Case and Stanley Bard, their attitudes to their respective establishment differs.

Stanley Bard became familiar with the hotel as a school child, when his father was its manager. Originally, Bard did not wish to follow in the footsteps of his father. Instead, he got a degree in the arts and accounting from the New York University after a stint at the military. Yet, his father decided to train him for the hotel and Stanley remained working there long enough to learn to appreciate its special atmosphere and clientele. He is quoted saying:

My father ... had a great deal of interest in human beings. He loved to sit and talk with all the characters that lived here over the years. He used to say to me that running the Chelsea was a twenty-four hour a day job. I used to laugh at him and promised myself that when my turn came, I'd do things differently. And here I am! Day in, day out, like him. ... I used to live here when I was a young man. I had a small apartment in the building but when I got married I realized that I couldn't combine being a family man with living at the Chelsea. (Bard qtd. in Ambrose 162)

His son, David Bard, adds about his father's ties to the hotel: "This place is his alter ego. It's in his blood, it's in his genes" (Leve 44). With David Bard jr. taking over the management duties from his father in 1995, there were three generations of Bards closely connected to the hotel, shaping the hotel with their particular vision.

---

17 The comment mirrors the one we have already seen in the Algonquin Hotel. Here, Frank Case was also seen as being one with his hotel. As Relph described it, this is an example of place-identity.

Accordingly, the Chelsea Hotel "is the story of one family, a dynasty now, three generations in an increasingly homogenous, multinational, corporate world who, through passion, a sense of history, and long hours, remain resolutely local, personal, and, for better or worse, unique" (Vowell 87).

Of the three generations managing the hotel, the largest contribution to the artistic atmosphere of the hotel came from Stanley Bard. When he took over the management of the hotel after his father's death in the 1960s, Stanley expanded his artist-friendly policy. While turning a profit was significant, according to Lough: "producing art and nurturing artists became the hotel's raison d'etre" (Lough 147). Bard's challenge was to achieve a balance between the different kinds of guests he checked into the hotel. He also needed to produce a profit for the board of the Chelsea Association, while offering struggling artists a place of refuge that they would not be able to afford without external support. About his vision, Bard states: "I don't ever want the Chelsea to turn into a normal place just in business to make money. ... I want to keep the atmosphere kooky but nice, eccentric but beautiful" (Dowd). The poet and longtime resident Rene Ricard confirms Bard's success in fulfilling this vision by stating: "Stanley Bard believes in an idea of the Chelsea Hotel and he is still creating this culture in this hotel and, the pressures of the marketplace notwithstanding, he is still trying to find room for a poet in this building. Poetry isn't just the bronze plaques on the facade for Stanley" (Leve 49). Over the years the hotelman transformed the Chelsea into an eccentric, yet most productive, artists' colony (Lough 145).[18]

These comments show that the Chelsea is to a large degree Bard's creation. The artistic atmosphere of the hotel and its peculiar creative space is seen as the achievement of one man. As Löw states, atmosphere arises from the spatial ordering as well as from acts of synthesis (44). The Chelsea certainly has been a considerate spatial effort from its conception as a utopian community experiment to its metamorphosis into a semi-transient/semi-residential hotel that attracts mostly people from the arts. Through all this, the Hotel Chelsea still remained a part of the network of New York hotels, a unique link in the hotel system of the city: "'It might not be the Waldorf or the Plaza, but it's my Waldorf, my Plaza'" (Bard qtd. in Leve 49). Ariel Leve writes in his article that the way Stanley Bard speaks about the hotel reminds him of a father talking about his child (49).[19] Bard had a strong

---

18 Some are even calling the Chelsea Hotel "MacDowell Colony South" (Lingeman), referring to the famous writers' colony in New Hampshire.

19 History seems to repeat itself, since Bard also called the Chelsea "his father's [David] 'second child'" (Bard qtd. in Vowell 87). According to Sarah Vowell who interviewed Stanley Bard during a stay at the hotel, he was often jealous of his "architectural sibling" (87) and suffered a form of orphanhood. Still, Vowell adds, Stanley Bard repeated the same behavior in his life, despite having three children.

feeling of responsibility for his 'tenants,' a relationship which was uncommonly close between this hotel manager and his guests: "I'm here to help them and protect them as much as I can – but I'm not their father. They have to carry their weight in society" (Leve 44).

Another important aspect is Bard's awareness of the uniqueness of the Chelsea's own character, which inspired so much creation of art. The manager believes in the material agency of the walls of the Chelsea Hotel: "There's not another building in the world that caters to this many creative people. ... There is something mystique within these walls that helps people produce art" (Bard qtd. in Dowd). He expands this statement in another interview, stating: "Ethan [Hawke] said there was something in this building that's unexplainable. Things happen within these walls. ... People were talking to the walls as a sounding board and the walls were talking back" (Bard qtd. in Morehouse 20). In these quotes the hotel gets the aura of a mystical place. It almost reminds the reader of the behavior seen in religious places such as the wall of mourning in Jerusalem, where people also use the physical walls of the former temple as the symbolic representative for a transcendental presence. According to Bard, art is created at the Chelsea hotel in such an abundant variety because "[t]his place affords that. There is a happy spirit. There's nothing more important to a creative person than to be in a good place, a happy place, a creative space" (Bard qtd. In Leve 49). In Morehouse's book *Life at the Top*, Bard states that he and his wife believe that places have a heart and a soul (20). This is the reason why he "keeps the mystery intact" (Matteoli 21) at the Chelsea. The quotes show that Bard sees the Chelsea Hotel and its peculiar space as being significant for his life, the lives of his guests, and for the creation of art by the residents. Even more than in the hotels discussed so far, the residents and the manager of the hotel are acutely aware of the agency of the hotel which actively influences them.

Stanley Bard is the human face of the hotel, "without whom this bizarre and wonderful institution would never have been possible" (Hamilton 320).[20] In an

---

20 Besides having "the inspirational talents of a coach, the patience of a babysitter, and the tact of a diplomat" Bard also needed to transform himself "into the hectoring debt collector, a role he performed with aplomb" (Lough 11). By less successful guests, Bard's personality has been described as fluctuating between benevolence and hard-hearted business greed, a Dr. Jekyll and Mr Hyde type of character (150). Bard's way of running the hotel is described by some as "steel fist in velvet glove" (147). As he was for a long time the only person who decides on new tenants, Bard wielded an enormous power concerning the composition of guests at his hotel. All statements and life narratives are consistent on the fact that the appointment with Bard was a decisive moment in their life at the Chelsea and all of them felt that he only accepted them because of some special creative quality they displayed. Some writers state that getting

article for *Vanity Fair*, resident and acclaimed costume designer William Ivey Long describes the manager's understanding of his clientele:

I'm very sentimental about it. Stanley Bard and the Chelsea Hotel saved my life. He certainly saved my artistic life. Stanley accepted the Bohemian biorhythm. This biorhythm is endangered. Stanley was determined that he wasn't going to be the one to put the lid on anyone's career. The people who could pay, did pay. The rich Italian tourists paid. The even richer rock-and-roll people paid. The people who couldn't, he supported them. I had some depressive moments there. But Stanley was one of the few people in New York saying, 'You can do it.' His belief in talented people will be his legacy. (Long qtd. in Rich)

In the end, Bard's ousting from the hotel by the board of the hotel was allegedly due to his unprofitable way of managing the hotel. For years, the occupancy rate of the hotel was said to have been between 65% and 80%, which for the location is considerably low, with an equally low return rate. Additionally, large renovation work was needed, even though Bard already had some work done at the hotel in the 1990s. Many guests believe that the reason for selling the hotel in 2011 was mostly about making money for the corporation.

After he was barred from the hotel, Stanley Bard started a quite aggressive campaign to return to his former management position with the help of the remaining Chelsea inhabitants. He is widely present in newspaper articles, websites, and video blogs. There, he continues to discuss his vision for the hotel, his hurt feelings after the ousting, and his criticism concerning the new developments at the Chelsea after its sale. Bard maintains that his vision for the Chelsea Hotel was of greater importance than the revenue that the hotel business brought. His summary of his time at the Chelsea resembles very much what Fourier had formulated in the early nineteenth century and what Hubert tried to create of 23nd Street:

I created something over a lifetime that I thought was beautiful and worth preserving, and so respected ... by everyone. I felt it would be a shame to have that disturbed in any way. I never wanted the Chelsea to be a conformist community. It's uncomfortable to me, to say the least. I have to protect the integrity, the people ... and I feel these are my friends, and they're worth protecting, and that's the beautiful part of it. ... It took me one lifetime to create that, I hope I live another lifetime to see that it's preserved. (qtd. in Carlson)[21]

---

into the Chelsea was seen as being more difficult than entering an Ivy League College (Hamilton 192).

21 As the reader might have noticed, in contrast to the Waldorf, where guests are preferably called patrons, and the Algonquin, where Case most often uses the term guests, people residing at the Chelsea are most often described as tenants, as we can see in this quote by Bard. Since 1905, the Chelsea was a hotel catering to both transients and residents. Yet,

Considering the abundant material that can be found on Stanley Bard and his own comments on the Chelsea Hotel, an ambiguous picture emerges. He is highly praised by many of his former residents and artist friends, and celebrated in articles as the last fair landlord of New York, protecting a vanishing race of liberal artists who fight against gentrification and the cult of sameness. Yet, he is also described as hard, unpredictable, easily irritable, unfair, and arrogant. Still, it is impossible to not take his achievements into consideration: Making the hotel a unique living environment in the heart of Manhattan. The Chelsea has inspired a great number of artists and visitors, and can be seen as forerunner of a current movement in hotels to become deliberately places for artists and creation (Volland 250f). New York's society and culture was influenced by the institution, which Stanley Bard created with the Chelsea Hotel. Edgar Lee Masters, whose hotel experience will be analyzed next, lived at the Chelsea before Bard's management. This explains why his experience there was caught between the tension of liberating atmosphere and lack of comfort and security.

3.1 THE HOTEL AS THE ARTIST'S REFUGE

Edgar Lee Masters, born in Kansas in 1868, grew up in a small town in Illinois in an atmosphere that he found oppressive and un-stimulating. Continuously writing throughout his career as lawyer, he had his breakthrough with a collection of poems, *Spoon River Anthology* (1915), a demystification of small town life in America. Ezra Pound said of Masters: "at last, America has discovered a poet" (qtd. in Primeau). For decades the collection was the bestselling book of American poems. Although Masters was already of an advanced age at his breakthrough, he decided then to concentrate on writing full time. He could never repeat the triumph of the *Spoon River Anthology*, yet he produced numerous poems, biographies, and dramas to moderate critical acclaim. To concentrate more on his work, Masters moved to New York, taking residence at the Chelsea Hotel in spring 1930, just when the Depression hit hard (Russell 274). In contrast to the narrow-mindedness of his Midwestern home, the city and the hotel allowed Masters to live a life free from conventions. Over the years, it became for him a refuge artistically as well as emotionally, even though he was also quite critical of the place.

There are contradicting accounts on Masters' relationship with the Chelsea. In some texts, he harshly criticizes the run-down situation of the hotel, lamenting

---

despite this circumstance, most long-term residents treat the Chelsea like a community housing project and do not use the more typical hotel jargon when writing about it. This choice of language is noteworthy as it tells us about the way people position themselves in relation to the Chelsea and how they rate their experience there.

about the noise, dirt, and confusion of New York and his lack of funds which would allow him to live in a better place (Swenson qtd. in Edinger 18). In others texts, he praises the creative atmosphere of the Chelsea, even recommending it as a workshop for writers such as Thomas Wolfe (Tippins, *Inside* 59; Russell 328). It is known that his second wife Ellen found the hotel and its infestation with vermin disgusting and moved out, leaving Master alone in the hotel to focus on his creative work. In 1936, the poet fell in love with Alice Davis, a fellow hotel resident, whom he employed to type his papers. Their correspondence is now part of the Manuscript and Archive Division of the New York Public Library. The papers reveal that the two met in the lobby of the hotel and lived 'together' in the two rooms they occupied in the hotel, Masters on the second floor, Davis on the tenth. The age difference between the two was pronounced (Russell 304f). This caused critical remarks by friends.[22] Still, Masters dedicated many of his poems to Alice, sometimes hidden behind the pseudonym 'Anita.'

The relationship between Davis and Masters at the hotel is documented in the letters of Masters which are held by the New York Public Library. They also contain information about Masters's difficult affiliation with and contradicting emotions toward the Chelsea. In the poem "To Miss A.D."[23] (no date given, presumably 1936) Masters writes: " I saw you several times in the lobby,/ And you gave me a lift./... The next time I pass you in the lobby/ If you feel friendly just smile/ I might come up to you and talk/ For a little while." Meeting her in the lobby is an act of fate for Masters: "So you and I here to day – both from Kansas, trailing a long and circuitous way to this hotel and to this union of our live" (Letter to Davis, 15 April, 1936). While he is aware of the shortcomings of the hotel, he is still grateful that it brought the two lovers together: "And I say now, call not those rooms of yours shabby – they are holy. In them we found each other, and went from hearty, happy, Dionysiac hours to hours of admiration and mystical ecstasy. In the entrance room I came one morning and confessed to you that I loved you, and I have never said that to you before" (Letter to Davis, 26 March, 1937). For him, the function of a hotel as meeting place, its open character enabling the mingling of strangers, made the love affair with Davis possible in the first place.

Masters also refers to the hotel outside his relationship with Alice, commenting on his regular life there. It is clear that the hotel occupies his mind repeatedly. The Chelsea is a place he strongly reacts to (Letter to Davis, 24 November, 1937). Masters writes Davis as a response to her question about the hotel: "I have no news of this hotel, only to say that some of the literati are drunk every time I see them,

---

22 The poet remained married to his second wife until he died.
23 The poems and letters by Masters, mentioned in this part, belong to the collection of the Masters-Davis Papers in the Manuscripts and Archives Division of the New York Public Library, donated by Alice Davis in 1978. I have researched them in spring and fall 2013.

and naturally incapacitated for deep thought, normally so natural to them" (Letter to Davis, 1 December, 1937). This is an interesting remark as it shows, as will also be seen in his poem "The Hotel Chelsea," that Masters is very aware of the artistic scene existing at the hotel, yet also of the destabilizing character the place seems to have on its inhabitants. In a poem written at the end of his time at the Chelsea, when he was already very sick, Masters paints an impressive image of the hotel and its role for the surrounding city: "Imprisoned in this dark hotel/ Like a lone spider in a well/ I am caught as in a spell/ Seemingly forever …" (19 June, 1943). "Imprisoned in this dark hotel" seems to refer more to a hotel's structural similarity to a prison than to the liberating character, which it had for Master when he first moved in. While this negative impression at the end of Masters's stay at the hotel might have more to do with his deteriorating health, it nevertheless gives the reader a glimpse of the less hopeful and darker side of the institution Chelsea Hotel.

Masters had to move out of the hotel in 1943, after twelve years of residence, due to a severe illness, and returned to his wife Ellen, who took care of him. With the move he cut all ties with his former Chelsea acquaintances. Davis continued to live at the Chelsea into the 1960s and is said to have been very disappointed that the hotel did not commemorate Masters's time at the hotel with a plaque, as it has been done for other writers like Dylan Thomas, Brendan Behan and Arthur C. Clarke (Turner 11). Especially, since with his poem "The Hotel Chelsea"[24] Masters is until today connected to the hotel and his lines are repeatedly reprinted, quoted and alluded to in texts about the Chelsea.[25] The poem contains several interesting statements about the hotel's past and reputation, and tells us how Masters felt about the place as I will analyze in the following.

Masters wrote the poem at a time when the hotel was in dire financial troubles because of the Great Depression as well as due to mismanagement.[26] It was a time of great insecurity for the residents. The poet reacts to this at the poem starts with: "Anita! Soon this Chelsea Hotel / Will vanish before the city's merchant greed" (l. 1-2). His predictions of the hotel's demolition turned out to be wrong, yet the poem accurately shows that the Chelsea was at an important point in its existence, changing ownership and with that facing new, unknown developments. Masters paints a very detailed picture of the hotel in his poem. He describes the elegant interior, part of a better time in the history of the Chelsea: "Then who will know /

---

24 The date of the poem is unknown, yet it is clear that it has to fall in the time span between 1935, when Masters met Davis and his departure in 1942, as it is part of the writings he undertook there. I have used here the version of the poem as printed in Turner 10f.

25 For example, Edinger, Turner, Hamilton, Tippins, and several blogs and webpages about the Hotel Chelsea quote Masters.

26 This allows the assumption that it was written in the years 1938 to 1940 when the sale of the hotel was immediate but not yet finalized.

About its ancient grandeur, marble stairs, / Its paintings, onyx-mantels, courts, the heirs / Of a time now long ago?" (l. 5-8). The Chelsea poet also refers to the well-known guests that resided in the Chelsea during its first fifty years. Mark Twain is mentioned as a representative for all famous artists who made the hotel their home, their workshop and their meeting place: "Who will then know that Mark Twain used to stroll / In the gorgeous dining-room …" (l. 9-10). These guests and residents made up "its soul" (l. 12).

The most often quoted stanza of the poem is

What loves were lived here, what despairs endured,
What children born here, and what mourners went
Out of its doors, what peace and what lament
These rooms knew, long obscured (l. 17-20)

In these lines, Masters seems to have caught the essence of the *genius loci* of the hotel and its function as agent and container for all human feelings and activities. As a hotel, the Chelsea is a place where the broad range of human existence is displayed and where human society is represented in a condensed way. The hotel rooms of the Chelsea have seen it all. They are anthropomorphized as spectators and agents, interacting with their human inhabitants. Masters speaks in these lines for all generations of artists living at the Chelsea.

One of the strongest points the poet makes about the Hotel Chelsea is that to him it is storage for memory, a stone monument for the artistic people who lived in its walls. Master writes: "Who will remember me when wrecking shears / Clip like a leaf this room of troubled aims" (l. 27-28). Masters sees the sturdy walls of the Chelsea as a preserver of his legacy. When they are gone, he fears his memory will be lost to oblivion. The poet knows that, despite its strong structure, the Chelsea Hotel is not safe from "the culture of demolition" (Koolhaas 138) that continuously changes the face of New York. The greed for making money from its high real estate value dooms the hotel to this fate of demolition. Even though Masters understands that this is how the city and its society works, he still laments these circumstances: "There will not be a seat for any ghost / No room left for a musing ghost to smile" (l. 33-34).

Masters is acutely aware of space in his poem. He uses the concept space both on a metaphorical level and on a physical level. He is aware of the importance of spaces and places for humans; that they have to live in a place, bodily, and need mental space for creativity and memory. Both spaces are in danger if the Chelsea is torn down. This is the reason why he writes of the Chelsea Hotel in his poem, to give it another space of existence, being remembered in his text. It is interesting that in the second but last stanza Masters confesses that he "sought for peace [in the Chelsea] and found it not" (l. 56). He deliberately selected this place, the Hotel

Chelsea, to be free from outside influences, free from his boring and conventional life, free for his creative work. Yet, considering the modest success of his writings during this phase, Masters did not achieve this peace due to the financial pressure that he felt in his old age, and lacking the support which later poets had in Bard.

As the poem "The Hotel Chelsea" shows, Masters's relationship with the hotel is very complex. In his essay on the Chelsea Hotel, Pete Hamill states that in Masters's texts, "there is a sense, in some of the poetry he wrote about the Chelsea, that the hotel had served him as the true convalescent home of his art and his bruised spirit" (qtd. in Edinger 18). The reason for the poem's popularity, in my opinion, lies in the fact that it seems to catch so successfully the atmosphere of the Chelsea, this elusive relationship between the artist and his surrounding space. It presents the artist's mood as well as the hotel's character convincingly.

The poem "The Hotel Chelsea" is a rich source for understanding the hotel experience at the Chelsea. By the 1930s, the hotel had the reputation of a refuge for artists, offering them space as workshops and for living. As described in the hotel's biography, its bohemian spirit of place is even older than that. Before Bard's arrival, Edgar Lee Masters experienced the Chelsea Hotel as an artistic refuge and unconventional home. While he arrived at a downtime of the Chelsea, Masters still perceived the spirit of place that attracted Howells and Twain to the hotel. The Chelsea has moved through several cycles of success and crisis. Despite all changes in the hotel and in its surrounding area, the words of Masters still ring true for Chelseaites, expressing most fittingly what the structure on 23rd Street means to them. The hotel was for Masters a "convalescent home" for the creative spirit. The most active phase of the hotel, however, was yet to come.

Arthur Miller's Time of Recovering at the Chelsea

Writers were not as defining a group of guests at the Chelsea as they were at the Algonquin. Still, they created a great number of texts that made the hotel's atmosphere vivid for outsiders.[27] This is the case in Arthur Miller's recollections of his time at the Chelsea. Miller moved into the hotel in 1960 and remained there for

---

27 The Chelsea Hotel was also famous for musicians, photographers, filmmakers, artists, and weirdos. A list of famous writers includes: William Dean Howells, O. Henry, Mark Twain, Tennessee Williams, Joseph O'Neill, Edgar Lee Masters, Thomas Wolfe, Dylan Thomas, Brendan Behan, the Beat Poets Jack Kerouac, Allen Ginsberg, William S. Burroughs, and Herbert Huncke. The Beat Poets motto "to make the private public" seems to fit the hotel surrounding extraordinarily well and explains why the specific environment of a hotel seemed so attractive to writers.

more than eight years.[28] The playwright needed a well-hidden, inconspicuous shelter after the break-up of his marriage with Marilyn Monroe. The Plaza Hotel being to public, he got the recommendation from writer Mary McCarthy to take a room at the Chelsea, which was not yet as famous as it would become in the midsixties. Instead, it was informal and decent enough to not attract too much attention.[29] For Miller's friends, his move to the Chelsea was seen as a sign of social decline and they reacted almost shocked at the mentioning of his address. Yet, Miller writes in his memoir *Timebends* (1987): "I felt at home there almost at once. Relaxing in the Chelsea charm, its unique air of uncontrollable decay..." (513). As with Masters, the hotel became his convalescent home, and allowed him to let down his guard. Miller writes about his time at the Chelsea in his autobiography *Timebends* and dedicates an essay to "The Chelsea Affect" ("TCA") in 2002, only a few years before his death. Both texts impressively catch his living experience at the Chelsea.

The Chelsea Hotel in the 1960s was an energetic place at the heart of New York, and here Miller witnessed all the changes of this era front row: "The Chelsea in the Sixties seemed to combine two atmospheres: a scary and optimistic chaos which predicted the hip future, and at the same time the feel of a massive, oldfashioned, sheltering family. That at least was the myth one nurtured in one's mind, but like all myths it did not altogether stand inspection" (Miller, "TCA" 242). Again, the concept of atmosphere is important, especially at the Chelsea, because it seems to describe best the mutual dynamic between the physical structure and its inhabitants. Although life at the hotel was vibrant and chaotic, Miller also highlights its sheltering quality, the security it projects. Another Chelsea quality, which Miller highly appreciates, is that, "whatever else it was, [the Chelsea] was a house of infinite toleration. This was the Bards' genius, I thought, to have achieved an operating chaos which at the same time could be home to people who were not crazy" (243). Miller confesses that he never fully understood David Bard and later his son Stanley in the way they acted proudly in their hotel, yet, he recognizes the Chelsea's atmosphere as their lives' achievement.[30] At the same time he is critical

---

28 Miller's check-out date is nowhere precisely stated, and historians and journalists give different timespans in their texts. From Miller's own writings it is clear that he stayed there at least until 1968.
29 Being "the closest thing in America to a European hotel" (Miller, *Timebends* 512), it was also the preferred New York home of his future wife Inge Morath.
30 Stanley Bard took over the management after his father's death in 1964, during Miller's time at the Chelsea. Miller writes: "It was not, one thought, that Stanley cultivated weird people, potheaded layabouts, and some extraordinary as well as morbidly futile artistic types, but simply that he seemed to think these dreamers were normal; it was the regular people who made him uneasy" ("TCA" 242).

of the influence the place has on the Bard family. After being shown around by Stanley forty years after his first visit to the place in the 1950s, he writes: "Was this clan fated to go on forever reproducing itself and repeating the same things? A hundred years from now would a Bard be showing the brand new faucets to some hapless possible tenant?" (249). Time and space seem to work differently at the Chelsea. Other writers have also commented on the uncommon timelessness at the Chelsea Hotel (Hamill qtd. in Leve 9). That the hotel has been in the hands of the same family, whose names even repeat themselves, increases this effect.

From Arthur Miller's texts the reader gets the impression that the hotel is a place of stark conflicts and paradoxical conditions. The Chelsea's aura does not allow for simple experiences. In Miller's writings the hotel comes alive as a place harboring an almost impossible combination of liberty and self-destruction, of tolerance and aggression, of peace of mind and constant struggle. For the playwright, the hotel meant the acceptance of its shabbiness and lack of 'classic' hotel services, but that "it was certainly more *gemütlich* than living in a real hotel" ("TCA" 239). The question if this really is a hotel in the American sense is discussed several times in his writing. He claims: "It [The Chelsea] was not part of America, had no vacuum cleaners, no rules, no taste, no shame" (*Timebends* 513). The lack of cleanliness bothered him, yet he seems to have been attracted by the other elements, the lack of rules, taste, and shame: "The surreal had its citadel in the Chelsea long before its spirit was lifted by the Vietnam War into radical protest" (*Timebends* 513). And while he calls the hotel on 23rd Street the world's "compost bin" he adds in the same sentence: "whose nutrients, however, were far from wasted on the resident creative types" (*Timebends* 513). This metaphor, the Chelsea as a compost bin is a quite unusual metaphor, yet, it seems to be a very precise way of describing the impression many New Yorkers had of the hotel. At the same time, it neatly states also the nurturing effect it has on its residents.[31] While the hotel could be disgusting with its dirt and weird inhabitants, it was also highly attractive for those who needed this kind of unconventional shelter: "The Chelsea, with all its irritants – the age-old dust in its drapes and carpets, the rusting pipes, the leaking refrigerator, the air-conditioner in which you had to keep pouring pitchers of water – was an impromptu, healing ruin" (*Timebends* 513f).

---

31 Arthur Miller befriended other Chelsea residents such as George Kleinsinger, who created a jungle in his apartment on the top, complete with snakes, monkeys, and 12ft tall trees. Miller accepted this kind of behavior as being completely in tune with the Chelsea environment. However, he harshly criticizes the destruction the Chelsea's spirit caused with friends such as Dylan Thomas and Brendan Behan. Both died shortly after taking up residence at the hotel. Commenting these sad circumstances, Miller states: "The Chelsea's walls could tell a lot about the self-loathing of talented people" ("TCA" 245).

Writing the texts years after his time at the Chelsea, Arthur Miller reflects that, despite the quiet of the apartments and the feeling of isolation, he could never really concentrate there. This, however, seems to belie his considerable output of three plays, which he wrote during his stay: After The Fall (1964), Incident at Vichy (1964), and The Prize (1968). Yet, it is one reason why he does not consider moving back to the hotel after living there for almost a decade. Another reason were Arthur Miller's two children with Inge Morath, who were born at the Chelsea. At the end of the decade, Miller and Morath decided that the Chelsea was not an acceptable childhood home and they moved out.

In his final statement of "The Chelsea Affect," Miller summarizes his hotel experience:

With all my misgivings about the Chelsea, I can never enter it without a certain quickening of my heartbeat. There is an indescribably homelike atmosphere which at the same time lacks a certain credibility. ... As in dreams things are out front that are concealed in other hotels, like the wooden bins in the corridors in which the garbage pails are kept, and for some unknowable reason this sort of candour seems so right that you smile whenever you pass the bins. It may simply be that nobody is urgently concerned about what it happening because nobody quite knows what is happening, or maybe there is a kind of freedom or severe disconnect with plain reality, or, as the saying goes, a sense that the inmates have long since taken over the asylum, which can be irritating but perhaps not altogether a bad thing, at least in a spiritual sense. ("TCA" 253)

The Chelsea Hotel is a place between dreams and reality for Miller, always fluctuating between these two conditions, always remaining liminal, public and private, in-between a real hotel, an asylum, and an artists' colony. The Chelsea of Arthur Miller's description explodes the 'classic' American hotel, it is not modern, representative, or safe in the usual sense. Yet, its atmosphere and its mix of people is liberating which is important to its artistic clientele.

Joseph O'Neill and The Chelsea Hotel as Fictional Refuge

The colorful mix of people also attracted writer Joseph O'Neill and his family to the Chelsea Hotel. I will examine his novel *Netherland* (2008) as the last example of the Chelsea's function as a place of refuge. O'Neill used his experience of living at the hotel with his family during the 1990s and early 2000s in the novel. The book presents the hotel's most current image. *Netherland* is a highly acclaimed post-9/11 novel that won the 2009 PEN/Faulkner Award for Fiction. It focuses on the immediate time after the attacks on the World Trade Center, with flashbacks into the protagonist's youth. In the novel, Dutch immigrant Hans van den Broek narrates the disintegration that happened to his family after the attacks in 2001. He finds a temporary refuge from reality in the Chelsea Hotel and in his obsession with Cricket. The sport brings him into contact with Jamaican Chuck Ramkissoon, a Jay Gatsby-like figure, who changes his view of New York and American life, and challenges his assumptions that America is a place of utopian possibilities where everything is still possible (Synder 465). In the end, Hans leaves the Chelsea and returns to London and his family, leaving behind his illusions and idealism. Before I analyze the hotel's depiction in the novel, I will discuss the real hotel experience of O'Neill and his wife, *Vogue* journalist Sally Singer, as presented in interviews and letters.

The O'Neill family has an intense relationship with the hotel. The reason for this is that they once moved out of the hotel to live with their family in a 'normal surrounding' in Brooklyn and then moved back into the Chelsea because they could not live without it. They preferred living in this refuge for unconventional people to living in a 'normal' home. This place change triggered a special awareness for the unique spatial nature of the hotel. In an article about the Chelsea in 2007, Sally Singer, O'Neill's wife, explains the reasons for their moves. Singer states that they wanted to provide their children with an environment more fit for small children. However, outside of the hotel they were miserable: "We would 'ship out' our friends from the hotel – get a car service to bring them to Brooklyn. Our babysitters – it was a continuation of the community" (Singer in Leve 46). The family returned after only 18 months. Sally Singer states about their hotel life:

It surprised me how attached I am and how much it matters to me to live here. It's a village that I feel at home in. I like that there are transient people coming in every night. The fact that it is a hotel is key to its character. There is a continual stream of people to look at. I don't want to live in my own closed-off space. People just drop by. They knock on your door. I want to open my door and let the world in and let my kids out. You have to want to live in the *shtetl*. That's in my DNA. (Singer in Leve 49)

Her statement about her family's hotel life at the Chelsea is probably one of the most telling descriptions of the Chelsea hotel experience. While many of the residents indeed treat the hotel more as an unusual apartment building with sometimes maid service, Singer directly considers the issue of the Chelsea being a hotel. She even explains that the structure of a hotel is what makes the place special for her.[32] Singer clearly cherishes the hotel experience. She appreciates the special

---

32 Only after the new management stopped to take reservations from transients in 2011, some of the other residents started to realize that while they were often irritated by the short-term guests and their touristy behavior, this element of chance meetings and the constant possibility for coming into contact with total strangers was an integral part of the atmosphere at the Hotel Chelsea.

community feeling that developed in the Chelsea and how it benefited their family life. It is also interesting how she describes the dynamic between the private and public spaces of the hotel. Singer perceives both separately, but she enjoys the merging of the two conditions, the liminal feeling that she gets at the hotel. Here, she is not closed-off in her hotel room but continues to be part of the larger, osmotic hotel culture and her children can 'play outside' while still remaining in the security of a building. Finally, it is also the circumstance of being at the heart of New York City that made the Chelsea so special for her and her family. Being at the Chelsea "defines my existence in New York probably more than any other element. It's a grounding place. It's the truth of my life" (Vogel in Leve 49). Like few other statements by hotel guests, Singer's comment depicts the reciprocity between place and person, and the strong feeling of place identity it creates. Joseph O'Neill's attitude toward the Chelsea complements his wife's. He, too, considers the atmosphere of the hotel as inviting for families.[33] The only drawback for O'Neill is that "I (Joe) am not normally capable of writing a word in the Chelsea Hotel, and have to flee it … . The hotel is a place of children and children and writing don't mix" (O'Neill in Troeller 54).[34] The comments of Singer and O'Neill show that their time at the Chelsea Hotel is of great importance for their family. It is a source of inspiration and happiness, even if O'Neill's creative work has to happen outside the hotel.

Reading the novel *Netherland*, the Chelsea's impact on O'Neill's imagination and writing is apparent. It influences his way of seeing New York City. While

---

33 While it is Sally Singer who describes her impression of the Chelsea here, it is known that her husband Joseph O'Neill feels similar about the place. In Troeller's photography book Joseph O'Neill writes in his love letter to the hotel: "Stanley's intuitive, haphazardly rapacious system of letting seems to work because the residents, a mix of creative types, no-hopers, secretive millionaires cause that the Hotel comes as close to Utopia as any singly building with terrible plumbing and soaring rents can. It's a pleasingly insular place. ... Where else could our sons Malachy, Pascal and Oscar (Chelsea Hotel babies) babble with Arthur Miller, play the piano with Bruce Livingston and party with Suzanne Bartsch" (O'Neill in Troeller 54). There were indeed a number of children growing up at the Chelsea over the years. In 2013, an article on actress Gaby Hoffmann in *The New York Times* states that her mother, Warhol muse Viva, co-authored a yet unpublished book, entitled "Gaby at the Chelsea," about her daughter's growing up at the Chelsea Hotel (Brodesser-Akner).

34 Considering the hotel's reputation as a place of creativity, it is indeed curious that, while the hotel fulfils and exceeds all other expectations for O'Neill, it fails him in the one sector for which it is famous: enabling the creation of art. However, the main reason might be the proximity to his young children, which even in the circumstances of a 'normal' private home is seen as a challenge for the concentration of the parents.

Netherland is not an autobiographical novel, it might be safe to assume that O'Neill's decision of placing the main protagonist in this hotel is founded in his own experience. In the *Chicago Tribune* review of the book, Art Winslow writes:

In *Netherland*, Hans and his wife move into the Chelsea Hotel, the legendary bohemian refuge on West 23rd street ... . With its cramped space and community of exiles and eccentrics, the hotel acts as a kind of idealised microcosm of Manhattan, an island unto itself. In reality, O'Neill also lives in the hotel with his wife, Sally Singer, ... and their three young boys. (Winslow)

Scholars have discussed the importance of the book as a post-9/11 or a postcolonial novel and have come up with very mixed reviews of what Joseph O'Neill achieved or failed to do on both counts. The novel is an interesting reanimation of Fitzgerald's *The Great Gatsby*. The author meant it to be a "farewell" to this great American novel because for O'Neill America is no longer the place where Gatsbies and their belief in never-ending possibilities can exist (Snyder 465). My focus here lies less on those two great issues mentioned above, but I am more interested in the use and function of the hotel space and the depiction of the Chelsea in the novel.

I agree with Andrew Anthony of the *Observer*, who wrote that, "if *Netherland* has a point it's that our surroundings shape who we are and how we feel. And the more detached we are from our environment, the more disengaged we become from ourselves" (Anthony). *Netherland* is a text of dislocation and very much concerned with space. One essential place in the novel is Hans's temporary home, the Chelsea Hotel. The book's protagonist "lives in the suspended reality of the Chelsea Hotel, a kind of urban Neverland" (Anthony). The hotel is the ideal spatial embodiment of the sense of unreality in which Hans and his family are caught after the events of 9/11. It is because of the well-known reputation of the hotel as a liminal space, hovering between the real and the surreal, living among famous artists and urban low-lives, that makes it such a perfect setting for the novel and its topics. The hotel provides the story with a place that is already projecting this liminal atmosphere and makes surreal moments credible. It is a 'mithandelnder Schauplatz' as Alexa Weik von Mossner calls it.

In *Netherland*, Hans van den Broek's dislocated condition and his fragile state of mind find a home at the Chelsea. The description of the hotel by the narrator shows that after 9/11 the Chelsea is a welcome refuge for him. The narrator's description presents not only a detailed picture of the physical structure of the building but it is already an analysis of its atmosphere:

Not counting the lobby, the Chelsea Hotel had ten floors. Each was served by a dim hallway that run from an air shaft on one side to, on my floor, a door with a yellowing pane of frosted glass that suggested the ulterior presence of a private detective rather than, as was actually the case, a fire escape. The floors were linked by a baronial staircase, which by virtue of the deep rectangular void at its center had the effect of installing a precipice at the heart of the building. On all the walls was displayed the vaguely alarming artwork of tenants past and present. ... Occasionally one overheard by-the-night visitors – transients, as the management called them – commenting on how spooky they found it all and there was a story that the hotel dead were secretly removed from their rooms in the middle of the night. But for me, returning from the office or from quick trips to Omaha, Oklahoma City, Cincinnati – Timbuktus, from my New Yorker's vantage point – there was nothing eerie about the building or the community that was established in it. Over half the rooms were occupied by long-term residents who by their furtiveness and ornamental diversity reminded me of the population of the aquarium I kept as a child ... . That said, there was a correspondence between the looming and shadowy hotel folk and the phantasmagoric and newly indistinct world beyond the Chelsea's heavy glass doors, as if the one promised to explain the other. (O'Neill 33f)

The narrative voice in this excerpt tells the reader that, despite the immigrant's Dutch background, Hans identifies himself as a New Yorker. Furthermore, he is now part of the Chelsea community and not only a transient visitor. Even though he has no close contact with his neighbors, Hans is aware of them. Most of all, the paragraph displays the microcosmic quality of the hotel for people in post 9/11- New York. The narrator claims that the hotel could explain the "newly indistinct world beyond the Chelsea's heavy glass doors" (O'Neill 33) and vice-versa. The city has become as chaotic as the Chelsea. While a city like New York can never be fully explained, especially after a traumatic event like the attacks on the World Trade Center, the hotel at least seems to offer a starting point and some insights into the city's deeper nature. As the paragraph shows, for the moment Hans identifies with his surroundings. The Chelsea has a soothing effect on him. He remains there even after his wife leaves him with his son because she considers New York no longer safe enough for them.

The novel highlights the hotel's calming nature, its function as a refuge for uprooted people. The narrator's words seem to echo Arthur Miller's experience: "[o]n my own, it was as if I were hospitalized at the Chelsea Hotel" (O'Neill 31). For Hans "[t]here was something anesthetizing about the traffic of people in the lobby" (O'Neill 32). The protagonist takes comfort from the staff, who, out of pity, allow him to spend time with them behind the counter and include them in their group. The Chelsea community becomes an unlikely surrogate family, including "a cross-dressing angel in wings and a wedding gown" (Winslow), whom Hans befriends and who symbolizes the weird but at heart innocent and liberating spirit of the place.

As the story develops, the protagonist realizes that the Chelsea does not only fit his state of mind but also provides him with place-identity. Being a resident of the

Chelsea means that he is at the heart of the New York experience. A temporary girlfriend tells him with "mock bitterness" that by visiting him at the hotel and seeing the place for herself "I finally feel like I've arrived in New York. It's only taken me four years" (O'Neill 112f). Hans shows her around the hotel and leads her down the famous art-cluttered stairwell. The experience of this downward journey is so weird to him that "I was startled when we reached the bottom of the stairs not to run into chuckling old Lucifer himself and instead find myself on the surface of earth and able to walk out directly into the cold, clear night" (109f). That they are met in the lobby by a roaring birthday party given for the dog of a resident only seems the logical consequence of life at the Chelsea.

Toward the end of the book, before he finally returns to his family in London, the Chelsea offers Hans one last, typically Chelsean unsettling yet comforting moment. One of the great summer power failures of New York happens and the hotel community reacts in Chelsea style: they make a party out of it. Hans first contemplates fleeing the island in a moment of panic, afraid of being captured on the island of Manhattan. However, he decides instead to join the ad-hoc rooftop party which "grew more and more raucous as the entire population of the building, it seemed, rose upward to laugh in the warm night" (195). Like Nick Carraway in *The Great Gatsby*, after his return to 'normalcy,' Hans feels a certain nostalgic longing for his unconventional home in New York. However, he realizes that his Chelsea time was only fitting the unique, liminal circumstance in which he found himself in the post-9/11 city.

In *Netherland*, O'Neill presents the Chelsea to the reader as a wacky, yet lovable shelter for people who have either lost their direction or deliberately refuse to have one. It becomes a healing place for protagonist Hans. This mirrors the real life experience of many people who lived at the hotel for any amount of time. This post-9/11 novel works to a large degree due to the clever choice of setting, by using the Chelsea Hotel as the focal point to present the unusual living experience in New York. The Chelsea makes a fragmentary and unsettling narration credible. In addition, the novel shows the more nurturing side of this hotel, which is often lost behind the glamor of its wild, radical, and hip image.

Considering his own understanding of the concepts 'home' and 'identity' Joseph O'Neill states in an interview that he finally has come to terms with his rootless status, seeing it as an advantage: "'You don't have a functioning substantial identity as a writer ... . You have a notional identity. ... I used to be quite exercised by nationality, but really I was an early member of the global flotsam. And if you stop thinking in terms of countries, you're left with cities'" (Anthony). The Hotel Chelsea in the novel is a microcosmic version of the artistic community of New York City. For the "global flotsam" as O'Neill calls himself, hotels are essential go-to places when they leave behind one city and move to the next. The Chelsea became his home as well as the source of inspiration for his work. Joseph O'Neill and his family are true Chelseaites and modern representatives of the century-old Chelsea hotel experience.

3.2 THE CHELSEA AS THE ARTIST'S PLACE OF INITIATION

Many writers have lived at the Chelsea and have used it as subject and setting in their works. Yet, writers are not the only artistic group that has been inspired by the institution on 23rd Street. Musicians also made the hotel their home, stopping place, or meeting spot in New York City. One can say that songs are the artistic product which have established the reputation of the hotel the most and which have helped to make it iconic. The songs best known for their Chelsea connection are Joni Mitchel's "Chelsea Morning," Bob Dylan's "Sad-Eyed Lady of the Lowlands," and Leonard Cohen's "Chelsea Hotel #2." All three spent some time in the establishment, Cohen and Dylan are also commemorated with plaques on the Chelsea facade. Their presence at the hotel has attracted thousands of visitors to the hotel, in particular young artists, who became residents themselves, hoping for the inspiration that lingers in the hotel's walls. For these young artists, the Chelsea became a place of initiation. It offered them a way into New York's counterculture, the world of artistic revolutionaries.

Patti Smith was one of these aspiring artists that came into her own through her hotel experience at the Chelsea. She describes this in her autobiography *Just Kids* (2010), which was awarded the National Book Award for Non-Fiction and was a finalist for the National Book Critics Circle Award in 2010.[35] Smith, most famous for her album *Horses* (1975), is a poet, a rock musician, and an artist, accomplished in all these fields. She creates a bridge between writers and musicians of the Chelsea. Her book is currently the best known text on the hotel. In it, Patti Smith writes of her time at the Chelsea with her first love and best friend Robert Mapplethorpe. According to an interview given to the German newspaper *Die Zeit* in 2010, Smith promised Mapplethorpe to write about their time together in New York (Amend). She fulfilled this promise more than twenty years after his death of AIDS in 1989, finally having the energy to write down her vivid memories of their lives during their early twenties. Patti Smith's account of these years is the tale of a survivor. In contrast to many of her contemporaries like Joplin, Hendrix, and Morrison, Smith survived the wild years of the late 1960s and 70s, and she survived

---

35 The book has been praised for the "power of observation and memory for everyday details like the price of automat sandwiches and the shabby, welcoming fellow bohemians of the Chelsea Hotel, among whose ranks these baby Rimbauds found their way" (Nissley). *Just Kids* is the only text of prose published by Smith.

the Chelsea, a feat not easily accomplished according to Miller.[36] Her survivor skills brought her to the Chelsea Hotel and there they enabled her to become a true artist. Patti Smith is aware of this in *Just Kids*. The Chelsea segment takes up more space in her narration than any other phase of her life. Her hotel experience is of crucial importance for her development.

Coming from a working-class family of modest means, Smith meets Mapplethorpe at the end of the 1960s, when both are broke and just hopeful youngsters, dreaming of an artistic career. Smith recalls that she needed to find a halfway decent accommodation for the two after Robert Mapplethorpe falls severely ill in 1969. She gets the recommendation for the Chelsea Hotel from a Brooklyn neighbor, who tells her that sometimes one can get a room there in exchange for art (Smith 93). This barter practice for artists is their only hope because the couple is unable to pay their rent in advance, and only Smith has the chance of a paying job at a Scribner's bookstore. As mentioned earlier, the one hurdle that one needed to take was to convince Stanley Bard of one's worthiness as future resident. According to Smith's matter-of-fact account, Bard gave them the benefit of doubt.

While Smith had heard vaguely of the reputation of the hotel, she does not select the place for the sake of its artistic image. She takes it because it offers shelter and security for the moment. In her book, she calls their residence at the Chelsea "a tremendous stroke of luck" (99). The time at the Chelsea Hotel turns out to be the two youngsters' most formative years, introducing Mapplethorpe to photography and the serious artist world of Manhattan, and providing Smith with an education in contemporary arts and thoughts that made her call the hotel her "new university" (138). Without a formal education, but a great interest in French poets like Baudelaire, Patti Smith starts her life at the Chelsea. In its lobby she meets Harry Smith, the legendary underground filmmaker, even before she secured rooms at the hotel. Through Harry Smith and other artists-in-residence like Sandy Daley, Smith gets to know the Beat poets Gregory Corso, Allen Ginsberg, and William Burroughs, who become her "teachers, each one passing through the lobby of the Chelsea hotel" (138). She first focuses on writing poems and is even able to publish

---

36 Surviving is an issue that repeatedly comes up in texts on the Chelsea. On the one hand, it is difficult to survive as an artist in Manhattan outside of the Chelsea, which is the reason why it seen as a refuge by them. On the other hand, however, it is also not an easy task to survive as a young artist inside the hotel without being devoured and side-tracked by the influence of the twilight world of the place has on its residents. In no other hotel discussed here are life and death so closely affiliated with the building. It has a truly liminal atmosphere. The Chelsea is as famous for the people who lived there as for those who died in it.

a collection of her work, inspired and energized by the building and its unique community.

Patti Smith's description of the Chelsea shows her almost loving relationship to the place and also the ambiguous experiences she makes there:

> The Chelsea was like a doll's house in the Twilight Zone, with a hundred rooms, each a small universe. I wandered the halls seeking its spirits, dead or alive. My adventures were mildly mischievous, tapping open a door slightly ajar and getting glimpses of Virgil Thomson's grand piano, or loitering before the nameplate of Arthur C. Clarke, hoping he might suddenly emerge. ... I loved this place, its shabby elegance, and the history it held so possessively. ... Here Dylan Thomas, submerged in poetry and alcohol, spent his last hours. Thomas Wolfe plowed through hundreds of pages of manuscript for *You Can't Go Home Again*. Bob Dylan composed 'Sad-Eyed Lady of the Lowlands' on our floor, and a speeding Edie Sedgwick was said to have set her room on fire while gluing on her thick false eyelashes by candlelight. (112f)

The author describes the microcosmic character of the Chelsea, calling each room "a small universe." Her perception of the special spatial quality of the hotel is very acute. What Patti Smith describes here is a veritable heterotopia. Only a hotel is able to connect different spaces and different spheres so closely with each other. Smith is very aware of the Chelsea's liminal atmosphere; she calls it "a doll's house in the Twilight Zone." Death and life merge at the hotel, and the residents are as much inspired by their living fellow-residents as they are by the lingering spirits of the former residents. This liminal element is also expressed in the "shabby elegance" of the building. It unites the former charm with the current energy of the hotel. The Chelsea has a strong sense of the past. Unlike a chain-hotel of supermodernity, a non-place which according to Augé does not contain history (Augé 78), the Chelsea has more of it than some of its guests can actually bear. For Smith, it is what fascinates her about the institution: "So many had written, conversed, and convulsed in these Victorian dollhouse rooms. So many skirts had swished these worn marble stairs. So many transient souls had espoused, made a mark, and succumbed here. I sniffed out their spirits as I silently scurried from floor to floor, longing for discourse with a gone procession of smoking caterpillars" (Smith 113). As the last remark shows, being at the Chelsea has for her the same feeling like falling down the rabbit-hole in *Alice in Wonderland*. It is adventurous and exciting. For Smith this "eccentric and damned hotel provided a sense of security as well as a stellar education" (99). It is her place of initiation as an artist.

At the same time, Patti Smith is also aware of the shortcomings of the hotel. While the shabbiness is somewhat charming, the room she occupies with Mapplethorpe, Room 1017, is allegedly famous for being the smallest of the hotel. It is just large enough to sleep there, yet it leaves them no space to work. She expresses her contradicting feelings poetically, writing: "How different the light in the Chelsea Hotel seemed as it fell over our few possessions, it was not natural light, spreading from the lamp and the overhead bulb, intense and unforgiving, yet it seemed filled with unique energy" (95). Due to the lack of space to create, her next goal, after getting into the hotel, is to move to a larger room.[37] This spatial move inside the hotel is important on two accounts: first, because it finally provides Patti Smith and her friend with working space, and second, because being on the second floor "gave me a sense that the lobby was an extension of the room, for it was truly my station [from where I] enjoy the din of the comings and goings" (120). The semi-public space of the lobby has a great influence on the twenty-two-year-old artist-in-the-making. The time she spends there inspires her to think beyond writing poems, making use of other fields of art, like music and painting. Due to the constant flow of people, a number of chance meetings occur which lead to new developments. Sitting in the lobby seems to offer endless opportunities: "I was thinking what a magical portal this lobby was when the heavy glass door opened as if swept by wind and a familiar figure in a black and scarlet cape entered. It was Salvador Dali" (133). This incident, which appears so striking to the reader, is actually "just another day at the Chelsea" (133) for Patti Smith, so much has she become adapted to the spirit of the place.

Because she feels secure and inspired at the Chelsea, Smith experiences a crisis when Robert Mapplethorpe expects her to leave the hotel to move with him into an artist's loft next to the hotel. Her move is necessary because only together they can pay the rent. Even though Smith has gone to great length to support the photographer at the beginning of their friendship, moving from the hotel "was the first and only time that I felt I had sacrificed something of myself for Robert" (151). The author confesses that she loves the hotel and that leaving the Chelsea also means for her to leave behind the hotel's "identification with poets and writers, Harry, and our bathroom in the hall" (145). The reader perceives how much the spatial surrounding of the hotel influences Smith's well-being. She knows that things will change for her after her move and she sees this as a break in her development. She worries about the consequences this might have on her creative work. She fears that they could "lose a certain intimacy as well our proximity to Dylan Thomas's room. Someone else would take my station in the Chelsea lobby" (150).

Although Smith is able to get more work done at the spacious loft, she repeatedly returns to the hotel, even though she now experiences it from an outsider's perspective. She continues to meet friends there such as Sandy Daley,

---

37 This is why she is one of the few residents who diligently pays her rent in the hope of getting a better room allocated. This materializes after several months of their stay, which she describes as an "energizing" change (119).

who presents Mapplethorpe with his first polaroid camera, sending him on his future way to become a professional photographer. Daley witnesses Mapplethorpe's and Smith's moments of initiation when she films the procedures of Robert getting his nipple pierced inside the hotel (an event which is also portrayed as his coming-out), and Patti getting a tattoo by a fellow Chelsea resident (183). These procedures are conceived as initiating moments into their existence as artists. Furthermore, these events highlight the hotel's function as setting for rites of passage.

Because the Chelsea is the location of Smith's liminal phase, as Victor Turner would describe it, it continues to be an important environment for her. When Smith and Sam Shepard become lovers in 1970, the reader realizes from reading Smith's description that one of Shepard's main attractions for her is that he has a room at the Chelsea. She loves staying with him, especially the feeling of "having a room back in the hotel" (179). Smith finds her calling as a poet and a rock musician through the people she meets at the hotel, among them the band Velvet Underground and Lee Crabtree. They inspire her to combine her poems with music. The hotel at this time was the place to stay for musicians in New York. There they could rehearse and jam with each other, and influence their styles mutually. Fittingly, Shepard's farewell present to his lover is a guitar which she still has at the time of writing her book and which accompanies her during her whole career.

For Smith the Chelsea and its surrounding area start to lose appeal in the summer of 1972 when Manhattan enters a phase of social and financial deterioration, and the situation of the residents at the hotel becomes tenser. Several of her former friends are evicted by Bard because they are not able to pay their rent or because of their increasingly bad behavior: "The Chelsea was changing, and the atmosphere on Twenty-third Street had a manic feeling, as if something had gone awry. There was no sense of logic" (207). For Smith it was time to go, especially since she by now knew what she wanted to do, having found her voice as an artist with the help of the hotel.

According to Smith's autobiography, the "vibrating arena of the Chelsea Hotel" (208) dominated her life during her forming years. It set her on a path that she would never have taken without her Chelsea experience. Smith profited from the unique opportunities the artists' hotel offered. In her 'love letter' to the Chelsea Hotel, published in Linda Troeller's photography book *Atmosphere,* Smith writes: "The Hotel Chelsea opened up a whole new thing for me, the rock&roll thing" (qtd. in Troeller 16). Her timing was ideal because she was able to witness the "halcyon days for art and artists in New York" ("Reviews/Non Fiction") at the Chelsea Hotel. Patti Smith's memoir *Just Kids* is another important piece in the puzzle of the larger picture of the Chelsea Hotel as a social and cultural institution in New York. Through Smith's account, the hotel will be remembered as "an energetic, desperate haven for scores of gifted hustling children from every rung of the ladder. ... Everybody passing through here is somebody, if nobody in the outside world"

(Smith 91). In the unstable years of the Vietnam War and of social unrest, the Chelsea provided the right mix of security and liberal openness, which only a hotel can provide.[38]

3.3 THE HOTEL AS SOURCE OF INSPIRATION

The Hotel Chelsea lived through its darkest decades in the 1970s and 80s. Like most of New York, it was considered unsafe, dilapidated, and at the edge of a breakdown.[39] The years following the murder of Nancy Spungen at the Chelsea in 1978 were very problematic for the institution. It took until the mid-1990s that the Chelsea became somewhat respectable again, after Stanley and David Bard jr. evicted some of the more problematic residents and renovated parts of the house. However, it is this gritty image of the Chelsea, always hovering between creativity and decay, which made this hotel the center of New York's counterculture and an icon for artists around the world. This spirit of place made the Chelsea a place of inspiration, a veritable artist's magnet. It would go beyond the scope of this work to discuss all kinds of art ever produced in and inspired by the hotel. Therefore, my main focus is on the works of photographers, as they played a crucial role in creating the iconic image of the Hotel Chelsea. A surprisingly great number of photograph artists lived and worked at the hotel over the years, and many of them made the hotel either their sole or at least a main focus of their creative output. Most of these artists will also only be remembered in connection with the hotel and not for their other creations. Hotels, being architectural structures, are visual entities. Their materiality is often prominent as they dominate the streets and the surrounding neighborhoods due to their size and the traffic of goods and people

---

38 There is an aftermath to Patti Smith's Chelsea hotel experience. In 1995, after the death of her husband and mounting medical bills, the hotel rescued her a second time. Poet Allen Ginsberg and musician Bob Dylan helped Smith financially as an act of solidarity to a former fellow Chelsea resident. Furthermore, Dylan arranged for Smith to be the opening act during his concert tour (Amend). She also took up residence again at the hotel for the time. It might be safe to say that the unique communal feeling at the Chelsea is the reason why the ties among the former neighbors remained so close. The relationship between Patti Smith and the current Chelsea residents, however, was tested in 2012, when Smith gave a concert at the hotel, arranged by the new owner Chetritt. Because several residents were evicted at that time, critics among the tenants saw this as Smith's selling out ("Patti Smith comes under fire for planned Hotel Chelsea Gig").

39 Some long-term residents stayed throughout those years, like Julie Eakin, Tim Sullivan, and Dimitri Mugianis, whose testimonies of their time during the Chelsea's darkest years is collected by James Lough in his oral history *This Ain't No Holiday Inn* (2013).

they create. Thus, photography seems to be an ideal medium to transport its meanings.

Almost all calendars of New York, coffee table books, and similar paraphernalia of the city contain a shot of the Chelsea Hotel. Its gothic, darkly looming facade has encouraged an uncountable number of photographers to catch their personal angle of the building, trying to tell their story of the hotel in their pictures. The Chelsea Hotel thus became a visual icon of New York, like the Empire State Building or the Chrysler Building, inextricably linked to the world's image of the city, an important sight, and part of the visitors' expectations. While the spiraling art-deco skyscrapers represent the city's progressive and powerful side, the Chelsea speaks of its history, its sub-cultures, its gritty parts, and the last vestiges of the faded Victorian glamor of the Gilded Age. The pictures of the Chelsea have become an important part of New York's visual culture. The Chelsea's atmospheric quality, its identity of place, has helped to shape the image of New York and inspired artists to come to the city. By depicting the uncommon clientele of the hotel together with its building the camera artists preserve this part of the city's history. Their works will allow future generations to learn more about this platform of New York's artists when the hotel itself will have been transformed once more.

Today, as the hotel is no longer open for visitors, the Chelsea's facade has already gained a greater importance in the minds of tourists and New Yorkers. For tourists, the impressive exterior is the only part they can still experience of the hotel. In their pictures of the hotel they try to capture at least a hint of authentic New York and the haunting atmosphere that the hotel exuded for almost 130 years. For New Yorkers, the facade of the Hotel Chelsea has taken on an additional meaning. It has become the symbol for the battle between the power of real estate sharks and the resistance of wacky artists, dividing the city's population into those who would like to see progress in this more run-down part of New York, and those who want to fight for the creative soul of Manhattan, which is driven out of the inner-city by exploding rents.

Over the years, several photographic artists, mostly residents of the hotel, presented their view of the hotel in their art books. Among the best known examples are Claudio Edinger's *Chelsea* (1983), published for the centennial of the Chelsea Hotel, Rita Barros's *Fifteen Years: Chelsea Hotel* (1999),[40] Julia Calfee's

---

40 Rita Barros's *Fifteen Years: The Chelsea Hotel* (1999) is now almost impossible to get, even though it is praised by art critics. There are only a few copies left, among them one in the Library of Congress in Washington D.C. Her website provides some basic information on the book. Barros decided to take black and white pictures of those artists who use the hotel as a backdrop for their films and videos, while using color images when depicting the residents of the hotel, whom she has photographed in their own

Inside: The Chelsea Hotel (2007),[41] and Linda Troeller's *Hotel Chelsea Atmosphere – An Artist's Memoir* (2007). All four artists lived at the hotel for an amount of time. While Barros's stayed there longest, collecting her impressions over the period of fifteen years, the others also spend several years in the Chelsea, a condition which is seemingly necessary to get the right feel of the building and to get closer to its core. Their pictures do not only depict the hotel's architectural structure, its furnishings, and the art displayed on its walls, but most often show how the people inside the hotel interact with the building, what their position is inside and toward the Chelsea Hotel, and how they stylize themselves before its historic background. While all four artists use a slightly different approach and bring to their projects their own way of seeing the Chelsea, some impressions converge with each other.

---

apartments. This provides the viewer with vibrant impressions of the people who kept the hotel alive with their residence. In contrast, those who have made the hotel an artistic object are captured as artistic monochrome objects themselves. Like with Edinger, each photo is also connected to a quote referring to life at the hotel (Barros "Fact Sheet"). Barros's pictures have been taken over the span of fifteen years. They show the hotel's development from its grittier years in the mid-80s to the time when the neighborhood and the Chelsea Hotel itself became attractive again. For Barros, the Chelsea creates an "environment which influences the art emerging from the hotel" (Barros "Fact Sheet").

41 Julia Calfee lived at the Chelsea from 2003 to 2008, a time, when the hotel had already gotten its much needed renovations and the neighborhood of Chelsea was again considered to be trendy. Like Edinger and Barros, Julia Calfee pairs her 81 black and white pictures with short texts of the residents on the hotel's atmosphere. For Calfee, "The Chelsea Hotel is a place where excess is welcome, where the psyche can be annihilated or resurrected. It has a magical potential for transformation, whether it be rebirth or destruction" (Calfee "Inside"). The liminal character of the hotel is seen as part of its lasting attraction. Calfee describes her vision for the book as "a visual quest for the unifying elements of the people who chose to live in this place and the ghosts who still lurk in its shadows" (Calfee "Inside"). The book is very conscious of its own aestheticism. Because of this, Calfee's book met mixed reactions. Its artsiness makes it appear inauthentic. Co-photographer Antonin Kratchovil says about *Inside: The Chelsea Hotel*: "You got the vibration of the place and also captured the experience of these strange characters. …You don't have to run around the world to capture humanity, you've captured it here and all you have to do is take the elevator" (Kratchovil qtd. in Calfee). The hotel here is understood as a vertical village; lives stacked upon each other that can be reached by the simple ride on an elevator.

In the following, I will focus on Claudio Edinger's book *Chelsea Hotel* (1983), as he was the first to publish a collection of photographs on the Chelsea,[42] especially during its most problematic phase, the early 1980s, and on Linda Troeller's *Atmosphere*, who published one of the most recent accounts,[43] which captures the hotel already in its gentrified condition. Both included a number of essays by fellow residents in their books, which are useful for connecting the visual impressions with the hotel experience of the presented individuals.

Claudio Edinger: Portraying the Chelsea During Its Time of Decay

Edinger's book is a combination of photographs and essays by noteworthy residents. At the beginning, the reader learns of Edinger's own connection to and impression of the hotel in his introductory text. Each picture in the book is either paired with quotes of the persons represented in the picture or, if it is a shot without human interaction, with quotes by Stanley Bard or newspaper quips. The essays by Pete Hamill, Arthur C. Clarke, Clifford Irving, William Burroughs, Viva, and Richard R. Lingeman deal with the relationships between the residents and the hotel, their personal hotel experiences there, and explain what the Chelsea means to them.[44]

Edinger's introduction establishes the tone of the book. It tells us about the dynamic between the artist and the hotel, and his feelings toward the place. We

---

42 It is unclear when Claudio Edinger moved into the hotel. By the time of the publication of the book in 1983, the year of the hotel's centennial, he had lived at the hotel for several years. Some of his earliest Chelsea pictures are from 1978, so it might be reasonable to assume that this was around the time he took up residence there.

43 In August 2013, Victoria Cohen published her book of photographs of the Chelsea, entitled *Hotel Chelsea*. She took these picture after the hotel was sold and before renovation started. Yet, reviews note that not much of the original atmosphere is captured in these pictures. Most come across quite sterile and stark. This is the reason why I have decided against analyzing it in depth.

44 Arthur C. Clarke calls the hotel his second home (47). William Burroughs used it as his favorite meeting place, getting together there with his fellow beat poets (63). Viva, Warhol's muse, had both her children at the hotel and praises the staff for helping her raising them (87). For Clifford Irving, the Chelsea was his "hideout and hideaway" when he needed a "secure nest, friends, buffers" in a time of personal crisis (111). Journalist Richard R. Lingeman compares it to a film set, resembling a "raffish Grand Hotel waiting for a Lubitsch or Fellini to cry: 'Quiet on the set. Camera! Action!'" (127f). Finally, Peter Hamill boils the Chelsea Hotel experience down to its essence: "at once ruin and monument, this artifact of everybody's lost city, this human habitation so often compared to a dowager ... offers the tale of lost New York" (11).

learn that the photographer's first reaction to the hotel was one of instant dislike when he visited a friend there, relating it to "a zoo" (Edinger 7). The main argument for even considering to stay there was the low rent and the necessity to move out of his former apartment. Yet, this friend sparked an interest by suggesting to Edinger that it would be worthwhile to make a book of photographs on the hotel: "The Chelsea is for you" (Edinger 7). It is interesting that it is the prospect of the hotel as an art object that convinces Edinger to try the place. From then on, he sees the hotel as an inspiration for his work. He experiences his life there as that of an artist in residence.

At the time of Edinger's arrival, the hotel was at its lowest point, shortly after the stabbing of Nancy Spungen, when it, like the rest of New York, was precariously close to collapse. The Chelsea's dark, forbidding appearance was an extreme contrast for Edinger who is originally from Brazil. Still, he acknowledges that with the "finely contoured ironwork balconies" and eclectic mix of Beaux Arts and Gothic themes it was "[t]he closest thing to Europe in New York" (Edinger 7). The photographer is treated to the typical introduction of the building by Bard, who praises the comforts of the hotel, despite its obvious derelict state, and promises him free answering service, towels, and a refrigerator, with the toilet down the hall. The artist compares his first days at the Chelsea with "the beginning of an unforgettable summer vacation in an exotic retreat full of offbeat, inquisitive people" (7). Slowly overcoming the cultural shock he experienced, he awakes "with a strange feeling of affection for the place. I was like a reluctant husband, one month into an arranged marriage to a woman he'd neither known nor cared about. Who little by little has grown accustomed to his wife" (7f). The struggle of emotions which Edinger experiences is remarkable. As an aesthete, the shabbiness and weirdness of the place irritate him, yet as an artist he also sees the potential of a place peopled with residents who seem to have myriad of stories to tell about the Chelsea (8). Living at the hotel, learning to see it through the eyes of its residents, he discovers "that the Chelsea is a veritable hothouse of creative talent" (8). Edinger pins the reason for this on Bard, and his special management style and attitude: "If there is a catalyst for all this creative energy, it has to be the freedom and sense of tolerance that pervade the hotel" (9). The people of the Chelsea, according to Edinger, can be safe in the assumption that "Stanley will understand" (9). Edinger's prime example of the uniqueness of a Chelsea Hotel resident is George Kleinsinger, who created his own, special living surrounding in the hotel, complete with a jungle, exotic animals, and an aquarium. According to Edinger, Kleinsinger took the penthouse studio in the Chelsea "to escape the cultural abyss of suburbia" (9). He left the hotel "feet first," as he hoped he would.[45]

---

45 As with other well-known former residents, "[i]n the hotel there was the feeling that George had never left" (9). For the photographer this is the case because "[t]here is a

Edinger ends his prologue with the poem "Chelsea Hotel" (1982) by professor of literature B.H. Williams, who writes: "Poets, artists, and musicians /Parade in by the score, / And, occasionally, somebody famous / Will walk through the front door. / And there stands Stanley Bard saying, / 'We hope everything goes well, / because we want you here forever / at the Chelsea Hotel" (qtd. in Edinger 9).[46] Edinger's book of photography is his personal contribution to the legacy of the Chelsea and its enduring reputation as *the* artists' hotel. It lives on as his particular gift to the hotel.

The photographs in the Edinger's book are all black and white, evoking the film noir feeling of the Chelsea Hotel and the tradition of New York pictures in monochrome. On the pages of Edinger's prologue and the introduction by Hamill, the pictures of the hotel are small, and mostly of the staff and of behind-the-scenes actions, like the cleaning of the rooms and operating the hotel telephones. Afterwards, one moves with Edinger's camera eye into the building, through the main entry and the lobby, climbing the staircase, and entering the apartments of the Chelseaites. He captures the residents around the house and in their rooms, in postures that express their self-understanding and the identity they wish to perform at the hotel. This is, for example, the case with Suzanne Bartsch, *the* fashion-stylist and event planner of the 1980s in New York. Despite her financial success, she prefers the Chelsea as home because it underlines her flamboyant image and allows her bohemian lifestyle. In the book, she is quoted as saying: "This is a vertical village, ... with all conveniences of a villa" (qtd. in Edinger 50).[47] By photographing Bartsch in a dramatic robe and hat, combined with her comment, Claudio Edinger captures the spirit of a bohemian who did good.

---

strange timelessness about the people of the Chelsea, something that has worn off on the place itself, something I've tried to find through my pictures" (9).

46 The poem, which in the full version describes the most important members of the staff and some memorable guests, reminds one of the song "Hotel California" and similar to the lyrics of that piece, the Chelsea Hotel, too, seems to be a place that "you can never leave."

47 Bartsch's word choice here is noteworthy: while the metaphor "vertical city" has become a set phrase for skyscrapers and can also be used for skyscraper hotels, the connotation of a "vertical village" is slightly different. It contains the connotation of being a condensed version of the larger world outside, yet, by calling it a village it evokes the impression of a more rural, simpler place. The comparison, in my opinion, fits very well with the Chelsea because, other than in the more refined Waldorf-Astoria and Hotel Algonquin, the atmosphere here is more communal and down-to-earth. The Chelsea's occupants are often not very compatible with the big city life. In the hotel, they have the feeling of being away from the corporate power of the city and, instead, are sheltered and protected here.

To discuss Edinger's style and his presentation of the Chelsea in more detail, I pick out the picture of Sophia Delza. Delza, who introduced Tai Chi to New York and continued teaching it at the United Nations for years, is portrayed doing one of the Tai Chi positions in her apartment. She is dressed in a traditional Asian dress, which fits perfectly with the simplistic, Asian style of her furniture. Delza is at the center of the picture and looks straight at the camera. Her gaze appears authoritarian and dignified, especially since the camera angle is low-view, which means that Delza looks down on the viewer. Behind her, the viewer sees a great fire place, which adds to the dignified impression of the picture. The photographer played with the light in the shot. While Delza is well-lighted, the background remains in twilight, which gives the room a mysterious note. Overall, the picture of Sophia Delza presents the Chelsea Hotel as a place of mixed cultures and liberal tradition. The place appears surprisingly dignified and presentable. The hotel's residents, represented here by Delza, exude a creative, mysterious aura, which feeds of the hotel's atmosphere and at the same time adds to it.

The pictures in Edinger's book capture the huge variety of people who are housed under the same roof: writers, painters, and musicians. They live next to families with children, night club owners, exotic dancers, activists, and the painter Alpheus Cole, who lived for decades at the Chelsea, rent-controlled, before he died there at the age of 112 years in 1989. The quotes of the residents reflect the wide range of needs that the hotel fulfills for the tenants. They express the many, often creative functions which the Chelsea has taken on. It is "second family" for some, "a Fortress of Solitude," "a state of mind," "a cross between the Plaza and the Port Authority Bus Terminal," "a sanctuary," and the pianist Gerald Busby writes, having the honor of the last quote: "Everything is so unstable. The hotel makes you create your own stability through your work" (qtd. in Edinger 144). Taken together, the comments confirm the hotel's identity as an artist's home, studio, and source of inspiration.

In every picture, the subject of the photography looks directly at the camera, often from low-view. By this, the facial expressions of the residents exude a protective attitude toward the hotel, a look of defiance with which they seem to declare their solidarity with the once elegant, but now shabby appearance of the hotel. The shots do never directly display the decay happening in the place. Instead, the pictures of the book seem to be more a celebration of the Chelsea's power of endurance. While the hotel is not blemish-free, it appears amiable in Edinger's book, which focuses more on the many tales the people can tell of their stay there than on the stark reality of much needed repairs and evictions. On the back cover, Edinger allows also the voice of a leading New York newspaper to enter the discourse on the Chelsea. The quote by *The New York Times* seems to capture Edinger's view of the hotel at its centennial: "The building sits on 23rd Street with the air of a great dame who finds herself in the midst of a party of her social inferiors but instead of complaining decides to join right in the fun" (qtd. in Edinger, back cover). Life at the Chelsea for Edinger is a celebration of the bohemian lifestyle. The hotel gives the permission to live according to one's own rules, free from conventions.

Love Letters to the Chelsea: Linda Troeller's Photographic Memoir

As the title of Linda Troeller's book *The Chelsea Hotel Atmosphere: An Artist's Memoir* (2007) implies, this art book is meant as a very personal approach to the institution on 23rd Street. It is another form of life 'writing,' a photographic record of her hotel experience as well as that of her fellow residents. Troeller comes from New York, yet she has worked around the world. Her main mission as an artist is to convey authenticity and simplicity in her pictures, capturing that instance between photographer and model that can seduce an audience (Juan Gaviria qtd. in Troeller 5). At the time of the publication, Troeller has lived at the Chelsea for twelve years, which overlap with the last years of Barros and with Calfee's stay. Like Calfee's, Troeller's mission is the preservation of the Chelsea's spirit for a time when the hotel has fallen prey to the real estate developments in Manhattan. The Chelsea is her muse and the place where she creates her art. It is her artist's studio.

The difference between her approach and that of the others is that she encouraged her fellow Chelseaites to write 'love letters' to the Chelsea. They all start with "Dear Chelsea Hotel" and continue to tell something about their attitude toward this establishment. The first picture is a shot of the Chelsea's key rack, stuffed with mail, and a handwritten letter by Stanley Bard on the famous Chelsea stationary, in which he states his pride in Troeller's development and her achievements during her time as his tenant. He applauds that her projects changed from focusing on herself to now including "the entire Chelsea family" (Bard qtd. in Troller 7). He acknowledges her as a real artist. Bard's letter also expresses his self-perception as a supporter of the arts and his paternal interest in his guests' progress.

Before presenting the love letters of other residents, Troeller starts with her own. In it, she marvels about the variety of people she daily meets at the hotel, like fashion-designer Alexander McQueen or beat poet Herbert Huncke, and how they influence her artistic expression and her self-understanding as an artist. Observing Huncke, she learns that the creation of art can be a life-long process. For Troeller "[t]he hotel intensifies human relations" (Troeller 8). She feels, for example, consoled by her room maid, not left alone and alienated. The Chelsea Hotel to her "is a cave to excavate suitcases of memories" (Troeller 8). She pairs a self-portray with her letter which only shows her blurred silhouette as she ascends the famous gothic staircase. She places the hotel in the foreground and depicts herself as only another link in the chain of humans that make the Chelsea an artists' hotel.

The photos in her book are a mix of close-up shots of the hotel, panorama shots of the halls and staircase, and portrays she made of those residents who contributed letters to the book. In contrast to Edinger's and Calfee's work, Troeller uses color pictures, which creates a very different, more vivid impression of the hotel. The Chelsea appears less artsy and more like a real-life place, where people live. Edinger hid the shabbiness of the 1980s appearance of the hotel by taking monochrome shots, the chiaroscuro effect giving the Chelsea a more dignified aura. Troeller, instead, captures the hotel when it has already been gentrified and become hip again. The color pictures stress the regained attraction of the hotel. She also takes pictures from the outside and by this connects the hotel more to its location in New York. The mix of people she combines in her book is as diverse as Edinger's or Barros's. Again, the pictures present people from all walks of life. Many residents are, of course, artistically inclined. Their letters are all quite personal. Most of them recollect a specific moment with specific people at the hotel, and they consider the mood and atmosphere of the place. Namedropping occurs repeatedly. The tone of the letters varies between wholehearted praise and grumbling acceptance, for example when librettist Arnold Weinstein calls Stanley Bard "a mad curator of this crazy museum," where the residents are "just his humble statues" (Weinstein qtd. in Troeller 41). Continuity is another issue in these letters because many residents consider the former tenants of their rooms. The interesting impression one derives from the residents' portrays in their apartments is that many of them live a surprisingly mundane life. It is also noteworthy how different the same space can look depending on the character of the inhabitant. Some hotel rooms have the appearance of a college dorm, while others indeed resemble museums and again others look like 'normal' homes. The picture of Joseph O'Neill's family looks just like an everyday family shot. The only bohemian element is the Warhol-like print on the wall behind them.

The two most remarkable contributors of love letters to the Chelsea, who have not been included in any of the other texts, are Stanley's daughter, Michelle Bard, and Catherine Klemann, the great great granddaughter of Philipp Hubert, the Chelsea's architect and one of its original owners.[48] These two women feel a special connection to the place and can actually claim the hotel as part of their family heritage. It is important for their identity. In her picture, Michelle Bard sits on a divan in the center of an elegantly furnished room. Behind her is a large fireplace with a gilded-framed mirror and a piece of period furniture. The whole setup looks very sophisticated and underlines Michelle Bard's profession as an interior

---

48 In contrast to her brother, Michelle is not often mentioned in texts on the Chelsea. Yet, it is clear that her career path has also been influenced by the hotel. She became an interior decorator because of her connection with the hotel.

designer. It also shows that her style is quite unlike the eclectic mix of the Chelsea Hotel. In her letter, Michelle Bard confesses that she once

wanted to make monumental changes, unfairly, because I was more interested in feeding my own ego rather than the hotel's ego. With time and maturity, I grew to appreciate the eclectic atmosphere and what the Chelsea represented to so many people world-wide. I have made it my mission to maintain the integrity and the character of the Chelsea. (Bard qtd in Troeller 80)

For her, the hotel is almost a family member. She anthropomorphizes the Chelsea, and considers its ego and its character. The building is part of what her family stands for.

Catherine Klemann gets the place of honor as the last letter writer in the book. Like Bard, she is connected to the hotel 'via bloodline.' However, she has a different relationship with the building.[49] Klemann learned rather late of her connection to the Chelsea. In her letter, she describes how she found out about her family's history with the hotel, and the growing fascination with learning more about the place her ancestor had created. Klemann writes about her shyness entering the building and the problems to connect to it. She never really became a part of the hotel: "I hardly got to know you." However, she feels "happy for the generations who found an enriching and vital community with you" (Klemann qtd. in Troeller 111). There is no picture of Klemann in the book. The reason might be that she has not actually lived the Chelsea experience and therefore remains on the outside, of the hotel and of this photographic memoir.

Troeller's selection of contributors and the pictures she pairs with the texts create a vivid impression of the hotel which has gone through several metamorphoses, yet remained in large parts the same. In the review of Troeller's book, blogger *The Fashion Informer* writes: "The overriding impression is of a soulful haven that encourages (or, at least, tolerates) eccentricity, nurtures creativity, and inspires individuality. ... More than anything, though, 'Atmosphere' is one woman's moving paean to the place that ignites her passion and feeds her dreams on a daily basis" ("'Atmosphere' by Linda Troeller"). Troeller's approach to the Chelsea is a very intimate one through the combination of love letters with pictures and portrays of residents and the hotel. *Atmosphere* highlights the personal hotel experience of the people connected to the Hotel Chelsea. It tells about the residents' existential insideness. As the title promises, the book is about atmosphere. The Chelsea's atmosphere is not only produced by people, and not just

---

49 Klemann has become a supporter of the fight for the preservation of the Chelsea in its artist tradition. At the 125th year's celebration of the hotel, she stated that it was time to get the Bards back as managers of the hotel because that is what the residents really want.

inherent in the walls but it is the combination of material goods and social practices, as Löw describes it. The Chelsea Hotel's special atmosphere made it the muse of many artists. This is its most unique legacy.

The volumes of photographs published on the Chelsea Hotel show an important genre of art created at the institution. They present the hotel's relevance for New York and literally enable different viewpoints on what the hotel stands for. By making use of the residents' participation, these books are testimonies to the social centrality of the Chelsea. In the letters, the comments, and the pictures, the importance of the place for these people becomes apparent. It is clear that they are united by the structure, that their identification as a community is based on their residency at the Chelsea. Over its almost 130 years of existence, the Chelsea has become an iconic structure in the city. Its fame has spread world-wide by the means of photography. As mentioned at the beginning of the chapter, the Chelsea is protected as a Historic National Landmark. Its facade is still intact behind the current scaffolding. Yet, its interior with its art and its color schemes, which contributed so much to the place's atmosphere, is already largely gone since the sale of the building and the start of the remodeling. The books of photography are the chronicles of the "Inside" of the Chelsea Hotel. They will allow later generations to re-experience the unique mix of shabbiness and elegance that made the hotel's spirit. For this kind of spatial preservation work photography is the best fitting medium.

An interesting fact about the Hotel Chelsea is that is has inspired an uncountable amount of people to produce art. According to many guests, already the act of sitting in the lobby and watching the traffic is a form of entertainment, a source of inspiration. The Chelsea's inspirational quality is not limited to Chelseaites, the insiders of the hotel. The hotel also had an impact on outsiders, artists who knew about the place and its unique reputation and who made use of it in their works. This is especially the case for performance artists, some of them even used the hotel as the actual location for their performances. In the following, I will discuss two different examples, which shall act as representatives for the number of art works by non-residents that have been inspired by the Chelsea.

Using the Chelsea as Stage: En Garde Arts's Performance *At The Chelsea*

The art project literally connected to the Chelsea Hotel is the performance *At The Chelsea* by En Garde Arts, Inc., which consists of three one-act-plays taking place in actual rooms of the hotel. In 1985, the site-specific performance group En Garde Arts, Inc., was founded by Anne Hamburger, a Yale Drama School alumna, whose vision was to create a total work of theater closely connected to the space in which it was performed ("En Garde Arts, Inc." 52). The company was to present "on-location productions using the ever-shifting landscape of Manhattan as its urban stage" (Grubb). For Anne Hamburger, site-specific theater has limitless potential and opens the city's space to realize new ways of performing ("En Garde Arts, Inc." 52).[50] In addition: "[p]art of the fun of site-specific work is infiltrating a neighborhood in a good way – figuring out the local politics and getting people involved in the production" ("En Garde Arts, Inc." 54). The great attraction of this kind of theater is that people become aware of their surrounding space in a new way, and reconsider their relationship with the places which they daily interact with. Especially in a city as diverse and complex as New York, the performances provide the possibility of seeing specific location with new eyes.[51] The way En Garde Arts, Inc. uses places like the Church of St. John the Divine, the Central Park, or the Chelsea Hotel "shed[s] new light on their significance – socially, politically, historically and artistically" (En Garde Arts, Inc., "Mission Statement" 1).

Anne Hamburger does not create the projects herself. Instead, she confronts artists with selected places, such as the Chelsea Hotel, and encourages them to develop their own acts in connection to these places. For Hamburger, the Chelsea "is a real 'if-walls-could-talk' place' [where] the audience will be able to cross the threshold into complete worlds created by the artists" (Pacheco). With this vision, Hamburger was able to capture Bard's imagination and support. He provided the company with three rooms "for this tribute to one of New York's most important landmarks of art, architecture and community" (Killmer 1). The timing was right for the project because, in 1989, the hotel was still before the great renovations of the 1990s, and Bard needed to improve the hotel's reputation.

The run of *At The Chelsea*, in the hotel's rooms 302, 322 and 502, took place from January 12 to February 5, 1989. As the playbill states, it is "A Festival of Performance Art, Music & Theater based on the history of the Chelsea Hotel" (En Garde Arts, Inc. "Playbill").[52] During the first two weeks, the three one-act-plays performed were "A Quiet Evening With Sid And Nancy" by Penny Arcade, "Little House on the Prairie" by the Squat Company, and "The Room" by David van Tieghem and Tina Dudek. The second two-weeks run consisted of the one-acts "Letters from Dead People" by Frank May, "Embedded" by Ann Carlson, and "A

---

50 Site-specific theater has already existed since the 1920s, to break down the fourth wall.
51 Besides raising awareness of places, Hamburger also wants to strengthen community bounds with the theater projects and bring together city planners, municipal agencies, and local businesses in the process (En Garde Arts, Inc., "Mission Statement"1).
52 One playbill of the performance looks like an advertisement for a vacation package at the hotel, promising the future guest "A return to the eras of good times and room-service! With a special evening of performances and partying at the Chelsea Hotel" (En Garde Arts, Inc., "Brochure *At The Chelsea*").

Way with Words" by John Kelly alias Dagmar Onassis. However, only a part of the second run took place at the Chelsea Hotel because the New York Fire Department closed the production at the hotel temporarily due to the violations of regulations.[53] Alternatively, parts of the production were shown in the hotel lobby and in a nearby private loft.

"A Quiet Evening With Sid And Nancy" enables the audience to 'observe' a quiet evening of the punk couple in their hotel room. The performance ends with the actress of Nancy Spungen lying bleeding on the tiles of the hall's bathroom, which reminds the audience of her murder at the hotel. In "Letters from Dead People," Frank Maya reads from fictional complaints of famous people staying at the hotels, amongst others Janis Joplin. Dagmar Onassis sings songs by Joni Mitchell in "A Way with Words;" however, she leaves out her song "Chelsea Morning." The reviews of the performances were rather mixed. For some, it was a great way of seeing the Chelsea as a truly artistic space. For others, some of the one-act-plays were silly and not developed enough. In *High Performance*, the reviewer states that "[t]he best works made the environment a participant in the performance rather than a backdrop" ("Penny Arcade"). Here, the hotel becomes a 'mithandelnder Schauplatz.' John Milward writes about the play that it is "a campy compendium ... captur[ing] a certain *je ne sais quoi* that has made the Chelsea the hotel of choice for generations of bohemian artists" and, while it is not great theater, it "is at least as entertaining as watching the passing parade in the Chelsea lobby" (Milward). Interesting are also the comments of the reviewers on the fact that the second part of the run of *At The Chelsea* was removed to a place outside of the hotel. For Robert Massa, "[t]he Chelsea was all the more present by its absence" (Massa). So, while the site-specific aspect was undermined because of the fire department's regulations, the atmosphere of the Chelsea Hotel was still palpable in the one-act-plays.

At The Chelsea was not En Garde Arts most successful play. However, the hotel was among the theater group's most famous settings. It seems that the New York audience was indeed most interested in seeing the unique setting of the hotel "in action." They wanted to perceive its atmosphere for themselves. In so far, En Garde Arts actually achieved to catch the *je ne sais quoi* of the Chelsea, this element of the hotel *genius loci*, which is impossible to grasp, but gives a place character.

---

53 The single room used was not licensed for the number of the audience, which was 75 people per show.

Save the Last Dance: Earthfall's Interpretation of the Chelsea Hotel

My second and last example of the Hotel Chelsea as a source of inspiration for 'outsiders' is the production *Chelsea Hotel* by the Welsh dance company Earthfall. In fall 2013, Earthfall toured with its Chelsea-inspired dance production through England and Wales.[54] Unlike *At the Chelsea*, Earthfall's performance does not use the physical Chelsea Hotel, but builds on its reputation and the stories surrounding it. The critically acclaimed show combines dance choreography with music commissioned for this project, which was inspired by the hotel's former residents. The Chelsea itself is present in form of videos and pictures, which are shown in the background. The show's producers, Jessica Cohen and James Ennis, have been inspired by Patti Smith's memoir, *Just Kids,* and Andy Warhol's work at the hotel, especially the film *Chelsea Girls*.

Cohen became aware of the Chelsea Hotel in 1980, when she visited a friend in New York, who lived in the hotel. At that point, the building was seen as an actually dangerous place, where drug deals and suicides happened. Yet, Cohen felt awed by the hotel and its legacy, which has inspired "an exceptional gallery of art works" (Cohen qtd. in Mackerell). For the performance, two long-term residents of the Chelsea supported the dance company, the artists' couple Bernard and Judy Childs. In 2011, they showed the choreographers around the hotel, which was already in its remodeling process, and told them stories of the famous and not so famous residents. Even though Cohen and Ennis researched that the hotel does not have a great history with the art of dancing, "[i]t was so fascinating that we felt that we had to do a piece about it in its own right" (Cohen qtd. in Mackerell).

The show focuses on four couples, who represent some of the actual residents, yet in a fictionalized, universal way. One couple is inspired by Patti Smith and Robert Mapplethorpe, and another by Sid Vicious and Nancy Spungen. In addition, there is also a couple of two male dancers, who perform a homoerotic dance which expresses the struggle of contradicting desires for each other. They stand for the variety of people living at the hotel and not for specific persons. With the dance project, the producers want to "reveal the poetry and tragicomic events from this iconic hotel and its place in contemporary culture" (Earthfall). Cohen and Ennis see the hotel not only as a visually iconic place in New York, but they understand it as an important influence on New York's culture and a source for the creation of art.

---

54 Jessica Cohen and James Ennis's dance company Earthfall was founded in Wales in 1989 with the mission to "engage, excite, inspire, stimulate and provoke the audience through the creation and touring of original high-quality mixed-media dance theatre performance" (Earthfall). The company's concept is to forge "radical choreography with live music and strong visual imagery" (Earthfall).

Their work shows the Chelsea Hotel's spatial agency. The way the hotel is depicted in the dance performance, it plays a greater role in the lives of its residents than being only a temporary accommodation and background setting.

The *Chelsea Hotel* tour was a success with the critics. According to Judith Mackerell of *The Guardian*, "[t]his portrait of the Chelsea is far more than an homage to one building, it's a sharp and tender elegy for our collective youth" (Mackerell). The show convincingly takes the audience back to the time when the hotel was a concentration of extraordinary talent, similar to Paris in the 1920s (Mackerell). While *Chelsea Hotel* seems to be a swan song to the hotel, which was already being transformed into a more commercial structure at the point of the performance, it still captures the hotel's power for inspiring people. The dance performance *Chelsea Hotel* by Earthfall is the most recent example of the rich legacy of the Chelsea's power of inspiration. It is a celebration of its ongoing fascination, which affects not only Chelsea insiders but also artists, who did not live at the hotel.

The Chelsea Hotel has never fulfilled the classic expectations that people have of modern American hotels. There are no little shampoo bottles or fluffy towels in its rooms. As Arthur Miller wrote in his memoir *Timebends*, it is not American in that way. Yet, the artists' hotel presents a unique example of what the institution can also be in New York, and what it can accomplish for its society and culture. In 2011, the Chelsea was sold by the Chelsea Hotel Corporation after seventy years of continuous ownership. Ed Scheetz, the current owner of the Chelsea Hotel, is the embodiment of the Bloomberg type of developers, who transform New York at the moment. According to an article in *The New Yorker*, the new owner's vision for the hotel is a continuation of the hotel's legacy. Scheetz claims that the new Hotel Chelsea will welcome "a community that is diverse – socio-economically, age, everything ... . We want young people that don't have a lot of money to be able to experience it, and interact with somebody who may have the greatest suite in the hotel" (Scheetz qtd. in Mead 22). The article mentions that the price range he is talking about is between $200 and $1000 per night. Scheetz acknowledges the hotel as a special place. He claims that he even intends to live there himself. However, he wants to revamp it, with a club on the roof top and top-of-the-line amenities in each room.

The remaining Chelseaites, who hold on to their rent-controlled apartments despite the impairments of the construction work, fear these changes. They have taken the fight for the hotel's soul, as some advocates of the hotel call it, to a very public level by using the instruments of modern social media. In Ed Hamilton's blog, *Living With Legends: Hotel Chelsea Blog*, but also on other websites by urban activists like the *gothamist.com*, Scheetz's plans are publicly torn to shreds. Hamilton, a writer and resident of the Chelsea, has become the mouthpiece of the activists fighting to preserve the hotel in its old way. He is a sought after interview partner and commentator on all things connected to the Chelsea neighborhood. On Hamilton's webpage, in addition to his own entries, one finds a large collection of articles on the developments at the Chelsea from the residents' point of view. These texts are often emotional, and their tone is very sharp. Scheetz reacts with lawsuits and money offers to buy out those residents with justified legal claims. About the current state of affairs at the Chelsea Hamilton writes: "It's definitely quiet here now. Funereally quiet. It used to be really lively. ... At the Chelsea, there were parties all the time in the heyday... . Unfortunately, that's over. That's the sad thing; that's the thing I hate worst. They can evict me and the others. But they're sort of ending a way of life" (Buckley). His comment, as well as those by other residents published in newspaper articles and online blogs, are from a subjective point of view. Still, they tell us about the Chelsea's importance for individual bohemians, their community, and New York's society and culture. Edward Relph writes: "In both our communal and our personal experience of places there is often a close attachment... . It is this attachment that constitutes our roots in places; and the familiarity that this involves is not just a detailed knowledge, but a sense of deep care and concern for that place" (Relph 37). This rootedness and resulting sense of deep care can be seen in the case of the Chelsea Hotel and its inhabitants. For some residents, the hotel has achieved an almost sacred character. In Ariel Leve's article, there is a picture of one resident with the hotel tattooed on his arm. It reminds one of religious rites of native tribes. The Chelseaites are often compared to a tribal community. This also fits Hetherington's understanding of social centrality of certain countercultural places. They are willing to fight for the place, despite inconveniences and harsh disputes.

At the moment the Chelsea is closed during constructions. Its once unique atmosphere, "composed of self-reliance, self-adulation, self-confidence that would all be dissipated in the atmosphere of orthodox living" (Turner 19), created by the people and inspired by the hotel's unique walls, is mostly gone. Not everything in the Chelsea was worth preserving, and it was not idealized by all inhabitants and visitors. New Yorkers were fascinated by the place, yet, at the same time, the majority was also put off by its shabbiness and bad reputation. As Leve wrote in his article, the Chelsea was full of contradictions. While the art mix in the lobby was quite democratic, combining trash and high art, the hotel itself had its own type of hierarchy. The tenants did not always mix, contradicting some of the nostalgic tales by former hotel residents. Stanley Bard later preferred famous artists to aspiring young artists. The rooftop was closed-off to those residents who did not live in the spacious penthouse and duplex studios on the top floors. The loud, run-down first two floors were often the homes of junkies, immigrants, and those who had not yet achieved fame and fortune. I have not discussed at length how many people were destroyed by the powerful atmosphere of the hotel and the temptations that existed there. Not all accounts on the hotel discuss this disparate nature of the place. They gloss over the differences and those elements that do not fit their utopian image of the Chelsea Hotel as the sanctuary to all who want to make the world a better, more interesting place. My reason for not focusing on this side of the hotel in the case study is that it would not do justice to the strong utopian quality of the Chelsea. The place saw the destruction of some of its guests. There are critical voices who blame the hotel for this destruction. However, considering the texts on this hotel, the creative, constructive side of the hotel appears to be the decisive one. It represents the experience of most tenants of the Chelsea Hotel.

The Hotel Chelsea is very different from the Waldorf, and even though it shares an artistic clientele with the Algonquin, its bohemian nature differs clearly from the sophisticated hotel on 44th Street. As Ed Hamilton, author of *Legends of the Chelsea Hotel* (2007), puts it, the hotel on West 23rd Street is a rebel mecca. Because of the extensive material and the deep ties that exist between the former residents and the Chelsea, its legacy will continue and it will remain a special place in the history of New York. Sherill Tippins, the author of *Inside the Dream Palace*, remains optimistic for the future of the Chelsea. She believes that the hotel will always reincarnate into something unique: "It is almost as though the Chelsea itself has said it's time for a change. You do get that feeling about the building after a while. I feel like as the Chelsea goes, so goes the city" (Tippins qtd. in Meade 23). Even if the hotel is gutted and revamped, its *genius loci* still determines its next incarnation. The Chelsea Hotel is currently closed as a hotel. It shares this fate with the Hotel Theresa and the Hotel Grossinger. In the following I will discuss these two hotels that have also fulfilled important functions for their communities.

4. Hotel Theresa – Harlem's Center of African-American Self-Manifestation

> "When we saw people who were going to be in New York, we'd say, 'Meet me at the Theresa.' We knew we would stay there and it gave us a sense of security. ...There was a solidarity among blacks who gathered in the hotel – a kind of solidarity that we don't have today. And I doubt if we will ever have a place like the Theresa again."
>
> CHUCK JACKSON/QTD. IN WILSON 20F

The three case studies, which have been discussed so far, show the wide range of hotels in New York. The Waldorf-Astoria, the Algonquin, and the Chelsea provide all the classic requirements connected to the institution hotel, yet they all also go beyond this and become important places for the city's society and culture. They differ in their clientele and management style. However, the three hotels also shared some of their guests in the past and offered their services to the American mainstream which is predominately white. The Hotel Theresa, which has become famous as "The Waldorf of Harlem" ("The Waldorf of Harlem" 8), stands apart from these other three well-known hotels. Not because its patrons were less glamorous, not because it had a different style of management, but because this hotel was one of the first and undoubtedly the greatest, black hotel in New York.[1] The Hotel Theresa was located on 125th Street and Seventh Avenue, which was also called "the Great Black Way" (Mallory 46). It mirrored Harlem's life. It was at the heart of what became the center of black culture in America. The Apollo Theater was its neighbor, and the big department stores of upper-Manhattan were all located around it. The Hotel Theresa developed into *the* meeting place of African-American entertainers, sportsmen, and politicians. Its bar was legendary. In and around the Theresa, African-American leaders had their offices, and regularly met with their

---

1 The Hotel Theresa was indeed the most famous hotel for African-Americans in America.

friends and clients in the hotel lobby and bar to discuss the situation of black people in New York City. With the end of segregation, it ceased to exist as a hotel in the 1960s.

While the Theresa did not actively exclude other ethnic groups, it was clear that the hotel catered mainly to the black community. The hotel became a symbol for an increasing African-American self-confidence, symbolizing to blacks and whites alike that people of color had made another significant step toward joining the American mainstream. Finally they had their own fine hotel in which they could live the high life just like the white people did in the grand palaces of mid-Manhattan.[2]

The number of texts written about the Theresa is much smaller compared with the other hotels discussed in this study. It is caused by a deficiency of good collections of African-American documents and historic material, which was often disregarded or only sporadically preserved due to insufficient funding, lack of awareness, and prejudices. As the situation is even worse for other historic black hotels, the Hotel Theresa functions here as a representative of a whole range of African-American hostelries which developed all over New York and America as a result of segregation. While I can only provide a limited insight into how important the institution of the hotel was for the African-American community, it is nevertheless crucial to include their example in the discussion of the impact of hotel experience on New York culture. The pretty terracotta building of the Theresa still exists, yet it was turned into an office building in 1967. Some Harlemites fear that with the transformation of the hotel into a business building they may have lost the heart of Harlem (Wilson 48). This already tells us something about the great significance that African-American people granted to the Theresa. The following analysis will discuss three important aspects of hotel experience at the Theresa: the hotel as the center of the African-American community; the hotel as a stage for black pride and as a symbol of black achievement; and the hotel as a stage for politics and as a victim of desegregation. I will end by examining the Theresa's role as training ground for an African-American leader.

In this case study the focus is on the hotel's central position for the people in Harlem and the fact that the Theresa became a platform for racial self-manifestation. This was to a large degree possible because of the hotel's multi-functionality and because the hotel as an institution had such an important standing in the white American community. While the Theresa was a comfortable hotel, it never reached the same level of luxury as a grand hotel like the Waldorf-Astoria, a circumstance that remained a problem for leading figures of black society. Yet, the hotel provided security against discrimination and rejection at a time when this was

---

2   Many hotels of Midtown still mostly excluded blacks as customers until the late 1950s.

still an everyday occurrence. The Hotel Theresa is a fascinating example of the urban development of Harlem and the mixed blessings of social change.[3]

The Theresa in Harlem was the climax of a movement that started decades before the hotel opened to black customers. Therefore, I will first provide some background information on the ambiguous relationship between hotels and African-Americans and the important function that hotels and inns played in the history of black equality. The history of black traveling and tourism is an often-overlooked chapter in the history of hospitality, and also in the fight for African-American equality. If we consider it in more depth it will deepen the understanding of the central role of the Hotel Theresa for Harlem.

A Short History of Black Travel and Tourism

From the beginning of modern American hotels, the presence of African-American customers in hostelries was problematic. Although there were often no official legal barriers which prevented blacks from entering hotels as customers in order to use the advertised services, an unwritten understanding existed which enabled many innkeepers to turn them away. Sandoval-Strausz describes in his book *Hotel: An American History* that in 1851 Frederick Douglass, probably the most famous African-American of his time, suffered discrimination at the hands of a front desk clerk in a hotel in Cleveland and could only obtain the requested room because of his well-known reputation (284). This was at least possible for Douglass in the Northern States. South of the Mason-Dixon Line African-Americans were still slaves at that point, and they would only enter a hotel as house servants with their masters or as hotel workers through a separate entrance. While the situation changed for all black Americans with the Emancipation Proclamation in 1863 and the following 13th Amendment to the Constitution of the United States of America, the question of whether African-Americans had a right to enter hotels was still a hotly debated topic.

Hotels became a focal point in the discussion of desegregation. Supporters of the rights of African-Americans claimed the law of the innkeeper as leverage to open all public spaces to them. The common law of innkeepers requires "the owners of public houses to provide shelter and refreshment to all travelers" (Sandoval-Strausz 290). This simple definition encompasses all members of society, including minorities like African-Americans. During Reconstruction, from 1865 to 1871, Senator Charles Sumner of Massachusetts stressed this point in his efforts to achieve equality for the newly freed black population. Accordingly, when the Civil Rights bill was discussed in the 1870s, hotels were one of the institutions at the heart of the debate.

---

3 See also Levander 10.

Controversies ignited on the issue of whether the right of guests for shelter was seen as more important under the innkeeper's law than the proprietor's right to control his or her own premises, i. e., the right to his or her private property (Sandoval-Strausz 293). Advocates of civil rights tried to use hotels as "the key to racial equality in public places" (Sandoval-Strausz 295). Starting with hostelries, they also wanted to achieve the opening of all other public institutions. Hotels foreshadowed "the numerous contemporary privatized public spaces (like theme parks, cruise ships, shopping malls, and resorts) that have come to define urban modernity" (Levander, *Hotel Life*, 2). Opponents wielded the ideology of the free market as their weapon of defense, admonishing law makers that an opening of all commercial places to all people could endanger the business of these institutions. As a compromise, the Civil Rights Act of 1875 limited the types of places of business which were open to everyone. In its final form the act states:

all persons within the jurisdiction of the United States shall be entitled to the full and equal enjoyment of accommodations, advantages, facilities, and privileges of inns, public conveyances on land and water, theaters, and other places of public amusement; subject only to the conditions and limitations established by law, and applicable alike to citizens of every race and color, regardless of any previous condition of servitude. (Civil Right Act of 1875 as qtd. in Sandoval-Strausz 295)

Because of this limitation, the act passed the Senate as well as the House of Representatives and became the law. "Inns" are named as the first place affected by the Civil Rights Act, which shows their importance in the previous discussions. They provided the key to the passing of the bill. Sandoval-Strausz states: "The passage of the act wrote the law of hospitality into the federal statute books" (Sandoval-Strausz 295). The act required that people who denied African-Americans entry into hotels and places of amusement were to be fined $500, payable to the aggrieved person.

Reactions to the bill were mixed. Northerners accepted the law, yet expected African-Americans to refrain from overly asserting their rights, while Southerners reacted hotly. Many establishments closed down and reopened as private boarding houses to prevent the necessity of catering to African-Americans. Blacks naturally saw the act as a starting point for more participation in public life and acted in a coordinated fashion to make use of the new law. The main problem lay in the circumstance that the federal officials, who were meant to enforce the law, were not well-prepared and often failed to fulfill their role. Partly because of their lack of action and partly because of changes in the law, African-Americans were quickly prevented again from entering public institutions by *de facto* segregation in American cities. In 1883, only eight years after the Civil Rights Act was passed, the Supreme Court declared it unconstitutional, and exclusionary practices flourished again, not only in the South but all over the United States.[4] Between the 1880s and the 1960s, African-Americans were segregated in most public institutions, *de facto* in the Northern states and *de jure* in the Southern states, and were commonly denied access to hotels, theaters, and public transportation because of their skin color. In his "I Have a Dream" speech in 1963 Martin Luther King still had to state that blacks could "never be satisfied as long as our bodies, heavy with the fatigue of travel, cannot gain lodging in the motels of the highways and the hotels of the cities" (King 104). The reason given by white businessmen for the heated struggle against inclusion was officially that their white customers did not wish to dine, sleep, or be entertained next to black customers and that the businesses would lose money if they accepted a black clientele. A hundred years after the end of the American Civil War, this ideology of the free market kept segregation a normal practice in the hotel business in many parts of the United States. Although several states started to include civil rights acts in their state laws, it took until the mid-1960s before another attempt for a national solution was made. This time the advocators of black equality were successful and desegregation became federal law with the Civil Rights Act of 1964.[5]

A fact that has not been discussed much in the three preceding case studies, yet which needs to be pointed out here, is that hotels are first and foremost commercial establishments that work under the system of capitalism. Although they perform the ancient rites of hospitality, hotels need to make money by providing shelter and refreshment. In the case of minorities, it is therefore even more important to look closely at the roles which hotels performed for these ethnic communities and how they impacted the communities' culture. Hotels catering to groups on the margin were under more stress and scrutiny to fulfill their roles successfully as sanctuary, retreat, and palace of the public. As I will show with the Hotel Theresa, the discrimination existing in mainstream hotels, resorts, and entertainment halls did

---

4   The concept behind declaring the act unconstitutional was that the federal government did not have the right to limit the individual rights of a person. Thus the private status of the innkeeper was accepted and protected (Sandoval-Strausz 301).

5   The Act outlawed discrimination in "any inn, hotel, motel ... any restaurant, cafeteria, lunchroom, lunchcounter, soda fountain ... any motion picture house, theater, concert hall, sports arena, stadium or other place of exhibition or entertainment" (Sandoval-Strausz 307). Because the Civil Rights Act of 1964 so closely resembled the one of 1875, it also needed to prove its constitutionality. This was largely achieved in the case of Heart of Atlanta Motel vs. United States, where the Supreme Court Justices used the law of hospitality and the need to protect travelers to affirm the constitutionality of the Civil Rights Act. Discrimination against minorities in the 1960s would have "a far greater impact upon the Nation's commerce than such practices had upon the economy of another day" (Sandoval-Strausz 309).

not mean that African-Americans were excluded from the institution hotel in general. To fill the gap, an alternative hotel-network developed that catered specifically to African-Americans.[6]

Since the middle of the nineteenth century it became a "patriotic exercise" (Armstead, "Revisiting Hotels" 151) to tour the country and visit historic sites across America, in short to travel America as a tourist. Through resorts owned by colored people or by white proprietors who catered specifically to them, African-Americans, too, could take part in the increasing development of tourism in America. Some of the best-known examples are the resorts in Idlewild, Michigan, and Highland Beach in Maryland (Armstead, "Revisiting Hotels" 137). Frederick Douglass's son, Charles, started Highland Beach in Arundel-on-the-Bay in Maryland as a summer retreat for African-Americans in 1893 after he had been refused service in white hotels (Armstead, "Revisiting Hotels" 144). Over the years, it became the vacation spot for the Washington D.C.-based black elite.[7] The resort in Idlewild, Michigan, was founded in 1912 in Lake County and was the preferred leisure place for Chicago's leading black class. The houses and bungalows of Idlewild, built in a rustic and simplistic style, offered all modern amenities like electricity and exuded adequate luxury with their Oriental rugs (Armstead, "Revisiting Hotels" 145). During the late nineteenth and early twentieth century, photographs taken of black vacationers of both places show that the black customers behaved themselves in the same decorous, Victorian fashion as white people did and that they enjoyed the same events and activities that mainstream Americans liked, such as Croquet and picnics. In these resorts, African-Americans lived in a kind of de-racialized atmosphere, where they could unwind from the stress of their jobs without needing to fear discrimination (Armstead, "Revisiting Hotels" 150). Furthermore, by taking part in the tourist movement of the early twentieth century, blacks could also affirm their status as American citizens, doing the same kind of things all other Americans did during vacation. Historian Marguerite S. Shaffer states that tourism, which "solidified into a popular leisure activity" (Shaffer 170) in the nineteenth century, helped to shape an American identity. Building these resorts, owning hotels, and managing them allowed African-Americans to feel like a part of the larger American nation. It provided them with the security of ownership and a sound business network of hotels, restaurants, and entertainment places. Black hospitality institutions enabled them to join "in the celebration of the nation with which they identified" (Armstead,

---

6   For more information, see Myra B. Young Armstead, "Lord, Please Don't Take Me in August," African Americans in Newport and Saratoga Springs, 1870-1930 (1999). Also see the chapter "Vacation Spots for the Black Elite" (151-81) in Lawrence Otis Graham, Our Kind of People: Inside America's Black Upper Class (1999).

7   Highland Beach was incorporated as the first black town in Maryland in 1922.

"Revisiting Hotels" 151). By the time of the Great Depression and the Second World War, the consumption of everything American-produced, including vacation trips and stays at American-owned and run hotels, was seen as a patriotic act.

This new black self-confidence was also expressed in travel guides specifically written for African-Americans like *The Negro Motorist Green-Book*, first published in 1936 and continued until 1967, which listed an ever growing number of hotels, motels, and restaurants which welcomed Blacks (Armstead, "Revisiting Hotels" 154). In 1940, it already included 43 states and Washington D.C. Establishments in the Southern States were mentioned shortly in a section labeled "Southward." Under President Franklin D. Roosevelt's administration during the New Deal the federal government also understood the importance of using the increasing consumer base of African-Americans for the recovery of the national economy by printing the *Directory of Negro Hotels and Guests Houses in the United States*, which was distributed by the National Park Service in 1939 (Armstead, "Revisiting Hotels" 155). Both publications show that, on the one hand, specific guides were still needed for African-Americans, as they were still turned away from many establishments due to their skin color. On the other hand, the publications show that blacks found a way to deal with this situation by creating their own alternative network of hotels, resorts, and restaurants and that their presence as customers was acknowledged by parts of the America society by the middle of the twentieth century.[8]

By 1940, it was no longer necessary for many African-American business travelers to stay at private houses during their journeys to cities. Instead, professional institutions catered to them, which underlines the increasingly self-confident community of blacks and the progress in their struggle for full equality. This affected not only travel plans of black tourists but also hotel employment practice. After years of picketing and legal battles, former Whites-only hotels were forced by the Civil Rights Act of 1964 to employ African-Americans in more visible positions such as the front office. In the TV-series *Hotel* (1983-1988) by Aaron Spelling the success of this change in hiring practice was symbolically expressed in the role of front desk manager, Julie Gillette, played by Shari Belafonte, and head of hotel security, Billy Griffin, played by Nathan Cook. The example of this popular TV show makes it clear that African-Americans both as executive staff members and as guests had become an everyday occurrence in American life by the 1980s.

---

8   Although the hotel is a capitalistic enterprise and can be elitist and exclusionary, Levander writes: its "enduring popularity as an important crossroads has made it a highly conducive, logical, and often inevitable setting for protest, for awakening, for historic drama" (Levander 11).

The situation for African-American travelers in New York City was similar to that of the rest of the nation during the early twentieth century. Except for some notable exceptions like Booker T. Washington, whose reputation allowed him to stay for many years at the first-class Hotel Manhattan in Lower Manhattan, most black guests were refused entry in Manhattan's hotels. As could be seen in Langston Hughes's poem on the opening of the second Waldorf-Astoria, African-Americans were not allowed as guests or white-collar professionals. Black travelers needed either to stay with friends or to take up residence in one of the shabby hotels in upper-Manhattan, which allowed colored guests as they often did not attract white customers. Two notable institutions for black travelers in New York in the early twentieth century were the Marshal Hotel and the Maceo Hotel, which can be seen as "vanguards" for the Theresa (Wilson 52). Yet, continued racism combined with increasing numbers of black customers showed that these hotels were no longer sufficient. The situation was unsatisfactory for the aspiring African-American middle- and upper-middle class who easily could pay the rates of a good hotel in Mid-Manhattan, yet were not allowed to stay there due to the color bar. Even well-known entertainers like Lena Horne or Duke Ellington could not stay in the hotels where they were booked as star guests on the stage, but needed to remove themselves to an uptown spot (Scherman 13).

By 1940, Harlem was already the heart of the black community in New York City.[9] Known as a district for well-to-do Irish and later Jewish-Americans during the real estate boom of the late nineteenth century, the area between 110th and 155th Street and the East River and Hudson River, slowly but surely turned into a black neighborhood during the 1910s and 20s. The Great Migration brought large numbers of African-Americans from the South to northern cities. As the rents and housing prices in Harlem decreased after the real estate bubble burst and the housing market consequently collapsed, blacks took up residence there. In the years, which became known as the Harlem Renaissance in the 1920s and 30s, the black population grew to 180,000 people (Alleyne and Anderson 83). Still, during the Harlem Renaissance many of the entertainment places like the Cotton Club were for a white-only customer base. Blacks were only allowed as service staff and entertainers. The same was the case for many other businesses, like the department stores, the restaurants, and hotels owned by white Harlemites. With the beginning of civil rights actions after the second world war, for example, the double victory campaign and activities of the NAACP, the situation slowly started to change.[10]

---

9   The name Harlem goes back to the original European settlers of this part of town, the Dutch, who called it Haarlem after a town in the Netherlands.

10 Black customers were, for example, encouraged by the NAACP and other organizations not to buy in shops, which did not offer employment for African-Americans. This was one path of action, which helped to change the business practices in Harlem.

More businesses were bought by African-American entrepreneurs, and entertainment places also started to allow black people in the audience. The Hotel Theresa was in the midst of the changes happening in Harlem and it is exemplary of these developments in many ways. Next, I will discuss the history of this hotel and consider its location and structural appearance before I will examine the different aspects of the hotel experience at the Theresa.

The Biography of the Hotel Theresa

The thirteen-story Hotel Theresa was opened in 1913 and was the highest building at the time in Harlem (Hirsh 116). It remained the tallest for forty years. The lot on which the Hotel Theresa was erected was formerly the location of the Winthrop Hotel, built in the 1880s. It was six-stories tall and owned by Alva S. Walker. The Winthrop was torn down to make way for the Theresa in 1911 (Dolkart 2). This new hotel contained three hundred bedrooms and was an imposing presence on 125th Street.[11] The Theresa was developed by clothing manufacturer Gustavus Seidenberg who named it in honor of his late wife, Theresa Seidenberg. The manufacturer actually first planned to erect a department store on this location, which was considered prime real estate in uptown Manhattan.[12] Yet, reading the signs of the times correctly, he figured it would bring more money to have a respectable middle-class hotel built in this convenient location, also known as the "heart of Harlem." As Image 8 below shows, the hotel's direct neighbors were the Apollo Theater (erected between 1913 and 1914, renamed as the Apollo in the 1930s), the Victory Theater (1917), and Blumstein's Department Store (1921) (Dolkart 3). The architectural firm for the Theresa was George & Edward Blum. The building's outstanding appearance is achieved through its white brick and terra cotta façade, which is adorned with geometric ornamentation (Johnson 26). The ornamentations were said to have been inspired by Islamic decorations of the 14th century Alhambra, which is apparent in the image below (Image 9). Others saw in it

---

11 According to William and Rivers, Harlem's main thoroughfare, 125th Street, is said to have gotten its prominence partly because of the hotel: "The other streets of Harlem which might have developed prominence, you will notice, have no hotels of the importance and standing of the Theresa and, despite stores, theaters, and transit facilities, must be content to play second fiddle" (Williams and Rivers 144).

12 In the article "12-Story Hotel For Harlem" in *The Evening Mail* from March 21, 1912, Seidenberg is reported to have come to an agreement with L. M. Blumstein in 1911 to erect a department store. The plan was canceled in 1912 as the article states without giving reason and instead the Theresa was built. It is mentioned that the public transport situation was ideal for a hotel, since it was only one block from the subway and the elevated train.

a foreshadowing of the Art Deco elements of the 1920s (Gray). It is important to note that the hotel was run as an all-white place for the first thirty years. It was not built as a hotel for African-Americans. It was "the golden girl and grand dame of the Renaissance" (Holland 21).

Image 8: The "Great Black Way": The Apollo Theater with the Theresa in the background

125th Street View. Private.

In all texts on the hotel, the Theresa is called a handsome building and a decisive presence in Harlem. It quickly became known as the "Waldorf of Harlem" as, similar to the Waldorf, it dominated the scene and provided as great a comfort as the downtown Waldorf hotel. The Theresa catered to an all-white clientele for almost thirty years before it was finally desegregated in 1940 due to declining occupancy rates and lawsuits. The owners decided to hire a black manager, Walter W. Scott, a university graduate and hotel professional. Scott ran the hotel until 1947 when he retired due to illness. The management was taken over by William (Billy) Brown. Brown, who had already conducted federal housing programs in Washington and Boston, remained the manager of the hotel for ten years and returned, after an absence of a year, for another two years in 1958.[13] At this time the lease was taken over by the well-known African-American businessman and hostelry owner, Love B. Woods, who dreamed of turning the hotel into a real 'Waldorf of Harlem.'[14] Woods invested heavily in the hotel. However, already weakened by age and illness, Love B. Woods lost the struggle for the Theresa against financial pressures and decreasing occupancy rates, as well as the race riots in Harlem in 1964. The Hotel Theresa, in a dilapidated condition, was closed in 1966. It was sold to a white corporation, which turned it into an office building, called the Theresa Towers, in 1967.

Due to its importance for the history of African-Americans, the hotel was one of four buildings granted landmark status in Harlem by the city of New York in 1993, the first ones to be recognized as such in the uptown neighborhood. The commission found that the "Hotel Theresa, built in 1912-13, is significant in the history of Harlem, America's most prominent African-American community, as one of the most important social centers of this community" (Dolkart 12). The other three structures were churches of historical and spiritual importance. Councilwoman C. Virginia Fields, Democrat of Harlem, commented on the decision of the landmark commission: "I believe this is long overdue ... and it does a lot to move forward looking at Harlem for more landmarks as a way of preservation and development" (Dunlap). In 2009, the Theresa Towers was renovated and there is still talk of a future remodeling of parts of it into a hotel. Besides a number of offices, over the years it contained the Campus of Teachers College of the Columbia University, and also the Institute for Urban and Minority Education (IUME), which continues to celebrate the building's great history ("The Hotel Theresa").[15] With the Theresa, Harlem lost its only commercial hotel for many years. Even today, there are only a handful of hotels in this part of town. The opening of the Aloft Harlem in 2010, a boutique hotel-chain and member of Starwood Hotels, was seen as a first important step forward in years. It is the first new hotel development in Harlem since the early 1960s. While the neighborhood has become increasingly more attractive to middle-class people of all ethnicities in the last few years, especially white families, Harlem is still lagging behind the rest of Manhattan when it comes to business and infrastructure developments. Part of this might be caused by the lack of hotels in the area.

---

13 Brown had a falling out with the building's owner. However, his success as manager forced them to bring him back after the occupancy rate was sinking.

14 Woods was the owner of the other well-known black hostelry, the Woodside Hotel, immortalized by the song "Jumping the Woodside." He was also the owner of several cheap hostels, called flophouses.

15 IUME moved into the building in the early 2000s. However, recently they moved back to the main campus of Columbia University, see *iume.tc.columbia.edu*.

As historian Sondra Wilson points out in her book *Meet me at the Theresa* (2004), the only monograph focusing on the Theresa Hotel, the literature on the hotel is "minuscule" (Wilson 245). Unlike in the case of the other hotels of this study, there are no autobiographies and memoirs that focus specifically on the hotel experience at the Theresa.[16] Yet, there are a number of personal comments collected in newspaper and magazine articles as well as discussions of the hotel in historiographies of the neighborhood dealing with the importance of the Theresa for Harlem.[17] In addition, there are two biographies on Ron Brown, former Secretary of Commerce during the Clinton administration, who was raised at the Theresa as the child of its second manager Bill Brown.[18] Together with the interviews about the Theresa that Wilson undertook, they provide fascinating material and allow us to understand the importance of the hotel experience at this institution for the black community.[19]

The large question that looms behind many of these texts is: with the demise of the Hotel Theresa, has the black community lost the soul of Harlem? While this might seem exaggerated, the following analysis will show that the hotel and the

---

16 In my opinion, this has to do with the marginal situation of African-Americans in the years in which the hotel was the most important institution in Harlem. Besides the well-known obstacles such as limited education and the lack of leisure and money for writing material, a lack of a market for and interest in their stories caused this shortage in texts. The short comments in the autobiographical texts by Malcolm X and Maya Angelou show that the hotel was perceived as having great significance for the black community, however, none of the hotel managers, residents, or staff member received enough encouragement to put their story to paper.

17 The Hotel Theresa is mentioned, often only shortly, in Jervis Anderson, *This was Harlem: A Cultural Portrait 1900-1950* (1981); Noreen Mallory, *Harlem in the Twentieth Century* (2011); Aberjhani and Sandra L. West, *Encyclopedia of the Harlem Renaissance* (2003); Lloyd A. Williams and Voza Rivers, *Forever Harlem: Celebrating America's Most Diverse Community* (2006); Lawrence Otis Graham, *Our Kind of People: Inside America's Black Upper Class* (1999).

18 One was written by his daughter, Tracey L. Brown, *The Life and Times of Ron Brown: A Memoir* (1998), the other by Stephen Holmes, *Ron Brown: An Uncommon Life* (2001). Again, with Ron Brown we have a hotel child who experienced some of the well-known elements of hotel life as discussed earlier. However, there are also particular differences occurring in the life of the "Theresa's version of Eloise" (Holmes 21) which make his experience especially interesting.

19 Sadly, Sondra Wilson died in 2010, so a communication with her and insight into her material was not possible. This is why I have to use her book more extensively than planned, as it is the only source for the interviews she undertook with members of Harlem's community and Theresa conoscenti.

experiences it provided fulfilled a very important role for African-American New York. The Hotel Theresa was also an important part in the hotel network of the city. The case study on the Theresa Hotel provides the African-American perspective on hotels as cultural institutions.

4.1 THE HOTEL AS CENTER OF THE AFRICAN-AMERICAN COMMUNITY

This short history of the Hotel Theresa already opened up some questions about the importance and the function of the hotel for the black community in Harlem. How did the hotel experience of people at the Harlem hotel transform it into a center and platform for the African American community? I will start by examining the transformation of the Theresa from a white to a black institution and what implication this change had for the relationship between the building and the community.

Image 9: The Façade with Ornamentations at the Top of the Theresa

Hotel Theresa, Harlem. Private.

When it opened in 1913, the Hotel Theresa was built by a white textile merchant and operated as an all-white business. At this point there was still a large white population in Harlem, even though the number of African-Americans inhabitants was rising. The hotel was the first large hotel in upper Manhattan and was a stylish building. It was similar to the Algonquin Hotel in mid-Manhattan, as it too was catering to the upper-middle class and provided its clientele with genteel comfort. The Theresa was not built in the neoclassic hotel style but already leaned toward new architectural designs influenced by the Beaux Arts movement and the upcoming Art Deco style. While it was not as large as some of the grandiose downtown hotels, it was already a substantial hotel enterprise and meant a significant change in the makeup of the area around 125th Street and Seventh Avenue. The coming of the hotel to Harlem was an important step for the community. It showed that Harlem was now connected to the national hotel network of America and was willing to welcome visitors and foreigners. It was also an important signal for commercial enterprises, signifying progress in uptown Manhattan.[20] For the first twenty years, the hotel did not attract much media attention. It was a typical hotel operation of the twentieth century with an average mix of residential and transient guests of white middle-class stock. By the time of the Harlem Renaissance, the white hotel, literally and ethnically, was perceived as a symbol of the Jim Crow system. Like the Cotton Club, it lived the paradox of being in close proximity to establishments that offered African-American culture to a white audience while not integrating blacks in the audience and clientele.

It is interesting to consider the appearance of the building in more detail. The building was by far the tallest one in Harlem, easily standing out in its surrounding environment with its thirteen-stories. It was built to be slender, not massive like the downtown hotels, and it had extensive, if not overly ornamental decorations around its top floors. The facade was and still is very white, a striking contrast to the typical brownstones of New York. From the way the building is described in newspapers and histories of Harlem, it is attributed female, almost Victorian, characteristics: slender, ornamental, white, and handsome (Hirsch 116). This is topped by its name "Theresa," named for Seidenberg's wife, which additionally personifies the building as female and anthropo-morphizes the structure.

The circumstance that the Theresa was a Whites-only institution for many years was the reason for much criticism and hurt in the Harlem community. The hotel was at the heart of Harlem's black community, yet it still functioned as a reminder of white supremacy and discrimination. This hurt was expressed, for example, in two lawsuits by African-American businessmen, who were denied entrance to the Theresa in 1937. They sued the hotel and the Gustav Seidenberg estate on account of violating Section 40 of the State Civil Rights Law, which "forbids discrimination

---

20 By the early twentieth century, hotels were recognized as essential American institutions that represented the reputation of the city to guests from around the country and from abroad (Raitz 17f). It is the first place visitors approach when coming to an unknown city.

by hotels and other 'places of public accommodation' on ground of race, creed or color" ("Hotel Sued By Negroes"). They demanded $500 damages each. This is a typical example of the use of the state law of hospitality. It shows that this kind of racist behavior still existed in the heart of Harlem's black community until the late 1930s, in defiance of the state constitution.

By the late 1930s, the occupancy of the Theresa hotel had decreased so much that a change was necessary. To survive, this slender 'lady' needed to adapt to reality, in a sense, and turned inwardly from white to black. The transformation of the establishment was perceived as an important moment for the black community on its way to equality in America as the "fates of the Hotel Theresa and Harlem were inextricably linked" (Wilson 4). The Hotel Theresa became the safe haven and sanctuary of black Americans during the most difficult years of desegregation and the rise of the Civil Rights Movement, when people started to realize that times were changing in America. This tense situation in New York and the importance of the hotel for the African-American community is expressed in interviews that Sondra Wilson undertook for her book on the Theresa. She quotes Judge James Watson, who said: "We [blacks] really didn't want to go downtown. We had a luxurious hotel now and the burden of being rejected and despised was lifted" (Watson qtd. in Wilson 18). To have a 'luxurious' hotel of their own meant a significant step toward equality in the minds of Harlemites. They could partake in the life of America's middle-class. The Theresa contributed as an enabler of a new self-confidence.

Like the other hotels discussed in this study, the Theresa was not only a stopping place for travelers from across the states and for black visitors from other countries, but an important agent in its local community and home to a number of long-term guests. The bar was *the* meeting place of uptown New York, in importance comparable to the Algonquin's famous dining room. It was so crowded that Billy Rowe, journalist for the *Pittsburgh Courier* and the hotel's columnist, wrote: "a man could lose his pants and walk the length of the place without anybody noticing him" (Rowe qtd. in Scherman 14). The Theresa's public rooms, such as the Orchid dining room and the later added Skyline Ballroom, were locations where the "top-shelf" of black society socialized, had their debuts and weddings, and where the achievements of fellow Blacks were celebrated, such as the Nobel Peace Prize for Ralph Bunche in 1950. Trumpet player Joe Wilder remembers: "The Hotel Theresa was one of the showcases of the community ... . The only one on that level. There is no place today of that status" (Wilder qtd. in Wilson 82).

The hotel's interior, its pomp and decorations together with the flair of the new manager Walter Scott, created an atmosphere of refinement that reflected back on the customers. For Blacks, it was status-confirming to come to the Theresa as it proved to the world that one was able to take part in the high life: "The large mirrors behind the bar allowed beautiful ladies decked out in jewels and furs to admire themselves. The Theresa bar was to blacks what 'Meet me under the clock at the Biltmore' was to whites" (Wilson 94). This is further elaborated in an article on the Theresa in the African-American magazine *Ebony* in 1946, published a year after the foundation of the magazine in the hotel by John H. Johnson (Mallory 47). The writer states that

> The Theresa is social headquarters for Negro America, just as the Waldorf is home for white elite. ... And to its registration desk flock the most famous Negroes in America. It is the temporary home of practically every outstanding Negro who comes to New York. It is common knowledge that Joe Louis stays there along with every big-time Negro fighter. So does Rochester and the Hollywood contingent, all the top bandleaders who haven't the good fortune to have their own apartments in town. Negro educators, colored writers, and the Liberian and Haitian diplomatic representative. Big men in the business world jostle top labor leaders in the flowered, mirrored lobby. ... Today the hotel makes money with Negro business. The building and land are worth about one million dollars. Rooms are booked months in advance and its rooms are always jammed. ("The Waldorf of Harlem" 8)

This excerpt shows that the hotel was perceived as the place in town with which one wanted to identify oneself as an African-American. It was in the Theresa where many members of the black community went for celebrations and where they expressed their self-perception as a strong people. The quote also shows that the Theresa connected the local community of Harlem with the larger world. Harlem writers met foreign diplomats here and local business men came together with entertainment stars. The *Ebony* article repeats several times that the hotel is frequented by African-Americans. It stresses the fact that they are its chief clientele and that these people in return make the hotel important and famous. By mentioning that the Theresa is always booked, a clear sign of the establishment's profitability, the article also tells the reader that the hotel itself is a successful black business. This again reflects well on the advancement of African-Americans in the mid-twentieth century.

The article's title shows that the hotel had already gained its nickname as the "Waldorf of Harlem." While it could not command the exact same level of luxury, it was perceived as a step in this direction. With this hotel, in contrast to the palatial Waldorf, the importance did not lie so much in the rich furnishing and decorations but in the mix of people and the special atmosphere of racial self-awareness it created. As described earlier, hotels often functioned as essential places for their community by showcasing its achievements. They are privatized public places where everyone can see their fellow people's progress and partake in it. The Theresa was the 'palace' of the black people in Harlem.

Walter Scott – Harlem's Leading Black Hotelier

Walter W. Scott, the hotel's first black manager, was instrumental in making the Theresa the center of Harlem society and embodied the new professional class. His taking over of the Theresa in 1940 meant a great change in the African-American community and stood for a significant shift in the power structure between black and white people in uptown New York. As we have seen earlier, the position of a manager has great visibility and is highly respected in the larger American society. George Boldt, Frank Case, and Stanley Bard were well-known figures in New York and were perceived as representatives of their clients. Walter Scott's position as manager of the greatest black hotel in town was also pushing him to the front of the black community. The public saw him as a prime example of what African-American professionals could be like and what they were able to accomplish. His personality and leadership transformed the Theresa into Harlem's mecca for society. The manager's personality and attitude defined the space of the hotel. Scott decided who was part of black society and who was not by including them on his guest list. It was another form of discrimination, but it worked along the lines of W.E.B. Dubois's concept of the "talented tenth" of African-Americans (Rabaka 94). Descriptions of Scott's relationship with the Theresa and his position in Harlem's community show that the manager was an essential element in making the Theresa a center for African-American society and culture. Scott's behavior and actions largely defined the hotel's impact on the community and the people that frequented it. He played a decisive role in the Theresa Hotel experience.

Walter Scott was introduced as manager to the Theresa with the following announcement in the *New York Age* in 1940:

Harlem Hotel Seeks Negro Trade; Picks Manager: The Hotel Theresa at Seventh Avenue and 125th Street, which catered to white patronage for several years, has changed policy as of March 20 and will cater to both races, under Negro management with a Negro staff, according to an announcement by Richard Thomas, publicity manager of the hotel. In carrying out its new policy for the accommodation of Negroes and whites, the Gresham Management Company, operators of the Theresa, appointed Walter Scott as the hotel's manager. Extensive renovations and improvements of the services and facilities of the hotel have been undertaken. A staff of 80 persons has been employed. (qtd. in Wilson 65)

This advertisement for the Theresa fulfills an important purpose: it makes clear to Harlemites and people beyond the borders of New York that there is now an uptown hotel that is integrated and specifically welcomes blacks as customers. As the hotel catered for whites-only for almost three decades this change in policy needed to be made as public as possible. It might be surprising that the hotel also catered to white people, yet as the Theresa already had long-term residents before its change of management, the operators of the hotel were unwilling to send away good permanent customers and instead offered them to stay on for a reasonable rate. More than a dozen white residents accepted the offer and remained for years. They were a last vestige of the white past of the house, yet their comments make clear that they enjoyed their stay at the hotel and felt well taken care of by Walter Scott and his staff. Long-term white resident Isabel Jones remembers: "My, when the colored people took over I was so frightened! ... I thought they'd make me go away, that they want their hotel all for themselves. But mercy, they've been so *kind* [sic]" (Jones qtd. in *Ebony* 9). Another reason for this strategy, besides securing occupancy, was probably to show white New York that while blacks were discriminated against in New York's downtown hotels this was not a practice used at the black-run Theresa. At the hotel, both races lived together without perceivable conflicts. This showed a high level of foresight on the side of Walter Scott and the hotel's operators, and underscores the fact that Blacks wanted to be a part of mainstream American society, not separate from it.

Manager Walter Scott was an example of the promising young black man growing up in America in the early twentieth century. He graduated from New York University and, having gained some experience as bellhop and porter in hotels, was appointed business manager of a YMCA. When he became the Theresa's manager in 1940, Scott moved into the hotel with his family. They occupied a six-room suite on the tenth floor. His wife Gertrude and teenage daughter Gladys lived a relatively invisible life at the hotel because Gertrude Scott was educated in the Victorian fashion and did not approve of the practice of mixing with strangers in the public rooms of the hotel. Sometimes she entertained guests with her husband. However, he fulfilled most of his duties as host alone. The Scotts' daughter graduated from college and studied psychology at New York University during the tenure of her father as the Theresa's manager. Like her father, she was a prime example of the rising professional class of blacks in Harlem. In contrast to the Case family, the manager operated the hotel without familial support. One reason was that middle and upper-middle class African-Americans were at pains to prove that they were respectable, and another was to show that, like the wives of white professionals, the wives of black professionals did not necessarily need to work.[21]

---

21 The Victorian principles of formality were still highly regarded at that time, and being too closely connected to the sometimes very lively crowd of the hotel could be seen as improper and accordingly was not done by Scott's family. It seems like a contradiction that the manager's family should keep themselves separate from a clientele that was said to be made up of the best that black America had to offer and that one should be proud of being identified with. However, it was still a balancing act.

Walter Scott was reportedly very proud of his hotel. He is quoted as saying: "We've got the top hotel in Harlem here … . Bellboys, room service, cleaning and pressing, phones in the rooms, beauty parlor, a restaurant, and a bar right in the building" (qtd in Wilson 66). He drew his self-confidence from his position as the manager of the world's leading hotel for Blacks. Scott's polished personality reflected on the hotel and the good name of the hotel reflected on his character. In an interview, barmaid Ruth Guzzman remembers: "Walter Scott was pure class. ... He was gold brown and tall – good-looking and very distinguished. I was young and I thought he was serious all the time. But now I know he was trying to put forth a good image for the hotel" (qtd. in Wilson 66f). The quote shows the intricate connection between the character of the manager and the character of the hotel. It also shows another typical attribute of the leading black class of the early and mid-twentieth century: leading people in the black society often needed to be of a light skin color (Gatewood 158). Significant parts of the "aristocracy of color" were made up of African-Americans with white ancestry, able to pass for whites. African-Americans with a dark complexion were usually not employed for visible positions like managers, clerks, sales people. The black community saw a light skin and smooth hair as attractive until the second half of the twentieth century.[22]

As the quote above shows, besides being a comfortable accommodation for weary travelers, the hotel also provided good jobs for the people of Harlem. At the Theresa, they were not only employed as dishwashers and maids, but they worked in highly visible positions such as bell men, front desk clerks, barkeepers and managers.[23] It is true that most of the employees in this front-of-the-house position were light-colored African Americans, but they were obviously black according to the racial spectrum and would not have been able to pass as white. Scott was aware that he needed to advertise the blackness of the new Theresa to the people outside in order to make it the preferred new meeting place for people of color. According to contemporaries, he devised a clever plan to do so. Walter Scott put Big Steve, the only black bartender who was already part of the hotel staff before the integration of the hotel, right next to the window of the Theresa bar where he was most visible.[24] Tap dancer Leroy Meyers recalls: "There was a joke around Harlem that Walter Scott put Big Steve in the window so that black people would know that it was all right to come to the hotel. Steve had never worked in the window till Walter

---

22 This particular type of intra-race discrimination continued until the 'Black is Beautiful' movement of the 1960s.

23 Accent was equally important. Blacks who could speak like whites were considered to be higher on the social ladder. There was also the practical consideration that they could be easily understood by whites when they spoke.

24 Even before 1940, a small number of blacks were on the staff of the hotels, and some well-known, rich blacks could also get rooms at the hotel at the end of the 1930s.

Scott put him there" (qtd. Wilson 68). This action shows the balancing act that was necessary to successfully integrate the hotel into its community. To put a staff member, who was more or less hidden during the time of segregation in the hotel, metaphorically on the platter shows the power of visibility which helped to transform the formerly white institution into a meeting place for black society.

Walter Scott actively tried to shape Harlem's society according to his visions, which often very closely resembled the tastes and behavior of New York's white leading class. On his second anniversary at the hotel he is quoted in the *Pittsburgh Courier* stating:

Our staff feel that we have answered a definite need in Uptown New York for comfortable facilities; and all of us are deeply pleased that we have had the opportunity to serve so many fine people from every walk of life and from practically every section of the country, as well as many persons from foreign countries, during the two years we have conducted the Hotel Theresa. ("Hotel Served over 125,000 People")

This quote can be seen as Scott's mission statement for the Theresa. He wants to make it a center for the black community. In addition, it invokes the communal spirit he tried to foster in the hotel and expresses the pride that he felt in his establishment. In the 1940s, the Hotel Theresa under Scott developed very much along the lines of Booker T. Washington's concept of 'accommodation.' The style of the hotel's interior, the mix of the people entertaining at the hotel, the way they behaved, and what they liked was heavily influenced by white American culture. While the hotel was perceived by the guests of the 1940s as their Waldorf and a haven amid a still racist white culture, the hotel and its clientele nevertheless emulated this white culture. The Theresa was a symbol for ongoing changes in society, but it could not yet claim to be a breakthrough for black culture. Still, during the hotel's early years as a black institution Scott enabled members of the leading black class of Harlem to come into contact with each other and with blacks from all over America and the world. A new kind of self-confidence and awareness developed in African-Americans frequenting the hotel. The hotel was the news exchange venue of Harlem and the starting point to learn about happenings in the neighborhood. After the war, Judge James Watson remembers: "When I returned from the army, I headed straight for the Hotel Theresa. ... I knew that I could find out all I needed to know in the Theresa bar. I could catch up on all that had happened while I was away" (qtd. in Wilson 105).

The guests of the house spread the word about the achievements at the Theresa from mouth to mouth. Yet, it was spread even more by the newspaper men and women who wrote of Harlem in their columns and often focused on the going-ons in the Hotel Theresa because everything of importance for black society seemed to happen right here. Therefore, I will discuss in the following the importance of the hotel as the home of the black press. This further underlines the hotel's central position for Harlem.

The Hotel Theresa and the Black Press

John H. Johnson, famous African-American publisher and business man, was a regular at the Theresa. Due to the hotel's convenient location, he opened the offices for his magazines *Jet* and *Ebony* right in the hotel. Both publications were seen as "trailblazing" (Mallory 47) for the black community, starting a movement for more African-American-owned and -run magazines and newspapers. Johnson himself became the first black entrepreneur to appear in the Forbes 400 list. *Ebony* and *Jet* were not the only publications who had offices in the Theresa. It also became the headquarters for most major black New York and American newspapers, such as *The New York Amsterdam News* and *The New York Age* and provided office space for reporters from the *Pittsburgh Courier*, the most important black magazine of the mid-twentieth century (cf. Mallory 45). Starting in the 1940s the Black National Newspaper Publishing Association also had offices on the hotel's second floor, where reporters from all kinds of print media passed by to get the latest news on and for the black community.

The most famous among the journalists connected to the Theresa was Billy Rowe, who wrote for the *Pittsburgh Courier*. He frequently commented on the events happening at the hotel in his column "Billy Rowe's Notebook," the most widely read column of its time in a black newspaper. Having his office directly opposite the hotel and often frequenting its bar to pick up the latest gossip, he was best equipped to tell black America about this mecca of African-American culture. From these stories and accounts of guests, many readers gained the impression that whoever was able to stay at the Theresa was comfortably rich and that living there was the fulfillment of one's dreams. Billy Rowe covered the Theresa until the middle of the 1950s. The hotel helped establish his name, while reciprocally Rowe's column made the hotel a catchword in the African-American community nationwide. By reading "Billy Rowe's Notebook," blacks across the country felt that they took part in the high life at the Theresa. They felt what Edward Relph describes as vicarious insideness, this 'secondhand' experience of a place that still allows for "deeply felt involvement" (Relph 52). Evelyn Cunningham was another reporter for the *Pittsburg Courier* who wrote about happenings at the Theresa. She recalls that people loved to act out the role of the big man around town when coming to the institution on 125th Street: "You are at the world-famous Hotel Theresa so you stand outside to let everybody see you. It used to tickle me to death" (qtd. in Holmes 20). Cunningham worked for the *Courier* until 1962. She became especially known for her covering of lynchings and the Civil Rights Movement. Later Cunningham entered the political world as special assistant to governor

Nelson Rockefeller and made herself a name as a leading force in the battle to better the situation of black women. The press coverage of the Theresa stressed the almost utopian quality of this heterotopia for the black community. By providing space and stories for the press, the hotel empowered black media and gained for itself its well-known reputation as the "center of black existence" (Nails qtd. in Wilson 151).

Hotels, more than most other public institutions in urban society, do not only provide shelter and refreshment but also space for reinvention and power (cf. Levander 14f). While entry to these American institutions was long barred or limited for blacks, the Theresa opened a way into this world. The hotel's importance for the Harlem community and African-Americans nationwide can hardly be overstated. As we could see above, the hotel played a significant role in making Harlem the center of black society and culture. It was the headquarter of black media. The Hotel Theresa, led by role model businessman Walter Scott, provided Harlem with the crucial space for social meetings, information exchange, and as a secure haven – a home away from home without the fear of rejection. The Theresa gave its patrons the hope that the fulfillment of their dream of finally arriving in American society was near. The hotel was perceived as a semi-sacred institution, an iconic place that has been described as an "elegant temple filled with the riches of the black world" (Wilson 4). For the black people of New York and beyond, this hotel had gained social centrality, it provided "a focus for the articulation of identity and a sense of belonging ..." (Hetheringon 34). We could see this social centrality already in the cases of the Algonquin Hotel and the Chelsea Hotel. However, the social centrality of the Theresa is even more important for the community of African-Americans at midcentury because they did not voluntarily live outside mainstream society but were forced into this position by the dominant social stratem of America.

4.2 THE HOTEL AS STAGE FOR BLACK PRIDE AND AS SYMBOL OF BLACK ACHIEVEMENT

The Hotel Theresa under Walter Scott fostered the dream of many black Americans to enjoy the same opportunities and lifestyle that white Americans enjoyed. He himself embodied black achievement and he was responsible for seeing that visitors and guests experienced the Theresa as a stage for black pride and as a symbol of black achievement. Walter Scott's vision for the hotel was to create "a place for the better element of the race – certain entertainers, the professionals, the successful businesspeople, the eminent achievers, and other of unblemished social, moral, and ethical background" (Wilson 139). During his years as the Theresa's manager, Scott worked to improve the place, for example, by opening new public spaces in the hotel such as the Orchid Room. This dining room is reported to have been the manager's pride and joy, a special place in which he only allowed the cream of Harlem society, educated professionals, and writers. Wilson writes: "When *Native Son* was released, there in the orchid room [sic] Richard Wright's masterpiece was celebrated by Harlem's elite authors and artists, including Langston Hughes, Ralph Ellison, and artists Romare Bearden, Aaron Douglas, and Ellen Tarry" (Wilson 112). When Scott needed to retire in 1947 due to a severe illness and moved out of the hotel with his family, he had not yet fully realized his goal of African-American betterment. However, he had given Harlem a respectable public institution for blacks with the Theresa. It was a starting point for further improvements of the positions of African-Americans in New York and the nation.

For Harlemites and black Americans nationwide, the integration of the Hotel Theresa in 1940 meant that for the first time they had a hospitality institution that could be compared to those of the white people. Built by a rich white businessman and run as a white hotel for almost thirty years, it was certainly up to the standard of white America. Mentally, the existence of a black hotel in Manhattan meant that blacks now had a safe place to go to when visiting the city, without fearing rejection and discrimination. As Horace Carter said: "Black people preferred being at the Theresa. There was a psychological security for celebrities and others being in Harlem ..." (qtd. In Wilson 153). While a white company owned the hotel, it was an important change in the 1940s that the general manager of the enterprise was indeed a black man. Both Scott and Billy Brown, Scott's successor, were prototypes for a new generation of black businessmen: well-educated, well-groomed, highly professional at their job, and imbued with the *je ne sais quoi* of a good host. Like the early hoteliers of the nineteenth century, the manager of the Theresa was an important figure in the community of Harlem. He was respected and understood as a representative of the neighborhood by people visiting from outside New York, the first contact many of them had with New York's African-American population.

In the case of the Hotel Theresa, it was segregation that made the institution important and successful in the first place. Although the building was beautiful, even for New York standards, and it had a prime location in the heart of Harlem, the services and the interior decorations would not have set it apart from a large number of Midtown hotels. As a white establishment it would not have been remarkable. One can say that the hotel's fame and importance in Harlem was a product of its time and of the nation's racial ideology. The Theresa was indeed a microcosm for Harlem's position in New York: it contained all achievements and represented the hope of its people for full acceptance in American society, and, at the same time, it mirrored all the shortcomings and the amount of challenges still ahead of them.

Sondra Wilson captures the glamor and hopeful spirit of the place in her description of entering the hotel, as imparted to her by former guests and staff members whom she interviewed:

The double doors beneath the marquee opened to a wide foyer that revealed a lighted lobby. When visitors walked in, they were struck by the glistening mirrors and green and beige floral paper that covered the high walls. Freshly polished white, square tiles with black stripes covered the entire first floor. Eloise Scott, a slender, golden brown lady with a friendly face, stood behind the registration desk to greet visitors. ... A set of elevators was adjacent to the registration desk. Three public telephone booths were next to the elevator. While waiting to register, a number of guests greeted old friends, waited for dates, and looked for celebrities who were usually on the scene. (Wilson 84f)

The hotel, as it is depicted here, was experienced as a civilized, warm, and inviting place. The adjectives used, "open," "light," "glistening," "fresh," "golden,"[25] "friendly," immediately produce an impression of an attractive and civilized surrounding. Besides pleasing physical attributes, the hotel offers something even more important: "Although the hotel's character and appearance were significant, it was the action that occurred within its walls that was most compelling. In other words, the amenities offered by the hotel were secondary to the star-studded guests who stayed under its roof" (Wilson 82). This quote makes clear that the hotel's fame was not so much founded on its structural comparability to the white hotels of the city, but more so on the meaning with which the people of Harlem and African-Americans elsewhere imbued it. The manufacturing and resulting celebration of achievements in business, the arts, and the entertainment industry are a great part of the hotel's special *genius loci*. Black celebrities and society leaders needed the Theresa as their stage, as their 'community hall.' Its physical structure together with the activities that occurred here defined the Theresa's central position and its function as a symbol for black achievement.

The hotel was a stage for black pride from its early years onwards. The boxer Joe Louis belongs to a handful of people who already stayed at the hotel before it was integrated. Famous for his success over Max Schmeling in 1938, Louis was a national hero for both black and white America and always drew crowds when he came to Harlem: "After knocking Hitler's man off his Aryan pedestal, Joe Louis was undisputedly the most celebrated figure in the world in the late 1930s" (Wilson 131). The Theresa was his preferred home in New York, and here Louis's famous victory parties took place. Billy Rowe commented on the effect of a Louis fight on the Theresa in his column, writing: "But an even bet will get you anything, except a room, that it will be a sure defeat for [manager] Walter Scott of the Theresa Hotel.

---

25 Here meaning "light-skinned."

If he had twice as many rooms, he wouldn't be able to lodge all the folk who have been trying for more than a year to sleep and be seen there during the fight" (Scherman 14). People wanted to be close to their idol and staying at the hotel meant that one was part of the in-crowd.

Because of his success, Joe Louis was able to break some of the color barriers still left in Harlem, not just in the Theresa but also in public places around the hotel, such as Frank's Restaurant. His celebrity status gave him power, and he used it. While Louis was never as active a member of the Civil Rights Movement as Muhammed Ali was, he gave Harlemites a reason to be proud and made the hotel the place to celebrate this new racial pride. Because of his iconic status in Harlem's community, June 19, 1946 was declared Joe Louis Day in Harlem and celebrated with a parade (Wilson 132). On the day of Louis's death in 1981, President Ronald Reagan honored Louis, stating: "But Joe Louis was more than a sports legend – his career was an indictment of racial bigotry and a source of pride and inspiration to millions of white and black people around the world" (Reagan).

Louis's conduct in the hotel was not always orderly, and his extramarital love affairs at the Theresa were a hot topic in the bar. In that, Louis was similar to many other famous customers of the hotel such as Sugar Ray Robinson and his wife Edna Mae, who all "let their hair down" at the hotel and disregarded puritanical conventions. The atmosphere at the Theresa in that way was more akin to the one in the Chelsea than to the Algonquin's. Even under the more serious management of Walter Scott, the hotel was famous for the parties that went on in its public parts and private bedrooms, and for the good times people had there. Joe Louis is just one hero in a long line of black celebrities, who stayed at the hotel. The Theresa was also home to entertainment stars like Duke Ellington, Lena Horne, Dinah Washington, and Jimi Hendrix. Hendrix is known as the last famous resident of the hotel before it closed. Rejected by white hotels, here the stars of black America were celebrated by the community and spoiled by the staff: "In its heyday [the Theresa] sparkled, a stylish response to an ugly reality – the Jim Crow policy of the big Midtown hotels" (Scherman 13). The Theresa Hotel was for the 1940s and 50s "Harlem's mecca, the home away from home for black entertainers, sports heroes, politicians, and other public figures" (Brown 40).

Because of the increasing number of African-American celebrities visiting the establishment on 125th Street, a stay at the Theresa gained an almost mythical importance in the black community. People imagined that 'things could happen' at the hotel. While it might not change one's whole life, a stay there at least allowed one to act like everything was possible for the time of a visit. Caroline Levander comments on this phenomenon at hotels, writing: "Within this structure of shifting possibilities, the hotel guest can seemingly become anything, too. ... Racial fantasies can be temporarily hardened or obliterated. An ordinary person can, for a limited time, become a king or queen" (Levander 15). This almost utopian possibility and dream-like quality is apparent and strong at the Theresa:

> The Theresa represented a utopia for thousands of blacks from the rural South and other parts of the country. Dream chasers viewed it as the ideal setting to reinvent themselves. They could pretend to be anyone they desired, if only for a short time. A number of the Theresa's guests built their lives on a foundation of fabrication. And the Theresa played a role in keeping those dreams alive; it was a stage for dreamers and wannabes. (Wilson 121)

Once more, as we could see in the earlier case studies, the hotel's nature allows it to be a playground for the guests' desires and temporary identities. The Theresa was Harlem's stage for black pride, sometimes rightfully gained, sometimes only as a game of pretend.

This stage-like quality of the hotel was further encouraged by Walter Scott's successor, William Brown, better known as Billy Brown, in 1947.[26] As his predecessor Walter Scott, Billy Brown's personality had a strong impact on the way the Theresa was perceived by Harlem's community. Brown was the very public face of his institution and spread the fame of the hotel even farther. He was adept at public relations and had a fitting personality for the glittery hotel world: "Brown had a natural flair for public relations and he had personality galore – attributes that his predecessor lacked. He produced more stories for the press on the hotel in his first few months than Walter Scott had generated in his eight-year tenure" (Wilson 142). Fitting the multifaceted nature of a hotel, Brown had the ability to interact with all of his customers and with the locals from the neighborhood, rich businessmen as well as street hustlers. He was well aware that the Theresa was the only respectable hotel for blacks. Under Brown, the Theresa turned even more into a hotspot for black society, and was frequented by all of the great names from sports, entertainment, politics, and the arts.

Due to the rationing limitations imposed by the Second World War, Scott had not been able to develop the public spaces of the Theresa as glamorously as he had envisioned. Brown was the one who opened the rooftop ballroom that lay dormant

---

26 Similar to Scott, Brown, too, belonged to the growing black middle-class. He was born in 1916 in Bressler, Pennsylvania, to a family who owned their own farm. Brown graduated from Howard University and during the Franklin D. Roosevelt administration got a job at the Federal Housing and Home Financing Administration, focusing on poor family housing in Boston. He married Gloria Osborne, a very light skinned, pretty Washingtonian, whom he met while studying at Howard. The Brown family with their then seven-year old son Ron moved to Harlem in 1947, where shortly afterwards Brown was appointed manager due to his experience with federal housing.

for several years after the transformation of the Theresa to a black establishment. The Skylight Ballroom became the great attraction of the Theresa and was the place for society initiation in Harlem. A press release from 1948 stated: "For the first time in Harlem's history, or anywhere else in America, there will be a hotel catering to colored people with a spacious, sumptuous large capacity ballroom right in the Theresa Hotel" (Wilson 151f). Those Harlemites who could hold their debuts, weddings, and anniversaries at the hotel signaled to America's black community that they had socially advanced. Entertaining in the Skylight Ballroom became the symbol for black achievement and pride. Horace Carter describes the hotel's position in society after 1948 in the following way:

I think of it now as a Mecca. I say that because everything that was important to Harlemites and to African-Americans happened in the Theresa – the rallies outside, the political meetings inside, the cotillions, the weddings, the business meetings. Especially after the Skyline Ballroom opened, the hotel could accommodate every aspect of our race's needs and desires. (Carter qtd. in Wilson 153)

The last part of this comment is especially interesting. The hotel was indeed perceived by Harlemites as an almost utopian place that could encompass the desire and dreams of a whole race. It also spells out that the hotel stood for more than shelter and refreshment. It had acquired a symbolic meaning that went beyond its basic function; it was a mecca, an almost sacred place for Harlem's community.

To achieve the high-class atmosphere of the Theresa, Brown, too, saw it necessary to conduct a kind of social ordering inside the hotel. A selection of the 'right kind of people' took place. For this the Theresa's managers not only encouraged entertainment stars to use the hotel for their events, but they also reached out to black intelligentsia. For example, James Weldon Johnson's literary group met occasionally in the Orchid Room in the 1940s. In 1944, Zora Neale Hurston took a single room in the Theresa to recover from her divorce and to conduct work on a play (Hemenway 298). Bill Brown and his wife entertained quite regularly inside the hotel, in their private quarters as well as in the public rooms. Both were light skinned, and Gloria Brown was even able to pass as white. They carefully selected their guests and surrounded themselves preferably with the celebrities of their house. One of Brown's life mottos was "There's no excuse for being an ordinary Negro" (Holmes 26), and he lived according to this maxim at the hotel. The hotel provided him with the necessary power and background to be an extraordinary African-American, and people who were entertained in style at the hotel were of the same class.

The Theresa was seen as a sign of black achievement. It was the cultural center of this uptown community, the meeting place of celebrities, and a secure haven for blacks, especially the race's talented tenth. While it was elitist to a certain extent, mostly due to a still fragile self-confidence, it brought a new kind of racial pride to Manhattan's northern community. Those who stayed and entertained at the hotel often belonged to the richer section of black America. The hotel offered the opportunity for locals to mix and mingle with these people. The Theresa was a focal point in Harlem's African-American community and connected it to the wider world. As a result, the Theresa's prestige and reputation made the corner of 125th Street and Seventh Avenue the soapbox corner of Harlem, the place to be for black politicians.

4.3 THE HOTEL AS PLATFORM FOR POLITICS AND AS VICTIM OF DESEGREGATION

Besides being the center of the community and the stage for black pride, the Theresa Hotel was also the political heart of black America, the platform for their fight for equality: "the hotel also became known as a crucial pit stop for anyone participating in the world of politics. If you had something to say and you wanted the people of Harlem and beyond to hear it, then a stop at the Hotel Theresa was practically mandatory" (Mallory 49). I will now discuss this very significant function of the hotel. It is its lasting legacy and an important part of the hotel experience at the Theresa.

As I have already pointed out in the introductory chapter, American hotels have a long history with politics. They were used as accommodation for candidates on election tours, conference facility for party conventions, and stage for speeches. In many cities and small towns, they took over the role of a town hall. Since the beginning of the institution hotels played an important role in the democratic making of America. They brought people together, locals as well as visitors, and were centers of information (Sandoval-Strausz 233f). The Hotel Theresa is a worthy successor of these early 'palaces of the public' and has functioned as the most important location for political discussions in Harlem between the 1940s and the 1960s. The intersection of 125th Street and 7th Avenue was, and still is, the leading thoroughfare of Northern Manhattan. Due to this, many people move through it on a daily basis, making it a place where one's message could be heard. The Theresa was part of the political network of black America from its transformation to a black institution in 1940 onwards. The hotel rented office space to many leading figures of black America who made use of the prime location of the hotel in Harlem's heart. Among the first black politicians active in the Theresa was Philip A. Randolph, who planned a march on Washington in 1941 and finally realized it together with Martin Luther King in 1963. He was one of the earliest widely known black politicians, and his message was well heard from his position in the Theresa. Other famous regulars with political connections were Adam Clayton Powell Jr., the first black representative for New York in the House of Congress and Charles Rangel, who later took over Powell's seat in Congress.[27] Powell was celebrated as the first independent black politician and while he did not live at the Theresa, he regularly took part in events hosted by the Brown family and had exchange there with local leaders and his voters. Not only black politicians used the special reputation and symbolism of the hotel for their message but white politicians also campaigned in Harlem to gain the support of the community. For example, Richard Nixon visited the Theresa to campaign in 1952 for Dwight D. Eisenhower, whose vice-president he became.

The hotel's bar was an especially good place to mix and mingle with the people of Harlem because here politicians could hear what the word on the street was. The Theresa's bar was the nerve center of the hotel and the larger community. It was also known as "Harlem's unofficial intelligence center" (Scherman 13). Here, black businessmen sat next to members of Harlem society, people from the arts and entertainment industry, and even comrades of the Communist Party.[28] As mentioned above, the hotel was also the seat of several newspapers, and many reporters frequented the building on 125th Street. After Presidential speeches it was a common custom to check at the Theresa to learn how they were perceived by America's black population (Wilson 165). This was the case, for example, in 1947 when Truman gave his "Truman Doctrine" speech. From the reactions at the Theresa, journalists deduced the overall reaction of the African-American community. The hotel, however, not only provided space inside the building for political exchange and confidential meetings, it also famously functioned as a symbolic background for political rallies and speeches by black politicians. Due to this, the hotel and its direct surroundings have been compared with Hyde Park's well-known Speakers' Corner (Holmes 20) and called the "village green in Harlem" (Benjamin). In *The New York Times*, reporter Philip Benjamin stated: "[p]oliticians hold rallies in and around [the Theresa], and Negro celebrities receive the acclamation of the multitude there. It has been described as Harlem's Waldorf-Astoria" (Benjamin).

The issue of politics shows once more the similarity between the Theresa and the Waldorf-Astoria. They both functioned as leading establishments for their communities. The Waldorf-Astoria, as described earlier, has the closest ties to the United Nations and its representatives in New York. On a smaller level, the same was true for the Theresa, as it became the home away from home for diplomats from countries like Haiti and Liberia. Several African countries made the hotel their

---

27 Rangel worked as a desk clerk at the hotel for some time before entering politics (Wilson 233).

28 The Communist Party had a long-standing strong foothold in the Theresa, using it as their base for recruiting in New York.

representatives' temporary residence. Here they connected with local leaders and with America's black community. Wilson writes that the United Nation's location in New York enabled African-American activists in Harlem to overcome the divide-and-conquer rhetoric often used by white politicians and enabled them to get into direct contact with African leaders (Wilson 202). The hotel fostered this kind of communication. It provided the necessary space for meetings and due to both its public and private character, it could react to its political guests' wishes and needs. The Hotel Theresa provided blacks from America and around the world with a safe environment where they did not need to fear discrimination due to skin color. Despite the circumstance that the hotel remained in white ownership throughout its existence, this leading black hotel of Harlem fulfilled the function as social, cultural, and political meeting place for colored people successfully. Wilson writes: "That African leaders used a platform in front of the Hotel Theresa to address African independence and the ills of American racism was a clear indication of the hotel's prominence as black America's headquarters and of Harlem's significance as the black headquarters of the world" (Wilson 203).

During the 1950s, the Theresa Hotel became more and more a symbol for black nationalism. After the Accommodationist years of the hotel in the 1940s, the atmosphere turned more radical as the climactic years of the Civil Rights Movement, 1954 to 1968, drew nearer. Frustrated by the slow changes in American policy after the decision of *Brown vs. the Board of Education of Topeka* on May 17, 1954, many black people saw communism as a possible choice. In contrast to the American mainstream during the tense years of Cold War, African Americans made it clear that they did not have problems with Russian communists as they had never enslaved Africans. Harlem was internationally positioned when it came to politics. Because of the downtrodden position of blacks in America, its political leaders looked beyond the borders of America. The fight for racial equality knew no national boundaries, therefore in the 1950s and 60s it moved to the international level at the United Nations. Malcolm X led this movement for black America. He announced in his speech "The Ballot or the Bullet" that the United Nations had to be the next stage for African-American activists, in order to move their demands outside of Uncle Sam's borders to the more powerful international community. After he broke with the Nation of Islam in 1964, Malcolm X established the headquarters for his new organization at the Theresa, where he was a regular customer for several years. He called the hotel's site "one of Harlem's fuse-box locations" (Malcolm X 322).

The ties between Malcolm X and the hotel are manifold. He had already learned of the importance of the structure on 125th Street and Seventh Avenue during his first visit to Harlem. In his autobiography he writes: "I saw the big, tall, gray Theresa Hotel. It was the finest in New York City where Negroes could then stay, years before the downtown hotels would accept the black man" (Malcolm X 76). It is important to note here that the activist does not describe the hotel as white, but calls it gray, which moves it closer to the dark skin color of its neighborhood and breaks with the white history of the building. Additionally, he does not call the hotel unreservedly "the finest of New York" but the finest in which "Negroes could then stay." The existing shortcomings of the place are considered by Malcolm X, but its importance for the community remains nevertheless strong. Its location, the malleability of the institution hotel, and its great reputation explain why Malcolm X declared in 1964: "OAAU [Organization of Afro-American Unity] and Muslim Mosque will have its headquarters in the Hotel Theresa in Harlem" (Malcolm X 323). He wanted it to be his working base for an action program "designed to eliminate the political oppression, the economic exploitation, and the social degradation suffered daily by twenty-two million Afro-Americans" (Malcolm X 323). Love B. Woods, the last manager of the Theresa Hotel, gave him large parts of the hotel's second floor, not only for offices but also to operate a mosque. On his return from Mecca in May 1964, Malcolm X also held his first press conference at the Theresa. Following Malcolm X's break with Elijah Muhammad, however, people started to avoid being close to the activist in the hotel. It was known throughout Harlem's community that an assassination plan against him was on foot. In 1965, Malcolm X was shot in the Audubon Ballroom without being able to start his new organization and open the mosque in the hotel.

Some years earlier, Malcolm X met Muhammed Ali, the professional boxer, at the Theresa and became his mentor. Ali is another crucial figure of black politics, who is connected to the hotel. The boxer later joined ranks with Elijah Muhammed of the Nation of Islam and distanced himself from Malcolm X. Muhammed Ali lived at the Theresa for some time after his breakthrough as World Heavyweight Champion. About his selection of the hotel for his residence he said:

I could be living all exclusive, downtown, in some skyscraper hotel. I could be living right up in the hotel's penthouse. ... I am up here in the heart of blacktown. I can't find nothing wrong with that, but it seems to bother everybody else, it looks like. I been around my own people all of my life. ... The white people don't want integration: I don't believe in forcing it and the Muslims don't either. (Ali qtd. in Haley 78)

By the 1960s, the tone in political speeches in Harlem was increasingly separatist and anti-integrationist. Ali saw the hotel as a place that symbolized the separateness between the white and black races which was for him the right way for African-Americans to proceed.

Fidel Castro's Visit at the Hotel Theresa

As these comments show, the Theresa Hotel was perceived by its own community as the place where the fate of African-Americans was fought for and even decided. The one event that made the hotel known to all Americans as black America's icon and place of power, even far beyond the borders of New York City, was the visit of Fidel Castro and his Cuban entourage in New York in 1960. Castro came to New York to give a speech at the United Nations. Originally, the Cuban representatives were meant to check-into the Shelbourne Hotel in mid-Manhattan. Out of necessity, they finally took up residence in Harlem's Waldorf, the Hotel Theresa.[29] Love B. Woods, the current manager of the hotel, accepted them after some considerations, and allocated 40 rooms to the Cubans. They moved in on September 19, 1960, and remained at the hotel for ten days. Their stay was widely covered by the local, national, and international press, pushing the Theresa Hotel into the spotlight.

The visit to Harlem was a chance event. About his arrival in Harlem Castro is quoted saying: "I had always wanted to come to Harlem, but I was not sure what kind of welcome I would get. When I got news that I would be welcomed in Harlem, I was happy ... I feel very warm here" (Castro qtd in Wilson 207). Castro's stay shows that one of the important features of hotel business is the flexibility with which it is able to react to new situations. Due to the tense political situation, it would have caused severe problems to allocate the Cubans to a state or national institution. However, it would have been even worse not to find a place for Castro and his men on this important occasion.[30] The Cubans had a right to be heard at the United Nations, even though its location on American ground made the whole event problematic from the start. The Theresa Hotel functioned as a diplomatic in-between actor. It was a profitable development for the hotel, yet the stress it created

---

29 There are two differing accounts why they moved into the Harlem hotel. One story stated that Castro and his supporters brought live chicken with them to the Shelbourne and because of that were ousted from the place. According to another story, which is backed by more sources, the Shelbourne's management was put under pressure by the American government and consequently demanded $10,000 in advance from the Cubans. They refused to pay, insulted by the distrust. Due to this, they needed to find new quarters. As only a few hotels were willing to take in the notorious communist in 1960 at the height of the Cold War, the search was a difficult one. According to Wilson, the black nationalist James Lawson, an American supporter of Castro's visit, suggested the Theresa to the Cubans. According to Ralph Crowder, a member of the Cuban party brought up the hotel after having had communication with Malcolm X (Crowder 80).

30 At one point, Castro threatened to camp with his men in Central Park. This would have been seen as a significant embarrassment to the American government.

for the community and the bitterness it caused outside of Harlem also have to be taken into consideration.

Most Harlemites celebrated Castro's coming to their neighborhood. African-American writer Maya Angelou remembers the Cuban leader's visit at the Theresa:

> To our amazement, at eleven o'clock on a Monday evening, we were unable to get close to the hotel. Thousands of people filled the sidewalks and intersections, and police cordoned off the main and side streets. I hovered with my friends on the edges of the crowd, enjoying the Spanish songs, the screams of 'Viva Castro,' and the sounds of conga drums being played nearby in the damp night air. (Angelou 223)

The hotel was the epicenter of the actions surrounding Castro's visit in New York. His defiance of U.S. leaders was considered by African-Americans as an important sign that white America's racial and ideological policies were not accepted by all. Most newspaper articles on Castro's visit make mention of the Theresa and its position at the heart of Harlem. It is considered the hotel's great symbolical moment, this meeting of Cuban and black American culture. The close ties were underlined by the circumstance that the Cuban leader reserved his interviews for black American journalists only, refusing to talk to white reporters at the Theresa. His meeting with Malcolm X at the hotel was momentous, as they greeted each other like two heads of state, black America meeting Cuba, making the Hotel Theresa again a true equivalent of the white man's Waldorf-Astoria (Wilson 207). Malcolm X himself said in 1964: "The Theresa is now best known as the place where Fidel Castro went during his UN visit, and achieved a psychological coup over the U.S. State Department when it confined him to Manhattan, never dreaming that he'd stay uptown in Harlem and make such an impression among the Negroes" (Malcolm X qtd. in James 107). The difficulties of finding acceptable shelter in New York "were transformed into a momentous opportunity for cultural-political expressions of solidarity and anti-racism (James 107). Looking at the Theresa's position in this historic moment tells us much about the political attitude of Harlemites and their fears and aspirations for the future. The hotel functions as a condensed version of the neighborhood. Inside its walls the struggle for African-American acceptance and equality was at a boiling point. Another consideration that also comes up with Castro's Theresa visit is that the usual marginal status of Harlem and its leading hotel, seen from the perspective of Midtown, is inverted here. The neighborhood and the Theresa are suddenly in the center of attention, for the first time since the Harlem Renaissance, and this time it is even more internationally recognized.

Castro's residence at the Hotel Theresa also brought in other politicians. The atmosphere around the hotel heated up even more when Khrushchev came to the Theresa to talk privately with Castro. This was a strategic move for the Russian leader as it was widely covered in the national and international press and made the close ties between the two communist nations highly visible. A meeting of the two only at the United Nations would have been far less conspicuous as they would naturally meet there. However, Khrushchev going out of his way to meet Castro at his chosen accommodation showed the high regard he had for the Cubans and the threatening implication this close relationship might have for America.[31] Historian John Henrik Clarke describes the powerful implications of this get-together at the Theresa in the following way: "The symbols were absolutely magnificent. ... Fidel Castro in a black-owned hotel, Khrushchev meeting him in the lobby, the community surrounding the hotel day and night. Castro occasionally coming to the window to wave. It was an event in the development of consciousness in the community" (qtd in Wilson 212). Khrushchev's example was followed by other heads of state, such as President Gamal Abdel Nassar of Egypt, India's Prime Minister Jawaharlal Nehru, and Bulgarian leader Tedor Zhivkov (Crowder 84).[32]

The whole housing incident was famously included in Fidel Castro's speech in front of the United Nations General Assembly. He presents the incident as one more sign of America's disregard of other ethnicities. He starts his address by saying:

When we were forced to leave one of the hotels in this city, and came to the United National Headquarters while efforts were being made to find accommodation for us, a hotel, a humble hotel of this city, a Negro hotel in Harlem, offered to rent us rooms. ... The reply came when we were speaking to the Secretary General. Nevertheless, an official of the State Department did all in his power to prevent our staying at that hotel. At that moment, as though by magic, hotels began appearing all over New York. ... Out of simple reciprocity we accepted the Harlem hotel. We felt then that we had earned the right to be left in peace. But peace was not accorded us.

Once in Harlem, since it was impossible to prevent us from living there, the slander and defamation campaigns began. They began spreading the news all over the world that the Cuban delegation had lodged in a brothel. For some a humble hotel in Harlem, a hotel inhabited by Negroes of the United States, must obviously be a brothel. (Castro)

The problem of accommodation and the stay at the Hotel Theresa was used by Castro as a prime example of the difficult situation of minorities in America and of

---

31 Two years later, in 1962, the close connection between Russia and Cuba would lead to the Cuban Missile Crisis, the hottest moment in the Cold War, catching the American public off-guard.

32 Not only politicians visited Castro at the Hotel Theresa at that time. It is also reported that Langston Hughes, civil rights activist Robert F. Williams, historian John Henrik Clarke, poet Allen Ginsberg, French photographer Henri Cartier-Bresson, and Professor C. Wright Mills met there with the Cuban leader (Crowder 85).

the still unresolved racial tensions. It was an instrument to show capitalism's inhumane side. The hotel was at the heart of this message. Without its cooperation Castro's visit to the United Nations would have had a different spirit. It manifested the good relationships between Cubans and African-Americans for the future.[33]

Castro's visit at the hotel was not just an immense stroke of luck for the Theresa. Concerning the capacity of the institution, a visit like this almost exceeded its possibilities. Most people in the hotel and in Harlem were relieved when the Cubans left. While Woods stated to the press that the visit was the thrill of his lifetime, he also conceded that he would only take them in again if forced, not voluntarily, as the pressure it put on the hotel was immense ("Cuban Pay Bill in Cash"). While some staff members reported that Castro treated them exceedingly nicely, others complained that the Cuban delegation had made many demands without ever tipping them. The claim that they would rename a famous hotel in Havana "Theresa" in honor of the hotel in Harlem, a story which was also printed by *The New York Times*, turned out to be only a rumor. It also needs to be mentioned that not everyone in the black community sided with the communists. Adam Clayton Powell Jr. saw Castro's visit as a publicity stunt that was not really meant to help the situation of African Americans.[34]

The strong effect that the visit had on American politics could be seen in the speech of John F. Kennedy, which he gave in front of the Theresa in 1960, shortly after Castro's stay. While other members of his campaign had already visited Harlem, among them Senator Henry Cabot Lodge and Robert Kennedy's wife, Ethel, the presidential candidate came to the famous intersection in Harlem on October 12, 1960, after the place had become so symbolic. Kennedy directly referred to the famous incident in his speech, stating:

I am delighted to come and visit. Behind the fact of Castro coming to this hotel, Khrushchev coming to Castro, there is another great traveler in the world, and that is the travel of a world revolution, a world in turmoil. I am delighted to come to Harlem and I think the whole world should come here and the whole world should recognize that we all live right next to each other, whether here in Harlem or on the other side of the globe. (Kennedy)

---

33 Despite the fact that in Cuba racial discrimination also existed among light skinned Cubans and Afro-Cubans.
34 Castro reinforced his gratefulness when he made a return visit to Harlem in 1995: "I remember with such appreciation those days [when] I was here in this neighborhood. Those were unforgettable days for me, the days when I came to the Theresa Hotel, many years ago. There was such hostility [in the U.S.]. There was such a campaign against our country. ... But everything changed when I came to Harlem" (Castro qtd. in Tyner). Over thirty years after the event, the stay was still recalled fondly as a sign of true hospitality in a country that did not show many friendly gestures toward the Cubans.

Kennedy's metaphor of the world revolution as a great traveler fits the setting of the speech in front of Harlem's most famous hotel. Hotels are key players in the system of travel and Kennedy's invitation to people to come to Harlem needs the existence of a hotel like the Theresa to make the visit possible. The quote also uncovers the need of white politicians to connect to the people in Harlem as they realized at this point that they were in danger of completely losing African-Americans to communism and black separatism. Choosing this very symbolic location, in front of the Theresa, and connecting the hotel and its neighborhood to larger America is a clear attempt to build a bridge to Harlem's people via its best known institution. Until today the visit of Castro to Harlem and the Theresa is remembered as a high point in Harlem's influence on America's policy making. It was one of the few times when New York's focus was clearly on Manhattan's northern tip, not because of racial riots, but because of political commitment. The Hotel Theresa's function as political and social heart of Harlem was essential in this.

The stay of Castro at the Theresa had strong repercussions in politics and also in popular culture. In Alfred Hitchcock's espionage thriller *Topaz* from 1969, based on the novel of the same title by Leon Uris, the Hotel Theresa was famously used as a setting for the movie, functioning as the temporary home of Cuban representatives. The movie directly alludes to Castro's stay at the hotel which was still well-known enough for the viewers to make the connection and lend authenticity to the story. The scenes are shot at night, giving the building a dark and looming atmosphere. The famous marquee of the hotel and its lights are shown several times to remind the viewer of the symbolism of this location. The audience is first presented with the outside view, which shows a frenzied mob before the hotel celebrating the Cubans. One then enters the building with the undercover agent through the camera's eye, and sees the modest, sparse interior of the hotel. The hotel is depicted as quite run down which matches authentically the condition of the hotel in the 1960s, as at that time it was already past its prime and declining. At the same time, the poor condition of the place highlights the underdog situation of the Cubans in contrast to wealthy white America. It also functions as a contrast to the cheering crowds outside the hotel, again alluding to the real historical visit. With the movie, this famous occasion at the hotel was immortalized in American pop-culture, and it is an interesting testimonial to this important event of the Cold War era.[35]

---

35 *Topaz* is one of the few examples where the Hotel Theresa is used in a fictional text. The only other use of the Hotel Theresa as setting in a movie, is in the Academy Award winning film *Precious* – based on the novel *Push* by Sapphire (2009). The former hotel's use in the movie, in a way, still represents the centrality of the structure for the black community in Harlem.

Castro's stay was financially a success for the hotel as the bill was paid in full by the Cubans and the press coverage was immense. Along with Kennedy's speech, it was the last great event in the history of the Theresa. Manager Love B. Woods planned large renovations at the hotel with the money from the Cuban visit. Years before, he already had the vision of making the Theresa into a real grand hotel with the kind of luxury to be found in the white Waldorf-Astoria. However, in the months following the Cubans' visit, it quickly became clear that with desegregation the need for a hotel catering to blacks was diminishing, and the hotel was losing clients to downtown institutions. Although it sounds paradoxical at first, the Hotel Theresa was a victim of desegregation. In the following I will show how the acceptance of black people in formerly white institutions caused the closing of Harlem's famous establishment.

Desegregation and the Hotel Theresa

It has already been mentioned that the hotel had its shortcomings and was more famous for its glamorous clientele than for its rich interior. Despite the attempts of Scott, Brown, and Woods to make the Theresa a luxurious venue for its guests, it never reached the same level as the palace hotels of mid-Manhattan. African-Americans who had travelled more extensively and who had reached a certain level of fame knew of the gap between the comfort of America's best black hotel and an institution like the Waldorf-Astoria. For example, entertainer Sammy Davis Jr. never stayed at the Theresa. Instead, he checked into whatever five-star hotel downtown would cater to him because of his fame. He is quoted as saying: "The [blacks] haven't made a hotel that's luxurious as I want to live in" (Davis Jr. qtd. In Wilson 21). The Theresa was a significant step up from the hotels available to blacks before 1940. It was an important symbol for African-American achievements, yet as Davis's quote shows, it was not yet on the level of white grand hotels. This difference in quality was also discussed in the *Ebony* article of 1946. In the article, the reporter recites the conversation between a young woman and an elderly woman, which took place on the Theresa's mezzanine floor, a more private part of the hotel. The young woman is quoted as saying:

How much longer are they going to treat us as if we had never seen any place nicer than the Theresa? How much longer they going to pass off good-enough on us when we deserve the best? I've passed downtown – a thousand of us have gone to conferences and appeared at benefits in New York's white hotels; we can pay for what we saw there – space and beauty, well-cooked, original food, shaded lights, color in the rooms, a flower on the table – you'd think there weren't any good cooks or decorators in Harlem. ("The Waldorf of Harlem" 12)

The article continues with the older woman's reply, trying to explain to the younger generation the challenges a hotel like the Theresa has to face:

> Just be patient, dearie. It's the war that made them go so slow. And you have to realize this it a small hotel, and not many rooms are big enough to call for an $8 rent. It may be where the most famous of our race stay, but it's a small hotel for that, and not very rich. Besides, we didn't build it with funny lights and tiled floors. We didn't put in this dusty statue ... or make the outside fancy so it would catch all the dirt in Harlem as it blows by. This was a white hotel, honey. Mr. Scott's only been here six years. ("The Waldorf of Harlem" 12)

This conversation provides deep insight into the importance of space for one's self-perception and how the surrounding environment influences one's mood and state of mind. It also shows the limits of a black 'luxury' hotel during the time of segregation and the amount of effort that was still needed for African-Americans to be really treated as equal in American society. The young woman clearly perceives her surroundings as reflecting on her own persona. She argues that the lack of style of the Theresa, especially in contrast to the white hotels of downtown Manhattan, makes her feel inferior. It infuriates the young woman that the most elegant institution that blacks have is the Theresa with its perceived shortcomings. For her it represents to the larger society that African-Americans are still easily satisfied with second best. The older woman's words also carry important information. She takes in the shortcomings but also knows where the limitations come from and considers the hotel as being on the right track. Furthermore, she also sees the reasons in the circumstance that the hotel was originally a white middle-class hotel and not meant as an African-American palace hotel. The older woman still sees hope in the future for the hotel and her race, represented here by professional black businessmen like Walter Scott, the manager of the Theresa.

The article in *Ebony* magazine is the most elaborate contemporary document on the hotel. In this feature story the writer takes pains to not only show the achievements of the Theresa, but also to give an objective and critical account of the place. The reason for this might be to avoid sounding over-enthusiastic and naïve. Already at the beginning the article makes clear that while the Theresa is the social headquarters of the African-American community and venue of their most glamorous parties, "there the resemblance to the Waldorf ends. With its dimly-lit hallways, drab, colorless bedrooms, dingy, ancient furnishing, and limited room service, the Theresa is anything but a first-rate hotel. But it is the best that Harlem has" ("The Waldorf of Harlem" 8).

The article was written in 1946, and indeed at that time the hotel's shortcomings where also due to the rationing caused by the war. Over the years, the Theresa saw some new additions to its public rooms and renovations of the existing ones. However, the prophesy of the old woman did not come to pass. The Harlem hotel never caught up luxury-wise to the hotels of mid-Manhattan. In June 1959, an article in the *New York Age* stated: the "Hotel Theresa, for years the proud queen of Negro hotels in America ... [is] today only a maudlin burlesque of her former greatness" (Scherman 18). Ironically, the reasons for the decline of the hotel lay mostly in the improving situation of blacks in New York and in the Supreme Court decision *Brown vs. the Board of Education of Topeka*. Hotels in the city center, which offered the luxury that the young woman in the article craves for and that Sammy Davis Jr expected, abolished their segregational policies by the end of the 1950s. As soon as this was the case, black guests started to leave the Harlem hotel for downtown New York. Now, the Theresa was only a reminder of racial injustice.

Segregation had made the Theresa the center of Harlem community, and desegregation led to its slow but certain demise. Historian Preston Wilcox commented on the reaction of African-Americans to desegregation: "The white man made us think that Harlem was worthless, and we bought his crap. Soon as they opened up downtown, we went running down there trying to be around white folk. Some of us would come back uptown bragging about being at the Waldorf or the Plaza" (Wilcox qtd in Wilson 48). The attraction of finally being able to enter the great white hostelries and dining establishments was too much to simply pass. That this behavior often destroyed black businesses like bars, restaurants, and the Hotel Theresa, was a realization that only set in years after the damage was done and most institutions had already closed in Harlem. Wilcox concludes: "We don't know what we have lost when we lost the Theresa. The old Harlem is gone and the Hotel Theresa went with it" (Wilcox qtd. in Wilson 48). Desegregation was a gradual process, and it took years until New York was fully integrated. Due to this, and the preference of black nationalists to remain in Harlem and in its establishments, the Hotel Theresa continued to serve black Americans until 1966 when it was sold. One year later, it was reopened as an office building, the Theresa Towers, which contained a mix of service offices and businesses, yet it did not regain the position of social centrality that the hotel once held.

By the 1980s, although the structure still physically existed, the memory of the place was fading.[36] This was encouraged by the new management of the Theresa Tower. They did not want people to visit the building and talk about its famous past as a hotel. Until today, Harlem does not have a hotel that plays a similarly important role as the Theresa formerly did. In my opinion, the neighborhood's marginal position in New York is at least partly founded in this circumstance. A hotel would help to revitalize the neighborhood and reconnect the people with each other, functioning as Oldenburg's third place. This is especially important nowadays, since Harlem has become more heterogeneous in recent years and is said to have lost its identity as the black mecca of New York.

---

36 Until today, one can still read the name Hotel Theresa at the building's top.

4.4 THE HOTEL AS TRAINING GROUND FOR AN AFRICAN AMERICAN LEADER

To round out the chapter on hotel experience at the Theresa I want to discuss the impact the hotel had on an individual, manager Billy Brown's son, Ron Brown. Brown's biographies are among the few life writing texts which focus on the relationship between one person and the Hotel Theresa. Through these books, which were published after the death of Ronald H. Brown in a plane accident, the Theresa was granted a kind of second life in the memory culture surrounding his life. Brown was the first black elected chairman of a leading national party, the Democratic Party, and the first black Secretary of Commerce during the first Clinton administration (1993-1996). As the son of Billy Brown, he was considered a true son of Harlem.[37] The discussion of his hotel experience will serve to connect the case study of the Theresa to the other hotels of this work and will show the similarities that exist across racial differences. Family members, and intimate friends, as well as unrelated newspaper reporters see a clear link between Ron Brown's personality and career, and his growing-up at the Theresa. To them, the hotel's atmosphere as well as its close connection to politics prepared him for his later positions. On the other hand, he became the embodiment for the people's memory of the hotel. Today the Hotel Theresa is most often mentioned in articles in connection to Ron Brown, the house's most important son.

According to his daughter, Tracey Brown, Ron's life changed dramatically when his father became the manager of the Theresa Hotel. He arrived there as a seven-year-old boy and continued living in the hotel until he left for college. The new position of his father as one of the most important men in Harlem influenced Ron's Brown self-perception. Contemporaries say that he behaved as if his parents were not only running the hotel but Harlem. He was the black Eloise of Harlem, having free run of the hotel. His daughter writes: "If he got an urge for an ice-cream soda – or any other treat he wanted – he'd go into the coffee shop for it. Living in the Theresa, and being an only child, Dad was spoiled; he was a little kid in an adult world and many hotel guests paid special attention to him" (Brown 42). Like Margaret Case and Michael Colby, Brown can be described as a spoiled and neglected child at the same time.[38] To pass time he was 'helping' staff members

---

37 Because of his premature death, there is no autobiographical text by Brown himself. Accordingly, the hotel experience depicted here comes from secondary sources. Yet, as he is often quoted directly in the texts, one is able to gain at least a useful insight into his relationship with the Theresa.

38 Besides the similarities to Harriman Case's and Colby's texts, Ron Brown's life at the hotel shows also many parallels to the autobiography Hotel Kid (2002) by Stephen

running the elevator or working the soda fountain. The employees accepted the sometimes annoying little boy because he was the boss's kid. Brown's preferred place in the hotel was its rooftop where he was allowed to play ball and walk his dog. Being the 'dauphin' of the black Mecca gave Ron Brown an envied and powerful position with his peers: "My father's childhood friends were always eager to visit him at the famous Theresa Hotel. Dad would lead them through the lobby and public areas, but eventually they'd end up on the roof to play Dad's favorite game" (Brown 44).

Yet, except for those visits by his friends, the world of the Theresa was clearly an adult one. Here he came into contact with grown-up topics and the social practices of the black society. Nick Jones describes Ron Brown's childhood at the Theresa in the following way: "Being exposed to all kinds of people in the hotel – the celebrities, the sports folks – made him more sophisticated than his peers. That within itself was a tremendous education. Nothing after that experience came as a shock to him .... He had seen it all before he left the hotel as a teenager" (Wilson 150). The Theresa was a condensed version of Harlem, a microcosm that taught him the most important lessons. Brown started early to regularly read newspapers and converse with guests on politics and current topics. The special environment of the hotel had great advantages for Ron Brown, yet it also produced a precocious strain in him that sometimes made him too noisy in the guest's affairs, transgressing the hotel code.

Education was highly regarded by his parents and the rising black middle class. However, the vibrant atmosphere at the hotel did not always provide him with the right learning environment and challenged his ability to focus on his school work. Nevertheless, he graduated from some of the most prestigious schools. Brown was subsequently enrolled in Hunter's School for gifted children and later went to white private schools in mid-Manhattan. He lived a kind of "racially schizophrenic existence" (Holmes 18), departing for white America in the mornings and returning to the heart of black America in the afternoon. Brown's bridging of worlds was also expressed in his perception of his environment. From his bedroom window he could see "west down 125th Street to the Apollo Theater and, far west, to the distant George Washington Bridge and New Jersey" (Brown 43). The combination of sights described here is also a combination of the black and white parts of town. His bedroom window was allowing him to see both sides at the same time. This special position, of being able to perceive the inner tensions of New York society, is not only commented on by Ron's daughter, but is also picked up by a *Time Magazine*

Lewis. Lewis grew up in one of New York's biggest hotels, the Taft Hotel on Times Square and relates very similar impressions in his text. I recommend his text for those interested in the life accounts of hotel children and their special life-long connection to their former environment.

article on Brown. In the article, Brown is quoted, saying: "'I'd be peeking around the hotel, always conscious of who people were and how they operated...'" The article continues: "From the roof of the Theresa, 13 floors high, Ron and his friends would gaze out on the excitement of 125th Street – the Apollo Theater, the street-corner orators, the hustlers – and the poverty beyond" (Isaacson). It is important to take this into consideration: at the hotel Ron Brown was part of black society and lived in abundance and comparable splendor. This upbringing could have left him spoiled for life.[39] Yet, living in the heart of Harlem also showed him the problems of the community and the lack of equality that blacks still experienced. Not only the impressive sights of the city were visible from his vantage point at the Theresa, but also the poverty.

According to childhood friend John Nails, Ron Brown started to escape the hotel atmosphere more regularly as an adolescent because it was limiting his abilities to get into contact with peers and the opposite sex. This was one of the things the hotel did not provide, girls of his age that he could date without surveillance. Still, John Nails, who later became a famous heart surgeon in the city, considered the hotel surroundings as being always more of an advantage than a disadvantage in Ron Brown's life:

He believed he could do anything. It made him a lot more sophisticated at an earlier age. He matured quicker. He developed a tenacity to his personality. It came out of the Hotel Theresa environment. It was definitely that unique experience of growing up in the Theresa. To grow up in the center of black existence had to have an impact on his life – but in the most positive way. (John Nails qtd in Wilson 151)

This quote from an interview of Wilson with Nails is the most expressive comment on the powerful influence of the Theresa's hotel environment on the life of an individual. Ron Brown gained a strong place-identity from living at the hotel. According to his intimate friend, it provided him with insights and experiences that were only possible in the unique combination of culture, politics, and society that existed at the Theresa. He shows many similarities with other hotel children, yet his experience is clearly colored in the most literal sense by his ethnicity and the uniqueness of the hotel's position for the black community of Harlem. While, for example, Margaret Harriman Case's upbringing at the Algonquin influenced her own career path, Brown's childhood at the Theresa had an impact beyond his individual life, it would resonate throughout the African American community of the United States.

---

39 Later it was sometimes commented upon that he behaved almost more white than black; and, not unlike Obama, he had to justify himself as black repeatedly.

Ron Brown left Harlem when he started college in 1958 and did not return for more than thirty years. Yet, when he showed his family his former childhood home and neighborhood in 1992, he still considered himself a Harlemite. His daughter writes of this special trip to Harlem:

> He took me, Michael, and Mom on a tour of the Theresa, now an office building, then he led us to his old playground, the roof. ... He pointed out Harlem landmarks, and the view of the Apollo Theater from his bedroom window. ... It had been thirty-seven years since Dad left home, seeking and finding success and influence in Washington's halls of power. But those years and those successes made no difference, and he remained true to his beginnings. He remained a native son, a child of Harlem. (Brown 51)[40]

Ron Brown toured the building with his family to relive some of the impressions that he had when growing up at the Theresa.[41] To also share with them the view from his bedroom window once more underlines the importance it had for him and his understanding of Harlem. The Apollo Theater functions here as a signifier of the pride of the African-American community in their cultural achievements. Together, the Theresa and the Apollo made up the center of Harlem, business and culture, global and local elements, the core of black America.

Ron Brown died in a plane crash in Croatia in 1996 while he was on a business trip for the Department of Commerce. Over thirty people lost their lives in that crash. It ended the career of the most promising black politician before the arrival of Barack Obama. National and international newspapers reported on the death of Brown and a large number of obituaries and articles on the secretary were published in the following weeks. Many of them comment on Brown's early life in Harlem and the influences that shaped his career path. Almost all make mention of his ties to the community's lodestone, the Theresa, as for example *The New York Times* which starts their obituary by writing: "Reared in the celebrity-filled cacophony of the Hotel Theresa in Harlem, where his father worked as manager, Mr. Brown quickly learned the art of making connections and closing a deal – first for the autographs of Joe Louis and Jackie Robinson, and eventually for the chief

---

40 Biographies are not unproblematic sources. It is impossible to verify emotions or ideas from a third person perspective. However, his daughter's text nevertheless allows us a glimpse into Brown's mind and his emotion toward his former home. Tracey Brown at least was personally present at the moment, and it can be assumed that she was more intimately privy to his thoughts than an unrelated biographer.

41 It seems that his position as powerful black politician enabled him to get entry into the office building, even into parts that are usually off-limits, such as the roof. In contrast to other former residents who were barred from entering the building to reconnect to the hotel years, Ron Brown can even take his family around with him.

executives that he led to China, Southeast Asia and, in recent months, to many of the world's trouble spots" (Sanger). In obituaries, these remembrances and recollections of an individual's life, not only the most influential people but also the most formative places of the deceased are often mentioned. The readers are able to create a fuller picture of the person when they can also place him geographically and connect him to his formative environment.

The Hotel Theresa, Harlem's former social, cultural, and political center, lives on in articles and books also because of its ties to Ron Brown, the neighborhood's most important politician. In the introduction to Tracey Brown's book, former president Bill Clinton writes:

As the first African-American commerce secretary, and a man who never forgot where he came from, Ron focused especially on those Americans who had traditionally been left behind. He treated African-Americans as people with economical potential rather than economic need, and he challenged minority businesses to join the new global economy. The son of a Harlem hotel manager, Ron had lived the American Dream. (Clinton qtd. in Brown, xiv)

In this statement both ideas are combined: that of Ron Brown as enabler for his people and that of Ron Brown, who was enabled by his surroundings in the Hotel Theresa, the heart of Harlem. It is quite American that a man, coming from a hotel background, which is glamorous yet also sometimes morally dubious, gains such an appointment in the American government. It confirms the innkeeper's important position in American society. From a publisher's point of view it is clearly attractive to write that Brown's father was the manager of the best black hotel, at least more interesting than if Bill Brown had been a teacher, doctor or lawyer. By stating that Ron Brown reached his American Dream as the son of a hotel manager, reminds one also of the several instances we have seen by now in which American hotels are seen as the place were the pursuit of happiness is made possible. Boldt, Tschirky, Case, and Bard all lived their American Dreams, and their hotels were their means to reach them. Because of the obstacles that still existed for a man of black color in the 1960s, Bill Brown did not succeed in the same way. However, his son was able to fulfill the promise not least due to his hotel background. He honored his father's life motto and did not become an "ordinary Negro," but a positive example for future generations of African Americans.

The Hotel Theresa is the hotel with the shortest lifespan of all the establishments discussed in my work. It did not become as financially successful as the others and it did not get the same media attention as the Waldorf, the Algonquin or the Chelsea Hotel. Yet, in many ways the Hotel Theresa is at least as exemplary as the other hotels when it comes to the importance of the institution for New York's society and culture. The connection between the Theresa and its immediate community was stronger than in the case of the other hotels. Furthermore, this establishment did not only stand for Harlem and its people but for blacks across the nation and, in some incidents, even for blacks worldwide. This "glamour castle" (Wilson 134) became the platform for the rising racial pride and the increasing self-confidence of African-Americans from the middle of the twentieth century onwards. It was a successful instrument to reduce the stress and pain of segregation, and it enabled a lively exchange among the "talented tenth" in Harlem, the community's elite, who helped to change the situation of blacks in America. While the hotel clearly had its shortcomings, its symbolic meaning for the people was more important than its furnishing, cooking, or services. The two managers who shaped the hotel according to their visions can be seen as prime examples of the rising black middle class and the increasing professionalization in all fields of the economic sector. That the hotel declined with the coming of desegregation and the increasing equality for blacks after the Civil Rights Act of 1964, is, on the one hand, a sign of success for the acceptance of African-Americans in mainstream American culture. On the other hand, it also shows the compromises; sometimes foul ones, that come with integration. The loss of the Theresa in 1966 was seen by many as a great loss for African-American culture, a loss of communication, and some even say, the loss of the heart and soul of black Harlem. The institution Hotel Theresa might have proven an important asset during the racially difficult years of the 1970s, 80s, and early 90s. It is an interesting exercise to imagine a victory party for Barack Obama at the Theresa in 2008. Would it have been similar to the ones given to Joe Louis and Muhammed Ali half a century earlier?

The Theresa Hotel shows the possibilities, the achievements, and the failures of the heterotopic institution of the hotel for the black community. Talks of a new kind of Theresa are resurfacing repeatedly in the news surrounding the business redevelopment of Harlem. Sondra Wilson herself considered it almost certain that another Theresa is coming in the near future. It would not be the same, but it should have become clear that the potential of such an institution for society and culture can be far larger than that of any other business venture. Hotels are still carrying in them the seed for another American Dream as we will also see in the last case study of this work.

5. Grossinger's Hotel and Country Club – Acculturation in Style

> "But Grossinger's is also much more than a resort hotel. It has, in a very real sense, become an authentic institution – symbolic representation of an affluent life style for an entire ethnic class that rose from the ghettoes to positions of wealth, power, and importance during the first half of the 20th century.
> ... to many an upward-striving individual, coming to Grossinger's was indisputable evidence of having 'arrived' – of having 'made it!'"
> POMERANTZ 277

The chapter on the Hotel Theresa shows that the institution of the hotel can become a central place for a specific community and a symbol of social change and cultural achievements. From its structure and operation, the Theresa was a classic city hotel of the modern American type with its mix of transient and residential guests. Psychologically and emotionally it became the mecca of black culture in the middle of the twentieth century. The white building on 125th Street and Seventh Avenue transformed into a platform for the developing African American self-confidence.

The last hotel that I am examining in this thesis, the Grossinger's Hotel and Country Club, appears to be very different from the four hotels discussed so far. In contrast to them, it is not located in Manhattan and it is not a city hotel, but a resort hotel in the foothills of the Catskill Mountains in New York, a region which became famous as the 'Borscht Belt.'[1] Yet, despite these differences, Grossinger's fits well into my discussion of hotel experience and its impact on social and cultural

---

1   The nickname 'Borsch Belt' for the dominantly Jewish part of the lower Catskill Mountains derives from the Borscht soup, one of the most popular dishes in the region. This soup has been brought to America by Eastern European Jewish immigrants and stands here for the whole culture.

life in New York: it also provides people with a unique space which enables changes in social behavior, inspires the creation of culture, and is a platform for developing a successful group identity.

As we will see in this chapter, this is not only possible in a city hotel but also in a resort hotel. Resort hotels are urban institutions situated in the country that tie together large cities with their hinterland and thereby construct an important network among city and country people. They bring urban infrastructure, professional jobs and progress to less developed parts of the country, while enabling city people to connect again with nature and to experience open space. The Catskills region became the preferred holiday area for New Yorkers in the 1930s and had its heyday in the 1950s and early 60s before it started to decline in the late 1960s. This region played a far larger role in the development of entertainment culture and especially in the integration of Jewish-Americans into the American mainstream than is often considered. Therefore, an analysis of the Catskills resorts and Grossinger's as the exemplary representative of these unique social and cultural institutions will add another facet to the hotel experience in New York and to the important place of hotels in its culture and society.[2]

The three main aspects of the hotel experience of the Catskills' hotel world and in particular of Grossinger's discussed here are the hotel as point of entry to American culture, the hotel as site of female empowerment, and the hotel as site of identity struggle. I will show how these holiday establishments enabled Jewish immigrants to become American, while at the same time keeping their religious and ethnic identity. They even influenced American culture in turn, a process described as acculturation.

The first part of this chapter will highlight the historical development of the Catskills and their growing importance for Jewish-Americans. They had escaped their Eastern European homelands because of the pogroms, the brutal persecution in czarist Russia, but continued to face anti-Semitism in the new country for several decades. The Catskills provided them with a secure surrounding in which they could reestablish their culture and slowly overcome the prejudices that they faced in their adopted country. Until the 1950s Jewish-Americans had to deal with discrimination similar to that which African-Americans faced, so it is interesting to see how they used the hotel to create a safe haven for their people (Sandoval-Strausz 99). They managed to turn their small farms with space for boarders into a commercial enterprise that exceeded all expectations of those connected to the rise of the Borscht Belt. No one did it more successfully than the Grossinger family, who, under the lead of Jennie Grossinger, the matriarch of the clan, operated the

---

2   Al Hine writes in an article on the hotel: "Grossinger's...partakes of an infinite variety of Catskill characteristics. Its clientele is vast and varied, its acreage expansive, its plant impressive. It may well stand as a symbol of the whole vacation area" (Hine 99).

most famous resort of the Catskills. The Grossinger's resort's story will be used exemplary for the whole region.[3]

The second discussion focuses on Jennie Grossinger, the leading lady of the Mountains. She has become an icon in Jewish-American culture and has attracted much interest, praise, and criticism over the years. Her hotel experience and her way of using the hotel presents a special, feminine example that adds an important element to this study. Up until now, the focus lay exclusively on the achievements and actions of hotelmen, as they dominated this business sector.[4] Yet, women play an essential role in the hotel network and shape hotel life in a different way. Jennie's life story and her attitude toward her hotel have been discussed in two biographies as well as several articles and private documents.[5] I will examine them to present and make comprehensible the overall importance of Jennie Grossinger for the Borscht Belt.

The analysis of the last aspect, the hotel as site of identity struggle, will also focus on Grossinger's. It is based on the experience of two hotel children, Tania and Richard Grossinger, and will highlight the importance of the hotel for their life.[6] Tania and Richard are distantly related and approach the resort from very different points of origin; Richard as the heir-apparent and Tania as the child of a hotel employee. Tania struggled with growing up at the resort hotel, which offered certain advantages but which was also a major challenge. For Richard, the hotel was his private paradise as a child. Yet, as an adolescent and adult, his family's legacy turned into a burden that threatened his self-perception. Their two accounts

---

3 The reason for this approach is that one has to consider the 'Borscht Belt' as one, more or less, homogenous entity, where people had very similar hotel experiences. Grossinger's Hotel and Country Club reigned as the 'queen of the mountains' for several decades and can be seen as the most expressive institution of this cultural phenomenon. This approach of discussing the Catskill hotel region as one entity has also been used successfully in an article on the Borscht Belt hotels in the German-Jewish magazine *Aufbau*. In this issue they presented the cultural and social importance of a variety of specific hotels around the globe. Yet, they also decided to treat the hotel region Catskills as an equivalent to the articles on specific hotels. In the text on the Mountains they, too, put a special focus on Grossinger's as the leading institution of this region.

4 The only small exception was Mary Bodne. However, she operated the Algonquin closely together with her husband, Ben.

5 I will use the first names of Jennie, Tania and Richard Grossinger in my analysis because they could otherwise be confused with the hotel, which carries the same name.

6 Again, the hotel experience of the Grossinger children is exemplary for other hotel children of the Catskills. Phil Brown has collected a number of life accounts of children growing up in Catskills resorts as either children of the staff or of the owners. There are several parallels between Tania's and Richard's and theirs.

throw a very different light on the resort. They show its darker side of abuse of power, sexual promiscuity, lack of privacy, phoniness, and an often still fragile hybrid Jewish-American identity. Their narrations discuss the challenges and the struggles to come to terms with this unusual kind of environment, a task especially difficult for children and young people. Despite the clear criticism in both texts and their different perspectives, Tania and Richard nevertheless agree in their conclusions that Grossinger's helped them become the people they are today and is inseparably part of their Jewish-American identity.

The religious and ethnic identity of these establishments of the Catskills region allows me to present the importance of hotels for a religious group that plays a significant role in New York. After examining the impact of the other essential identity categories on the hotel, such as class, race, and profession, in this last part I will consider religion and gender. Hotels in the Catskills like Grossinger's, drew a large part of their self-perception from being Jewish institutions with kosher food, obeying Sabbath rules and presenting a stage for Jewish-American rituals, life-style, and entertainment. Grossinger's was described as the Waldorf in the Catskills. This nickname of the grand Jewish resort also brings us full-circle in the discussion of hotels in New York and once more shows the close interconnections between the institutions examined in my study.

A Short History of the American Resort Hotel

To better understand the Catskill region and the importance of Grossinger's, a short definition and history of the hotel type called a resort is useful. Resort hotels belong to the oldest types of hotels in America, evolving at the end of the eighteenth century.[7] Best known among them are Saratoga Springs, New York, Newport, Rhode Island, and the higher Catskill Mountains. As their clientele was mostly made up of the better class of city dwellers, who had the time and money to go vacationing at these resorts, they were not located too far from larger towns. While they proclaimed to be structures close to nature and refuges from the crowded and dirty cities, resort hotels were not anti-urban but rather part of the urban system, providing modern amenities and allowing customers to return to the city in a day's travel (Sandoval-Strausz 87). They created a link between the city and its

---

7 Since the second half of the eighteenth century, Americans started to visit mineral springs for health reasons, inspired by the European habit of going to baths and spas. In Europe, this kind of health traveling had already existed for several centuries, but the eighteenth century brought the building of the first great spa resorts. To catch up with European developments at Baden-Baden and Carlsbad, enterprising Americans started to build their own resorts in the late eighteenth and early nineteenth century along the Eastern Seaboard (Sandoval-Strausz 88).

hinterland. Resort building brought much needed commercial development and revenue to parts of the country which until the nineteenth century were largely undeveloped and not connected to the nation's economic progress and prosperity.

While the health aspect was an important reason for the establishment of resorts, during the nineteenth century another stimulus for journeys to the countryside was the increasing appreciation of the beauty of the American landscape and the cultural meaning of unspoiled nature. The period of American Romanticism, expressed in writings and paintings of groups like the Hudson River School, made people aware of the untapped riches of America's mountain regions and sea sides and encouraged the nation's citizens to visit these idyllic places. As a direct consequence, one of the first great resort hotels was built in the Catskill Mountains in 1823, the Catskill Mountain House (Gregory 20). Tourism at that time became more than a pleasure activity and was seen as a patriotic duty because one was exploring one's own nation and discovering its richness and beauty (see Chapter 4). Instead of traveling to Europe, Americans set out to create their own version of a Grand Tour.[8]

During the second half of the nineteenth century the most important reason to stay at a resort for weeks and sometimes months at a time were the social opportunities and activities. Different from the high-class European spa towns, Alexis Gregory writes that in American resorts "brass, not class, set the tone" (Gregory 20). Hotel resorts in Saratoga Springs, Newport, and the Catskills provided stages to flaunt one's wealth and to strike up connections with people similarly well-endowed. While transient guests of city hotels usually stay only for a couple of days, resort visitors remained at their hotels for much longer periods, sometimes even for the whole season, which on the Eastern seaboard usually lasted from Memorial Day to Labor Day. This circumstance provided the resort hotel with a more or less fixed group of people, a returning social scene that in itself became an attraction. To entertain these people, hotels provided concerts, games, nature walks, and dances, which made them also the perfect background for conducting courtships among the daughters and sons of well-to-do families. The resort environment was often exclusive and safe enough to become a veritable marriage market for young upper and upper-middle class Americans. As they were chaperoned in the hotel by parents, siblings, and female relatives young women could display their advantages to young gentlemen without fearing for their reputations. Resorts were so popular for courtships that "[t]he young beaus and belles searching for a profitable marriage partner at fashionable resorts and hotels

---

8 In his *Notes on the State of Virginia* (1785) Thomas Jefferson already proposed building accommodations close to the Natural Bridge in Virginia so that people could enjoy its romantic beauty. The concept of resort tourism in the nineteenth century became a national project and was almost "sacred" (Sandoval-Strausz 88).

quickly became a stock figure of periodical fiction" (Brucken 206). Writers like William Dean Howells, Kate Chopin, and Edith Wharton set their society novels in resort hotels as they provided authentic background and fertile ground for complex social interactions as in *Their Wedding Journey* (1871/1887), *The Awakening* (1899), and *The Buccaneers* (1938). The social life at resort hotels remained their main attraction for decades, a fact that can still be seen in the developments of the Jewish Catskills in the first half of the twentieth century. The "enormous resorts" of Grossinger's and Brown's were the best-known examples for this phenomenon and "achieved a certain status in matchmaking: many happy marriages can be traced to weekends in what is known today as 'the Borscht Belt'" (Gregory 21).[9]

During the late nineteenth century and the early twentieth century, resort hotels became more inclusive. Some of them actively undermined the segregating practices of city hotels. As could be seen in the case of African-Americans and as I will show for Jewish-Americans, certain resort hotels became the places where minority groups could experience for the first time the American way of life by partaking in typical American leisure activities. At the same time, they could preserve their own customs and adapt them. By opening and operating resorts themselves, Jewish-Americans expressed a new kind of self-confidence. Similar to city hotels, resort hotels were also microcosmic versions of American society. Joel Pomerantz writes about the Catskills institutions:

A resort hotel that never closes its doors is no less than a microcosm of the larger world. Children have been born at the hotel while the elderly have died. People have fallen in and out of love. Marriages have been performed. ... Celebrated artists – from Irving Stone, the

---

9   The Eastern seaboard was only the first resort region of America. Resort-building in Florida, California, and the Rocky Mountains have also been important enterprises in the nineteenth century. Resort hotels often became the starting places for settlements, where people could stay until their own homes were finished, and where visitors from the Northeast could experience the natural beauty of the American South and West. Florida only developed into a modern state because of the early enterprises of Henry Morrison Flagler. Almost singlehandedly, Flagler opened up Florida for settlement via tourism. With his money, railroad lines were built and the marshes were dried and readied for human habitation. His actions turned Southern Florida into a fashionable winter tourist destination. Out of these early enterprises developed cities like Palm Beach and Miami Beach. As this chapter focuses on the hotel experience of Jewish-Americans, it should be mentioned that the history of tourism in Florida is also an example of the discrimination against this religious group. Palm Beach was an all white, Anglo-Saxon, Christian environment and exclusionary. Anti-Semitic practices were a common occurrence in its hotels. As a reaction to this, Miami Beach developed into *the* predominately Jewish resort, a division which still exists (Gregory 26).

novelist, to Paddy Chayefsky, the playwright – have come to work or re-kindle creative energies. Man's communion with God is often celebrated. (276)

For Jewish-Americans the Catskills hotel world seemed to fulfill all needs of their daily life during vacation, including the desire for religious and ethnic community. Despite the fact that a resort hotel with its frivolities and superficiality seems to be the antithesis to a religious site, the hotels, bungalow colonies, and summer camps of the Catskill Mountains were able to cater to both corporeal and spiritual needs in a condensed space.

There is one more peculiarity connected to resort hotels that I want to mention shortly, as it is of importance for the hotel experience in the Catskills. In contrast to city hotels, resort hotels were usually not open year-round. Instead they opened for *the season*, which in the Catskills started around Memorial Day (or Decoration Day) in May, and ended with Labor Day in September. The climate in the Catskills attracted most guests in the summer. The whole area of the Mountains lived and worked according to this seasonal cycle. Great waves of migrant workers arrived in the spring to bring the houses and summer camps up to date and left the mountains again in fall, usually for the Floridian resorts.[10] The proprietors themselves often had to work and live in New York City during the winter, but returned to their mountain properties in spring. Grossinger's Hotel and Country Club was one of the first winterized hotel resorts. They started to open up the hotel again for the Christmas Season in the late 1930s. After that, many of the larger hotels were open all year long but the busy time of the year still remained the summer season.

This life cycle had many repercussions on the hotel families' lives. For them it created a distinctively different kind of experience than those hotel experiences which we have already seen in the case studies of the city hotels. First, it meant that hoteliers needed to earn as much money as possible during the busy season, working extremely hard for three months. Second, it often meant the uprooting of the family twice a year. Hotel children, like Esterita Blumberg, regularly changed schools during the school year. Also, the perception of their living environment and the larger region was heavily influenced by the season: former hotel children describe a feeling of acute loneliness that overcame them in fall. Part of their growing up was to learn that this had to do with the vacation business of their

---

10 Other resort regions such as South Florida attracted most of its clientele in winter. Because of this, in the middle of the twentieth century many Jewish hotel people from the Catskills moved to the Jewish-American hotels and resorts in Florida for the winter. They established a close connection between the Catskill Mountains and Miami Beach. This made Florida the preferred vacation spot for New Yorkers for decades.

parents and the region in which they lived.[11] With resort hotels, the dimension of time plays an important role, even more so than in the cases of the city hotels already discussed. The procedure to close a hotel for the winter break was full of rituals of seasonal change and prepared the hotel family for the quiet, isolated time lying ahead of them. This was not necessarily something negative, as these families often worked themselves close to the breaking point during the busy season and needed the rest period to recharge and also to make repairs and improvements. Esterita Blumberg describes that with the end of summer, the main building of the hotel became a private home again: "Difficult as the farewells were, the other side of the coin involved the conversion of our property back to a family habitat, with no sharing strangers" (Blumberg 51). Accordingly, depending on the time of the year, the resorts exuded a very different atmosphere. In late fall and winter, the remaining hotel families lived a very quiet and secluded live. In summer, when the hotels and camps filled with people, the region housed a lively community: "It was the time when our quiet countryside came alive. The village streets were vibrant with a steady stream of humanity. The county's population, so small in winter, swelled a thousandfold" (Blumberg 75). In contrast to city hotels, where the flow of strangers remains constant and the home in the hotel is always a shared living space for the hotel family, here two different experiences alternate: being a host and being a private person; being co-workers and being family. Due to this circumstance, resort families experience their hotel life even more consciously than those who live it without interruption. In the life writings of Esterita Blumberg, Alvin L. Lesser, Carrie Komito and Tania and Richard Grossinger, the level of awareness of the hotel space and perception of their life as being uniquely shaped by this environment is striking. The seasonality of hotel life shaped the Jewish Catskills and caused a strong feeling of place-identity, as we will see in the following.

The Jewish Catskills, the foothills of the geographic region of the Catskill Mountains, are a prime example for these resort developments. At the beginning of the twentieth century, a unique kind of culture developed here which remained legendary even after its decline in the 1980s. I will provide an introduction into the history and the special religious culture of the Jewish Catskills before discussing the first aspect of hotel experience at the Jewish-American resorts.

The Jewish Catskills

The Catskill Mountains attracted travelers and tourists from the early nineteenth century onwards. The countryside close to the Hudson River was first inhabited by

---

11 Alvin Lesser, a Catskills hotel kid, remembers: "During the season, we had guests who brought their children and with their presence, that feeling left me. Gradually, I began to understand that what I was experiencing [in the off-season] was loneliness" (Lesser 38f).

Dutch settlers and during the nineteenth century saw German and Austrian immigration, gaining the region the nickname "The American Rhine" (Gregory 20). It was eternalized by Washington Irving's stories "Rip van Winkle" and "The Legend of Sleepy Hollow." It is necessary to consider the geographical outline of the Catskills for a moment. The Catskills Mountains, with its high peaks and beautiful views, are located in New York state and consists of six counties: Greene, Delaware, Sullivan, Ulster, Schoharie, and Otsego. Parts of Albany County are also included at times (Brown, *Catskill Culture* 23). This area covers nearly four million acres and counted almost half a million inhabitants in the 1970s. The so-called "Jewish Alps" are much smaller.[12] They are located mostly in Sullivan County and parts of Ulster County, at the foothills of the Catskill mountains. This made them more attractive for tourists in the twentieth century, as reaching them was far easier and less dangerous. The most popular way to get there was first by train and then by car from the 1940s onward. In the first decades of the century, it took almost a whole day to travel up to Sullivan Country. With the modern expressway, today it takes no longer than 90 minutes to reach the area from New York City.

The first Jewish-Americans already tried to establish religious communities in this part of New York State in the 1820s and made another attempt was made in 1837 (Brown, *Catskill Culture* 24). However, it was not until the 1880s and 1890s that permanent Jewish settlements developed. There are several reasons why these European immigrants turned the foothills of the Catskill Mountains into the greatest Jewish vacation region of America. At the end of the nineteenth century a large wave of Eastern European Jews emigrated to the United States to escape the Russian pogroms. The unprecedented influx caused rising nativism and racism in American society and the religious refugees experienced anti-semitism in many parts of the country. Starting in the 1870s, hotels, which earlier accepted Jewish guests, barred them from their properties.[13] This spurred the building of Jewish-owned resorts, starting in the 1880s. One of the earliest successful resorts from which a whole town developed is Fleischmann's in Griffins Corner in eastern Ulster County, which was built by the rich Hungarian Jew Charles F. Fleischmann, from

---

12 While the Catskill Mountains is geographically the correct description of the northern mountaneous region, most New Yorkers refer to the Jewish parts of Sullivan and Ulster county as "the Catskills".

13 Most famous was the Seligman/Hilton controversy of 1877, in which a rich Jewish-American businessman was barred from entering a hotel, which he had frequented for several years (Sandoval-Strausz 298-99). The reason was that the hotelier Judge Henry Hilton believed his shrinking profit was due to his acceptance of Jewish guests. His manager explained that Mr Hilton "came to the conclusion that Christians did not like their company, and for that reason shunned the hotel. He ... gave us instructions to admit no Jews" (*New York Times*, 19 June 1877).

Cincinnati, who was a U.S. Senator and a successful manufacturer (Brown, *Catskill Culture* 25). The "Silver Age"[14] (Conway i) of Sullivan County ended with many new Jewish settlers taking over the old, no longer profitable hotels. Conway writes: "[t]hese ambitious neophyte owners not only breathed new life into their hotels, but expanded and modernized them" (i). A few decades later they caused a "Golden Age" in this region. Starting in the 1920s these new operators also introduced a new building style, called *Sullivan County Mission*, which shaped the image of this region. While the number of Jewish people was increasing in the area and they were becoming more accepted by their neighbors, there were still years of tension ahead. In the 1920s, the Ku Klux Klan was very active in New York State. Blumberg describes in her autobiography that anti-Semitism was still alive in the 1930s. Throughout the years of the "Borscht Belt," the Jewish population, despite their strong cultural influences, remained a fifteen percent minority in the area (Blumberg 53).[15]

The experience of exclusion is only one reason why people started to form their own Jewish communities in Sullivan and Ulster County. At the beginning, the future settlers mostly came to the Catskills for health reasons and because of its likeness to their old country in middle and Eastern Europe. Many Jewish immigrants who worked in the crowded textile industry of the Lower East Side contracted tuberculosis for which there was no successful therapy available at the turn of the century. The best chance for recovery was a move from the polluted areas of Manhattan to the fresh air and open space of the Catskill Mountains.[16]

---

14 This term describes the phase of the first resort building by Gentiles lasting between the 1890s and 1915.

15 The issue of discrimination in the region is difficult. Jewish culture dominated the area in summer, yet among the locals, they were a minority. This fluctuation caused unpleasant encounters at times, when Gentile locals felt outnumbered. In the memoirs of a Jewish Orthodox girl, who worked in the mountains in the summer of 1963, a Gentile local explains: "When I grew up, a Jew was just a metaphor. We didn't think youse guys really existed like real people at all. We used to drive by and scream stuff at the summer freaks with beanies on their heads. Like they was from another planet. Jews was just our summer fun" (Maidenbaum 18). Many of these locals, derogatorily called Bimmies by the Jewish hotel people, did not realize that in the hotels and their cafés "Jews thought the same about them. ...No one outside of the Jewish Orthodox 'group' really counted. They were something of a joke" (Maidenbaum 18).

16 In Liberty, Sullivan County, the banking mogul J.P. Morgan had already subsidized a sanatorium for Gentile patients at the end of the nineteenth century, from which Jews, however, were barred. As a reaction, in 1910 the Workmen's Circle, a benevolent political and cultural Jewish group, which consisted mostly of unionists and socialist

Many guests of the first Jewish boarding houses and hotels came to the Catskills to heal and over the years many hotels and health institutions held by Gentiles were sold to Jewish families who transformed them into resort hotels and bungalow colonies.

Many future hotel owners of the Catskills themselves moved to the area because members of their families were sick and needed to recover in the countryside. Jennie Grossinger's father recovered in Sullivan County after a physical breakdown. As a consequence the family decided to start over as farmers in the mountains to prevent a relapse of Selig Grossinger. Their first boarders also included many who came to the region to recover their health or to recharge their energy, away from the crowded life of the Lower East Side. Most operators of Catskill establishments came from this part of Manhattan and most guests of these establishments were their former neighbors and family members. This created the close connection between New York City and New York countryside as described in the historical overview of resort hotels. This fact is important for the later developments discussed here.

For many Jewish immigrants another reason to move to the Catskills and out of the closely-knit *shtetl* life of the Lower East Side was the wish to own one's own land.[17] Many Russian Jews were barred from having their own land in their home country due to anti-Semitic laws which limited them to trade jobs. On arriving in America the greatest goal for them was to obtain their own piece of land and the feeling of security that comes with owning land. While most of these settlers had never worked as farmers,[18] they saw this as the right kind of occupation for a new start in America as it enabled them to live a free, self-sufficient life in open space.[19] The farms, which Jewish settlers purchased, were often of low quality, not very fertile, rocky, and difficult to make arable. But because of this, they were cheap. The lack in quality quickly led to the transformation of farms to boarding houses and later hotels. Esterita Blumberg narrates the experience of her grandparents:

---

supporters, opened their own sanatorium through a community effort for a quarter of a million dollars (Brown, *Catskill Culture* 27).

17 *Shtetl* is Yiddish for a small town or village in Eastern Europe (OED). It derives from the German word for little town. Today it is used in English to describe a predominately Jewish part of the city, often crowded and with a tightly-knit community structure.

18 There are some exceptions with Jews from Poland and Hungary who, in contrast to the Russians, also had farmers and land managers among them, yet farming was generally not widely spread among the Jewish population of Middle and Eastern Europe.

19 The admiration for farming in the recollections of later hotel people reminds one of Jefferson's Agrarian Ideal. Jefferson perceived the farmer as the backbone of democracy and an uncorrupted and upright active citizen of the country. This might have played a role in the process of Americanization of Jewish immigrants.

All too soon, the reality of their inexperience, difficulty in growing crops in the poor soil, and a short growing season led to many farm failures. Those who found no alternatives returned to New York City. There were others, however, who discovered that they had 'commodities' that were indeed saleable. The scenery was magnificent, there were eggs from the chickens and milk from the cows. The fresh air promised a cure for the disease stemming from the pollution that plagued those left behind in the city – a ready-made clientele. The farmers could offer cool breezes to people whose backyard was a fire escape: *landsleit*, fellow workers, kith and kin. The families moved to their barns for the summers and the farmhouse rooms were rented. They were accustomed to cooking for large families, so adding a few more plates was not difficult. Taking in boarders was a way of augmenting their meager incomes. They could stay on the land – the resort industry was born! (Blumberg 25f)

It helped these new boarding house owners that around the same time, 1890-1920, the Progressive Era, unions successfully introduced the idea of vacation for workers. Many textile workers saw spending a week at one of the farmhouses as "a week in heaven" (Blumberg 26). The situation of the Grossinger family was similar as Selig Grossinger, Jennie's father, also started the family enterprise with the dream of owning his own place and soon, due to the hardship of farming land in the Catskills, transformed his house into a boarding facility.

The early years of the resort region of the Jewish Catskills can be seen as a revival of the ancient laws of hospitality in America. While some of the narrations are covered by a nostalgic gloss, they still present the importance of these hotel experiences for the Jewish-American communities realistically. They recount that in the 1910s, guests still helped out in the boarding houses if the work became too much for the host family. As a consequence, the rates were extremely low and the atmosphere in these forerunners of the great Jewish resorts was very familiar. The return rate among the guests was high, resulting from the feeling of belonging to a seasonal family. While city hotels in New York had already developed into professionally organized hospitality institutions, the early hotels of the Catskills brought in just enough revenue to continue. Accordingly, the 1910s and early 1920s were still years of amateur hotelkeeping, as none of these early hotelmen and women had any kind of formal training in this business sector. However, over the years the hotelkeepers of the Catskills progressed to become professionals for this particular type of hotel business by learning-by-doing. With their increasing knowledge, their houses changed from small boarding houses on farms with no running water to real hotel structures, which differed architecturally yet could claim a similar type of comfort and amenities as the small city hotels of New York.[20]

---

20 In contrast to the high-rise city hotels, these resort hotels had a horizontal line of architecture in tune with the landscape.

The Catskills entered a most important yet very difficult time in the late 1930s and early 1940s. With the rise of the Nazi-regime in Germany, America experienced a renewed rise of anti-Semitism (Michael 170). Many Americans did not want to get involved in the European conflict and famous anti-Semitists like Henry Ford even blamed Jewish fellow citizens for the nation's entry into the war (see Frodon 143, Perry & Schweitzer 105). The Catskills had an air of insularity about them at this time. Here, Jewish-Americans could safely exchange news from Europe and discuss the rumors about the persecution of their landsmen, which were considered to be gross exaggerations by the American mainstream. At the same time, people also traveled to the "Jewish Alps" to escape the terrible news from Europe and to relax and celebrate despite the catastrophic situation that developed across the Atlantic.

The atmosphere at the Catskills resorts is very difficult to describe. Three neglected novels set in the Catskills try to preserve it: Reuben Wallenrod's *Dusk in the Catskills* (1957), Harvey Jacob's *Summer on a Mountain of Spices* (1975) and Martin Boris's *Woodridge, 1946* (1980).[21] In his book Wallenrod expresses the Catskill experience from the perspective of a disillusioned hotelkeeper. He writes:

Every morning you read the papers, the heart thumping with fear of surprises. You kept telling yourself that the Nazis would be beaten. It was impossible otherwise. But...[h]ere, in Brookville, in a little village in the Catskill Mountains, Jewish men and women, brothers and sisters of those tortured Jews in Poland and Holland and Slovakia, came and demanded pleasure with eagerness, with anxiety. ... The grounds were bright and colorful with flower beds; on the tennis court young men and women jumped, one opposite another; and no one paid attention to the monstrosities that cut into the brain. (Wallenrod 234)

The terrible reality of European Jews and the carefree attitude of American Jews affect the narrator. It was a difficult balancing act to continue one's daily business and to follow one's conscience. A former hotel owner later regretted "how little we all had to say about what was happening to European Jewry. It was almost as if by not mentioning the event we might dismiss it from reality" (Kanfer 172). However, it needs to be mentioned that a number of Jews, who escaped from Europe, also found shelter and recovery in the Catskills. After the war, the region became an important place for the rebuilding of Jewish culture. The smaller establishments often offered direct familial care. Here, Holocaust survivors could heal, reconnect with emigrated family members, and learn about America (Kanfer 172).

---

21 As the dates of the publications of these books show, it took the people time to come to terms with their experiences in the Catskills during the years of the Holocaust. For more details see Kanfer 195.

After the Allies' victory over Nazi Germany, the Catskill resorts experienced their boom years. Now not only Jewish customers but also Gentiles came to the hotels and, after lifting the limitations of war economy, the resorts were expanded to include Olympic-quality sport facilities and high-class entertainment that transformed the region into a tourist area of great reputation. The 1950s and 1960s were perceived as the region's "supernova period": "the Catskills grew large and bright, before exploding" (Brown, *Catskill Culture* 43). According to writer David Boroff, "[b]y espousing luxury and glut, the Catskills have invited criticism as vulgar and ostentatious" (60).[22] Starting in the late 1950s, many hotel families invested too much in new amenities. They wanted to keep up with the competition in the tourism industry and were no longer able to pay their debts when the Catskills became less attractive because of innovations like air-conditioning, changes in the Jewish community, and the new availability of exotic travel destination by airplanes.[23] By the mid-1960s, many smaller hotels and boarding houses closed. Only some of the larger resorts survived until the 1980s, when they too faced bankruptcy and foreclosure. The "Borscht Belt" was no longer fashionable, and despite some attempts at revivals, the decline could not be reversed. Today, only a handful of smaller hotels remain in Sullivan and Ulster County.[24] Several hotels were turned into rehabilitation facilities, while others were

22 Boroff softens his criticism, however, by adding: "For every guest engaged in maneuvers of upward mobility in mink and stole and Cadillac, there are a dozens of modest people interested in fresh air for their children. If the Catskills are raucous, they are also friendly and open. At bottom, pleasure is innocent and life-affirming" (60).

23 These changes include on the one hand a secularization of the Jewish community, with weakening ties to typical Jewish places like the Catskills. Young people no longer felt the need to go to Jewish places as they were now widely accepted in American hotels. David Boroff writes: "the gates of the ghetto have swung open" (50). On the other hand, it was a change in tastes. For the younger generation, the resorts were seen as too clannish and the entertainment and interior decor too old-fashioned. Many also no longer cared for Jewish dietary food laws. They did not require kosher food during their vacation. The large amount of food for which the hotels were famous, no longer fit the eat-healthy-and-stay-fit lifestyle that became popular in the 1960s and 1970s.

24 Since the 1990s, several scholars and witnesses of the great years of the Catskills started to collect memorabilia and oral histories to build up an archive and organize conferences on memory culture of this unique region. The outcome is the Catskill Institute, currently housed at the Northeastern University in Boston, where it is supervised by Professor of Sociology, Phil Brown. The Institute has a homepage where they continue to collect the memories and materials of the resort history of Ulster and Sullivan Counties. They have organized more than thirteen conferences on Catskill culture and books are published regularly on the topic of the "Jewish Alps," covering a wide range of genres including

taken over by orthodox and Hassidic Jews who created their own kind of institutions out of the former tourist establishments.

5.1 THE HOTEL AS POINT OF ENTRY TO AMERICAN CULTURE

After this short overview over the history of the Jewish Catskills and the reasons why the region developed the way it did, I will now focus on the resort hotels' function as point of entry for this religious and ethnic group into American mainstream culture. First I will examine how these institutions enabled Jewish settlers to keep their tradition and ethnic identity and at the same time helped them to become American. Then I will show how the resort hotels also made it possible for them to influence and add something to American culture. This process of becoming part of another culture and then to influence it vice-versa is called acculturation. Here I use Lawrence J. Epstein's definition of acculturation, which states: "Acculturation is a process by which two cultures borrow from each other so that what emerges is a new or blended culture" (Epstein 105).[25] In the process of adapting to American culture Jewish immigrants contributed to it. I will elaborate on this by using the example of the resort hotels of the Catskills.

What role did the resort hotel play in keeping the Jewish traditions and their identification as a group alive? The historical overview over the creation of the "Borscht Belt" showed that it was not a planned effort. Neither New York State nor any Jewish business association had drawn up plans to develop the foothills of the Catskill Mountains into a tourist destination and business community for Jewish people. America's once densest hotel region grew out of many separate projects and life decisions, often unconsciously, a mere reaction to the difficulties these immigrants faced and that they needed to overcome to become part of their adopted country. Community building quickly turned out to be a very important if not the

---

short stories, novels, memoirs, autobiographies, social and oral histories, and biographies of the region's great institutions and famous figures.

25 It is important to note that his definition of acculturation is bidirectional, allowing a reciprocal dynamic between two cultures (see also Taft 1977, Berry 1980, and Persky and Birman). Usually one culture is somewhat weaker than the other, which means that one is the host and the other is the immigrant culture, as in this case. Furthermore, the Jewish immigrants discussed here are of course not only Jewish but also Czech, German, Austrian, Russian etc. (Persky and Birman). Yet, for the sake of the hotel focus of this chapter, I am leaving out multidirectional acculturation processes which would also fit in this case. Here I am deliberately focusing on the religious identity alone.

main issue behind the successful development of this tourist resort area.[26] In the Catskills, many Jewish immigrants had, for the first time in generations, the possibility to own their own land. Their community finally had space to grow. In contrast to the crowded tenement houses of the Lower East Side, in the Mountains they could expand over the free space that was abundantly available. They could literally build something like a new Jewish "Promised Land" (Pomerantz 135). The awareness of this potential can be seen in the parallel construction of several synagogues in the area next to resort hotels and bungalow colonies. Most of the early boarding houses and hotels depended on each other's support for security and stability. They provided themselves with this emotional support by financing the building of their new temples as a group. Phil Brown writes that the building of synagogues "is one more piece of evidence that Catskill culture involved the creation of a community far broader than a collection of boarding houses and hotels" (Brown, *Catskill Culture* 30). He quotes a farmer turned hotelman who recalls:

Since the synagogues were so far away in Swan Lake and White Lake, ten Jewish farmers between the towns wanted to have a place of worship and to educate their children in Hebrew. One neighbor, Jake Rotship, donated a tract of land, centrally located, and they had a synagogue built. As money-poor as these farmers were, they felt it an absolute necessity to educate their children in Hebrew. (Shagrin qtd in Brown, *Catskill Culture* 30)

The early Catskills farmers-turned-innkeepers wanted to preserve their cultural identity and to hand it on to the next generation. Despite the challenges they faced, this was of the greatest importance for them. The money that they made with their boarding houses financed these community efforts, and the jobs they offered to the incoming immigrants secured the continuation of this tradition.

Keeping their Jewish culture alive among people of other faiths was a prime goal for these new hoteliers. A striking feature of the developing hotel world in the Catskills was the often-strict observance of the Jewish law and rites. Right from the beginning, kosher cooking was advertised as a distinctive selling point of the Catskill boarding houses. Although it was often a challenge to ensure this in the simple circumstances of the early transformed farms, the families took great pains to achieve it. Over the next decades, the larger resorts set up separate milk and meat

---

26 The focus on community building was not only important for Jewish immigrants but also for many other American immigrant groups such as the Germans, Irish, Italians, and Russians. A certain kind of clannishness could be observed in all these communities. The tightly-knit structure of their newly built communities provided them with a certain feeling of security, especially since the language barrier that they experienced in their adopted country often excluded them from participating in the mainstream culture.

kitchens, at great additional cost, which they, however, were willing to incur, if it secured the observance of their religious beliefs. Up until World War II, almost all big and small enterprises of the Catskills also honored the Sabbath and did not cook or entertain between Friday evening and Saturday evening. Instead they offered religious services on their grounds (Pomerantz 253).[27]

The continuation of Jewish culture in America was also actively enabled by the success of the resort hotels in the field of romance (Kanfer 267). As mentioned earlier, the Borscht Belt became known as the biggest marriage market for Jewish-Americans. Looking specifically for partners of the same faith, the resorts proved a most attractive meeting place for couples. A whole romance culture developed, which was specifically tailored to bring young people together with games and special single activities. Successful matches were rewarded with special honeymoon packages and lavish benefits for the returning couples. Although this often put much pressure on young people, especially on women who saved their money to spend it on weeks of vacation to find their partner, the overall success became part of the Catskills myth. Grossinger's Hotel took the lead here. Over a thousand couples are said to have found each other at the resort, helped by Jennie Grossinger's warm personality and guidance (Pomerantz 136, 290).[28] Romance in the Catskills became such a well-known fact, that even Hollywood movies were made about it like *Having A Wonderful Time* (1938) by Alfred Santell, staring Ginger Rogers and Douglas Fairbanks Jr.[29]

Besides encouraging romance, the Catskill hotels also preserved and even spread the use of Yiddish. This language was so prevalent in the regional towns that

---

27 One has to consider the great implication this means for a hotel business. In contrast to other sectors of the economy, in the hospitality industry the mantra is normally to provide guests with everything 24/7. To actually limit attractions of the hotel meant a certain risk to the profitability of the business. Yet, until the middle of the twentieth century, it was a risk the hotel owners were not only willing to take, but that also paid out, as the guests, being Jewish themselves, expected and wanted it that way.

28 This impression was a conscious effort of the public relations office of Grossinger's which was keenly aware of the financial potential of romances. The "Singles-Only" Weekends at Grossinger's belonged to the defining events of the 1960s in popular culture (Hendler 60).

29 The movie is based on a Broadway play of the same name produced by Marc Connelly (an Algonquin Round Table member) and written by Alfred Kober. In the play all characters are Jewish, as befits the location of the movie, a Catskill summer camp. For the movie, the names of the characters were changed to erase the Jewishness from the story. Leonard Maltin writes: "the original's satiric depiction of Jewish New Yorkers is completely homogenized" (Maltin 588). The reason for this move was the still strong anti-Semitism in America, which peaked in the interwar years (Sarna and Golden).

even Gentile shopkeepers, whose businesses relied on Jewish hotel and bungalow colonies, learned to speak Yiddish. Because the coexistence between Gentile and Jewish citizens in several of these small communities of the Catskills, for example, Woodridge, worked so well, a newspaper article described it as "Utopia in the Catskills" (Blumberg 66). Over the decades, the Yiddish language found entry into mainstream American English with words like bagel, chutzpah, klutz, and to schmooz, a development that can be partly attributed to the success of the Catskill hotel region. This was made possible because of the Gentile people working with and at these hotels, the hotel guests themselves, and especially the Jewish-American entertainment industry that grew out of the Mountains.

The Catskill hotel resorts enabled Jewish immigrants to keep their religious and ethnic identity and helped them to settle into their adopted country more easily. The resorts also helped them to develop a strong hybrid Jewish-American identity and functioned as a platform to influence American culture. In his study *Adapting to Abundance: Jewish Immigrants, Mass Consumption, and the Search for American Identity* (1990), Andrew Heinze argues for the importance of the Catskills for Jewish immigrants to fully arrive in their new country. He describes how the concept of leisure was something Jewish immigrants from Europe first needed to learn to become adapted to American ways. In their home countries they had been excluded from most forms of entertainment and "[t]raditional Jewish culture discouraged entertainment not connected to religious events" (Heinze 118). The existence of amusement parks like Coney Island was something unknown and new to the Jewish immigrants. Accordingly, becoming accustomed to leisure activities meant taking a step toward becoming American. Vacationing was an important element in this process. Heinze writes: "[w]ithin the realm of leisure, Jews found the vacation to be the most impressive component of the American lifestyle" (124). It also helped these immigrants to understand the social relationships between women and men in America and provided them with an "experience of a profound sense of fulfillment about their expectations of American society" (125). According to Heinze, Jews were the only immigrant group to adopt the concept of the "full-fledged" American vacation and found their ideal version in the summer resort.

The idea of a particular Jewish resort hotel experience was first fictionalized in Sholom Aleichem's *Marienbad* (1911), a satirical, epistolary novel that brought Aleichem the nickname "the Jewish Mark Twain" (Heinze 125). The book, however, was still set in Bohemia. Only affluent people could enjoy vacations there. Adapting to their new country, Jewish-Americans, however, did not consider vacationing as something limited to the wealthy but a "social necessity for city people" (125). The cheap rates asked for by the neophyte boarding house owners helped to fulfill this demand for a healthy break for city people. Jewish-Americans democratized vacationing in their summer resorts from the beginning onwards. While it was seen as fit for both genders to take a regular vacation during the summer, it was even more important for women, so they could be "good and healthy mother[s]" (129). This also marked the Catskills as an area dominated by women, with husbands, who needed to continue working during the week, only visiting on the weekends. For both, wife and husband, vacations in the mountains were described as 'a transformative experience,' on the one hand restoring health, and on the other hand merging with the nation's lifestyle, despite the Yiddishness of the resorts. The area was praised as the "best approximation of earthly paradise that could be imagined" (131).

An early American literary representation of this transformation of Jewish immigrants into Jewish-Americans through vacationing can be found in Abraham Cahan's novel *The Rise of David Levinsky* (1917).[30] The narrator depicts a dinner scene at the Rigi Kulm House, a fictional resort hotel in the upper Catskills. The first person narrator describes the rowdy atmosphere in the dining room and the impossibility of the dinner orchestra to be acknowledged and appreciated. When the band plays the "Star-Spangled Banner," as a kind of last resort to get the audience's attention, the main protagonist states:

The few hundred diners rose like one man, applauding. The children and many of the adults caught up the tune joyously, passionately. It was an interesting scene. Men and women were offering thanksgiving to the flag under which they were eating this good dinner, wearing these expensive clothes. There was the jingle of newly-acquired dollars in our applause. But there was something else in it as well. Many of those who were now paying tribute to the Stars and Stripes were listening to the tune with grave, solemn mien. It was as if they were saying: "We are not persecuted under this flag. At last we have found a home." Love for America blazed up in my soul. (Cahan 296)

The hotel brought Jewish-Americans together in a secure environment and it allowed them to feel part of the larger nation in this quintessential American institution. The entertainment offered to the guests, the abundance of food, and the possibility to display one's success to each other in the form of lavish dresses and jewelry all play part in this acculturation process.[31]

This tradition of entertaining in Jewish Catskill resorts became the region's most important legacy. The entertainment industry boomed in the Catskills in the

---

30 See also Heinze 131 and Brown, *Catskill Culture* 269f.
31 At the same time, this excerpt also already foreshadowed a recurring kind of criticism that was wielded against the resort culture of the Catskills. After the 1950s many perceived the area as being overly focused on consumption, affected social behavior, and empty of any authentic experience.

1940s, 50s, and 60s.[32] The big hotels such as Kutcher's Country Club, the Concord, and Grossinger's could claim world class acts of performers such as Tony Bennet, Irving Berlin, Robert Merryl and Jerry Lewis. Smaller places, while often not able to compare with them, still provided a solid level of entertainment and were a main reason for customers to return. Many famous entertainers started their careers in the playhouses of these hotels. Some of them even worked first as busboys to finance themselves before they were discovered for the stage. Many careers were also deliberately staged at Catskill hotels.[33] Most successful were comedians, who made the particular biting Jewish humor popular.[34] At the beginning, their style was still particularly European Jewish. Later, the types of jokes, the chronology of the acts, and the characters they played were all founded in the Yiddish tradition, yet more adapted to a broad American audience. The great advantage of the Catskills hotels and bungalow colonies was that they allowed artists to try out their programs before they risked the shark pool that is the entertainment industry of New York (Kanfer 131). As most of the guests were New Yorkers, a success in front of the famously critical audience of Catskill hotels almost guaranteed success in the city (Kanfer 231). In the Catskills, artists could hone their acts and also make themselves marketable. Many performed in the hotels under their birth names, but they changed their names for their careers in New York: Eddie Cantor, born Idisore Itzkowitz; Joan Rivers, born Joan Alexandra Molinsky; and Jerry Lewis, born Joseph Levitch (and related to the owners of the Brown Hotel in the Catskills).[35]

The music industry was also influenced by the culture of the Catskill Mountains. However, surprising as it might seem, the "Jewish Alps" were a driving force in establishing Latin American music in the American mainstream in the

---

32 While no precise date can be named for the inception of the entertainment industry in this area, its beginning can be traced to the 1920s and 30s and the tradition of the Jewish *tummlers*. Tummler means noise-maker. It is a traditional figure of storytelling and entertainment in Jewish culture.

33 This is described in Tania Grossinger's autobiography where she writes of Eddie Cantor's 'discovery' of Eddie Fisher at the resort, a publicity coup directed by the hotel's public relations manager, Milton Blackstone. Acting as a claqueur the night of Fisher's breakthrough she writes "I saw a page written in entertainment history" (T. Grossinger 80).

34 This type of humor makes fun of oneself and one's community. It makes the audience realize their own faults and teaches them to laugh about themselves.

35 This issue of name changing is a well-known element of adaption. Although not all stories are true concerning the radical way of changing people's name on Ellis Island, indeed many Jewish-Americans wanted to make sure that they would be able to have a fresh start in America and would be safe from discrimination by 'streamlining' their names (see Boyer 430; Organista, Marin and Chun 106).

1950s and 1960s. Instead of following Anglo-American music styles or the traditional Yiddish sounds of klezmer music, the Jewish community in Sullivan and Ulster County became the greatest supporter of Afro-Cuban and Puerto-Rican music, especially dance rhythms like the cha-cha-cha and the mambo, which led to the defining label of many young Jewish people in the mountains as mambonicks, meaning a Jewish mambo dancer (Twickel). Ethnologist and American Studies scholar Josh Kun describes the importance of this musical craze:

for some Jews in the fifties, Yiddish music was too Jewish while Latin music was not-Jewish, but also not-American. Latin music was outsider music, but it wasn't their outsider music, which made it a perfectly comfortable place to be, allowing Jews to be inside and outside at once. ...Latin music was the perfect mediating soundtrack for this transition from otherness to whiteness. (Kun 64)[36]

Latin music was an important element in creating a successful, hybrid Jewish-American identity. Again, it did not mean assimilation, but bidirectional acculturation. The hotel resorts in the Catskills provided the stage for this musical and social revolution, they were training ground and laboratory (Twickel). Most of the musicians playing Latin music, who were later successful in the American charts, trained in the Catskills and used its institutions as steppingstones.[37] Even sociologist Phil Brown, who was raised in the Catskills and had his first jobs in the hotel industry, describes himself as a mambonick in his youth in his interview with the *Aufbau* magazine. Due to its marginal location in American mainstream but its central position in Jewish culture, this successful kind of acculturation could only happen in the particular atmosphere of the Catskill hotels. The mambo craze of the Catskills is an important part of the Jewish-American hotel experience.

New York entertainment culture was influenced by Jewish artists who trained at the Catskill resorts and by the region's preferred musical style. At the same time, Jewish-Americans were influenced by American pastimes, especially in the form of American sports, which swept to the resorts. The sport star cult in the Catskills

---

36 Kun explains this close connection between the Jewish community and Latin-American music with the proximity of their neighborhoods. While racially differently categorized they shared the same area in the 1950s in East Harlem (Kun 57). Both cultures inspired each other, and Jewish business men would lead the establishment of Latin-American music in America by successfully founding record companies.

37 In her autobiography, Tania Grossinger describes herself as a mambo maniac. Playing the trumpet from time to time in the Latin-American combo of the hotel resort, for her "was more than a phase. It became, in fact, a way of life" (72). She experienced the music's influence on her in the Catskill environment as an important moment in her growing-up process, the first time she came into her own and identified with something.

started with Jewish boxer Barney Ross (born Dov-Ber David Rosofsky). In itself, it seemed a very unlikely starting point, as boxing was never known to be a preferred pastime in Jewish life. This, however, changed with Ross's success and his decision to make Grossinger's Hotel his training grounds. Stationed there during the preparations for his big fight, the Jewish-American population rallied behind him. When he won the lightweight world champion title in 1933, he became a hero for Jewish-Americans. With his heroic action in World War Two Ross also turned into an all American champion. Ross's example of training at a Catskill resort was quickly copied by many other sportsmen and women, among them golf pros and Olympic athletes, boxer Rocky Marciano, and baseball star Jackie Robinson.[38] Many of these had in common that they came from an immigrant and minority background. They were warmly welcomed in the Jewish resorts. Having this great mix of American sports heroes coming to the "Jewish Alps" connected the community closer to the American mainstream and gave its members a feeling of truly belonging to their adopted country.

Another lasting legacy of Grossinger's and its fellow resorts was that it provided summer jobs for the next generation of successful American Jews.[39] The bungalow colonies, summer camps, and resorts were a safe and often attractive environment for them to work. While the work was hard, one benefit was that the young men and women usually were allowed to use the facilities of the place after work hours. In addition they were surrounded by their peer group and built up a network that proved to be immensely useful in their later careers and lives. With tips and minimal costs of living over the summer, the jobs as busboys and camp counselors provided a foundation that enabled a generation of Jewish-Americans to follow high-achieving career paths and rise in American society.

The importance of the resort region of the Catskills for creating a successful hybrid Jewish-American identity can hardly be overestimated. Phil Brown writes: "In the Catskills, Jews could become Americanized while preserving much of their Jewishness. The resort was the vacationland and the workplace of Jews" (Brown, *In*

---

38 Jackie Robinson, the baseball player who integrated American professional baseball playing for the Brooklyn Dodgers, is the most famous example for the inclusive atmosphere of almost all Catskill resorts. Long before the city would desegregate all its public institutions, the resorts in the Mountains welcomed people of all ethnic backgrounds. Jennie Grossinger was a great friend of Robinson and his family and was said to have been a trailblazer in this development (Pomerantz 303).

39 A running gag was that one should treat the waiters, busboys, and porters friendly and tip them generously because next year they might operate your ulcer (Richler). This practice is shown in the movie *Dirty Dancing,* which is said to have been inspired by Grossinger's. The movie came out in 1987, riding on a wave of nostalgia for the old Borscht Belt.

the Catskills 12). A number of books on the adaptation and acculturation of Jewish-Americans to American culture have a chapter on the centrality of the "Jewish Alps." In *Tradition Transformed: The Jewish Experience in America* (1997), Gerald Sorin describes the transformation of Sullivan and Ulster Counties into a resort area as "an invention of the immigrant Jews and their social networks of relatives and landslayt" (95),[40] a development that is similarly important as the famous "Hollywood Eight" and their invention of the silver screen world. Lawrence J. Epstein stresses the importance of the Jewish Catskills for Semitic culture even more. In his book *The Haunted Smile: The Story of Jewish Comedians in America* (2001) he examines how the Catskills became an important center for Jewish culture, a safe retreat from the increasing anti-Semitism of the 1920s and 30s. The security of these resorts allowed them to work out a new hybrid kind of identity that enabled them to enter the American mainstream:

[t]here, in a thousand hotels and bungalow colonies, Jews could escape the heat of the city and the tensions of trying to fit into the wider American society. They could be themselves. They could eat all they wanted, play all day, relax, look for husbands and wives or more transient partners, and most of all laugh. The Catskills allowed the Jews to escape. (Epstein 109)

According to Epstein, these Jewish-American resorts were modeled "on the warmth of a Jewish home" (Epstein 111). He clearly stresses the special place-identity the Jewish resorts had for their customers, but also for the hosting families. Here, in this secure environment they could explore American culture and rehearse their hybrid identity as we have seen.

To conclude, the Catskills resort area helped Americanize Jewish-Americans and vice-versa to influence the American mainstream with the unique experiences made in their hotels, bungalow colonies, and *kuchalyns*.[41] However, with the growing acceptance of this religious and ethnic group, the decline of "the Mountains," the once the most densely built resort area of the world, was the natural result, similar to the fate of the Hotel Theresa in Harlem. From the 1950s onwards, segregation of Jewish-Americans was almost completely history. Accordingly, they moved away from their former vacation haunts and instead opted for mainstream resorts and West coast vacations. Some even began to visit Europe again. The "Jewish Alps" were seen as old-fashioned and too homely. For the more

---

40   *Landslayt* is Yiddish and means fellow countrymen.
41   *Kuchalyns* comes from the German word "Küchlein" (little kitchen) and means here a simple boarding house where boarders could prepare their own food in a common kitchen. It was the simplest category of accommodation in the Jewish Catskills resort region.

radical people of the 1960s they were seen as "exposing luxury and glut" (Boroff). Young people no longer wanted to be identified with this lifestyle in the "hip 1960s."

The Biography of Grossinger's Hotel and Country Club

One of the last resorts to close was Grossinger's Hotel and Country Club, the prime example of a Catskills resort. Al Hine described it "a symbol of the whole vacation area" (99). It was sold in 1986 and has not re-opened since. Grossinger's defined itself as a business with kosher cooking, and religious traditions and rituals, such as keeping the Sabbath and prohibiting smoking on this day. At the same time, it introduced the American way of life to their guests with sports, entertainment, and an abundance of space and food. The hotel invoked the spirit of the Catskills in a condensed, microcosmic way. In his article "The Catskills: Land of Milk and Money," Mordecai Richler writes: "Any account of the Catskill Mountains must begin with Grossinger's" (Richler). Historians confirm the fact that Grossinger's has earned an important position in the story of the Catskills. In his social history *A Summer World: The Attempt to Build A Jewish Eden in the Catskills* (1989), Stefan Kanfer states that "Grossinger's was once the epicenter of the Borscht Belt" (6). Many of the important elements of the Catskill resorts as described above can be seen in this particular hotel. It preserved Jewish tradition, while it enabled the Grossinger family and its guests to feel more American. Furthermore, the hotel itself developed a huge cultural presence that made it a household name in New York, America, and even in Europe. Grossinger's reputation reached beyond the typical fellowship of the rest of "the Mountains." During its heyday even its rival neighbor institutions would say about Grossinger's: "When the queen is in style, the peasants can smile" (Kanfer 7). In the following I will present a short historical overview of Grossinger's, focusing on major developments that set it apart and influenced the whole region. Against this background I will then discuss the hotel experience of members of the Grossinger family, reflecting their different perspectives.

The history of Grossinger's Hotel and Country Club, as it was officially called since the 1930s, is an exemplary Jewish success story of the twentieth century.[42]

---

[42] Its development from a small farm to America's most beloved resort hotel is told in the authorized historiography *Waldorf-in-the-Catskills* (1952) by Harold J. Taub, Joel Pomerantz's biography of Jennie Grossinger, *Jennie and the Story of Grossinger's* (1968), the autobiographies by Richard and Tania Grossinger, historiographies of the Catskills such as Frommer's *It Happened in the Catskills* (2004), and in articles and travel essays. While the publications authorized by the hotel present a glowing, censored picture of the hotel, together with the other accounts, most information could be verified.

The family originally came from Baligrod, Galicia, formerly part of the Austro-Hungarian Empire and today Southern Poland. Unlike the Jewish people in Czarist Russia, Austrian Jews were under the protection of Emperor Franz Josef and did not suffer the same harsh discrimination or persecution. Yet, due to the wide-spread poverty and lack of future prospects, Selig Grossinger, Jennie's father, emigrated to the United States in 1897 and was followed by his family three years later. Jennie was eight at the time of her emigration. Selig Grossinger was a trained land overseer. In the Lower East Side he got a job in the textile industry, performing physically hard work that quickly affected his health. Failing in health he quit and opened a small restaurant, "Grossinger's Dairy Restaurant." The restaurant became a kind of canteen for the neighborhood, frequented by neighbors and family members (Pomerantz 71). Selig suffered a collapse caused by overworking and the air pollution of Lower Manhattan, and was ordered by his doctor to recover in the countryside. His experience there inspired him to move to the countryside with his family. In 1914, following the advice of a successful relative, Grossinger bought a farm in Sullivan County, which was called "Longbrook House," a name that "had a nice 'American' sound" (Pomerantz 95).

Like many other Jewish immigrants, the family quickly took in boarders because the most successful crop of this stony and infertile land were "boarders" (Pomerantz 90). By taking in the first nine boarders in the summer season of 1914, the Grossingers were among the first Jewish-American families to open a boarding house in the Mountains (Kanfer 169). Due to an increasing demand for accommodation the Grossingers sold their first farm in 1919 and bought a former hotel on a considerable acreage, the "Terrace Hill House," located on the Nichols' estate near the small town of Liberty in Sullivan County.[43] In contrast to their first boarding house Terrace Hill House was a modern structure with electric lights, in-house plumbing, and a lot of space for guests.[44] In an interview from 1954 with Morris Freedman, Jennie recalls the difference she experienced: "'You can't imagine my pleasure when I went from room to room and pushed buttons to turn on the lights. After all that kerosene, just to push a button for light'" (Grossinger qtd in Freedman).

Grossinger's Terrace Hill House, later known only as Grossinger's, remained the site of the hotel until its closing in 1986. The main house was built in Sullivan County's mock Tudor style (Image 10). In the following years, the extensions were

---

43 The town is approximately 90 miles from New York City, an acceptable distance for a summer retreat in the first half of the twentieth century. The journey then was mostly taken on the New York, Ontario & Western Railway before New York State Route 17 was updated. From then on most guests arrived by car.

44 The appearance of Longbrook House is deliberately downplayed by the Grossinger's historians to create a striking contrast between the first house and the second one.

also constructed in this style to create a somewhat homogenous impression.[45] The outside appearance of these Tudor-style buildings looked old-wordly, reflecting the European heritage of its owners. The interior was mostly done in a rustic style, playing on the closeness of the resort to nature. Over the years, the style became more artificial, including the use of fake plants, pink and aquamarine colors, and chrome.[46]

Image 10: The Main Buildings of Grossinger's

Grossinger's Hotel and Country Club. By The Catskills Institute.

---

45 This, however, ended with building additions in the international style during the 1960s and 70s. These were multistoried buildings with flat roofs and no embellishments.

46 Already in the 1960s, newspaper articles criticized that more and more typical outdoor activities were covered up and put inside. The style changed from back-to-nature to a domestication of nature, an artificial environment only reflecting natural and rustic elements. For example, despite its lake, Grossinger's could also lay claim to the largest, Olympic-size indoor swimming-pool of the area. Other resorts started to build indoor skating rinks, so that guests would not be cold while ice-skating and could also skate in summer. In addition, the resorts often consisted of building-complexes which were connected to each other via glassed-in gateways and corridors, minimizing the exposure to the (already domesticated) outdoors. Activities like rowing on the Grossinger Lake were no longer attractive as they lacked the level of gregariousness wanted by the hotel's guests (Boroff). This reminds one of Henry James criticism from 1907, where he writes that American society always searches for "the supremely gregarious state" (105) at hotels which fulfills their happiness.

Throughout the 1920s and 30s Grossinger's slowly developed into a resort which was able to survive the Great Depression due to conservative financing and because vacationing in the Catskills was an inexpensive alternative to many other holiday options. Around the same time the hotel grounds were improved for their guests with new amenities such as tennis and volleyball courts, and in 1931 the first nine-hole golf course was opened, which became the basis for the large Grossinger's Golf Club still existing today (Taub 111).

Quicker than other establishments of the area, Grossinger's understood the importance of predicting its guests' expectations and their wishes for activities and entertainment. The hotel was a forerunner with its sports facilities. In short succession these were copied by surrounding hotels. The resort also started to offer professional entertainment and transformed the figure of the traditional Jewish *tummler* into the position of a social director with a full-fledged entertainment staff. In the 1930s, Grossinger's achieved nationwide fame when it became the training ground for the Jewish boxer Barney Ross, who won the World Championship in 1934.[47] Over the years, the resort not only focused on Jewish guests, but was open to all ethnic groups. Most visible was the presence of baseball player Jackie Robinson and his wife at the hotel. Publicity pictures underline the impression that the Grossingers wanted to make a point of inviting members of all types of ethnic minorities to their resort. Grossinger's perceived itself as a place of inclusion and tolerance. The hotel became Jennie Grossinger's instument to project this.

By the 1940s, the hotel was acknowledged as *the* resort place to be on the East Coast. This was also helped by famous newspaper reporter Damon Runyon calling Grossinger's in one of his sport columns "Lindy's with trees" (Kanfer 153), spreading its fame nation-wide. At the end of the 1940s Grossinger's even added its own airstrip, which developed into Liberty Airport. It underlined the trailblazer position of the resort, yet it also foreshadowed the exaggerated expectations people had of the Catskills for the future years. The 1940s also marked the beginning of charity programs organized by Grossinger's, such as selling war bonds, collecting money to rescue Jewish children from Europe, and the "Canteen-by-Mail" program which distributed food to thousands of American servicemen throughout the Second World War. These actions connected the name Grossinger's with good citizenship in the people's mind, putting it in a positive light despite the rising luxury and gluttony taking place at the resort. Jennie became a leading charity figure in New York.[48] Because of the amount of war bonds sold with her help, the army even named a bomber "Grossinger."

---

47 In the following years, the resort became the training ground of six more world champion boxers, among them Rocky Marciano.

48 A great amount of Jennie Grossinger's correspondence, which is held by the YIVO Institute for Jewish Research in New York, consists of texts connected to her charity

By the time Jennie Grossinger's biography was published in 1970, the resort consisted of 35 buildings and presided over 1,200 acres of land which made it "twice as large as the principality of Monaco" (Pomerantz 276). It offered night clubs, a swimming pool, a riding academy, a dining room for 1,300 people, an air conditioned card playing room, a dance studio, and a ski slope (Freedman). The resort could house up to 1,300 guests at full occupancy, and an additional 600 day guests. While this did not make Grossinger's the estate with most beds, it was considered to be the most elegant and personal one.[49] In 1954, in his article "The Green Pastures of Grossinger's," Morris Freedman writes of Grossinger's:

Roughly, Grossinger's is to resort hotels as Bergdorf Goodman is to department stores, Cadillac to cars, mink to furs, and Tiffany to jewelers, but only roughly. It has been called 'Waldorf in the Catskills.' Yet neither the old nor the new Waldorf ever had a strictly kosher cuisine, a full-time hostess to introduce unattached guests to one another, an Olympic swimming pool, an airport, a ski slope, or champion prize-fighters training on the premises— to mention a few of the more unusual attractions. (Freedman, Commentary, July 1954)[50]

Staying at Grossinger's in the 1950s was a statement of achievement. The possibility of rubbing elbows with men like Nelson A. Rockefeller, Chaim Weizman, Rocky Marciano and women like Debby Reynolds, Elizabeth Taylor, and Eleanor Roosevelt was unmistakable proof of this. However, this phase did not last long. Even before the death of Jennie Grossinger in 1972, the estate, like its surrounding region, started to decline. Grossinger's was sold in 1986 to the Servico company. Despite announcements about re-openings, the hotel remains closed and now deteriorates.[51]

---

efforts. This kind of work was very important for her and increased during the 1940s and 50s.

49 The Concord held this title with over 2,000 beds available.
50 In the historiography of the hotel entitled *Waldorf-in-the-Catskills: The Grossinger Legend* (1952), a comparison between the Catskills' resort and the New York grand hotel is often drawn. Similar to the case of the Hotel Theresa in Harlem, by this its owners and the larger Jewish-American community established their claim that they were now a fully equal part of American society.
51 Grossinger's represents the state of many other establishments in its current fate of becoming an attraction for "ruin porn" tourists and art photographers (Bartels). Grossinger's is the only hotel in this study that has not been preserved by the New York Landmark Commission, despite its almost mythical status as the favorite retreat of the emerging Jewish-American middle- and upper-class. A reason might be that it is outside of the city of New York and lacks a strong lobby. Also, it was probably too commercial and too mainstream to inspire preservation commissions to save it from destruction.

The hotel with its own postal code, Grossinger, NY, now lives on in the memories of its family, staff, and guests. Even though it was regularly criticized in the 1960s for its corniness and its assumed fake-happy atmosphere, Grossinger's is still recalled as a homely, comforting place: "Grossinger's was the mecca for those who honored a kind of innocent fun associated with early Hollywood and the pre-War era" (R. Grossinger 70). This homely, familiar atmosphere is largely the achievement of Jennie Grossinger, the matriarch of "the big G," who was one of the most powerful hotel women of New York in the twentieth century.

5.2 THE HOTEL AS PLACE OF FEMALE EMPOWERMENT

In all texts about Grossinger's, from its beginning in 1914 to its closure in 1986, Jennie Grossinger is the symbol of the resort, the "loadstar of the Catskills" (Kanfer 7), or, as Rachel Kranson puts it, "a priceless resource" (Kranson 185). She was the human face that gave the place "its tone, its dignity and hospitality" (Paul Grossinger in Freedman). With the nationwide success of her resort, Jennie became a Jewish-American icon. In books and blogs on Jewish success stories and on female leaders, she figures largely as a role model.[52] To understand Grossinger's and its function for the Jewish community, one needs to understand Jennie Grossinger and her vision for the hotel. Likewise, Jennie Grossinger can only be understood in connection to the hotel resort that bears her name. It is a strong part of her identity. Therefore, in the following I will examine Jennie's hotel experience as depicted in a collection of books and articles.[53] Similar to the other hotel leaders

---

Finally, it might also have to do with a lack of support from the Jewish community, who, with few exceptions, have turned their backs on the former vacation hot spot.

52 See Carol A. Weisenberger, "Jennie Grossigner," *European Immigrant Women in the United States: A Biographical Dictionary* (1994), 121-122; "Grossinger, Jennie," *American Women Managers and Administrators: A Selective Biographical* (1985), 96-97; "Jennie Grossinger," *The American Jewish Woman: A Documentary History* (1981), 671-676. In these accounts Jennie is celebrated as a prime example of the American Dream myth. As we could see before, hotel managers and owners are often seen as embodiments of the American Dream. As a female resort owner, Jennie Grossinger, however, seems to be unique among innkeepers in America. In the Catskills, many Jewish women took on managing positions. In that, they were more progressive than their Gentile neighbors.

53 Although there exists a correspondence between Jennie and Prentice-Hall Publishing about the first four chapters of her autobiography, co-written by Howard Eisenberg, the book has never been published (see letter by Bernard Geis of Prentice-Hall Publishing from January 27, 1958, and Jennie's response from February 13, 1958, which are part of the collection of Jennie Grossinger's correspondences at the archives of the YIVO

discussed in this study, she too formed the hotel after her vision and imbued it with her unique personality and atmosphere. She was perceived as one of the main attractions of the place. In contrast to the already discussed hosts, however, Jennie performed her role in a very feminine and motherly way. She did this so successfully that the resort hotel functioned for her as a place of female empowerment.[54] Diner, Kohn and Kranson write:

Jennie Grossinger used the resources at her disposal as a woman, a mother, and a Jewish immigrant to challenge the boundaries of the feminine mystique. Hotelier Jennie Grossinger ... became a national celebrity by playing into postwar gender ideals and promoting her own image as a nurturing, maternal figure. Ironically, it was this convincing portrayal of a Jewish mother that transformed her into a wildly successful entrepreneur. (8)

The role of hostess allowed her to project a caring, feminine image, while the success of her resort hotel gave her a powerful position in New York society, which she used for the advancement of the Jewish-American community.

Jennie Grossinger is a role-model example of Jewish immigration to America at the turn of the century. Her rise to becoming one of the best known innkeepers of the country has been presented as a clear-cut example for the American Dream. Born in 1892 in Baligrod, Galicia, and emigrated to America in 1900, Jennie quickly became independent and was used to work hard. Jennie was outgoing and people-oriented, even though her biographer describes her struggle with shyness in the first years of her life as a hotelkeeper. While the accounts of Taub and

---

Institute for Jewish Research. Geis even sent Jennie a copy of Conrad Hilton's recently published *Be My Guest*, so that she would have an idea how the finished product would look). Therefore, I will rely on a number of other sources that provide us with information about her close relationship to her hotel and her hotel experience there: her biography *Jennie and the Story of Grossinger's* (1970) by Joel Pomerantz (started by Quentin Reynolds, completed after his death by Pomerantz); Harold Taub's history of Grossinger's, *Waldorf-in-the-Catskills* (1952); the life accounts of her grandson Richard Grossinger, *Out of Babylon: Ghosts of Grossinger's* (1997), and her cousin Tania Grossinger, *Growing Up At Grossinger's* (1975, republished in 2008). All these texts define themselves as non-fiction. Still, it is necessary to remain cautious of their respective evaluation of Jennie. The accounts of both Pomerantz and Taub were ordered and published by the Grossinger's resort and are very adulating. In contrast, the texts by Richard and Tania Grossinger reveal personal tensions among the members of the Grossinger family and are also biased.

54 Hotels are ideal for this purpose, as they are meant to project a home-like atmosphere. The home belongs to the female, the private sphere. It is a most fitting place to empower female hosts, as they perform a role natural to them. By this they gain real power.

Pomerantz differ on who signed the papers for the "Terrace Hill House" that would later become the Main House of the Big G. (as it is called by guests and staff), it is clear that already in 1919 Jennie was the driving force in the expansion of the business and its professionalization. Much is made by the writers of the fact that the Grossinger family had no hotel training and no clear vision for the future of their boarding business before the expansions in the 1920s.[55] The family is stylized as naïve, yet hard-working, fitting the image of the immigrants who by luck and determination realize their success story. Pomerantz describes the Grossingers as a: "remarkable little family that came to the New World at the turn of the century poor in everything but hope, love and humanity" (275). The reason for this narrative strategy is probably to overcome the still lingering anti-Semitism, which saw any too active pursuit of business success as a sign of a Jewish conspiracy (Kranson 178). The publishing company stresses this wholesome impression on the book cover, stating: "It's a story of hardship and hard work, of family loyalties and love, the sublime evidence of the American dream come true" (Pomerantz back cover).

For the Grossinger's resort experience, it is important to understand how Jennie is presented to the public. One can divide her depiction in the texts into three categories, which all relate to her role at the hotel: first, she is presented as the gentle Jewish mother who imbued the resort with a cozy, familiar atmosphere and made good by it. Second, she is seen as a savvy businesswoman who by means of her instincts and her supreme ability to listen to people's wishes turned the resort into a national institution, making "Grossinger's ... the undisputed aristocrat of the mountains" (Pomerantz 278). And third, she is depicted as the embodiment of the Jewish immigrant success story and a role model for second generation Jewish-Americans. In all three roles, she remains a female force, a point that is an important part in her definition as America's beloved hostess.

Jennie Grossinger had two children, Paul, born in 1915 and her successor in business, and daughter Elaine, born in 1927, who later also joined the management of the resort. Per definition this makes Jennie Grossinger a Jewish mother. However, Rachel Kranson explains that the title "Gentle Jewish Mother" fits somewhat uncomfortably with Jennie, even though this is the way she is most often presented to the public. Even the very positive accounts of Taub and Pomerantz have stated that Jennie could not take much time for raising and educating her own two children because she was so involved in the daily business of the hotel. According to Pomerantz this was a constant source of guilt for Jennie. Paul Grossinger later recalls that he "was drug up," not lovingly raised, by the resort (Paul Grossinger in R. Grossinger 55). However, toward her guests and her staff

---

55 However, it is briefly mentioned that Malke, Jennie's mother, was the daughter of an innkeeper back in Galicia. A certain amount of knowledge and ability seems to have existed from the beginning on.

Jennie performed the role of a gentle Jewish mother very successfully. Jennie was an observant Jew and followed most of her beliefs' traditions and rites at the hotel until her death.[56] It was not until after the Second World War that she decided that the resort would continue its entertainment program throughout the Sabbath. According to Pomerantz and Taub, Jennie did this for the recovering soldiers, who visited the resort after the war and who deserved some form of escapism. To remain inside the Jewish law, the Grossinger's "handed over" the ownership of the hotel for the time of the Sabbath to a longterm Gentile staff member, a doctrine known as "Shtar M'Chirah" (Pomerantz 254). By stylizing the story this way Jennie's image as the caretaking Jewish mother is strengthened.

In the same vein other successful business ventures are explained by fitting them to Jennie Grossinger's motherly image. Some examples are the decision to let Barney Ross train for his welterweight boxing championship at the hotel and the establishing of Singles Weekends to foster successful, Jewish, marriages.[57] Jennie's image of the gentle Jewish mother was even attractive to the convention business that the hotel needed in the 1960s when changes in the style of vacation-making demanded the opening of new markets. According to Pomerantz, Jennie learned that the "same cozy, familial atmosphere that appealed to individual guests" (263) also appealed to convention-goers and their wives. In contrast to other hotels, the conventioners also brought their families to Grossinger's, which allowed the participants to spend some time with their families while working.

The relationship between the staff and Jennie is used as another piece of evidence for her comforting qualities. Hotel pay in the Catskills was low overall, yet, in contrast to most other places Grossinger's is reported to have paid better than the rest and focused on giving its staff the impression of belonging to a larger family: "One thing that separated the Grossinger staff from staff at many of the other hotels was the 'personal touch.' As much as possible they were really treated as if they were members of the family. Jennie tried to take their problems to heart whenever she could" (T. Grossinger 64). This familial relationship between staff and host family is further underlined by the fact that some longtime employees identify so much with the place that they select their burial plots on the Grossinger's acreage (185). While Tania's overall description of her cousin is very

---

56 Jennie's mother, Malke, was very religious and wore the traditional *sheitl* until her death. The texts point out that it was largely due to her that the resort remained strongly Jewish. Jennie kept the tradition in honor of her mother.

57 The way the Barney Ross episode is described in the books by Taub and Pomerantz one gains the impression that it was more out of kindness than economic consideration that Jennie allowed the training of Ross at the resort. In the positive, familiar atmosphere of the kosher hotel, the boxer, who was himself a strong follower of the Jewish faith, could become much more successful.

critical, she does not leave a doubt that this cozy feeling that was attributed to Jennie Grossinger was based on fact. When a fire destroyed a staff cottage and took the life of half a dozen staff members, Jennie Grossinger is recorded to have been deeply affected by this catastrophe and to have taken a very active role in the care-giving to the injured and surviving staff members. Despite the many honors that Jennie received for her philanthropic acts, according to her biographer, Joel Pomerantz, Jennie's proudest moment was when she received a plaque from her staff members, inscribed with the following text:

A few weeks ago, a distinguished committee on the West Coast named Jennie Grossinger one of the ten outstanding women of the world. To those of us who have worked with her during the years, she is far more than that. To us, she is the architect who poured her soul into the creation of this fabulous resort. She is the humanitarian who has helped endow hospitals, nurseries and schools in Israel and elsewhere throughout the world. She is the benefactor who made it possible for countless young men to go to college and become physicians, lawyers, engineers and teachers. ... She is the friend who always listens with a sympathetic ear and an understanding heart to the woes of even the humblest of us. She is a woman of great social genius and magnetic warmth. To us, she is the No. 1 woman of the world! We want, at this time, to wish her a long, long life, filled with further opportunities to give aid and comfort to her fellow-men. (Pomerantz 312f)

The text was signed by the 950 staff members of Grossinger's, underlining Jennie's quote: "The real hotel is the people who work here" (312). While this story is certainly placed in the biography to strengthen Jennie's image as the ultimate caring Jewish mother and humane businesswoman, it works as a powerful reminder for the reader of Jennie's warm personality and her strong connection to the hotel.

However, as mentioned above, the role as "Gentle Jewish Mother" did not fit too comfortably with Jennie. Anne Landau, the wife of the hotel's rabbi, writes that Jennie was respected and even feared by some members of her staff as a hard and focused businesswoman who, despite her warm appearance, ensured a clear hierarchy at the hotel (Kranson 189). This side of Jennie is also depicted in Tania Grossinger's autobiography where the writer comments repeatedly on the exaggerated heartiness of Jennie toward her guests, and the sometimes fake display of emotions toward family members.[58] Both perceptions seem to be true and show

---

58 Tania Grossinger writes of her reaction to Jennie's nightly speech at the Playhouse: "And it was no longer possible to sit with a straight face when Jennie, at the end of each Saturday night show, would go on the Playhouse stage and say dramatically, 'My wonderful guests. What would I do without you? My one wish is that when I go to heaven I'll have a large hotel and you will come and be my guests. And you won't need reservations either. Thank you, from the bottom of my heart!'" (T. Grossinger 122).

the conflicting character of Jennie Grossinger, the supreme Jewish hostess. I argue that this two sidedness is based on the particular nature of a hotel resort. As mentioned earlier, hotels are always public and private at the same time. Privacy at a resort hotel is even more difficult to get for the owners than in a city hotel as the family is expected to have personal interaction with the guests. In my opinion this is the reason for Jennie's Janus-like personality. She lived with her family, guests, and staff at the resort for more than fifty years. Playing the role of hostess for so long certainly had an effect on Jennie's psyche, manifesting her close identification with the resort.

Considering texts on the Catskills hotel, it is clear that the female side of Jennie, her neat appearance and motherly behavior, distinguished her hotel from others in the crowded market of the region. More than with any other of the hotels discussed in this study, the gender of the host plays a remarkably large role in the success of the hotel. As Kranson writes: "Unlike the immigrant tales of Jewish men, which attributed their success to determination, hard work, or 'ruthlessness,' Jennie Grossinger's biography credited her motherly kindness and decency for her triumph in America" (184). The most often used words for Grossinger's resort therefore are warmth, coziness, a familiar atmosphere, and a wholesome and healthy environment, fit for families, singles, celebrities, and business people alike. That the hotel was able to attract such a diverse group of people can be seen as proof for the success of Jennie's projected image. Jennie's motherly appeal was an important selling point of the Grossinger's experience and at the same time helped to disguise the business oriented cleverness of the famous hostess.[59] Her motherly aura indeed empowered her. The more successfully Jennie projected the image of herself as the gentle Jewish mother, the more successful was her hotel. Richard Grossinger writes about his grandmother in his memoir: "Perhaps she was no more than a clever businesswoman, but she *seemed* to be Eleanor Roosevelt and Molly Picon" (49).

Considering the success of Grossinger's, Jennie Grossinger was indeed a very savvy business woman, one of the first who operated under her own name and not her husband's. In Taub's account the purchase of the Nichols's Estate, which would become the home ground of the famous Grossinger's resort, was arranged for and signed by Jennie, and she is the one who took on the responsibility for expanding the boarding house into a real hotel. It is also clear from other accounts that often her decisions counted the most in the family business, especially since the death of her father in 1932. Coming from a conservative, Eastern European background,

---

Tania Grossinger writes that many ex-staff members would still laugh about the clichéd quality of this appearance years after the end of Grossinger's.

59 Freedman writes: "I was impressed, captivated possibly, by a graciousness that approached elegance, and by an embracing, glowing femininity that covered over and made unimportant her obviously sharp business sense" (Freedman).

Jennie grew up in a community where women usually were expected to let men make the decisions. But if we follow Richard Grossinger's account of the resort's history, then Jennie did not simply obey her father and her husband, but made decisions of her own. According to Taub and Pomerantz, the reason why the resort so often led the way in the developments of the Catskill hostelries was that Jennie was an extremely attentive listener to the wishes of her guests. The fruits of this were the establishment of tennis courts (unusual at this time), a large swimming pool (first considered unnecessary, as the resort already included a large lake), the Singles Weekends, as well as so-called "Grossinger's Reunion Dances".[60] By the late 1940s, Grossinger's was the leading resort of the East Coast. Her role as its hostess made Jennie a powerful role model for young women in America.

Another example of her sense for business can be seen in her way of dealing with her staff, especially an incident when the call for unionization arose in the Catskills region. According to Taub, Jennie believed that the staff would only ask for unionization if they felt unfairly treated by her. With the strategy of making the demand for unionization appear as her personal failure of being a good boss the situation is successfully overcome by Jennie. As a result, the staff withdrew its demands and unionization did not happen at Grossinger's until the 1960s. The staff even declared that they were happy to work for Jennie and would continue to do so. The whole union incident is portrayed as something manufactured from the outside, and not personally wanted by the Grossinger's staff members.[61] Not only for Jennie, but allegedly for her staff, too, the resort became a home, the place they identified with.

Pomerantz closes his book about Jennie and her resort by calling Grossinger's: "a kind of microcosmic social laboratory where the simple coming together of different races and religions has proved a more powerful antidote to bigotry than thousands of high-sounding words" (303). Indeed, there is no report of Jennie ever

---

60 For these dances former hotel guests were invited to a beautiful ball in the city's most prestigious hotels such as the Waldorf-Astoria in the winter season to refresh their contacts from the summer. That these reunions usually were organized as charity events, which collected money for Jewish-American causes was additionally positive. Jennie Grossinger, as personification of her resort, maintained close connections to the hotelmen of New York, making her hotel part of the city's network, despite the 90-miles-distance between Grossinger's and New York City.

61 The only critical voice raised in this context of staff treatment is Richard Grossinger's, but even in his text he only hints at the difficult working conditions for immigrants at the hotel. He does not elaborate on the matter. In contrast, in other text passages we learn that many of the hotel's staff have been there for many years, often even decades and that asked about retirement, longterm-employees did not know where else to go (Pomerantz 287).

acting in a racist or chauvinistic fashion. Quite to the contrary, Jennie Grossinger is reported to have actively sought the business of minorities, believing in their right to equal treatment. The famous African-American baseball player Jackie Robinson said about Jennie: "To Jennie, people are people! It's about as simple as that – not matter their skin, their place of birth, or where they happen to pray" (Robinson qtd. in Pomerantz 303). Grossinger's was a role model place for successful race relations. The resort was Jennie's platform to achieve change in New York society by bringing together politicians, intellectuals, and entertainment stars. Jennie met with society's leaders, such as Governor Nelson Rockefeller, and influenced them with her ideas. Her philanthropy and tolerant policy is part of Jennie's lasting legacy. It certainly also boosted business at her resort hotel.

Intertwined with her role as gentle Jewish mother and as savvy businesswoman is Jennie's status as an embodiment of Jewish immigrant success and role model for second generation Jewish-Americans. Jennie was seen as the prime example for a strong Jewish-American hybrid identity. She was praised for her ability to combine her ethnic and religious identity with being a good American citizen. Her friend, journalist Quentin Reynolds, even published a booklet in 1939 which just focused on her exemplary Americanness.[62] In the first decades of the twentieth century, members of the Catskills community still had problems with bringing together their Jewish roots with American mainstream expectations. Jewishness was repeatedly related to being backward and un-American.[63] Against this background, Jennie was perceived as an example for successful acculturation. In her biography and interviews, Jennie appears to be a person secure in her ethnic and religious identity, yet she is also eager to combine it with becoming American. There are several instances in *Jennie and the Story of Grossinger's* in which this is stressed. When they successfully complete the first nine-hole golf course at the resort, Jennie is quoted as saying: "'Who would ever believe that the Grossingers from the Lower East Side would ever own their own golf course! It's another miracle!' to which her father replies 'An American miracle,'" (Pomerantz 172). Pomerantz also quotes Jennie saying: "Living in this country is a privilege" (215). In speeches Jennie repeatedly mentioned that she is grateful for having been given the opportunity to

---

62 See Quentin Reynolds's publication *One Hundred Per Cent American* (1939), held by the Manuscript Division of the New York Public Library, which praises Jennie as America's leading hostess.

63 See for example Lisa Bloom, *With Other Eyes: Looking at Race and Gender in Visual Culture* (1999); Joseph Litvak, *The Un-Americans: Jewish, the Blacklist, and Stoolpigeon Culture* (2009); Ronald L. Jackson and Jamie Moshin, "Scripting Jewishness within the Satire *The Hebrew Hammer*" (2008).

live in America.[64] After all, the basis for her success was the possibility to own her own land as a Jewish immigrant in America and to become self-sufficient on it. Grossinger's Hotel and Country Club is Jennie's lived American Dream.

Jennie Grossinger advertised this in the way she lived but also in her philanthropic undertakings. Supporting the war effort by selling war bonds, Grossinger's under the lead of Jennie was doing a major patriotic work, showing to those still critical of the Jewish effort in the war that they indeed were actively helping to win it. Jennie also famously contributed to several institutions of higher learning, such as Brandeis college, as well as establishments for the preservation and education of Jewish culture, such as the Chaim Weizmann Institute of Science. She was aware that public charity would help the cause as well as her resort in the end.

Jennie's almost legendary desire for education is picked up by most books and essays on her. It furthermore manifested her image as a Jewish-American role model. She explains her desire in the following way: "I love learning and art, perhaps because I went to school such a short time. I wish I could read every book I ever see" (Jennie qtd. in Freedman). Jennie quit school at thirteen to earn money. She reportedly felt the need for compensating her lack of education in any way possible.[65] Realizing the potential of some of her guests concerning knowledge and

---

64 An interesting piece of evidence for this is a letter that Jennie received on November 28, 1954. In it, a Mrs John T. Willis from Forestburg, Texas, who describes herself as a farm housewife, asks Jennie for an autographed menu and a match folder from the hotel. She wants to use it for a scrapbook of "Americana" that she plans to give her daughter as her only heritage. She writes that she would like to have it represented in her book. Jennie replies to this on December 1, 1954. She praises the woman's idea as a way of instilling in her daughter's heart the greatness of American and by this keeping "America a shining example of democracy to the rest of the world" (Grossinger's Country Club. YIVO Archives).

65 Richler writes bitingly of "Jennie Grossinger's maudlin 'warmth' or 'traditional reverence' for bogus learning." Yet, throughout his text Richler can never fully disentangle himself from a certain fascination of Grossinger's leading lady. He writes: "Grossinger has everything – and a myth. The myth of Jennie, LIVING SYMBOL 'HOTEL WITH A HEART,' as a typical Grossinger News headline runs. ... 'A local landmark,' says a Grossinger's brochure, 'is the famous smile of the beloved Jennie.'" Although Richler calls her cynically "Dr. Schweitzer of the Catskills," he also states that in contrast to the cold and efficient Concord, Jennie's warmth makes the G. at least appear "a haimishe (homey) place, however schmaltzy." Richler's article is quite typical for the ambiguous kind of writing Grossinger's started to receive in the 1960s and 70s, which was impressed by the amenities of the place but also highlighted the loud, noisy

education, Jennie Grossinger encouraged them to become her personal tutors and also hired people for this specific purpose.[66] The hotel provided her with a varied mix of people that made this possible. Her efforts resulted in the establishment of educational lecturers at the resort. Scholars like Max Lerner and authors like Irving Stone gave talks at the resort and a full cultural program was instituted. Jennie's interest in self-improvement gave guests the chance to become more knowledgeable while on vacation. Over the years Jennie turned her private home, Joy Cottage, located on the Grossinger's grounds, into a salon where she entertained intellectuals and mixed them with personalities from politics and the stage: "[p]olitical, charitable and purely social banquets brought the illuminati" (Pomerantz 266) to Grossinger's. Pomerantz adds: "[i]n the post-war period, if you stayed at The Big G. long enough, the world would come to you" (266).[67] Overall, one can say that Jennie used the hotel and its public image to support her causes. Before the background of her resort she presented herself as the immigrant girl who made good and lived her American dream. I argue that it empowered Jennie to make her shortcomings public and to show how she eradicated them by using her resources, in her case the hotel. Freedman describes her manner as "a mixture of the humble and the confident." Jennie had proven that she had it in her power to change her fate and outgrow her earlier disadvantages. The hotel was her home and her stage, a testing ground for new developments and a tool to achieve her goals. The hotel, in its multi-functionality and complex nature, lent itself to this purpose. Her success at Grossinger's made her the mouthpiece of the Jewish-American community of the middle of the twentieth century. Jennie was perceived as an ideal role model for second generation Jewish-Americans.

Grossinger's Hotel and Country Club was a place that strongly relied on this human component. Its success was largely based on the motherly icon at the helm. For Mordecai Richler, like for many other progressive Jewish-Americans, the resort was a "Disneyland with knishes:" "Grossinger's is their dream of plenty realized, but if you find it funny, larger than life, then so do the regulars" (Richler). Similar to her hotel the real Jennie Grossinger was the result of a mixture of old Jewish values and modern American ideals. She was the gentle Jewish mother as well as

---

vulgarity of the resort. In the 1990s, the texts become more nostalgic again and Grossinger's is once again remembered as the Queen Bee of the mountains.

66 Jerry Weiss, her music tutor and later entertainment director at Grossinger's, remembers: "Jennie was always wonderful to me, and it was my pleasure to teach her. ... She knew little about classical music but had enormous interest, always wanted to learn, to improve herself" (Weiss qtd. in Frommer 47).

67 This quote echoes statements on the Peacock Alley in the Waldorf Hotel. It shows that the hotel nature is perceived very similarly, that hotel experiences can affect different people in different institutions in the same way.

the clever businesswoman and therefore an icon for a successful Jewish-American identity. At the end of his biography on Jennie, Pomerantz enters an anecdote, allegedly told to him by the hostess herself. It shows that with the hotel Jennie really was fulfilling her calling: "When I die, wherever I go, I hope they have a hotel there, too. And I hope they'll let me run it. I'll find a lot of our early guests there and I'll remember what they liked to eat'" (316).

Jennie Grossinger can only be thought of in connection with Grossinger's and the resort only operated successfully as long as Jennie was alive to create its unique homey, fun, and promising atmosphere. As Malpas's states: "It is through our engagement with place that our own human being is made real, but it is also through our engagement that place takes on a sense and a significance of its own" (Malpas 23). Thus, with Jennie's death in 1972, the Grossinger's myth was at its end. Bunny Grossinger, Jennie's daughter in law, concludes: "The last vestiges of spirit left this place with Jennie ... . The Zises took the brains, and Jennie took the soul" (363).

5.3 THE HOTEL AS SITE OF IDENTITY STRUGGLE

The name Grossinger was a door opener and a burden for those who carried it in the heyday of the resort. The resort's reputation and its legacy were so powerful as to define the life of the people related to it even beyond its demise. This shows itself clearest in the life accounts of Tania and Richard Grossinger. Both grew up in the Grossinger universe and both identify strongly with the place. Their accounts are critical responses to the kind of life they led as children in this complex and for them inescapable place. Tania needed to adapt as well as possible to this home allocated to her by her mother, and Richard had to learn to live with the fact that he was heir to a place that had a complex power struggle going on below its surface. Both writers experienced rites of passage at Grossinger's, they tested their limits and fought against preconceived expectations, and while it took them years to understand their conflicting feelings toward the resort, they also felt a kinship with it that defined their them. Both discussed the resort repeatedly in various texts; it became the topic of their lives. Due to their connection to the resort they are still in demand as interview partners and witnesses of this important part of *Americana*. Their love/hate relationship with the resort hotel provides a new perspective, not only on this hotel, but also on the conflicting nature of hotel living and the stress it can put on an individual living there. This criticism of a hotel insider was not available in the case of the life accounts of the other hotels discussed in this study. Grossinger's enables me to include this aspect in my dissertation by providing another facet of hotel experience. In this last part I will examine the aspect of the hotel as site of identity struggle. I will examine Tania and Richard Grossinger's peculiar growing-up experience at Grossinger's Hotel and Country Club. Key issues discussed here are the importance of religion, the experience of liminality in hotel space and the struggle with developing one's identity in a place that was famous for its hypocrisy and overacting.

Tania Grossinger – The Insider/Outsider

Tania Grossinger first published her autobiography *Growing-up at Grossinger's* in 1975, when the great era of the Catskills was waning.[68] It was her way of coming to terms with a growing-up that was difficult and often twisted, but at the same time provided her with irreplaceable life lessons. Tania was a born Grossinger. Her father belonged to the Chicago branch of the Grossinger family, which was related to the New York Grossingers through Harry, Jennie's husband. After her father's death, Tania and her mother Karla moved to the resort on Jennie's invitation. Karla was to become the Social Hostess and Director of Romance. The move was meant to give Tania the chance to connect with the "roots" (T. Grossinger 6) of her Jewish heritage and her father's family, which had been lacking in their former home in California.[69]

From the beginning, Tania narrates that she rejected the hotel because she saw it as a home that was forced upon her. Even though the hotel is just about to enter its most successful phase when Tania arrives there in 1945, she "already hated it" (2). Throughout the first years the resort for her is a place that affords her with almost no privacy. It is an operation only focusing on the well-being of the paying guests and not on her needs as a half-orphaned child. In this period, Tania and her mother move between different cottages on the acreage, often sharing rooms with guests during the season. This moving around and the complete lack of privacy for her and her mother cause tensions which led to Tania lacking any "sense of security" at Grossinger's (47). While Grossinger's is a longed for home-away-from-home for thousands of people each week during the busy season, for Tania the place does not really "qualify for a home" (48). She has the impression of being an insider-outsider. She is only the child of a staff member and, despite the same name, is not treated as a full member of the owner's family: "I felt like an outsider having an important name but none of the frills to go with it" (102). Up until maturity, Tania suffered from this feeling, especially because she was constantly identified with the great institution by the outside world. Only during her college years at Brandeis did she finally learn to accept that her identity was connected with the hotel but that did not define her personality. Her childhood friend Gail Cherne, daughter of Lena

---

68 The book was republished in 2008 and fed a revived nostalgia for the 'good old' times of the Catskills.
69 Karla and her husband moved from Illinois to California before Tania's birth.

Horne, teaches her: "Stop running away from who your are. You *are* a Grossinger. You *did* grow up at the hotel. You do know famous people. But most important, you are Tania" (Cherne qtd. in T. Grossinger 125). With the help of the dean of the college and the geographical distance from Grossinger's Tania learns "to make peace with [her] name – and [her]self in relation to it" (146).

The resort hotel has an immense influence on Tania. Her upbringing in this surrounding has far-reaching consequences on her identity and her self-perception. The autobiography focuses on the decisive years in which Tania came into her own. Due to the nature of such a coming-of-age text, her book is full of conflicting impressions and contradictions. Her mother's job of taking care of the guests makes Tania, in her own words, almost a full orphan: "I was having great difficulty identifying Karla the Hostess with the mother with whom I shared my room. Karla the Hostess always had something witty and uplifting to say to everybody. My mother never had time for me" (51). Yet, Tania finds surrogate care in the form of Jennie's mother Malke, and in many friends among staff and guests, such as Jackie Robinson, the African-American baseball player who becomes her life-long friend. Tania lacks privacy and suffers from this as any teenager would, but she also has the possibility of realizing talents and developing special skills that only this environment can offer her: "I wanted to know more about the entertainers who came up, what they were like, how they selected their material, and how they put together their acts. I couldn't have asked for a better place than Grossinger's at which to learn" (T. Grossinger 75). Even though Tania often resents Grossinger's (106), she also repeatedly sees the opportunities the resort offers to her. Life there is a balancing act.

One of the most positive factors that Tania sees in her life at Grossinger's, is the way it identifies as a Jewish-American place: "[w]hen Jennie told my mother I would have a chance to learn about my Jewish heritage if we came to Grossinger's, she was absolutely correct" (53). While she encountered anti-Semitism during her life in California, when she did not even know much about Judaism, living at Grossinger's provides her with a great insight into Jewish traditions and the religious roots of her people. As mentioned before, the Catskills, and from its beginning on Grossinger's, had a strong Jewish identity. Although it would go too far to consider Grossinger's as a strictly religious place (it remained a resort hotel in most aspects with all the frivolities), during the High Holidays, like Passover and Rosh Hashana, religious observance was expected by the guests, the staff, and the children. For Tania, when Grossinger's transformed the Playhouse for Rosh Hashana, it was "the most beautiful house of worship I had ever seen" (55). The transformation from entertainment hot-house to place of worship is remarkable. However, it is also quite typical for the Jewish community because a certain level of creativity and flexibility in worship has a long tradition with them out of necessity. The observance of religious tradition was also part of the commercial success of the resort, as Tania writes: "In the forties, I venture to say that Grossinger's attracted the cream of Jewish families, certainly in New York, if not in the nation" (54). She is impressed that Malke's directive "Yom Kippur [is] God's day, not the Grossinger Hotel's day" (57) is duly followed. This leaves a strong impression with Tania. She does not become the most observant Jewish person, but she keeps close ties to her Jewish family and their heritage, which becomes clear in her later writings and her life choices.[70]

For Tania Grossinger, the experience of Jewish culture at the resort was important to her. An aspect of life at the hotel, which is also intimate but far more problematic for her, is the issue of open sexuality at Grossinger's. In the Catskills summer resorts, marital intercourse, extra-marital affairs, and sex between staff members and staff and guests were all a normal part of everyday life, even if not officially allowed (Brown, *Catskill Culture* 186f). When Tania arrived at the resort she was eight years old, and she continues to live there until she leaves for college. The decisive years of her adolescence are spent in a place where sex "was one of the underlaying foundations of life at the hotel, and as such, it was part of my everyday existence" (T. Grossinger 90). One needs to remember that she writes about a time, the early 1950s, when sex before marriage and adult intimacy were mostly whispered about in America.[71] Overall, her upbringing at Grossinger's makes Tania very precocious. At the beginning, she and her friends react with pranks to the sexually charged atmosphere of the resort. Life at the hotel becomes more complicated when Tania grows older: "Being an adolescent in a crazy kind of environment, that of a resort hotel, was doubly hard on me because at the same time I was just getting ready to face my own sexuality" (90). She lacks a close and nurturing relationship with her mother and feels even more left alone.

In her text, Tania Grossinger is very outspoken about her first sexual experiences with a young man from the music staff of the hotel. Other members of the family saw her relationship with her boyfriend as problematic, as he was only a

---

70 Most of Tania's experience of Catskills-style Jewishness at the Grossinger's resort fits the findings of sociologist Phil Brown who discovered that summer resorts were often more about Yiddishkeit than the actual religious rites (Brown, *Catskill Culture* 218). He confirms that due to their way of performing Yiddishkeit and religiosity: "the Catskills contributed to the continuation of Judaism" (222). In this, the Catskills are quite unique. No other hotel area in America focused so much on one religious and ethnic culture as the Catskill Mountains. Grossinger's and the surrounding businesses provide a unique glimpse into the way hotels can become tools for religious communities and how this category of identity is also closely connected to places and the concept of place-identity.

71 It may have helped her land a job as public relation agent at the *Playboy* magazine in the 1970s, a time when women were rare in that part of the business sector.

staff musician.[72] In addition, a main problem of their intimate relationship is the lack of privacy and especially private space. To be together they need hidden places, like secret passageways and unused storage space that they can transform into their own private world. They manage this, but not to a satisfying, romantic degree: "When I look back, I realize that we never even got into a bed together until our third year. Until then, we hid a mat and blanket in a storage closet backstage. It's a miracle we were never caught. ... I understood only too well that the lack of personal privacy was one of the perils of growing up at a hotel" (97). This is an interesting statement about the importance of control over space in one's personal life. Tania lives in a place were there are hundreds of bedrooms and where romance is a part of the product sold at Grossinger's. Yet, she has to struggle on both points. Until she leaves for college Tania does not even have her own room but needs to share a room with her mother. Her special situation at Grossinger's makes her account of hotel experience and the role place plays in her life even more interesting. In her text, Tania is very conscious of the unusual environment that surrounds her, because of other people as well as her own spatial experience. Her awareness of the unique phenomenon of hotel space is acute. This has to do with her liminal position as teenager, staff member's child, and Jewish-American.

While she learns to come to terms with her hotel experience as an adult, her unusual life at the hotel causes friction in her short-lived marriage, as her husband has problems with understanding her background and the kind of life people lead at the resort.[73] At that point, Tania herself has not yet developed her own, stable attitude toward this place. It becomes clear that she first needs to understand her complicated relationship with the Grossinger resort before she can bring others to do the same. For a long time, Tania does not realize, or does not want to realize, the deep impact the physical surrounding that she grew up in has on her definition of herself as an individual.[74] Because of Tania's hotel upbringing she has no problem

---

72 Like all hotels, also the Catskill summer resorts had a very clear hierarchical structure. An important difference to the summer resorts is that they distinguished between jobs such as waiters, busboys, and pool boys which were mostly occupied by "insiders," the children of hotel guests and family members, and jobs, such as musicians, dance instructors, and handymen, which were fulfilled especially by Latinos and African-Americans. They were considered as "outsiders" and for them it was prohibited to date staff or guests.

73 This reminds one of Margaret Case's experience with her first husband. Her marriage also fails because her husband lacks understanding of the hotel space as important part of her individuality.

74 Proshansky, et al. discovered that children are even more impacted by their surrounding environment than adults are. For a long time, this spatial influence on the development of our personality had been neglected. The concept of place-identity helps us to realize how

with relating to other people, especially older ones. Instead she has problems interacting with her own peer group (T. Grossinger 101). While she feels she is at a disadvantage coming of age at a resort hotel, she also feels that "if I could adjust to Grossinger's, I could adjust to any place" (106). This is an important skill, especially in today's global world. Tania repeatedly struggles with the fact that Grossinger's is more deeply intertwined with her being than she wants to admit. It is only when she moves outside of the resort that she finally has the chance to see this. After college she starts a new job at a medical center in California to get away as far as possible from the hotel both geographically and professionally (147). Here she understands: "I also missed something – the sense of excitement at the hotel that I had never before realized was so much a part of my being ... the 'always something new' happening ... never knowing who or what to expect next. As interesting as my new environment was, I had to acknowledge that I wasn't quite ready to cut off my roots" (152). It is interesting that the author repeatedly states, sometimes almost unwillingly, that Grossinger's is not just a mere background to her life but that it plays an active part in who she is. Despite the frivolity and the lack of real substance that seems to go with a resort hotel, this place gives her roots.

Grossinger's Hotel and Country Club, like the other hotels in my study, has a certain material agency (Prescott 197). It is a place for encounters. It creates possibilities. It allows for people to develop a new kind of identity, which is especially important for second generation Jewish-Americans. Tania realizes as an adult that she profited from this agency of the hotel, despite the costs it claimed. As a teenager she often resented her life at the hotel and her constant connection with it, yet she cannot fully free herself from it. Writing the book years after she left the hotel helped her to understand her life there and also to make peace with her name, her family, and the hotel. The autobiography functions as her therapy for her hotel experience. Writing about the resort and the impact it had on her life she states: "Putting this collection of memories together has been a moving experience, one that has brought me closer not only to my childhood friends and family, but to myself as well" (T. Grossinger 187). When she visits the resort after Jennie's death she realizes: "I was amazed how much the 'feel' of the hotel was still in my blood. Despite all the changes, emotionally it was as if I had never left. The 'G' was still very much part of me" (186). She is comfortable with her new home in Greenwich Village, but she feels a wave of nostalgia for the warmth of Grossinger's, its style and the special spirit (180). At the end, after having made peace with her mother and coming to an "accommodation" (175) with Jennie, she also finally comes to

---

far the space that we live in and especially grew up in influences our self-perception (Proshanksy et al. 64f).

term with the concept of home and the place that represents it to her.[75] As a mature woman she realizes: "I've lived in the same apartment in Greenwich Village for over 40 years, but when I think of home, it was and will always be Grossinger's" (T. Grossinger qtd. in Mendelsohn). Peace with Grossinger's also means peace with herself. Despite the sometimes harsh choice of words, the troubling experiences she had, and the rejections she felt at the hotel, she states at the end of her autobiography: "for me personally, would I have had it any other way? Emphatically NO!" (T. Grossinger 187).

Tania Grossinger's autobiography is probably the most dense and spatially aware text on hotel experience examined in this study. Because of the liminal phase she describes, the growing up at Grossinger's, her text tells us a lot about the special space of the hotel and its effect on the people who live, work, and relax there. As a hotel child she is able to move between the fixed hierarchies of the resort. She meanders between guests, staff, and owners, building up relationships with all of them, yet also feeling separate from them. Her position as a more distantly related family member, in fact the child of a staff member, makes her the insider/outsider of the place and allows her to view the place with more critical distance than a real insider could. *Growing Up At Grossinger's* has the usual inevitabilities that all autobiographical texts have. It is very subjective, written from historical hindsight and presents a specific selection of the past of the Grossinger resort. Yet, for a study on hotel experience in New York, Tania's life writing text is a rich source.

Richard Grossinger – The Heir Apparent

Tania Grossinger's perspective of Grossinger's is that of a staff member's child. She is an insider/outsider of the resort. Richard Grossinger's connection to Grossinger's, in contrast, should have been that of an insider as Jennie Grossinger's oldest grandchild. However, in his non-fiction book, *Out of Babylon: Ghosts of Grossinger* (1998), his hotel experience is also a tense and increasingly complex one. Richard provides an intimate look into the inner power structure of the resort and the invisible but marked strain it puts on the hotel family. *Out of Babylon* belongs to the genre of life writing, yet the book is very different from Tania's more classical, chronologically ordered autobiography. The nature of Richard's text is, as he describes it, one of "collage and pop-culture" (R. Grossinger 575). A trained

---

[75] She struggled a long time with the term, as expressed in the following quote: "I never quite agreed with those who say, 'You can't go home again.' On the contrary, I spend more time wondering if you can ever really leave" (177).

anthropologist, his style and approach to the topic is unlike Tania's account.[76] While Richard Grossinger experiences emotions similar to Tania, his overall approach to the hotel differs largely. His text is less self-centered than Tania's, and he makes larger connections between the resort hotel, his own life, and the role of Grossinger's for New York's Jewish society and culture. His experience of Grossinger's resort is less intense than Tania's because, in contrast to her, Richard, the legal son of Paul Grossinger, did not grow up at the hotel but only visited it during the holidays. [77] Still, as the intended heir of Grossinger's, Richard's involvement with the Grossinger resort should not be underestimated. Moreover, while Tania's account of Grossinger's ends in the late 1970s, Richard Grossinger's account narrates the decline and the end of the hotel, and gives important impressions of the end of the era of Grossinger's and of the Catskills in general.

Richard's book is not only about the story of Grossinger's. Large parts of the text focus on Richard's academic life, his spiritual journey and New Age experiences, as well as his own family life. Yet, as the title already announces, the whole text is influenced by the "ghosts" of the resort and it pops up repeatedly throughout his life. Each time he takes his family on vacation at Grossinger's, each time he borrows (or smuggles) something from the hotel, each time he uses his resort connections to get special tickets for baseball, boxing, or any other kind of entertainment, each time he thinks of his parents, Grossinger's is mentioned. Richard appears to be not always completely conscious of the influence the place has on his life and development. Like Tania he often describes his attempts to cut the ties to Grossinger's. Yet repeatedly, he realizes that this is impossible. This

---

76 He dedicates the first 'book' of *Out of Babylon,* which consists of five main parts, to retelling the story of Grossinger's, largely put together from the books of Pomerantz, Taub, Kanfer, and comments of family members that he gathered. In the other four books he focuses on his mother's and his stepfather's (Richard Tower, the entertainment director of Grossinger's) families, as well as his brother's development. In the final part he writes about his life after learning of the name of his real biological father and about the end of Grossinger's. In his text Richard includes diary notes from his brother Jonathan, his own personal stream-of-consciousness impressions of parts of his life story as well as dreams, and excerpts from advertisements and newspaper articles. Despite this irritating mixture, his special relationship with Grossinger's is very apparent throughout the book.

77 One of the core topics of the book are the problematic family relationships of the Grossingers. The reader learns that Richard is not the biological son of Paul, but the offspring of a love affair between his mother and a Grossinger's guest while she was married to Paul Grossinger. However, for many years Richard believed his mother's second husband, Robert Towers, to be his father. Richard's own life is an example of the frivolous atmosphere and sometimes-loose morals at the resort.

highlights his strong place-identity: just like other personality categories like race, gender, and class, one can never really rid oneself of the place one is connected to and escape its influence. Both accounts of the Grossinger children are clear proof of this.

Image 11: A Grossinger's dinner menu, showing the abundance of food

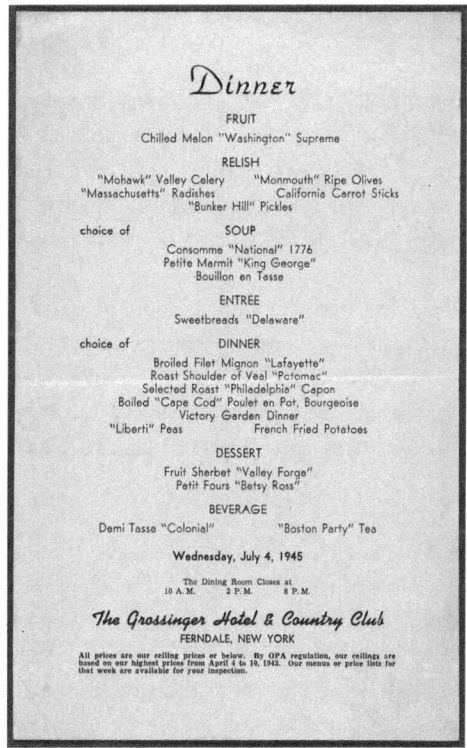

Grossinger's Dinner Menu. From the New York Public Library.

During his childhood, the days Richard spends at the resort instead of his stepfather's home in New York are described as "Edenic." His real home is a very dark place for him because of his mother's psychological problems and his position as the step-child of his mother's husband. Grossinger's, in contrast, is to Richard "a shamrock and rainbow land" with

parasol and cabanas, distinctive house buses and paintbox rowboats, the taste of frost and coffee nut, photo galleries of celebrities on vacation winding down corridors around posts to exotic dead ends at underground passages lit from ancient portals, cologned air blowers in washrooms, tables filled with prune and poppyseed Danish, coffeecakes, and cheesecakes, hard roles, onion roles, fat doughy saltsticks, and sweet buns... .(R. Grossinger 11)

The hotel is for Richard an explosion for the senses, with all desirable things in constant supply without the need for him to pay or to ask for them. As the son of Paul, he is handed it all. Richard feels free when he is at the hotel during vacation time. Instead of being the outsider, which is his role in his New York home, here at the big G. "I had two brothers, a collie like Lassie, a new mother, Big Milty, a bakery spilling out cookies, cakes, and rolls – a whole Emerald City" (92). Richard describes the resort also as "a yellow and brown city on a hill" (91).[78] These two labels "Emerald City" and "city on a hill" recall two American topoi.[79] In Richard's eyes Grossinger's is not so much an existing place, but a dream. According to Richard, the resort was more or less meant to fulfill the role of a "New Promised Land" for Jewish-Americans in the 1940s and 50s:

They sought a fleeting moment when the world exploded into gardens, palaces, tummlers, and vaudeville, and everyone remembered they were once happy – when romance ignited in rainbows (and show tunes), and icicles hung like jewelry from ski chalets – when a poor philosopher could become a millionaire overnight without losing Maimonides, when God restored Paradise and let the Hebrews back, before rigidity and greed set in. (R. Grossinger 70)

The description of the guests' expectations is a very telling statement on the symbolic functions of Grossinger's. Despite the abundance, which is on offer, as the dinner menu shows (Image 11), it also betrays the impossibility of fulfilling them. Richard asks himself repeatedly if Grossinger's, the dreamland he experienced as a child and that so many former guests keep in loving memory, ever really existed. Echoing the question of a former guest, he asks himself: "What happened to Grossinger's? Perhaps there was never a moment when it existed as

---

78 In her novel *Paradise, New York* (1998), Eileen Pollack makes a very similar statement about Grossinger's. The book is about a young woman who tries to keep afloat her small family resort hotel in the Catskills against the rising economic problems of the area. Perceived from her family's small hotel, the Eden, the protagonist states: "...I wished the Eden had been as successful as That Other Hotel – my grandmother wouldn't allow us to say its name in her presence – that splendid city on the hill, which started from beginnings as humble as ours but had only grown larger, more famous and more elaborate as the Eden decayed" (67).

79 The "Emerald City," the magical capital of L. Frank Baum's fictional world Oz, as well as the Puritan ideal of "a city [up]on a hill" are two utopian places, role models for a perfect world that is unreachable.

reality rather than a dream" (71). The concept of Grossinger's for Jewish-Americans was more utopian than the Chelsea's was for its artists or even the Theresa's was for Harlem's community.

Richard Grossinger experiences the hotel most directly during his childhood and teenage years. Like Tania, he is in his liminal, adolescent phase at the hotel. As a child he perceives everything to be wonderful there. Living at Grossinger's seems to be the best thing that could happen to him. However, a drastic change in his attitude toward the hotel takes place when he enters college. This change collides with the time when hippie America rebels against traditions and established institutions in the late 1960s and the Catskills start to decline. At that point Richard's experience of and his relationship with the place is markedly different. In his memoir he is unsure whether "the Hotel was deteriorating or I was outgrowing it" (118). He perceives his growing-up process and the downward development of the hotel to be closely linked. 'Seeing' the place through the eyes of his schoolmates and later through those of his fellow students at Amherst, he notices for the first time the inequalities among workers at the resort and the vulgarity of the new generation of guests. Richard turns away from the resort for the next years, even though he does not break with it completely.[80] The reader repeatedly encounters a paradoxical mix of emotions and viewpoints of the big G. that is similar to Tania's account. On the one hand, Grossinger's is "where Yankees came as real people. …It was where Grandma bought clothes for poor workers" (R. Grossinger 108). Richard is proud of his grandmother's philanthropic actions and her interest in her workers. On the other hand, he denounces the fakeness and hypocrisy of the place and calls the hotel's story banal, pure advertising copy: "[t]he heritage of the Hotel [is] one of corrupted wealth, missed opportunity, xenophobia, and greed riding the tiger for all he's worth" (448). Writing about Grossinger's is a difficult task for the author, an undertaking he started even before going to college and that he only manages to finish when he is already in his forties. He feels bound by the promise he gave to his grandmother Jennie, who appointed him to be her historian. For Richard, the telling of the story of Grossinger's becomes "an obligation and an omen much of my life" (5).[81]

As an adult Richard has great problems in coming to terms with the place. For years, Richard cannot make peace with his family and their resort, so he tries to find another way of removing himself from them. When he learns that he is not biologically a Grossinger, Richard tries to contact his biological father. However,

---

80 Until the end of Grossinger's, Richard revisits the place for vacations with his family.
81 In his memoir, Richard Grossinger makes many meta-comments about writing the text and what a challenge this is for him: "Sometimes it was all too much. It didn't seem just a book I was writing" (508). It is clear that for him, despite all struggles, the story of Grossinger's is of utmost importance.

the man refuses to even see him and dies before Richard can change his mind. Richard confesses that he wanted to contact his biological father because: "I want permission not to be a Grossinger anymore" (481). This permission is not granted. He later realizes that a permission would have been useless as his whole life is already influenced by the family and the eponymous resort. Through his name, Richard is always tied to the place.[82] Both Grossinger children struggle with the fact that their family name is the same as the name of the hotel. Because of the extreme success of the resort in the 1940s, '50s and '60s most Americans recognized the name and knew of the place. So both Tania, the insider/outsider, and Richard, the heir apparent who turns away from the hotel and follows an academic career, have to live with the legacy. They were part of an important moment in Jewish-American history. They experienced Grossinger's at a moment when it had become a piece of *Americana*. Yet, they also saw it change into a place of vulgarity, excess, and artificiality. By writing about it and revisiting their past at the hotel in their memoirs, they come to terms with their conflicting experiences.

Richard comes to a very interesting conclusion about his relationship with the hotel. During a painful visit to the empty grounds of the partly demolished Grossinger's in the 1980s, he realizes about his immediate family:

None of us were really Grossingers. The true Grossingers were the thousands if not millions of alumni who danced through while magic was in the air, then made their lives in other places – the Abe Lymans and Joel Greys, Robert Merrills and Milton Berles, Rocky Marcianos, Bill Grahams, and Leonard Lyons, the playwrights, restauranteurs, countless senators and judges, chiefs of surgery and psychiatry, lawyers and corporation heads who got their start as bellboys and waiters sentenced by curmudgeon Aunt Rose to run-down cottages six in a room ... plus the generation who fell in love and married in Jennie's temple. (449)

This is an interesting observation. While Richard clearly grew up as a Grossinger and was raised in the awareness of being something special in the same way that the hotel was something special, he discovers that a Grossinger is not necessarily someone related by blood. The experiences that people had at that place are more important to him. Those people who used the place as Jennie intended it, as a place for relaxation, romantic opportunities, and summer jobs on the way to a medical

---

82 At the Waldorf, the Algonquin, the Chelsea, and the Theresa, the names of the managers and owners differ from the names of their establishments. To those who are not familiar with the hotels, the connection would not be so immediately clear as in the case of the Grossinger's.

career, are really Grossingers.[83] This is confirmed by Bob Towers, Richard's stepfather and the former entertainment director at the resort:

Grossinger's didn't die. It's everywhere you look. Every other bigshot in this town got his start there. Do you know what Grossinger's was? It wasn't just a hotel. You never went to the Catskills; you went to Grossinger's – or you didn't say where you went. The Brickman, Paul's, Morningside, the other places; they never achieved that. Grossinger's was a fraternity. We wore its emblem on jackets and tee shirts. It was the Jewish Yale and Harvard combined. No one from the Ivy League ever had any more loyalty to a college than the alumni of Grossinger's. (Towers in R. Grossinger 460)

What is striking here is the huge emotional investment that many people had in Grossinger's and that connected them with the resort for decades, even after it disappeared. Towers left the place in the middle of the 1940s, yet in the 1980s he still speaks of it as if he were still actively involved in it.

The resort marks an important moment in New York, and in American cultural history. From the 1960s onward, Jewish-Americans were acknowledged more and more as a normal part of American society, not through assimilation but through acculturation. The culture that they created in the Catskills did not vanish but it was incorporated into the American entertainment and business sectors. While Jewish-Americans became more American in the Mountains, New York and its culture became more Jewish, due to the exchange of people vacationing at the Catskills resorts and living in the city.

After years of working on the book, Richard manages to fulfill his agent's request: "to personify Grossinger's at all its levels of majesty and scandal. ...Grossinger's is 'an ikon [sic] of Americana. ...It's a myth'" (R. Grossinger 8). As an anthropologist, Richard Grossinger was aware of Roland Barthes's use of the term myth.[84] As a Jewish-American myth, Grossinger's holds a special place in the consciousness of its people. During its heyday, the resort hotel wielded a certain amount of political and social power, with Jennie Grossinger at its helm as motherly leader of the enterprise. It was status-defining, confirming that one had arrived in

---

83   Richard Grossinger's revelation is confirmed by Jonathan Mark, who writes in an article for *The Jewish Week*: "Anyone who ever spent time in the Catskills knows that the celebrities and entertainers were the sideshow; the guests, like you, were the main attraction. ...The guests were the story" (Mark).

84   For Barthes, myths are stories "we tell each other as a culture in order to explain complexities and to banish contradictions, thus making the world seem simpler and more comfortable for us to inhabit" (Kean and Campbell 11). The challenge is to unravel a myth and to look behind its depoliticizing facade to find the groups and issues that are hidden there.

American society. However, the term myth also tells the reader that the great reputation of Grossinger's often leaves out the darker side of the resort, the exploitation of workers, the *shtetl*-like clannishness, and the power struggles going on between the family and their direct surroundings. It would be shortsighted to understand Grossinger's only as the luxurious, beautiful vacation mecca that its propaganda machinery sold so successfully to the people. Its vibrant legacy in personal memories, historiographies, newspaper articles, exhibitions, and pop-culture shows that the Grossinger's story is "a Biblical epic that happens to be an essential piece in the variegated puzzle of United States' cultural history" (Barry Gifford in R. Grossinger, back cover). Richard's account, like Tania's, is a very rich source for the history of Grossinger's and its importance for individuals and the community of Jewish New Yorkers.

The resort world of the Jewish Catskills had a lasting impact on the American vacation culture. Tania and Richard Grossinger, separately from each other, realized that Grossinger's was a forerunner of Las Vegas and its postmodern hotel world. About her first visit to the casino city Tania Grossinger writes: "In one sense, Las Vegas was a whole new world. In another, it was like a homecoming" (155). Very similarly, Richard Grossinger states that the heritage of the G. "ends in Vegas and Atlantic City, with resorts modeled on Grossinger's exploding through 'Star Wars' technology into robot/entertainment wars – performers who began in the Borscht Belt, now working glitter stages arising phoenix-like from New Jersey/Nevada debris – and no one missing a beat" (448). In that way, Grossinger's not only helped to integrate Jewish-Americans into the American mainstream, but it also started a pop-cultural tradition for which the U.S. is still famous throughout the world – the hyperreal glitz gambling palaces of Las Vegas. There, only signs are left over, a simulacrum without the foundation that Grossinger's, based on the Jewish-American tradition of the Catskills, still had. Grossinger's Hotel and Country Club was sold several times in the 1980s. Plans to redo Grossinger's failed. In 1986, the Playhouse, which was the core part of the hotel, was blown up, an event which brought Grossinger's once more into the news.

It is somewhat ironic that shortly after the destruction work started on the resort the movie *Dirty Dancing* (1987) opened, which produced a huge wave of nostalgia for the great days of the Catskill resorts. It became a cult movie of our time.[85] As

---

85 Unlike the Waldorf, the Algonquin and the Chelsea, Grossinger's Hotel did not attract much fictional writing. This is somewhat surprising as the place was the vacation spot for writers like Isaac Bashevis Singer. Singer, one of the most acute observers of Jewish life, visited the Catskills often, yet he dedicated only one short story to the Mountains, "The Yearning Heifer" (1975). There is also a small number of novels which comment on the outstanding position that Grossinger's had in the Catskill community, e.g. Harvey Jacob's *Summer on a Mountain of Spices* (1975) or Eileen Pollack's *Paradise, New York* (1998).

most people of the Mountains, but few people outside know, the film is based on the lives of dance instructors Jackie Horner and Michael Terrace, both working at Grossinger's in the 1960s (Jones). The screenwriter Eleanor Bergstein combined their recollections with her own childhood memories of vacation days at the resort. The movie is not a profound analysis of the cultural complexities and the existing power struggles of the Catskills and Grossinger's. Richard Grossinger calls it "a sanitized '80s version – Grossinger's lite." Yet, he admits: despite its "stagey sentimentality [it] carries a shard of the texture and mood." To him, "[i]t did feel like stardust and coming of age in Shangri-La" (R. Grossinger 449). The movie picks up on the famous commodification of romance at the hotel. Like its real-life model, the Kellerman resort is charged with the strong sexual tension that Tania Grossinger commented upon. The movie also highlights the resort's function as a starting point both for Jewish college kids, who work in the dining rooms in summers to finance their studies, and the mambo craze. It does this all in front of the background of the slow decline of the depicted resort, reminding the audience that the world they see on the screen has already stopped to exist and all that remains now is a strong nostalgic yearning for this stardust time. The movie is a kind of pop-cultural time capsule for what the Catskill hotel experience felt like. Jewish New Yorkers are reminded of their own experiences at Grossinger's when they hear the movie's title song "(I've Had) The Time of My Life" at the end of the film. Today the nostalgia for Grossinger's and the Catskills causes an increasing output of oral histories, pop-cultural collections and scholarly research. The creation of the Catskill Institute and the number of publications on the history of the Mountains, life writing texts of former hotel and bungalow colony owners, as well as exhibitions, testify to it.

Through its staff, its guests, and its infrastructure of purchasing and promoting, the Grossinger Hotel was part of the New York hotel network. Grossinger's Hotel and Country Club distinguishes itself from the other hotels in this study because it was a resort hotel, a place where people stayed for their vacations. The resort is a seasonal place, meant for those few weeks when people escape their everyday life in the city. Besides the family and some staff members it has no permanent residents. Yet, this is one reason why I decided to add it to my study, as it presents a different but important hotel type, which is also part of the hotel experience of New Yorkers. Here, other dynamics happen than the ones that we have seen in the urban counterparts. It is a place of indulgence, carefreeness, and contemplation. The resort hotel shares the classic elements of the institution of the hotel; it fulfills the same basic functions of shelter and refreshment and creates a communal feeling just like

---

In addition, there are the magazine essays by David Boroff or Mordecai Richler, and some of the cultural happenings at Grossinger's are collected in the book *It Happened in the Catskills* by Myrna and Harvey Frommer.

the city hotels do. While Grossinger's was outside of the city limits, it was still part of New York's culture, especially of the Jewish-American community. Similar to the Hotel Theresa in Harlem, the Catskill hotel world with Grossinger's at the helmet achieved the integration of Jewish-Americans in New York and American society. Grossinger's was just one resort of the Catskills, yet it was the prime example of the area and showed the active agency of a hotel for a religious community in America. The Catskill vacation region is now almost entirely gone. Coincidentally, the Jewish-American culture of New York is waning. Today's generation is mostly secular and Jewishness now is more a cultural than a religious identity (Goodstein). Except for the small increase of strict, Hassidic Orthodox Jews, the United States census shows a decrease of people identifying as Jewish. Lefebvre wrote that a society needs fitting places to remain viable. Perhaps the Jewish-American community needs a new kind of Catskills and Grossinger's for a revived cultural identity.

Conclusion

> "Of all the spaces in the city, ...the one that holds the most significance... is the space connecting all the others – the New York hotel."
> PETERS 69

The hotel is a most important institution for America. "Hotel" stands for the letter "H" in the NATO phonetic alphabet. Each episode of the famous television show "The Muppet Show" ends with a commentary by Waldorf and Statler, the two grumpy old men on the balcony, who are named after New York's once biggest hotels. Hotels show the dynamic mutuality between place and people, especially in the city of New York. Henry James wrote in *The American Scene* (1907) that a grand hotel like the Waldorf-Astoria contains "the essence of the loud New York story" (102). The hotel experiences made in the five institutions discussed in the case studies of this dissertation allow us to get closer to the essence of this city and to understand it better. Throughout the twentieth century, hotels have fulfilled important functions for New York. They are work-places for hotel people and their guests, inspiration for a number of influential artists, stages for social groups, platforms for the self-manifestation of minority communities, and transient and permanent homes for an uncountable number of people. While they remain commercial enterprises, which are operated to make a profit, hotels contribute to New York's society beyond the purely financial aspect. Since its beginning, the hotel is more than a mere business. It is a multi-functional entity at the heart of urban societies.

I have approached the five hotels using Elizabeth Bowen's three aspects of a great hotel: the historical, the social, and the organic. In each case study, the development of the respective hotel has been examined, "its character and its place in the human pattern" (Bowen 10) in New York, and its unique as well as its generic function as a hotel have been analyzed. It has become clear that all five institutions bring something specific to New York's multifaceted urban life. Taken together, these hotels help to unravel the underlying foundation of its society.

In the case studies I have looked at the selected hotels through the eyes of their respective hotelkeepers, of which four were run by men and one by a remarkable woman. I have presented the meticulous maître d'hotel Oscar Tschirky and the rugged self-made man Conrad Hilton; the suave New Yorker Frank Case and the charming Southerners Ben and Mary Bodne; the artist-friendly pragmatist Stanley Bard; the well-groomed host of the black upper-class, Walter Scott, and the attractive man-about-town Bill Brown; and the incomparable gentle Jewish hostess Jennie Grossinger. Their life accounts show that each hotel is very much the product of its hotel man or woman. At the same time, their hotel experiences also reveal the strong and dynamic mutuality, which exists between the building and its keeper. Each one of these people was deeply influenced by their institution and its spatial agency. Their stories confirm Relph's statement on essential insideness: they became part of their place and the place became a part of them (Relph 55). Together with the physical structure of the buildings, their interior furnishing, and the human interaction happening in these places, hotel people create atmosphere, this elusive quality of a place that is not only the projection of one's own feelings and ideas but which seems to come out of the walls of the institution. The Chelsea Hotel has been probably the most expressive example of this power of atmosphere, and many residents swear that the walls have inspired their works. For the hotel people presented in this study, the hotel is their work place. Compared to other professions, the site affects the worker on more levels because it encompasses so many facets of human life. This is one main reason why in the life writing accounts of hotelkeepers the hotel space becomes an integral part of their identity. Place-identity can be ideally studied in the cases of hotelmen and women.

All five hotels of this study were partly transient and partly residential enterprises, which is the most typical hotel form of New York in the twentieth century. The guests experience the hotel from the best-known perspective. They describe the institution in its classic function, as temporary home, and place of shelter and refreshment for travelers. The guest's perspective has been especially important in the cases of the Waldorf-Astoria, the Algonquin, and the Chelsea Hotel. Yet, in these three hotels the guests discussed were all more than transient visitors. They made the hotel their permanent homes because for them, hotel living was the most adequate form of living in New York. As The New Yorker writer Maeve Brennan states, a hotel is a "shelter without being shut away" (Brennan 256). For guests like Elsa Maxwell, Alec Wilder, and Patti Smith, their hotels are the sources of their inspiration, places of work, meeting places for their friends, and, most of all, homes. The Algonquin and the Chelsea Hotel are famous as theater or artist hotels. Throughout their existence, they have been home to an impressive number of artists who have used the hotel not only as a stopping place, but as an ideal alternative to the suffocating homes of American suburbia in the twentieth century. The two hotels also were the stages for their respective artistic clientele.

The Algonquin famously catered to those creatives already successfully established, and interested in a cultivated and enriching surrounding. The Chelsea, on the other side, has allowed aspiring artists to experiment, to be taken care of, and to soldier on amid a like-minded, tolerant community. The famous Chelsea tolerance has been essential for all its guests, on their way down even more than on their way up. The two hotels, the Algonquin and the Chelsea, both play an important role in the cultural history of New York. They are important for the city's self-perception because the hotel stories happening there are a crucial part of what New York is for New Yorkers.

Probably the most interesting insight into New York hotel experience comes from a unique and often neglected angle. In the cases of the Hotel Algonquin, the Hotel Theresa, and the Grossinger's Hotel, I have examined the hotels from the perspective of hotel children. The accounts of Margaret Case Harriman, Michael Colby, Ron Brown, and Tanja and Richard Grossinger allow us to the see the respective hotels from an 'unauthorized' point of view. Their experiences sometimes confirm but often contest the main narratives of the hotels, and they give us a very interesting insight into the power of place and the creation of place-identity. Their liminal position as well as the liminal phase they were in while living at the hotel, make their experience the most interesting example of what the hotel can mean to those who use it regularly. Even more than in the cases of the other two great actors of the hotel, the managers and the guests, the hotel is a microcosm of the larger New York for hotel children. The hotel is their home and playground; the staff members are their friends, educators, mentors, and family; the guests are playmates, role models, or annoying invaders of their territory. They are the least powerful actors in the hotel space and are most affected by it. But they are also most knowledgeable, and are able to transgress the hotel code and the hotel's hierarchy. They use the space to their advantage. Hotel children are a very American phenomenon. The children's book *Eloise* about the little girl who lives at the Plaza has given the phenomenon a face. It has immortalized the experience of hotel children in New York. The Waldorf-Astoria and the Algonquin have each created their own children's book on this model.

Finally, The Hotel Theresa as well as Grossinger's Hotel were both platforms for social change; in the case of the Theresa for the African American community of Harlem, and in the case of Grossinger's for middle- and upper-middle class Jewish-American families. Both groups adapted the hotel to their needs. Although they did not change them in their basic functions and operative structures, they made the hotels into their very own urban institutions. The Theresa became the epicenter of the awakening of black pride, political activism, and cultural achievements, and Grossinger's and its fellow Catskills resorts were perceived as symbols for the successful arrival of Jewish immigrants in American mainstream, and birthplace of a healthy hybrid identity.

All five hotels in this study display the concept of social centrality for their respective communities. This can be seen in the labels "Waldorf Crowd," "Algonquinites," and "Chelseaite," as well as in the centrality of the hotels for African-Americans and Jewish-Americans. As the textual analyses show, the hotels often became semi-sacred institutions for the respective groups. They are called meccas, shrines, and temples, the places of origin of strong group identities. The strong identification is described once or twice for other famous hotels in America, but nowhere is it as strong and as significant as in the cases of the New York hotels presented here.

The five institutions discussed in my thesis are very specific examples of hotels in America. The hotel experiences made in these New York hotels cannot be easily generalized. This specificity is what makes my study so interesting. There is no other city in America that has such a close connection with its hotels. In his book *The Guest List*, Ethan Mordden writes: "The Astors and their hotels were a gift to all of New York" (Mordden 5). Their dynamic relationship started with the Astor House, built by John Jacob Astor himself in 1836, and their legacy continued in the Waldorf-Astoria, the American grand hotel par excellence. Due to them, New York became undoubtedly "the greatest hotel city in the world" (Williamson 76). When E.B. White wrote about the city in his seminal essay "Here is New York" (1949), which is still celebrated as the best description of the city, he did so from "a stifling hotel room in 90-degree heat...in midtown" (696). This is the right place to write about New York because here White is "curiously affected by emanations from the immediate surroundings" (696).[1] New York just seems more approachable and comprehensible from the vantage point of a hotel room.

The institution hotel has changed in the twentieth century. As my examples show, hotels are still the places in New York where history is being made. The Big Four decided upon Europe's future in the Waldorf-Astoria in 1946, and today the United Nations still hosts events in the famous grand hotel. New York sophistication was born in the Algonquin and book publications are still celebrated in the hotel. New York became the epicenter of America's counterculture with the Chelsea Hotel, and the fight for its soul after its sale to developer Ed Scheetz continues to keep the artist community of the city on its toes. With the Theresa Hotel, Harlem moved into the center of the nation's and even the world's attention, in the case of Castro's visit to the hotel. Today, it is still remembered as the former heart of vibrant black culture in articles on the neighborhood. Grossinger's helped to make Jewish immigrants more American, at the same time as it helped to preserve Jewish traditions. It helped to influence New York with Jewish Catskills food and entertainment culture. Now, it has become a sought-after scene for

---

1   The stifling hotel room is, of course, located in the Algonquin Hotel, the place of reference for a writer for *The New Yorker*.

photographers interested in the aesthetics of industrial ruins and remainders of vanished worlds.

New York's hotels are still important for the city's society by providing space for social activities and for social functions, and by being meeting places and places of exchange. However, since the end of the twentieth and the beginning of the twenty-first century, hotels are no longer the vibrant democratic places they have been for most of the nineteenth and twentieth century. Hotel chains have transformed hotels into streamlined businesses. Standardized procedures have made hotel service more reliable, but less personal. The institution hotel has become an even greater player in the corporate business world than it had been a century earlier. While hotels become cheaper and more diverse, they lose something of their civic nature. Even the unique institutions that I have discussed in this study are not free from this development.

In her article "A Traveler in Residence: Maeve Brennan and the Last Days of New York" (2005), Ann Peters describes how the 1960s saw the destruction of a great number of well-known New York landmark hotels, such as the Hotel Astor on Times Square, and the transformation of many residential hotels into tourist accommodations, which had been traditionally homes to a large community of single women, low-wage earners, and old people.[2] For writer Maeve Brennan, who loved to live in hotels and who perceived residential hotels as a part of the city's soul, this meant the end of a life-style, the end of her New York experience. Established hotels like the Waldorf-Astoria and Hotel Algonquin moved through this crisis without too much damage. Yet, they needed to adapt to changes in hotel operation by either offering more attractive amenities such as air-conditioning in each room, or by stopping expensive traditions, such as the beloved entertainment shows in the Waldorf-Astoria. The Chelsea muddled through, more or less successfully, but almost foundered in the 1970s and 80s, when scandal and crime were a regular occurrence on 23rd Street. The Grossinger's survived until the early 1980s, but was losing customers each year. The Hotel Theresa capitulated and closed as a hotel in the 1960s. It vegetates as an office building that lacks its former significance.

After the end of the Hotel Theresa, community leaders in Harlem asked whether they lost Harlem when they lost the hotel. Maeve Brennan and other New York writers put forward more or less the same question in their texts. New York still has an incredible number of hotels per square-mile, and it houses flagship hotels of almost every great international hotel brand. Yet, in the last decades the city and its officials neglected to reconsider their strategies for the accommodation of New York's citizens and visitors. Regularly, texts are published in the city's newspaper

---

2   One of the last women residences remaining are the Webster Apartments on 34th Street and Ninth Avenue.

discussing how life in New York will look like in the not so distant future. The housing crisis of the 1960s has come back to haunt the city. With more and more dramatic and luxurious new high rises filling up the limited space of the Island of Manhattan, there is less living space for people with middle- or lower-class incomes. Some continue to move outside of the city, to the suburbs in New Rochelle and on Long Island. They join the unfathomably large number of commuters who enter the city each day and leave it in the evening. White middle-class families move north to Harlem and take over the picturesque brown houses there. By this, however, they drive out African-American families and other ethnic minorities who cannot compete with the increasing prices of the once affordable neighborhood. The newest idea of city officials is that every newly developed luxury apartment tower needs to include a certain percentage of cheaper apartments or provide affordable housing nearby. They construct so-called "mixed-income buildings." However, one result already shows itself in the form of "poor doors" (Satow). This means that some of these new apartment buildings have an official, representative entry, and another entry for those living in the cheaper part of the same house.

Until the 1960s, the solution for several of the problems described were the residential and semi-residential hotels for which New York was famous. They provided living space for a very diverse group of people. In addition, as my study showed, they caused the creation of a surprising amount of culture because of the special spatial experience that people made in them. Being "shelter[s] without being shut away" they allowed for community spirit to develop, they were part of the special New York experience. However, after their demolition, the city now needs to find new ways to fill the need for privatized public space. One way might be the "boutique hotel," as mentioned in the introduction. Building on the concept of boutique hotels, there are currently several hotel projects, which cater specifically to artists and creative communities, not only in New York (e.g. the Ace Hotel, New York), but also in Amsterdam (The Lloyd Hotel), Berlin (the Michelberger), and Vancouver (the Waldorf). In these establishments the artists' attraction to hotels is directly targeted. The hotels are built especially for a creative crowd, who can use their spaces as studios, work-places, salons etc. (Volland 250). It needs to be seen how successful these projects become and whether the artistic energy of a hotel can indeed be clinically planned, or if it needs to grow out of specific but difficult to define circumstances.

I have mentioned in the introduction of this study that, in the last few years, one can see an increasing scholarly interest in the institution hotel, with several conferences, exhibitions, and publications. However, it is still a surprisingly neglected field of study. There are many areas of research which merit a close examination by American Studies scholars. The history of hotels in New York continues to be under-researched, despite the amount of material available in the

New York Public Library, the archives of the New-York Historical Society, and the Museum of the City of New York. In my study, I was able to provide insights into this highly interesting field, however, it is too extensive for one single study. Furthermore, scholars have just started to analyze the relationship between America and the institution hotel, for example, Andrew Sandoval-Strausz and Molly Berger. Much work still needs to be done, especially for the twentieth century, which is often overlooked because of standardization. Furthermore, there are several studies on the *topos* hotel in German and British literature. However, there is not yet a systematic analysis of the hotel in American literature and, even more interesting, in film.[3] There are some preliminary texts, for example, Jann Matlock's "Vacancies: Registered Passing in American Cinema, 1929-1964" (2009), yet the amount of material justifies more research. Finally, this study is largely based on life accounts. Working with these texts taught me that this genre still lacks a systematic analysis of the importance of space in autobiographical texts. I realized that the influence of space on a person's life story, her or his essential place-identity, is still under-researched. I expect that a thorough analysis of the concept place-identity will yield interesting new perspectives on canonical texts.

In my study, the focus is on the experiences of people in New York hotels. The relationship between New York and its hotels can be described as a turbulent love story that is still going on. Writers add new texts each year to the growing corpus of what Pready has described as *hotel genre*. Artists still move into hotels each day; some only because they need to travel for their work, others to live in them, and again others to use them for their artistic process, just as Maya Angelou did for many years. With my thesis I intend to bring the topic of the hotel to the attention of American Studies in Germany, to help widen and deepen the understanding of this important institution for American society, and to encourage further research.

Hotel experience will continue to haunt me, even beyond the work on this study. I am myself a hotel child, as are my two sisters. Raised in the small city hotel of my parents in a midsized town in the heart of Germany, I share some experiences with the children whose life accounts I have discussed in my dissertation. Yet, as I learned in the process of writing this text, each hotel child makes her or his own discoveries. My hotel experience has inspired me for this research project, which opened to me, as Henry James once described it, the "amazing hotel-world" (102) of New York City. In a world, which becomes more globalized and more mobile each day, the institution hotel will continue to inspire people and will continue to play an important role in modern life.

---

3 In the last five years, a number of movies have been released which offer interesting new perspectives on the *topos* hotel and underline the continuous relevance of and interest in the hotel in texts, e.g. *Best Exotic Marigold Hotel* (2012), *Hotel Transylvania* (2012), *Grand Budapest Hotel* (2014), and *The Second Best Exotic Marigold Hotel* (2015).

Works Cited and Illustrations

"A Living Legend Evolves. The Algonquin." *The Hotel Algonquin,* 2014. Web. 12 Feb. 2014.
Achilles, Jochen, Ina Bergmann. "'Betwixt and Between': Boundary Crossings in American, Canadian, and British Short Fiction." *Liminality and the Short Story: Boundary Crossings in American, Canadian, and British Writing.* (Routledge Interdisciplinary Perspectives on Literature; 34). Jochen Achilles and Ina Bergmann (ed.). New York: Routledge, 2015. Print.
Aitken, Stuart. "Review: *Thirdspace: Journeys to Los Angeles and Other Real-and-Imagined Places* by Edward Soja." *Geographical Review* 88:1 (Jan 1998): 148-51. Print.
Alger, Horatio Jr. *Ragged Dick, Or, Street Life in New York.* Charlottesville, VA: University of Virginia Library, 1996. Web.
Allen, John. "The Cultural Spaces of Siegfried Kracauer: The Many Surfaces of Berlin." *New Formations* 61 (2007): 20-33. Print.
Alleyne, Sonia, Kim Renay Anderson. "Have We Lost Harlem?" *Black Enterprise* 33: 11 (June 2003), 76-90. Print.
Allsop, Erin. "The Digital Archive of the Waldorf-Astoria New York." *The Waldorf- Astoria New York Archive. Host to the World.com* 2014. Web. 20 Oct. 2014.
Ambrose, Joe. *Chelsea Hotel Manhattan.* London: Headpress, 2007. Print.
Amend, Christoph. "Patti Smith: Die Überlebende." *Die Zeit Online* 11 Mar. 2010. Web. 14 Mar. 2014.
Amin, Ash, Nigel Thrift. *Cities: Reimagining the Urban.* Cambridge, UK: Polity Press, 2002. Print.
Anderson, Jervis. *This was Harlem: A Cultural Portrait 1900-1950.* New York: Farrar Straus Giroux, 1981. Print.
Anderson, Linda. *Autobiography.* London: Routledge, 2001. Print.
Anderson, Wes. *The Grand Budapest Hotel.* Fox Searchlight Pictures, 2014. Film.
Angelou, Maya. "Castro in Harlem." *The Harlem Reader: A Celebration of New York's Most Famous Neighborhood, From the Renaissance Years to the 21st Century.* Herb Boyd (ed.). New York: Three Rivers Press, 2003. Print.

Anthony, Andrew. "Perfect delivery: How an unlikely tale of a New York cricket team turned Irish writer Joseph O'Neill into this year's literary sensation." *Culture: Books. The Guardian.* 6 Sept. 2008. Web. 14 Mar. 2014.

Armstead, Myra B. Young. *"Lord, Please Don't Take Me in August:" African Americans in Newport and Saratoga Springs, 1870-1930.* Urbana, Chicago: U of Illinois P, 1999. Print.

----. "Revisiting hotels and other lodgings: American tourist spaces through the lens of Black pleasure-travelers, 1880-1950." *The American Hotel. Journal of Decorative and Propaganda Arts* 25. Molly W. Berger (ed.). Cambridge, MA: MIT Press, 2005. 136-59. Print.

Arnold, Marilyn. "Two of the Lost." *Willa Cather (Modern Critical Views).* Ed. Harold Bloom. New York: Chelsea House Publishers, 1985. Print. 177-83.

Atherton, Gertrude. *Black Oxen.* Melanie V. Dawson (ed.). Buffalo, NY: Broadview Press, 2012. Print.

"'Atmosphere' by Linda Troeller: Live Well Lived At the Chelsea Hotel." *The Fashion Informer* 7 Oct. 2007. Web. 15 Mar. 2014.

Augé, Marc. *Non-Place: An Introduction to An Anthropology of Supermodernity.* 2nd English Edition. London: Verso, 2008. Print.

"Autograph Collection." *Brands. Marriott.com* 2013. Web. 15 Jan. 2014.

Avi. *City of Orphans.* New York: Atheneum Books for Young Readers, 2011. Print.

Bachelard, Gaston. *The Poetics of Space.* (transl. M. Jolas). Boston: Beacon Press, 1969. Print.

Bagli, Charles V. "Waldorf-Astoria to Be Sold in a $1.95 Billion Deal." *N.Y./Region New York Times* 6 Oct. 2014. Web. 14 March 2015.

Barros, Rita. "Fact Sheet." *Fifteen Years: The Chelsea Hotel. ritabarros.com* 2013. Web. 15 Mar. 2014.

----. *Fifteen Years: Chelsea Hotel.* Lisbon, PT: Camera Municipal de Lisboa, 1999. Print.

Baum, Vicki. *Grand Hotel.* (transl. Basil Creighton). Garden City, N.Y.: Doubleday, 1931. Print.

Benjamin, Philip. "Theresa Hotel On 125th St. Is Unruffled by Its Cuban Guests; They Are 'Very Nice and Well-Behaved,' Manager Finds Some Residents Say Elevator and Phone Are Monopolized." *The New York Times* 21 Sept. 1960: 16. Print.

Berens, Carol. *Hotel Bars and Lobbies.* New York McGraw-Hill, 1997. Print.

Berger, Molly. *Hotel Dreams: Luxury, Technology, and Urban Ambition in America, 1829-1929.* Baltimore, MD: John Hopkins UP, 2011. Print.

----. "The Rich Man's City: Hotels and Mansions of Gilded Age New York." *The American Hotel. The Journal of Creative and Propaganda Arts* 25. Molly Berger (Ed.). Cambridge, MA: MIT Press, 2005. 46-72. Print.

Berry, John W. "Acculturation as Varieties of Adaptation." *Acculturation: Theory, Models and Some New Findings.* Amedo M. Padilla (Ed.). Boulder, CO: Westview, 1980. 9-25. Print.
Bloom, Lisa. *With Other Eyes: Looking at Race and Gender in Visual Culture.* Minneapolis: University of Minnesota Press, 1999. Print.
Bloomer, Lucius. *Hotel Management, Principles, and Practice.* New York, London: Harper & Brothers, 1938. Print.
Blumberg, Esterita 'Cissie'. *Remember the Catskills: Tales by a Recovering Hotelkeeper.* Fleischmanns, NY: Purple Mountain Press, 1996. Print.
Boldt, George. *The Waldorf-Astoria, New York.* New York: selfpublished, 1903. Print.
Boorstin, Daniel. *The Americans: The Democratic Experience.* New York: Random House, 1973. Print.
Boroff, David. "Don't Call It 'The Borscht Belt'" *New York Times Magazine* 9 May 1965: 48-60. Print.
Bowen, Elizabeth. *The Hotel.* New York: Penguin Twentieth-Century Classics, 2003. Print.
----. *The Shelbourne Hotel.* New York: A.A. Knopf, 1951. Print.
Brennan, Maeve. *The Rose Garden.* Washington, D.C: Counterpoint, 2000. Print.
Brodesser-Akner, Taffy. "The Chelsea Hotel had its own Eloise," *Magazine. The New York Times* 8 Jul. 2013. Web. 20 Oct. 2014.
Brough, James. *The Dog Who Lives at the Waldorf.* Boston: Little Brown, 1964. Print.
Brown, Phil. *Catskill Culture: A Mountain Rat's Memories of the Great Jewish Resort Area.* Philadelphia: Temple University Press, 1998. Print.
----. *In the Catskills: A Century of the Jewish Experience in 'The Mountains.'* New York: Columbia UP, 2002. Print.
Brown, Tracey L. *The Life and Times of Ron Brown: A Memoir.* New York: William Morrow&Co, 1998. Print.
Brucken, Carolyn. "In the Public Eye: Women and the American Luxury Hotel." *Winterthur Portfolio* 31: 4 (Winter 1996): 203-20. Print.
Buckley, Cara. "Blogs, Books and Biscuits." *Sunday Routine. The New York Times,* March 30, 2012. Web. 15 Oct. 2014.
Cahan, Abraham. *The Rise of David Levinsky.* Minneola: Dover, 2002. Print.
Calfee, Julia. *Inside: The Chelsea Hotel.* Brooklyn: powerHouse Books, 2007. Print.
Carlson, Jen. "Video: Exclusive Tour of the Hotel Chelsea Circa 2007, With Stanley Bard." *Arts & Entertainment. Gothamist.com* 13 Apr. 2012. Web. 13 Mar. 2014.
Case, Frank. *Do Not Disturb.* New York: Frederick A. Stokes Company, 1940. Print.

----. *Feeding the Lions: An Algonquin Cookbook.* New York: Greystone Press, 1942. Print.

----. *Tales of a Wayward Inn.* New York: Frederick Stokes Co., 1938. Print.

----. *Tribal Tales of the Algonquin (Being a Reprint of a Series of Advertisements Appearing in* The New Yorker *during 1931). Hotel Algonquin: George B. Corsa Hotel Collection.* New-York Historical Society: New York. Print.

Castro, Fidel. "Speech to the Fifteenth Session of the U.N. General Assembly, September 26, 1960." *Official Records of the General Assembly*, Part I, Vol. I. New York: United Nations, 1960. 118-19. Print.

Cather, Willa. "Paul's Case: A Study in Temparament." *McClure's Magazine* 25 (May 1905): 74-83. Print.

Chamberlain, Lisa. "Change at the Chelsea, Shelter of the Arts." *N.Y./Region, The New York Times* 19 Jun. 2007. Web. 15 Oct. 2014.

Chavez, Marquita S. *"Inside: The Chelsea Hotel."* Review *Amazon.com* 13 Jul. 2009. Web. 15 Mar. 2014.

Chelsom, Peter (dir.). *Serendipity.* Miramax Films, 2001. Film.

Chopin, Kate. *The Awakening and Other Stories.* Judith Baxter (ed.). Cambridge: Cambridge UP, 1998. Print.

Colby, Michael. "The Algonquin Kid." *Theaterpizzazz.com* 20 Oct. 2013. Web. 14 Feb. 2014.

Conway, John. "Foreword." *Memories of the Catskills: The Making of a Hotel.* Alvin L. Lesser. Indianapolis: GSL Galactic Publ., 2013. i-ii. Print.

Corcoran, Judy. "Chelsea Residents Merge Art and Activism." *Manhattan Spirit* April 22, 1993. 34-37. Print.

Crane, Stephen. "The Blue Hotel." The Portable Stephen Crane. Joseph Katz (ed.). New York: Viking Press, 1969. 418-49. Print.

Craiutu, Aurelian, Jeffrey C. Isaac. *America Through European Eyes: British and French Reflections on the New World From the Eighteenth Century to the Present.* University Park, PA: Penn State UP, 2009. Print.

Cresswell, Tim. "Place." *International Encyclopedia of Human Geography.* N. Thrift & R. Kitchen (eds.). Oxford, UK: Elsevier 3 (2009): 169-177.

----. *Place: A Short Introduction.* 2nd rev. ed. Chichester, UK: Wiley-Blackwell, 2012. Print.

Crockett, Albert Stevens. *Peacock on Parade: A Narrative of a Unique Period in American Social History and Its Most Colorful Figures.* New York: Sears Pub. Co, 1931. Print.

Crowder, Ralph L. "Fidel Castro and Harlem: Political, Diplomatic, and Social Influences of the 1960 Visit to the Hotel Theresa." *Afro-Americans in New York Life and History* 24:1 (January 2000), 79-92. Print.

Crowninshield, Frank. *The Unofficial Palace of New York: A Tribute to the Waldorf-Astoria.* New York: Waldorf-Astoria, 1939. Print.

"Cubans Pay Bill in Cash." *The New York Times* 29 Sept. 1960: 15. Print.

Cukor, George (dir.). *Rich and Famous*. MGM, 1981. Film.
Dabney, Thomas Ewing. *The Man Who Bought The Waldorf: the Life of Conrad N. Hilton*. New York: Duell, Sloan and Pearce, 1950. Print.
Daniels, Lee, dir. *Precious – Based on the Novel 'Push' by Sapphire*. Lionsgate, 2009. Film.
Davis, Alice. "Master-Davis Correspondence, 1936-1944." *Master-Davis Collection, 1928-1978*. New York: New York Public Library Manuscript and Archives Division, revised 1998. (processed by Valerie Wingfield).
de Certeau, Michel. *The Practice of Everyday Life*. Berkeley: University of California Press, 1984. Print.
de Solier, Isabelle. *Food and the Self*. London: Bloomsbury, 2013. Print.
Dearing, Albin Pasteur. *The Elegant Inn*. Secaucus, N.J.: L. Stuart, 1986.
Demsey, David. "More Clues to a Life: The Alec Wilder Archive at the Eastman School of Music." *Notes*, Second Series. *Music Library Association* 46: 4 (Jun. 1990), 919-27. Print.
Denby, Elaine. *Grand Hotel: Reality & Illusion*. London: Reaktion Books, 1998. Print.
Dennis, Patrick. *Auntie Mame: An Irreverent Escapade in Biography*. New York: Vanguard Press, 1955. Print.
Diner, Hasia, Shira Kohn, Rachel Kranson. "Introduction." *A Jewish Feminine Mystique: Jewish Women in Postwar America*. Hasia Diner, Shira Kohn and Rachel Kranson (ed.). New Brunswick, NJ: Rutgers, 2010. 1-12. Print.
Dolkart, Andrew S. "Hotel Theresa (now Theresa Towers)." *Designation list 252, LP-1843*. New York: Landmarks Preservation Commission, 13 July 1993. Print. 1-9.
Donald, James. *Imagining the Modern City*. London: Athlone, 1999. Print.
Donzel, Catherine, Alexis Gregory, Marc Walter. *Grand American Hotels*. New York: Rizzoli, 1989. Print.
Dowd, Maureen. "The Chelsea Hotel, Kooky But Nice, Turns 100." *Metropolitan Report*. *The New York Times* 21 Nov. 1983. Print.
Dreiser, Theodore. *An American Tragedy*. New York: Signet Classic, 2000. Print.
----. *Jennie Gerhardt*. Lee Clark Mitchell (ed.). Oxford: Oxford UP, 1991. Print.
----. *Sister Carrie*. Mineola, N.Y.: Dover Publications, 2004. Print.
----. *The Titan*. New York: Dell, 1961. Print.
Dunlap, David. "4 Cornerstones of Harlem Life Are Designated as Landmarks." *The New York Times*, July 14, 1993. Print.
Earthfall.co.uk 2014. Web. 15 Mar. 2014.
Edinger, Claudio. *Chelsea Hotel*. New York: Abbeville Press, 1983. Print.
Ehrlich, Arnold W. "The Algonquin at 75." *New York Times Magazine* 16 Oct. 1977. 126-30. Print.
"En Garde." *TheaterCrafts* (Jan 1991): 52-58. Print

En Garde Arts, Inc. "Mission Statement." *Hotel Chelsea: George B. Corsa Hotel Collection.* New-York Historical Society: New York, 1985. 1-7.

----. "Brochure *At The Chelsea.*" Chelsea Hotel: George B. Corsa Hotel Collection. New York Historical Society: New York, 1989.

----. "Playbill *At The Chelsea.*" Chelsea Hotel: George B. Corsa Hotel Collection. New York Historical Society: New York, 1989.

Ensha, Azadeh. "The Chelsea Hotel's Resident Hairstylist Recalls Her Greatest Celebrity Clients." *Gallery, T - The New York Times Style Magazine* 3 Sept. 2013. Web. 15 Oct. 2014.

Epstein, Lawrence J. *The Haunted Smile: The Story of Jewish Comedians in America.* New York: Public Affairs, 2001. Print.

F., J. "Books: Sophisticates." *Time Magazine* 3 Mar. 1923. Web. 14 Feb. 2014.

Farrell, Frank. *The Greatest of the All.* New York: Giniger, 1982.

Ferrara, Abel (dir.) *Chelsea on the Rocks.* Wild Bunch, 2008. Film.

Fick, Annabella. "Conrad Hilton, *Be My Guest* and American Popular Culture." *European Journal of Life Writing* Vol 2 (2013): 18-34. Web.

"Fight For Hotel Algonquin: Mrs. Foster Says Lease Is in Her Name and Demands Control." *The New York Times* 14 Jun. 1904: 3. Print.

Fitzgerald, F. Scott. "The Hotel Child." *The Short Stories of F. Scott. Fitzgerald: A New Collection.* Matthew J. Bruccoli (ed.). New York: Scribner, 1989. Print.

Fitzpatrick, Kevin, Marion Meade. *A Journey into Dorothy Parker's New York.* ArtPlace Series. Berkley: Roaring Forties Press, 2005.

Fitzpatrick, Kevin. *The Algonquin Round Table New York: A Historical Guide.* Guilford, CT: Lyons Press, 2015.

Foucault, Michel. "Of Other Spaces." *Diacritics* 16 (Spring 1986): 22-27. Print.

Fowler, Gene. "Casing the Algonquin." *The New York Times Book Review* 20 Jul. 1956: 70-72. Print.

"Frank Case Buys Algonquin for $1,000,000; Hotel Long Home of Writers and Stage Folk." *The New York Times* 9 May 1927: 1. Print.

Freedman, Morris. "The Green Pastures of Grossinger's, Part I and II." *Commentary* 18, no. 2 (August 1954): 150-155. Print.

Frodon, Jean-Michel. *Cinema and the Shoah.* Albany: SUNY Press, 2010. Print.

Frommer, Laurence. "Review, Rita Barros's *Fifteen Years*: On the cusp of significance." *Amazon.com* 27 Aug. 2000. Web. 15 Mar. 2014.

Frommer, Mynra Katz, Harvey Frommer. *It Happened in the Catskills: An Oral History in the Words of Busboys, Bellhops, Guests, Proprietors, Comedians, Agents, and Others.* San Diego, CA: Hartcourt, 1991. Print.

Gaines, James R. *Wit's End: Days and Nights of the Algonquin Round Table.* New York: Houghton Mifflin Harcourt, 1979. Print.

"Gallery Nine: Counselor to the Republic." *Museum Exhibit Galleries.* Herbert Hoover Presidential Library & Museum. Web. 20 Oct. 2013.

Garcia, Olga. "Das Hotel im Spiegel der deutschsprachigen Literatur – Motiv, Kulisse, Bühne und Schauplatz." *Annuario de Estudios Filológicos* 34 (2011): 23-37. Print.
Gatewood, Willard B. *Aristocrats of Color: The Black Elite, 1880-1920. Black Community Studies.* Fayetteville, AR: University of Arkansas Press, 2000. Print.
Geller, Laurence. *Do Not Disturb.* Lost Angeles, CA: Volt Press, 2006. Print.
Ghigliotty, Damian. "Old New York: The Plaza Hotel." *Mortgage Observer. Commercial Observer* 14 Oct. 2014. Web. 22 Oct. 2014.
Giles, Judy, Tim Middleton. *Studying Culture: A Practical Introduction.* Oxford, UK: Blackwell, 1999. Print.
Gill, Brendan. "Algonquin: A Birthday on Forty-Fourth Street." *New York Public Library.* New York, 1977. Print.
Goeschel, Nancy. "Algonquin Hotel: Built 1902, Architect Goldwin Starrett." *Designation list 191, LP-1547.* New York: Landmark Preservation Commission, 15 Sept. 1987. Print.
Goldberg, Jonathan. "Willa Cather and Sexuality." *The Cambridge Companion to Willa Cather.* Ed. Marilee Lindemann. Cambridge: CUP, 2005. 86-100. Print.
Goldberger, Paul. "Preface." *Grand American Hotels.* Catherine Donzel, Alexis Gregory, and Marc Walter (ed.). New York: Rizzoli, 1989. 8-9. Print.
Goodstein, Laurie. "Poll Shows Major Shift in Identity of U.S. Jews." *U.S. The New York Times.* 1 Oct. 2013. Web. 10 Oct. 2013.
Graham, Lawrence Otis. *Our Kind of People: Inside America's Black Upper Class.* New York: Harper Perennial, 2000. Print.
Gray, Christopher. "Streetscapes: The Hotel Theresa." *The New York Times* 3 May 2009: 4. Print.
Gregory, Alexis. "U.S.A.: Size and Fantasy." *Grand American Hotels.* Catherine Donzel, Alexis Gregory, and Marc Walter (ed.). New York: Rizzoli, 1989. 10-37. Print.
Gross, Max. "Suite Dreams." *New York Post* 26 Apr. 2007. Web. 22 Oct. 2014.
"Grossinger, Jennie." *American Women Managers and Administrators: A Selective Biographical Dictionary of Twentieth Century Leaders in Business, Education, and Government.* Judith A. Leavitt (ed.). New York: Greenwood Press, 1985. 96-97. Print.
Grossinger, Richard. *Out of Babylon: Ghosts of Grossinger's.* Berkeley, CA: Frog Ltd., 1997. Print.
Grossinger, Tania. *Growing Up At Grossinger's.* 2nd Edition. New York: Skyhorse Pub, 2008. Print.
Groth, Paul. *Living Downtown: The History of Residential Hotels in the United States.* Berkeley, CA: University of California Press, 1994. Print.
Grubb, Kevin. "On Duty/On Stage: Space Available." *Taxi* 4:5 (June/July 1991): 1. Print.
Hailey, Arthur. *Hotel.* Garden City, NY: Doubleday, 1965. Print.

Haley, Alex. "An Interview with Cassius Clay." *Alex Haley: The Playboy Interviews.* Alex Haley and Murray Fisher (ed.). New York: Ballantine, 1993. 46-79. Print.

Halsall, Paul. "Modern History Sourcebook: Charles Fourier: from *Theory of Social Organization*, 1820." *Modern History.* Fordham University, NY. 1998. Web. 12 Mar. 2014.

Hamilton, Ed. *Legends of the Chelsea Hotel: Living with Artists and Outlaws of New York's Rebel Mecca.* Cambridge, MA. Da Capo Press, 2007. Print.

----. *Living With Legends: Hotel Chelsea Blog* 2005-2014. Web. 15 Oct. 2014.

Harriman, Margaret Case. *Blessed Are the Debonair.* New York: Rinehart Company, 1956. Print.

----. *The Vicious Circle: The Story of the Algonquin Round Table.* New York, Rinehart, 1951. Print.

Hayner, Norman S. "Hotel Life and Personality." *American Journal of Sociology* 33:5 (Mar. 1928), 784-95. Print.

----. *Hotel Life.* Chapel Hill, NC: University of North Carolina Press, 1936. Print.

Hayter, Sparkle. *The Chelsea Girl Murders: A Robin Hudson Mystery.* New York: Penguine Putnam, 2000. Print.

Heidegger, Martin. "Building Dwelling Thinking." *Poetry Language and Thought.* (transl. Albert Hofstadter). New York: Perennial Classics, 2001. 141-60. Print.

Heinze, Andrew R. *Adapting to Abundance: Jewish Immigrants, Mass Consumption, and the Search for American Identity.* New York: Columbia UP, 1990. Print.

Hemenway, Robert E. *Zora Neale Hurston: A Literary Biography.* Champaign, IL: U of Illinois P, 1980. Print.

Hendler, Herb. *Year by Year in the Rock Era.* New York: Greenwood Press, 1987. Print.

Hergesheimer, Joseph. *Linda Condon.* New York: A.A. Knopf, 1919. Print.

Hetheringon, Kevin. "Identity Formation, Space and Social Centrality." *Theory Culture Society* 13:33 (1996): 34-52. Print.

Hiller, Arthur (dir.). *The Out-of-Towners.* Paramount Pictures, 1978. Film.

Hilton, Conrad N. *Be My Guest.* New York: Prentice-Hall, 1987. Print.

Hine, Al. "Grossinger's." *Holiday* 6:2 (August 1949). 99-118. Print.

Hirsh, Jeff. *Manhattan Hotels: 1880-1920.* Mount Pleasant, SC: Arcadia Publishing, 1997. Print.

"History and Traditions of the Algonquin." *The Algonquin Wit Newsletter* (Winter 1995). *Hotel Algonquin: George B. Corsa Hotel Collection.* New-York Historical Society: New York. 1-5. Print.

Hitchcock, Alfred (dir.). *Alfred Hitchcock's Topaz.* Universal, (1969) 2005. Film.

Holden, Stephen. "The Song is Over, but Melodies Linger On: Oak Room at Algonquin Hotel Closes." *The Critic's Notebook. The New York Times* 3 Feb. 2012. Web. 14 Feb. 2014.

Holland, Joseph. *From Harlem with Love: An Ivy Leaguer's Inner City Odyssey.* Brooklyn, NY: Lantern Books, 2011. Print.
Holmes, Stephen A. *Ron Brown: An Uncommon Life.* Hoboken, NJ: Wiley, 2001. Print.
Hoover, Herbert. "Radio Remarks on the Opening of the Waldorf-Astoria Hotel, 30 Sept. 1931." *The American Presidency Project.* John Woolley and Gerhard Peters (ed.). University of California Santa Barbara 1999. Web. 20 Oct. 2013.
Horace, Smith. *Crooks of the Waldorf: Being the Story of Joe Smith, Master Detective.* New York: Macaulay Co., 1929. Print.
Horwitz, Murray, Richard Maltby, Jr. *Ain't Misbehavin.* 1978. Musical.
"Hotel Chelsea, 222 West 23rd Street." *Designation List 15, LP-0124.* New York: Landmarks Preservation Commission, 15 Mar. 1966. Print.
"Hotel Served over 125,000 People." *Pittsburgh Courier* 2 Apr. 1942: 14. Print.
"Hotel Sued By Negroes; Harlem Owners Accused of Discriminating Against Two." The New York Times 30 Jul. 1937: 22. Print.
"Hotels: The Key Man." *Time Magazine* 12 Dec. 1949: 87-95. Print.
Howells, William Dean. *Their Wedding Journey.* John K. Reeves (ed.). Bloomington: Indiana UP, 1968. Print.
Hughes, Langston. "Advertisement for the Waldorf-Astoria." *New Masses* Dec 1931. 16-17. Print.
----. *The Big Sea: An Autobiography by Langston Hughes.* New York: Hill and Wang, 1940. Print.
Hungerford, Edward. *The Story of the Waldorf-Astoria.* New York, London: G.P. Putnam's Sons, 1925. Print.
"*Inside: The Chelsea Hotel.*" *juliacalfee.com* 2013. Web. 15 Mar. 2014.
"Interesting Facts." *The Algonquin Hotel* 2014. Web. 13 Feb. 2014.
Isaacson, Walter. "Running As His Own Man: Ronald Brown." *Time* 133:5, 30 Jan. 1989. Print.
Jackson, Ronald L., Jamie Moshin. "Scripting Jewishness within the Satire The Hebrew Hammer." *Communication Ethics: Between Cosmopolitanism and Provinciality.* Kathleen Glenister Roberts, Ronald C. Arnett (ed.). New York: Peter Lang, 2008. 187-214. Print.
James, Henry. *The American Scene.* Leon Edel (ed.). Bloomington, ID: Indiana UP, 1968. Print.
James, Joy. "Review/Harlem Hospitality and Political History: Malcolm X and Fidel Castro at the Hotel Theresa." *Contributions in Black Studies* 12 (1994). Web.
"Jennie Grossinger," *The American Jewish Woman: A Documentary History.* Jacob Rader Marcus (Ed). Jersey City, NJ: Ktav Pub Inc., 1981. 671-76. Print.
"Jenny Grossinger Correspondence." *Grossinger's Country Club ca 1920-1983.* New York: YIVO Archives, YIVO Institute for Jewish.

Jewell, Andrew, Janis Stout. *The Selected Letters of Willa Cather.* New York: Vintage, 2013. 614-15. Print.
Jim, Bernard L. "'Wrecking the Joint': The Razing of City Hotels in the First Half of the Twentieth Century." *The American Hotel. The Journal of Creative and Propaganda Arts* 25. Molly Berger (Ed.). Cambridge, MA: MIT Press, 2005. 288-315. Print.
Johnson, Carolyn D. *Harlem Travel Guide.* New York: Welcome to Harlem, 2011. Print.
K., Anna, Isabel Canet. *Total Bedient: Ein Zimmermädchen erzählt.* Hamburg: Hoffmann und Campe, 2012. Print.
Kallis, Danny (creator). *The Suite-Life of Zac and Cody.* Disney Channel, 2005-2008. TV-Series.
Kanfer, *A Summer World: The Attempt to Build A Jewish Eden in the Catskills, From the Days of the Ghetto to the Rise and Decline of the Borscht Belt.* New York: Farrar, Straus and Giroux, 1989. Print.
Kant, Immanuel. "Toward Perpetual Peace." *Immanuel Kant: Practical Philosophy.* Mary J. Gregor (ed.). Cambridge: CUP, 1996. 311-52. Print.
Kaplan, Justin. *When the Astors Owned New York: Blue Bloods and Grand Hotels in a Gilded Age.* New York: Plume, 2007. Print.
Kennedy, John F. "Excerpts of Remarks of Senator John F. Kennedy, Public Rally, Hotel Theresa, New York, NY." 12 Oct. 1960. Ed. Gerhard Peters and John T. Woolley. *The American Presidency Project.* University of California in Santa Barbara. Web. 22 Oct. 2014.
Killmer, Ted. "Press Release: *At The Chelsea.*" *Chelsea Hotel: George B. Corsa Hotel Collection, New-York Historical Society.* New York, 1988/89. 1-4. Print.
King, Martin Luther Jr. *I Have a Dream: Writings and Speeches that Changed the World.* Ed. James M. Washington. San Francisco: Harper Collins, 1992. Print.
Klimasmith, Betsy. *At Home in the City: Urban Domesticity in American Literature and Culture, 1850-1930.* Hanover: University Press of New England, 2005. Print.
Knappett, Carl, Lambros Malafouris. *Material Agency: Towards A Non-Anthropocentric Approach.* Berlin: Springer, 2010. Print.
Koestenbaum, Wayne. *Hotel Theory: 8 Dossiers; Hotel Women: 18 Chapters.* Brooklyn, NY: Soft Skull press, 2007. Print.
Kolbe, Laura, Mary Sparks, Botakoz Kassymbekova. *The Rise and Fall of the Grand Hotel.* Oxford: Oxford UP, forthcoming.
Komito, Carrie. *Memoir of a Catskill Hotelkeeper Vol I & II.* Bloomington, IN: iUniverse, 2003/2006. Print.
Koolhaas, Rem. *Delirious New York : A Retroactive Manifesto for Manhattan.* New York: Monacelli Press, 1994. Print.

Kopytoff, Igor. "The Cultural Biography of Things: Commodization as Process." *The Social Life of Things.* Arjun Appadurai (ed.). Cambridge: Cambridge UP, 1986. 64-96. Print.

Koszella, Leo. "Menschen im Hotel." *Der Feuerreiter* 41 (1931): 662-64. Print

Kracauer, Siegfried. "The Hotel Lobby." *The Mass Ornament: Weimar Essays.* (trans. Thomas Y. Levin). Cambridge, MA: Harvard UP, 1995. 173-88. Print.

Kranson, Rachel. "The 'Gentle Jewish Mother' Who Owned a Luxury Resort: The Public Image of Jennie Grossinger, 1954-1972." *A Jewish Feminine Mystique?: Jewish Women in Postwar America.* Hasia R. Diner, Shira M. Kohn and Rachel Kranson (Ed.). Piscataway, NJ: Rutgers, 2010. 177-93. Print.

Krebs, Martina. *Hotel Stories: Representations of Escapes and Encounters in Fiction and Film.* Trier: WVT, 2009. Print.

Kreis, Steven. "Lecture 21: The Utopia Socialist: Charles Fourier (1)." *The History Guide.org.* 2000. Web. 12 Oct. 2014.

Kun, Josh. "Bagels, Bongos, and Yiddishe Mambos, or The Other History of Jews in America." *Shofar: An Interdisciplinary Journal of Jewish Studies* 23:4 (2005): 50-68. Print.

Künzli, Lis. *Hotels: Ein Literarischer Führer.* Frankfurt a.M.: Eichborn, 2007. Print.

Latour, Bruno. *Reassembling the Social: An Introduction to Actor-Network-Theory.* Oxford: Oxford University Press, 2005. Print.

Leao, Joao. "Review, Rita Barros's *Fifteen Years*: Postcards from a cruise on the 'Ship of Fools.'" Amazon.com 9 Aug. 2000. Web. 15 Mar. 2014.

Lefebvre, Henri. *The Production of Space.* Oxford, UK, Cambridge, MA: Blackwell, 1991. Print.

Lejeune, Philippe. *On Autobiography.* Paul John Eakin (ed.). Minneapolis: U of Minnesota P, 1989. Print.

Lent, Henry B. *The Waldorf-Astoria: A Brief Chronicle of a Unique Institution Now Entering Its Fifth Decade.* New York: Priv. Print for Hotel Waldorf-Astoria Corporation, 1934. Print.

Leonard, Robert Z. (dir.). *Week-end at the Waldorf.* MGM, 1945. Film.

Lesser, Alvin L. *Memories of the Catskills: The Making of a Hotel.* Indianapolis, IN: GSL Galactic Publishing, 2013. Print.

"Letter from Jennie Grossinger to Mr. Bernard Geis. 13 Feb, 1958." Folder 7, Box 1, RG 1195. *Grossinger's Country Club.* New York: YIVO Institute for Jewish Research. Print.

"Letter from Jennie Grossinger to Mrs. John T. Willis. 1 Dec, 1954." Folder 2, Box 1, RG 1195. *Grossinger's Country Club.* New York: YIVO Institute for Jewish Research. Print.

Levander, Caroline, Matthew Pratt Guterl. *Hotel Life.* Chapel Hill: UNC Press, 2015. Print.

Leve, Ariel. "Cover Story: New York Storeys." *The Sunday Times Magazine* 25 Mar. 2007: 40-51. Print.

Levy, Newman. "Songs of Hotels." *The New Yorker* 8 Dec. 1928: 36. Print.

Lewis, Sinclair. *Work of Art.* Garden City, NY: Doubleday Doran & Co, 1934. Print.

Lewis, Stephen. *Hotel Kid: A Times Square Childhood.* Philadelphia, PA: Paul Dry Books, 2002. Print.

Lingeman, Richard R.. "Where Home is Where it is." *The New York Times Book Review* 24 Dec. 1967. Print.

Litvak, Joseph. *The Un-Americans: Jewish, the Blacklist, and Stoolpigeon Culture.* Durham: Duke UP, 2009. Print.

Loos, Anita. *Gentlemen Prefer Blondes, But Gentlemen Marry Brunettes.* New York: Penguin Books, 1998. Print.

Lough, James. *This Ain't No Holiday Inn: Down and Out at the Chelsea Hotel 1980-1995.* Tucson, AZ: Schaffner Press, 2013. Print.

Löw, Martina. "Constitution of Space: The Structuration of Spaces Through the Simultaneity of Effect and Perception." *European Journal of Social Theory* 11: 1 (2008), 25-49. Print.

----. *Raumsoziologie.* Frankfurt am Main: Suhrkamp, 2001. Print.

Lunettes, Henry. *The American Gentleman's Guide to Politeness and Fashion.* New York: Derby&Jackson, 1858. Print.

Mackerell, Judith. "Earthfall – Review." *Stage. The Guardian* 6 Nov. 2013. Web. 14 Mar. 2014.

Madden, John (dir.). *Best Exotic Marigold Hotel.* Fox Searchlight Pictures, 2012. Film.

Madden, John (dir.). *The Second Best Exotic Marigold Hotel.* Fox Searchlight Pictures, 2015. Film.

Maidenbaum, Judith. "Confession of a New York Shrink." Unpublished. *The Catskill Insitute Archive.* Northeastern University, Boston. Viewed 16 Apr. 2013.

Mallory, Noreen. *Harlem in the Twentieth Century.* Charleston, S.C.: History Press, 2011. Print. Aberjhani, Sandra L. West. *Encyclopedia of the Harlem Renaissance.* New York: Facts on File, 2003. Print.

Malpas, Jeff. "Place and Human Being." *Environmental & Architectural Phenomenology* 20:3 (Fall 2009). 19-23. Print.

Maltin, Lenard (ed.). *Leonard Maltin's 2009 Movie Guide.* New York: Signet, 2008. Print.

"Manhattan Housing Opportunities for Artists Have Dwindled." *Artist-in-Residence. Curbed.com* Nov. 2013. Web. 15 Oct. 2014.

Mark, Jonathan. "Tania Grossinger's Book and the Real Catskills." *The Jewish Week* 1 May 2010. Web. 30 Oct. 2014.

Massa, Robert. "Sightlines." *The Village Voice* 34:7 (14 Feb. 1989): 95. Print.

Massey, Doreen B. "A Global Sense of Place." *Space, Place and Gender*. Minneapolis: University of Minnesota Press, 1994. 146-56. Print.

Masters-Davis Collection. Manuscripts and Archives. The New York Public Library. Astor, Lenox, and Tilden Foundations.

Matlock, Jann. "Vacancies: Registered Passing in American Cinema, 1929-1964." *Moving Pictures/Stopping Places: Hotel and Motels on Film*. David B. Clarke, Valerie Crawford Pfannhauser, and Marcus A. Doel. Lexington, KY: Lexington Books of Rowman and Littlefield, 2009. 73-141. Print.

Matteoli, Francisca. "Hotel Chelsea/Bob Dylan." *American Hotel Stories*. New York: Assouline Publ., 2009. 20-25. Print.

Matteoli, Francisca. *Hotel Stories: Legendary Hideaways of the World*. New York: Assouline Publishing, 2002. Print.

Matthias, Bettina. *The Hotel as Setting in Early Twentieth-Century German and Austrian Literature: Checking in to Tell a Story*. Rochester, NY: Camden House, 2006. Print.

Maxwell, Elsa. "Hotel Pilgrim." *The Unofficial Palace of New York: A Tribute to the Waldorf-Astoria*. Frank Crowninshield (ed.). New York: selfpublished, 1939. 127-38. Print.

McCarthy, James Remington. *Peacock Alley: The Romance of the Waldorf Astoria*. New York, London: Harper & Bros, 1931. Print.

McGinty, Brian. *The Palace Inns: A Connoisseur's Guide to Historic American Hotel*. Harrisburg, PA: Stackpole Books, 1978. Print.

McLennan, Rachel. *American Autobiography*. BAAS Paperbacks. Edinburgh: Edinburgh UP, 2013. Print.

McNeill, Donald. "The Hotel and the City." *Progress in Human Geography* 32:3 (June 2008): 383-98. Print.

Mead, Rebecca. "The Dream Palace." *The New Yorker* 28 Oct. 2013. 22-23. Print.

Meade, Marion. *Dorothy Parker: What Fresh Hell Is This?* New York: Villard Books, 1988. Print.

Meister, Ellen. *Farewell, Dorothy Parker*. New York: G.P. Putnam's Sons, 2013. Print.

Mendelsohn, Martha. "Interview with Tania Grossinger." *Interviews. The Catskill Institute* 28 Feb. 2008. Web. 14 Oct. 2014.

Michael, Robert. *A Concise History of American Antisemitism*. Oxford: Rowman & Littlefield, 2005. Print.

Miller, Arthur. "The Chelsea Affect." *Granta* 78 (Summer 2002): 237-54. Print.

----. *Timebends: A Life*. New York: Grove Press, 1987. Print.

Millhauser, Steven. *Martin Dressler: The Tale of An American Dreamer*. New York: Vintage, 1997. Print.

Milward, John. "3 Rooms of Theater at Chelsea Hotel." *Daily Magazine. The Philadelphia Inquirer* 16 Jan. 1989: C1-C4. Print.

Mink, Andreas. "New York - Expedition in die Catskills: Schlock und Wunder im Borscht Belt." *Aufbau: Das Jüdische Monatsmagazin* 72: 7/8 (Juli 2007). 6-13. Print.

Montgomery, Maureen. "Henry James and 'The testimony of the hotel' to transatlantic encounters." *Inns and Hotels in Britain an the United States in the Long Nineteenth Century.* Monika Elbert and Susanne Schmid (Ed.). Forthcoming.

Moody, Hank. *God Hates Us All.* New York: Simon Spotlight Entertainment, 2009. Print.

Mordden, Ethan. *The Guest List: How Manhattan Defined American Sophistication: From the Algonquin Round Table to Truman Capote's Ball.* New York: St. Martin's Press, 2010. Print.

Morehouse, Ward III. *Life at the Top: Inside New York's Grand Hotels.* Albany, GA: Bearmanor Media, 2005. Print.

----. *The Waldorf-Astoria: America's Gilded Dream.* New York: M. Evans, 1991. Print.

Morrison, William Alan. *Waldorf Astoria.* Charleston, SC: Arcadia Publishing, 2014. Print.

Murphy, J.J. *A Friendly Game of Murder.* New York: Obsidian, 2012. Print.

Nairn, Ian. *The American Landscape: A Critical View.* New York: Random House, 1965. Print.

New York Daily Tribune 23 Nov. 1902. Print.

Nissley, Tom. "Editorial Reviews – Just Kids: Patti Smith." *Amazon Best Books of the Month, January 2010. Amazon.com* Jan. 2010. Web. 15 Mar. 2014.

O'Neill, Joseph. *Netherland.* New York: Pantheon, 2008. Print.

Oldenburg, Ray. "Our Vanishing 'Third Places'." *PlannersWeb* 15 Jan. 1997. Web. 20 Oct. 2014.

----. *The Great Good Place: Cafés, Coffee Shops, Bookstores, Bars, Hair Salons, and Other Hangouts at the Heart of a Community.* Cambridge, MA: Da Capo Press, 1999. Print.

Pacheco, Patrick. "Chelsea Merges Art, Environment: An Artists' Hangout Stars in a Four-Weeks Festival." *Entertainment. New York Newsday* 12 Jan. 1989: 7-9. Print.

Parini, Jay. *The Norton Book of American Autobiography.* New York: W.W. Norton, 1999. Print.

Parker, Dorothy. "The Big Blonde." *The Portable Dorothy Parker.* Marion Meade (ed.). 2nd rev. ed. New York: Penguin Books, 2008. 187-210. Print.

"Patti Smith comes under fire for planned Hotel Chelsea Gig." *NME.com* 11 Jan. 2012. Web. 14 Mar. 2014.

"Penny Arcade, David Van Tieghem and Tina Dudek; Anne Carlson: At the Chelsea." *High Performance* 46:2 (Summer 1989). Print.

Perry, Marvin. Frederick M. Schweitzer. *Anti-Semitism: Myth from Antiquity to the Present.* New York: Palgrave Macmillan, 2002. Print.
Peters, Ann. "A Traveler in Residence: Maeve Brennan and the Last Days of New York." *Women's Studies Quarterly* 33:3/4 (Fall-Winter, 2005): 66-89. Print.
Pomerantz, Joel. *Jennie and the Story of Grossinger's.* New York: Grosset & Dunlap, 1970.
Pope, Virginia. "An Epoch Passes on With the Waldorf." *New York Times.* 28 Apr. 1929. 7-9. Print
Pready, Joanna Elaine. *The Power of Place: Re-Negotiating Identity in Hotel Fiction.* PhD Thesis, University of Notthingham. July 2009. Web. 13 Jan 2014.
Prescott, Holly. *Rethinking of Urban Space in Contemporary British Writing.* PhD Thesis, University of Birmingham. Sept. 2011. Web. 20 Feb 2014.
Presky, Irena, Dina Birman. "Ethnic Identity in Acculturation Research: A Study of Multiple Identities of Jewish Refugees From the Former Soviet Union." *Journal of Cross-Cultural Psychology* 36 (2005): 557-72. Print.
Primeau, Ronald. *American National Biography.* New York: Oxford UP, 1999.
Pritchard, Anne, Nigel Morgan. "Hotel Babylon? Exploring hotels as liminal sites of transition and transgression." *Tourism Management* 27 (2006): 762-72. Print.
Proshansky, Harold M, Fabian K. Abbe, Robert Kaminoff. "Place-Identity: Physical World Socialization of the Self." *Journal of Environmental Psychology* 3:1 (Mar. 1983): 57-83. Print.
Rabaka, Reiland. *Du Bois's Dialectics: Black Radical Politics and the Reconstruction of Critical Social Theory.* Plymouth: Lexington Books, 2009. Print.
Raitz, Karl, John Paul Jones III. "The City Hotel as Landscape Artifact and Community Symbol." *Journal of Cultural Geography* 9 (Fall/Winter 1988): 17-36. Print.
Rauh, Andreas. *Die besondere Atmosphäre: Ästhetische Feldforschungen.* Bielefeld: Transcript, 2012. Print.
Reagan, Ronald. "Statement on the Death of Former World Heavyweight Boxing Champion Joe Louis." 13 Apr. 1981. Ed. Gerhard Peters and John T. Woolley. *The American Presidency Project.* University of California in Santa Barbara. Web. 22 Oct. 2014.
Reedy, William Marion. "A Westerner in the Waldorf." *Reedy's Mirror* 13 (1903): 8. Print.
Relph, Edward. "A Pragmatic Sense of Place." *Environmental & Architectural Phenomenology* 20: 3 (Fall 2009): 24-31. Print.
----. *Place and Placelessness.* London: Pion, 1976. Print.
"Reviews/Non Fiction: *Just Kids* by Patti Smith." *Publishers Weekly* 1 Jan. 2010. Web. 15 Mar. 2014.
Reynolds, Quentin. *One Hundred Per Cent American.* Stamford, CT: The Pig Pen Press, 1939. Print.

----. "The Hotel That Refused to Die." *Esquire* (Feb 1950): 25; 116-20. Print.

Rich, Nathaniel. "Where the Walls Still Talk." *Vanity Fair Online* 8 Oct. 2013. Web. 13 Mar. 2014.

Richler, Mordecai. "The Catskills: Land of Milk and Money", *Holiday* 38 (July 1965). *HolidayMag.wordpress.com* 17 Feb. 2012. Web. 15 Apr. 2014.

Rose, Gillian. *Feminism & Geography: The Limits of Geographical Knowledge.* Minneapolis, MN: University of Minnesota Press, 1993. Print.

Rose, Kenneth D. *Unspeakable Awfulness: America Through the Eyes of European Travelers, 1865-1900.* New York: Routledge, 2014. Print.

Ross, Harold. "Vision for The New Yorker." 21 Feb. 1925. *University of Virginia.* Web. 13 Feb. 2014.

Roth, Joseph. *Werke 3: Das journalistische Werk 1929-1939*. Klaus Westermann (ed.). Köln: Kiepenheuer & Witsch. 1991. Print.

Rudolph, Alan (dir.). *Mrs. Parker and the Vicious Circle*. Fine Line Features, 1994. Film.

Russell, Herbert K. *Edgar Lee Masters: A Biography*. Champaign, IL: U of Illinois P, 2005. Print.

Rutes, Walter, Richard H. Penner, Lawrence Adams. *Hotel Design, Planning, and Development*. New York: W.W. Norton, 2001. Print.

Sanders, James. *Celluloid Skyline: New York and the Movies*. New York: Knopf, 2001. Print.

Sandoval-Strausz, A.K., Daniel Levinson Wilk. "Princes and Maids of the City Hotel: The Cultural Politics of Commercial Hospitality in America." *The Journal of Decorative and Propaganda Arts 25.* Molly Berger (ed.). Cambridge, MA: MIT Press, 2005. 160-85. Print.

Sandoval-Strausz, Andrew K. *Hotel: An American History.* New Haven, CT: Yale UP, 2008. Print.

Sanger, David E. "Crash in the Balkans: The Lives Broken Off; Ronald H. Brown, 54, Clinton's Commerce Secretary." *The New York Times* 4 Apr. 1996. Print.

Sarna, Jonathan, Jonathan Golden. "The American Jewish Experience in the 20th Century: Anti-semitism and Assimilation." *National Humanities Center.org* Oct 2000. Web. 27 Oct. 2014.

Satow, Julie. "Living in the Mix: Affordable Housing New York's Luxury Buildings." *Real Estate. The New York Times* 29 Aug. 2014. Web. 23 Mar. 2015.

Schaffner, Val. *The Algonquin Cat.* New York: Delacorte Press, 1980. Print.

Scherman, Tony. "The Theresa." *American Legacy* (Winter 1998): 12-20. Print.

Schloss, Dietmar. *Civilizing America: Manners and Civility in American Literature and Culture.* Heidelberg: Winter, 2009. Print.

Schrand, Brandon R. *The Enders Hotel: A Memoir.* Lincoln, NB: University of Nebraska Press, 2008. Print.

Schriftgiesser, Karl. *Oscar of the Waldorf.* New York: E.P. Dutton & Co, 1943. Print.

Seamon, David. "Place, Place Identity, and Phenomenology: A Triadic Interpretation Based on J.G. Bennett's Systematics." *The Role of Place Identity in the Perception, Understanding, and Design of Built Environments.* Hernan Casakin and Fatima Bernardo (eds). Oak Park, IL: Bentham e-Books, 2012. 3-21. eBook.

----. *A Geography of the Lifeworld: Movement, Rest, and Encounter.* New York: St. Martin's Press, 1979. Print.

----. "Body-subject, time-space routines, and place-ballets." *The Human Experience of Space and Place.* Anne Buttimer and David Seamon (ed.). London: Croom Helm, 1980. 148-65. Print.

Sedgwick, Eve Kosofsky. "Across Gender, Across Sexuality: Willa Cather and Others." *South Atlantic Quaterly* 88.1 (Winter 1989): 53-72. Print.

Seger, Cordula. *Grand Hotel – Schauplatz der Literatur.* Köln: Böhlau, 2005. Print.

Seitel, Fraser P, John Doorley. *Rethinking Reputation: How PR Trumps Marketing and Advertising in the New Media World.* New York: Palgrave Macmillan, 2012. Print.

Shaffer, Marguerite. *See America First: Tourism and National Identity 1880-1940.* Washington, D.C.: Smithsonian Books, 2001. Print.

Shields, Rob. "The Individual, Consumption Cultures, and the Fate of Community." *Lifestyle Shopping: The Subject of Consumption.* Rob Shields (ed.). London, New York: Routledge, 1992. 99-114. Print.

Shulman, Robert. *The Power of Political Art. The 1930s Literary Left Reconsidered.* Chapel Hill: University of North Carolina Press, 2000. Print.

Signoret, Simone. *Nostalgia Isn't What It Used To Be.* New York: Harper & Row, 1978. Print.

Simmel, Georg. *The Philosophy of Money.* (trans. Tom Bottomore and David Frisby). London: Routledge, 1978. Print.

Sirridge, Marjorie S. "Cather, Willa. 'Paul's Case.'" *Literature Annotations. Literature, Arts, and Medicine Database.* NYU, 24 Oct. 1997. Web. 14 Oct. 2013.

Slesin, Aviva (dir). *The Ten Year Lunch: The Wit and Legend of the Algonquin Round Table.* PBS, 1987. Film.

Smethurst, James. *The New Red Negro: The Literary Left and African American Poetry, 1930-1946.* New York: Oxford UP, 1999. Print.

Smith, Patti. *Just Kids.* New York: Harper Collins, 2010. Print.

Snyder, Katherine. "*Gatsby*'s Ghost: Post-Traumatic Memory and National Literary Tradition in Joseph O'Neill's *Netherland.*" *Contemporary Literature* 54:3 (Fall 2013): 459-90. Print.

Soja, Edward. *Thirdspace: Journeys to Los Angeles and Other Real-and-Imagined Places.* Cambridge, MA: Blackwell, 1996. Print.

Sorin, Gerald. *Tradition Transformed: The Jewish Experience in America*. The American Moment. Baltimore: John Hopkins UP, 1997. Print.

Spelling, Aaron (creator). *Hotel*. ABC, 1983-1988. Television.

Staggs, Sam. *Inventing Elsa Maxwell: How an Irrepressible Nobody Conquered High Society, Hollywood, the Press, and the World*. New York: St. Martin's Press, 2012. Print.

Stephenson, Walter T. "Hotels and Hotel Life in New York." *Pall Mall Magazine* 31 (September- December 1903): 253. Print.

Steve. "*Inside: The Chelsea Hotel*." goodreads.com 2 Sept. 2008. Web. 15 Mar. 2014.

Stone, Michael. "The Algonquin Faces Life." *New York Magazine* 2 Nov. 1987. 52-65. Print.

Sutton, Horace. *Confessions of a Grand Hotel: the Waldorf-Astoria*. New York: Henry Holt, 1953. Print.

Taft, Ronald. "Coping with Unfamiliar Cultures." *Studies in Cross-Cultural Psychology* 1. Neil Warren (Ed.). London, New York: Academic Press Inc., 1977. 121-153. Print.

Tartakovsky, Genndy. *Hotel Transylvania*. Columbia Pictures, 2012. Film.

Taub, Harold J. *Waldorf-in-the-Catskills*. New York: Sterling Pub Co, 1952. Print.

Thacker, Andrew. *Moving Through Modernity: Space and Geography in Modernism*. Manchester, New York: Manchester UP, 2003. Print.

Theroux, Paul. *Hotel Honolulu*. Boston: Houghton Mifflin, 2001. Print.

"The Algonquin as Literary Landmark." *The The Algonquin Wit Newsletter* (Fall 1996). *The Hotel Algonquin: George B. Corsa Hotel Collection*. New-York Historical Society: New York. 1-5. Print.

"The Hotel Theresa." *Institute for Urban and Minority Education (IUME)*. Teachers College, Columbia University. 2011. Web. October 22, 2014.

"The Most Splendid of Hotels." *The New York Sun* 15 March 1893: 2. Print.

The Oxford English Dictionary. 3rd ed. 2008. *OED Online*. Oxford University Press. Web. 20 Oct. 2014.

"The Waldorf of Harlem." *Ebony* 1 (April 1946): 8-12. Print.

Thompson, Kay. *Eloise*. New York: Simon and Schuster, 2005. Print.

Tippins, Sherill. "12 Famous Writers Who Lived in The Chelsea Hotel," *The Blog, Huffington Post* 3 Dec. 2013. Web. 15 Mar. 2014.

----. *Inside the Dream Palace: The Life and Times of New York's Legendary Chelsea Hotel*. New York: Houghton Mifflin Harcourt, 2013. Print.

Tomsky, Jacob. *Heads in Beds: A Reckless Memoir of Hotels, Hustles, and So-called Hospitality*. New York: Doubleday, 2012. Print.

Troeller, Linda. *Atmosphere: An Artist's Memoir of the Chelsea Hotel*. San Francisco: Blurb Inc., 2007. Print.

Trollope, Anthony. *North America*. Donald Smalley and Bradford Allen Booth (ed.). New York: Da Capo Press, 1986. Print.

Trollope, Frances. *Domestic Manners of the American's*. London: Whittaker, Treacher, and Company, 1832.
Tuan, Yi-Fu. "Space and Place: Humanistic Perspective." *Philosophy of Geography*. S. Gale and S. Olsson (eds.). Dordrecht, NL: D. Reidel Publishing Company, 1979. 387-427. Print.
----. *Space and Place: The Perspective of Experience*. 5th Edition. Minneapolis: University of Minnesota Press, 2001. Print.
Turner, Florence. *At The Chelsea*. San Diego, CA: Harcourt Brace Jovanovitch, 1987. Print.
Twickel, Christoph. "25 Jahre 'Dirty Dancing': 'Da kamen wohlerzogene jüdische Mädchen'." *Kultur. Spiegel Online* 8 Oct. 2012. Web. 28 Oct. 2014.
Tyner, Jarvis. "Fidel Castro Cheered at Harlem Meeting." *People's Weekly World* 28 Oct. 1995. Web. 20 Oct. 2014.
Van Orman, Richard A. *A Room For the Night: Hotels of the Old West*. Bloomington: Indiana University Press, 1966. Print.
Van Vechten, Carl. "'A Lady Who Defies Time'; published in *The Nation* (Feb 14, 1923)." *Black Oxen*. Melanie V. Dawson (ed.). Buffalo, NY: Broadview Press, 2012. 358-61. Print.
Volland, Jennifer M. *Grand Hotel: Redesigning Modern Life* (Vancouver Art Gallery). Ostfildern, Germany: Hatje Cantz, 2013. Print.
Vowell, Sarah. "Chelsea Girl." *Take the Cannoli: Stories From the New World*. New York: Touchstone, 2001. 81-94. Print.
Walker, Stanley. "Legendary Algonquin." N.Y. Herald Tribune 20 Nov. 1938. Print.
Wallenrod, Reuben. *Dusk in the Catskills*. New York: The Reconstructionist Press, 1957. Print.
Wang, Wayne (dir.). *Maid in Manhattan*. Columbia Pictures, 2002. Film.
Ward, Joseph A. "'The Amazing Hotel World' of James, Dreiser, and Wharton." *Leon Edel and Literary Art*. Ed. Lyall H Powers. Ann Arbor, MI: UMI Research Press, 1988. 151-60. Print.
Wasserman, Loretta. "*Alexander's Bridge*: The 'Other' First Novel." *Cather Studies* 4 (1999): 294-306. Print.
Watkin, David. *Grand Hotel: The Golden Age of Palace Hotels: An Architectural and Social History*. New York: Viking Press, 1984. Print.
Watkins, Ceri. "Representations of Space, Spatial Practices and Spaces of Representation: An Application of Lefebvre's Spatial Triad." *Culture and Organization* 11:3 (Sept. 2005): 209-20. Print.
Watson, Julia. "The Spaces of Autobiographical Narrative." *Räume des Selbst: Selbstzeugnisforschung transkulturell*. Andrea Bähr, Peter Burschel, Gabriele Jancke. Köln, Weimar, Wien: Böhlau, 2007. 13-25. Print.

Watson, Steven. *Prepare for Saints: Gertrude Stein, Virgil Thomson, and the Mainstreaming of American Modernism*. Berkeley: University of California Press, 2000. Print.

"'Week-end at the Waldorf,' With Ginger Rogers, Lana Turner, Walter Pidgeon, Van Johnson, Arrives at the Music Hall." The Screen. *The New York Times* 5 Oct, 1945: 27. Print.

Weik von Mossner, Alexa. "Abstract: A Cognitive Approach to Emotion and Cinematic Environment." *GWK*. Universität der Künste Berlin 2013. Web. 14 Oct. 2014

Weisenberger, Carol A. "Jennie Grossigner." *European Immigrant Women in the United States: A Biographical Dictionary*. Judy Barrett Litoff and Judith McDonnell (Ed). Collingdale, PA: Diane Pub Co, 1994. 121-22. Print.

Wharton, Annabel Jane. *Building the Cold War: Hilton International Hotels and Modern Architecture*. Chicago: University of Chicago, 2001. Print.

----. "Two Waldorf-Astorias: Spatial Economies as Totem and Fetish." *The Art Bulletin*, No. 85 (Sept. 2003): 523-43. Print.

Wharton, Edith. *The Bucaneers*. Marion Mainwaring (ed.). New York: Viking, 1993. Print.

----. *The Custom of the Country*. New York: Charles Scribner's Sons, 1972. Print.

----. *The House of Mirth*. New York: Scribner, 1972. Print.

White, Arthur. *Palaces of the People: A Social History of Commercial Hospitality*. London: Rapp & Whiting, 1968. Print.

White, E.B. "Here is New York." *Empire City: New York Through The Centuries*. Kenneth T. Jackson and David S. Dunbar (ed.). New York: Columbia University Press, 2002. 695-711. Print.

Wilder, Alec. "The Elegant Refuge: A Memoir of a Life at the Algonquin Hotel." Unpublished, 1976. Typescript, 300 pp. *Alec Wilder Archive*, Sibley Music Library, Eastman School of Music. (seen 3-5 Oct. 2014).

----. "The Search." Unpublished, 1970. Typescript, 176 pp. *Alec Wilder Archive*, Sibley Music Library, Eastman School of Music. (seen 3-5 Oct. 2014).

Williams, Lloyd A., Voza Rivers, *Forever Harlem: Celebrating America's Most Diverse Community*. Champaign, Il: Spotlight Press Inc., 2006. Print.

Williamson, Jefferson. *The American Hotel: An Anecdotal History*. New York, London: A.A. Knopf, 1930. Print.

Wilson, Sondra K. *Meet Me at the Theresa: The Story of Harlem's Most Famous Hotel*. New York: Atria Books, 2004. Print.

Winslow, Art. "'Netherland,' by Joseph O'Neill." *Chicago Tribune* 17 May 2008. Web. 14 Mar. 2014.

Wood, Roy. "The Image of the Hotel in Popular Literature: A Preliminary Statement." *International Journal of Hospitality Management* 9:1 (1990): 5-8. Print.

X, Malcolm, Alex Haley. *The Autobiography of Malcolm X.* New York: Grove Press, 1965. Print.

Zadra, Heather. "About 'Come to the Waldorf-Astoria' by Langston Hughes." *Modern American Poetry.* University of Illinois at Urbana-Champaign 2001. Web. 20 Oct. 2013.

Zeveloff, Julie. "Maya Angelou Always Rented a Hotel Room Just For Writing." *Life. Business Insider* 28 May 2014. Web. 14 Oct. 2014.

Zuhause in der Fremde. Hotels: Wo Kultur, Geschichte und Vergnügen aufeinanderstoßen. Aufbau: Das Jüdische Monatsmagazin 72: 7/8 (Juli 2007). Print.

ILLUSTRATIONS

Image 1
The Miriam and Ira D. Wallach Division of Art, Prints and Photographs: Print Collection, The New York Public Library. "City Hotel, Trinity & Grace Churches. Broadway. New-York." *The New York Public Library Digital Collections.* 1831. http://digitalcollections.nypl.org/items/5e66b3e9-0486-d471-e040-e00a180654d7.

Image 2
The Miriam and Ira D. Wallach Division of Art, Prints and Photographs: Photography Collection, The New York Public Library. "The Waldorf Astoria, New York." *The New York Public Library Digital Collections.* 1898 - 1931. http://digitalcollections.nypl.org/items/510d47d9-9b8f-a3d9-e040-e00a18064a99.

Image 3
Fick, Annabella. "The Second Waldorf-Astoria." 2013. Private, New York City.

Image 4
Music Division, The New York Public Library. "The Waldorf 'Hyphen' Astoria." *The New York Public Library Digital Collections.* 1899 - 1899. http://digitalcollections.nypl.org/items/510d47df-ef61-a3d9-e040-e00a18064a99.

Image 5
Fick, Annabella. "The Algonquin Hotel." 2013. Private, New York City.

Image 6
Rare Book Division, The New York Public Library. "Hotel Algonquin." *The New York Public Library Digital Collections*. 1945. http://digitalcollections.nypl.org/items/b6d31c6c-6e62-cb35-e040-e00a18061428.

Image 7
Fick, Annabella. "The Chelsea Hotel on 23rd Street." 2013. Private, New York City.

Image 8
Fick, Annabella. "The 'Great Black Way:' The Apollo Theater with the Theresa in the Background." 2013. Private, New York City.

Image 9
Fick, Annabella. "The Façade with Ornamentations at the Top of the Theresa." 2013. Private, New York City.

Image 10
The Catskills Institute. "Grossinger's Hotel and Country Club." Boston. Permission to use by Prof. Phil Brown.

Image 11
Rare Book Division, The New York Public Library. "The Grossinger Hotel & Country Club." *The New York Public Library Digital Collections*. 1945. http://digitalcollections.nypl.org/items/b6d31c6c-6ee4-cb35-e040-e00a18061428.

Cultural Studies

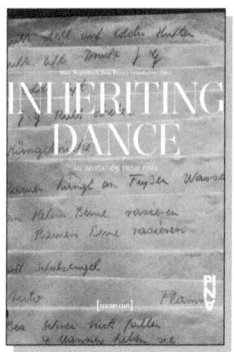

Marc Wagenbach, Pina Bausch Foundation (eds.)
Inheriting Dance
An Invitation from Pina

2014, 192 p., 29,99 € (DE),
ISBN 978-3-8376-2785-5
E-Book: 26,99 € (DE), ISBN 978-3-8394-2785-9

Gundolf S. Freyermuth
Games | Game Design | Game Studies
An Introduction
(With Contributions by André Czauderna,
Nathalie Pozzi and Eric Zimmerman)

2015, 296 p., 19,99 € (DE),
ISBN 978-3-8376-2983-5
E-Book: 17,99 € (DE), ISBN 978-3-8394-2983-9

Heike Paul
The Myths That Made America
An Introduction to American Studies

2014, 456 p.,
24,99 € (DE), ISBN 978-3-8376-1485-5
available as free open access publication
E-Book: ISBN 978-3-8394-1485-9

All print, e-book and open access versions of the titels in our entire list
are available in our online shop www.transcript-verlag.de/en!

Cultural Studies

geheimagentur, Martin Jörg Schäfer,
Vassilis S. Tsianos (eds.)
The Art of Being Many
Towards a New Theory and Practice of Gathering

2016, 288 p., 34,99 € (DE),
ISBN 978-3-8376-3313-9
E-Book: 34,99 € (DE), ISBN 978-3-8394-3313-3

Pablo Abend, Mathias Fuchs, Ramón Reichert,
Annika Richterich, Karin Wenz (eds.)
Digital Culture & Society
Vol. 2, Issue 1/2016 –
Quantified Selves and Statistical Bodies

2016, 196 p., 29,99 € (DE),
ISBN 978-3-8376-3210-1
E-Book: 29,99 € (DE), ISBN 978-3-8394-3210-5

All print, e-book and open access versions of the titels in our entire list are available in our online shop www.transcript-verlag.de/en!